The Nature and Essence of Economic Theory

The Nature and Essence of Economic Theory

Joseph A. Schumpeter

English edition and new introduction by **Bruce A. McDaniel**

Routledge
Taylor & Francis Group
LONDON AND NEW YORK

First published 2010 by Transaction Publishers

Published 2017 by Routledge
2 Park Square, Milton Park, Abingdon, Oxon OX14 4RN
711 Third Avenue, New York, NY 10017, USA

Routledge is an imprint of the Taylor & Francis Group, an informa business

Library of Congress Catalog Number: 2009042972

Library of Congress Cataloging-in-Publication Data

Schumpeter, Joseph Alois, 1883-1950.
The nature and essence of economic theory / Joseph A. Schumpeter.
p. cm.
Includes bibliographical references and index.
ISBN 978-1-4128-1150-7
1. Economics. I. Title.

HB75.S4566 2010
330.1--dc22

2009042972

ISBN 13: 978-1-4128-1150-7 (hbk)

This book is dedicated to
Ms. Johanna von Keler
Widowed Schumpeter

Contents

Preface

The following saying makes a lot of sense: To understand is to forgive. Better even: Whoever understands sees that there is nothing one has to forgive. And that is also true in the field of knowledge.

The layman sees perfection in the body of knowledge at his time. Axioms of former systems he sees as "wrong." For example, the "wrong" Ptolemaic system has to make room for the "correct" Copernican one, which is accepted now. If he would see that even the most modern theory is nothing but a temporary framework—to be replaced sooner or later by new descriptions (because sciences are nothing else than that)—he would lose faith in science. The term "failure of science" describes perfectly the impression that a lot of people have of this insight. In our area, that is not only the standpoint of "laymen." While physicists and mathematicians are like well-trained soldiers who stay in their foxhole even when the battle turns ugly, our authors do not display such steadfastness. This might be a sign of the relative young age of the social science that its representatives rather easily change directions and often ignore previous work in the area. It also seems that scientists in our area tend to ignore commonalities and rather stress differences, to the point that reforms are pushed through as radically as possible, or in other words: That one prefers a totally new construction instead of building onto an existing foundation. Therefore, the contrasts in our field seem to be so insurmountable, not only between the various directions but even in the underlying theory which will be discussed in this book.

This is not my standpoint, though. Like so many of my colleagues, I agree that each "direction" and every individual author is "right" with his claim: Compared to the aim or purpose of each claim, there are few that make no sense and can be dismissed as wrong. We may have reason to prefer a different viewpoint but that usually does not give us the right to dismiss the one that is opposed to ours. The old idea has fulfilled its function and a new one might not even be possible without the previous one. To think a thought all the way through is important, even if it turns out in the end that it was utterly useless. But most of the times we can gain something out of any theory.

We would like to work hard to understand and appreciate each and any of them, especially by spelling out their underpinnings, which are often neglected even by their authors. And then most of the times we find that the ideas are absolutely logical and any controversy would be mute. We want to understand, not fight; learn, not criticize; analyze and find what is correct in each sentence, not just simply accept or dismiss.

We not only want to do this with different opinions within the theory but also with the different "directions" of economics and we will always stress that there are absolutely no dichotomies, in the sense that one might be worthless and the other one "correct." In this way we do not share the partiality of most economists, but are absolutely willing to do justice to everybody, as long as we understand them. And today we are not alone with this viewpoint. But there is a point that makes understanding difficult in our field; and that is the problem that the researcher is at the same time politician and that his research is very often not unbiased; but we believe that theory and practice not only can be separated but they actually do not have anything in common. Even if you do not agree with us in this point, you could not disagree with us when we say that the quarrel between pure theory and history is a thing of the past. In any case, we do not want to be part of it and rather investigate in each separate case, whether the one or the other methods of investigation should be preferred. This way, we will not get to an all-encompassing answer but to separate ones for each individual case.

So, this book is not partial. The reader will find absolute composure in this book. We do not follow any type of scientific or political dogma. It would not have been difficult for me to write exactly the opposite of what you read here, if I would have thought it to be correct. And why not? I am far away from any practical politics and only try to find understanding; and there is no reason for me to prefer one specific method or different materials from the ones I used. If they would better lead to my goal, there would not be any reason to stick to my previous ways. On the contrary, it would be a pleasure—and I would expect a lot of stimulation and satisfaction—to switch to a different method and gain additional knowledge.

And I also do not care where an axiom that I support came from, what the origins of theories or directions are. It is the task of the dogma historian to be just in this case—we care about the problems not the persons.

Just in order to be clear, I do talk about "Ricardo's Systems" or "the Austrian School" etc. because these are common expressions. Everybody knows right away what is meant by them without having to go into long, intricate descriptions, although they might be more correct.

On the other hand, in order to fully understand a theorem we must understand its dogma-historical background. But we cannot and we will not strive for perfection in this regard. Since this book is not geared towards the beginner or layman, we expect the reader to have a certain background knowledge of our science and will understand my abbreviated outlines. Only with a rather exact previous knowledge base of our science the reading of this book will be fruitful. I have to stress, though, that unfortunately beginners in our field all too often do not have this background of all aspects of our science and its theory due to the fact that they specialize too early. I had to write the way I did in order to prevent this book from becoming too unwieldy. For example, when I talk about the "Boehm-Bawerk Theory," I do not go into all its details. All the theory's elements will be discussed but that will not be sufficient for a full understanding if the reader of this book has not also read the original work. But I will pay special attention to my German audience by providing as much background information as possible in an area, which they might not know as well.

In general I try to avoid citations and names as much as possible. Here I follow the English tradition, which seems to have a lot of advantages: completeness in the discussion of the literature is impossible and it is unjust to praise or blame individual writers. The reader has to know which approaches or lines of thought are being discussed when we use the phrases "a popular theory" or "it is often said"—individual writers do not play a role here. And the reader will also have to be able to judge what in this book is an original idea and what is just a summary of previous knowledge. If someone finds common knowledge, which I thought to be my own original thought … that would only make me happy.

The work of the latter grows organically out of the work of the former and I happily cling to the old views where it is possible. The less new we have to do the better. The author of this book seems to be closest to L. Walras and von Wieser.

Although you will not find many names mentioned in this book, it nevertheless contains most ideas of the current science of theoretical economics, and it therefore gives a complete overview of our discipline. I hope I have included all points of departure for further development. It was always my aspiration not to deconstruct but to develop our field further. Any exact science has to build its rocky path, step by step, and not care that the general public sees our efforts as insignificant. Unfortunately, that does not happen enough in our area—often it seems every new book wants to found a new economy. That will improve with the maturation of our discipline. We want to remember and appreciate all the previous work in our field but also not deny that there is a lot more left to do. The number of basic thoughts is small; quite a few—but not all yet—are complete.

But still, the reader might not find full satisfaction in this book. Some points, which we think are especially important or previously not addressed well enough, we discuss in depth but others we only touch upon briefly. What we see as having been discussed thoroughly in the past—even if it is very important—we might not cover at all. Please, dear reader, remember that this book is neither a textbook nor a systematic work that sees it as its task to cover all aspects of our discipline in equal depth.

What is being offered here is supposed to add to the existing knowledge, not repeat what already has been done. We want to look forward—backwards only when necessary. Furthermore, we are not very interested in the theorems as such, but more in their nature and their place in the system of our science. We use important practical questions just as examples for the types and findings of our thinking processes. So, we probably will sometimes stop our discussion at a point, where it will become interesting to some readers and in those places our incompleteness will become apparent. But it lies in the nature of this cause that only few questions can be discussed in depth. I still do not think that anybody who bothers to read this book will accuse us of superficiality or a lack of knowledge in our area.

The topic of our discussion is just a very narrow area of the social sciences, which allows for a very exact discussion.

It may be that just the term "exact economics" will make some readers shudder. Those of you who do not like exact disciplines … please put down this book without reading it. I would not want to blame anybody for it. And those of you who are of the opinion that we cannot deduct answers to practical questions … you are right! Some things are important for the practitioner, others are important for the theorist.

The classic system of national economics lies in shambles. Nevertheless, it is still seen by some as *the* economics. Many authors turned their backs on it and instead dedicated their work to other areas, which do not have much in common, neither methodologically or content-wise. In addition, a new theory was developed, based on different basic assumptions and different goals. That looks confusing, even chaotic.

What is the relationship between the theory and the other directions and what is the relationship between the old and the new theory? And what can we expect from these relationships? And in general: what now? Are there paths that lead forward and where are they? All this has been discussed in detail but the picture has not gotten any clearer—although an answer starts to shine through. We got to this point through basic, general, and *a priori* argumentation—often from outside from our field—but never going into details. The discussion looked more like a political fight: slogans used by partisan supporters instead of calm analysis piled up many misunderstandings, which will be hard to get rid of. Although advanced researchers are beyond this bickering over methods, we can say without exaggeration that many economists are utterly confused by these questions and do not know where to go from here. Every one of them can say where he stands and defend his stance with commonplace arguments but they cannot say anything about the basics, about national economics in general, about its problems, its nature, meaning, and future; unfortunately, all these areas are shrouded in a fog—and not only for people at the fringes of our field.

We want to try to find answers here. But not with common argumentation, which would not be wrong but would lead nowhere; not through a "dialectic approach" that proves everything and nothing; but rather through our work.

We always will try to clarify each of our theorems, its value, and its nature. Thus, we will develop something like a "cognition theory of economics" or at least try to move into that direction. I am convinced that only this way we can solve all problems, not through common argumentation. Up to now, every economist has started his analysis with *a priori* axioms about the nature of economic activities or human activities and then deduced assertions for this or that method. That cannot lead to any results. The sentence "Everything that happens is subject to causality, therefore exact laws have to be possible in the area of economics" does not prove anything. Aside from the fact that the modern theory of cognition would reject it, the question still is whether the causal connections are simple enough to allow for axioms of a sufficient interest. And that's what is important.

On the other hand, a sentence such as "Laws like we have them in the natural sciences cannot be used in the humanities" is also worthless. Again, besides the question whether and in what sense it is correct, it does not exclude the existence of regularities, which can be described exactly. And whether they really exist can only be shown by the analysis of individual problems. That leads us to a second point that often is neglected. General methodological books often do not deal with concrete problems; they discuss common assertions; often they show a lack of knowledge of details of the theory—and that is not only true for the works of Wundt and Siegwart but also of trained economists. Even the field of economics is staked out through general reflection. And even methodological discussions in prefaces of books that deal with concrete problems show this dilemma: There is no connection between these discussions and other followers but they rather are nothing more than a mere creed that belies the reality of human actions. They, for example, profess the necessity to include historical materials or that they do not just want to compile data but rather find "laws"—but in reality they do not do that. They say that they would not make any practical suggestions, only for the reader to find out that they do exactly that. They talk about the necessity of statistical basics but in reality they often just mention statistical data in examples but their conclusions are being reached through reasoning not through statistical analysis. So, it is no wonder that we can sometimes totally agree with the argumentation of an author although there is a total bewilderment of his direction.

It is our opinion that we should not cobble together methodological concepts in *apriority* but rather do what takes us the furthest regardless of our expectations. Especially the field of economics should not be staked out in advance. Instead, we should calmly approach the questions that interest us and clarify them. The method that seems to be the most useful to this goal still does not have to be generalizable. Of course, we will continue using the methods, which might or might not work but the latter does not mean our method is a bad one, nor does it mean the former is good. The tendency to generalize the usefulness of certain assertions (which are good to solve certain problems), leads to the odd situation that they can be defended through general reasoning and through certain examples without really satisfying anybody. It is easy for an opponent to prove exactly the opposite by using a different reasoning and different examples. And since both look at those aspects close to their heart, they will not be able to agree on anything. Each of them is totally convinced that he is right (and can actually prove it!) but the beginner in the field cannot get a grasp of anything.

These words summarize the whole history of the method dispute. It is not our goal to find generalizable axioms; the only actual axiom that is generally applicable is: act rationally. We also do not want to support one side or the other. We want to put those axioms that we deem to be correct in relation to each other, want to show their limits and their range, and apply them to individual cases in order to see whether or not they pass muster.

One cannot separate the analysis of methods from concrete problems. Only then do methods make sense. The details are important … great generalities have no substance. Only through our work we can come up with laws, which will then be subject to improvements, changes, and rejection. The description of the method should not be the first chapter but rather the last one. They are of little help to us. Besides … economists still ignore the latest—which in our eyes is the best.

Just one example is the discussion about induction and deduction. First it was conducted in a very general language. The best that was said about it was that both processes were equally important—who would have expected differently? That was just obvious and does not help us very much. Interesting in this context is only the analysis of the character of each of our axioms, each of the steps we take. That is necessary to evaluate the meaning and value of it. And then it shows that some axioms were arrived at through deductive methods others through inductive ones. Each path, if based solely on one or the other method, had to be dissatisfying. When the field of pure economics was defined as "deductive," the field was not treated fairly: While some of these attacks are not totally baseless, they went way too far. The controversies within the pure theory are quite similar. One example is the so-called "value controversy." At first, people operated with the terms "false" and "true" instead of "useful" and "not useful." That the sun "rises" is not "false" and does not contradict the axiom that that phenomenon is caused by the movement of the earth: both axioms are descriptions of the same process and are in themselves both true and false; towards some goals the one is more practical, for other goals the other one is—that is all. We then will not even try to have a *general* discussion about value or cost hypothesis. Instead, we will indicate why in the one case we use the one and the other one in a different case—if we do not use both. This—let me call it "pragmatic" approach—has not been used up to now. It allows our findings to be much more precise as if we would try to be very general. In addition, the controversy loses a lot of its edginess, it dissolves automatically, and it will become clear that justice and injustice can be found on both sides.

This approach to our problems might seem a little odd. But it is in line with the modern *cognitive* theory, which has grown out of practical work of the exact natural sciences. We do not want to go into more detail, because we want to avoid being perceived as biased: our comments should be seen as natural and impartial, as they were written unaffected by any axioms. Just in case that some of my comments or phrases will be seen as partial, I would like to note that I am not alone with my view of the cognition theory. I am prepared to take criticism for my comments on the value hypothesis and some related questions. I still believe that my approach is the only one that can expose the nature of the economic theory. And it should not be sacrificed for a more popular approach.

In this context I also want to mention that I do avoid the terms "cause" and "effect" but rather use the more poignant *functional concept*. We cannot go into a more detailed discussion at this point about how important it is, how it can add to the clarity and purity of reasoning. But I believe that it is especially important for exact economics to use rigorous correctness, even if the writing becomes dry and lifeless. For people in our field it is much more important than for people in those disciplines, which already have achieved a certain level of clarity in their foundations and reliability in solving concrete problems.

Clarity in the foundations and reliability in the solving of specific problems: That is what we are striving for, something for which we admire the exact sciences, and to which we want to contribute. There are many stumbling blocks in our path before we can even tackle the real problems in our science, and all the discussions we have already had have not been able to push them aside completely. Our task is not so much to find new ways to solve problems but more to prove that it is possible to navigate around them and not get stranded. The questions of "Telos" and "Causa" cannot be solved in the framework of an exact discipline, they can just be neutralized, so to speak: One can show that they do not barricade our path—and that is the same with many other similar difficulties.

It would be unnecessary to quarrel whether economics is a "life science," as it is often described, and therefore closer to biology as, for example, mechanics, if one can show it is utterly irrelevant for our results. And such comments have made a big impression on a lot of people and shaken their trust in our discipline. There are a lot of such slogans and all contributions to a "cognitive theory" of our science are full of them. We finally have to respond with precision to the question what of that is actually true and which implication they have. And this response to many important points will come out of this book.

We want to work out what we should think of today's pure economics, what its nature is, what its methods and findings, and where we should go from here. We want to show its limitations and weaknesses and we want to show to the reader how the latter can be improved. Even in this point people are too rigorous: Either one thinks the existing is perfect and does not need any further development or one rejects it totally. Both are equally superficial and convenient. Looking at individual cases, though, we see that neither of these two opinions is totally correct but rather each has elements of the truth. Everybody feels that without being able to say which of the two fits which concrete axiom: this is something we will do here.

You will not find here the general arguments, neither about political nor methodological nor other basic questions. What has to be said about them has already been said and is common knowledge. Only in very few areas will we add to this knowledge but we will not waste our time on generalities which are true and cheap: Our work on concrete problems teaches us our method and gives us our basic stance on the basic questions and in the individual directions of our science. We do not assume beforehand that economic facts show enough regularity that would allow us to come up with exact rules, but some will rather reveal themselves to us including their nature, their limitations, their weaknesses, and their value. We will see that we will be able to use certain axioms and that these axioms will form a consistent, self-contained system and will show its value and whether it can be generalized, and also in how far it is based on arbitrary presuppositions and definitions or on observations of facts. The results of this work on details will be quite different from those general *a priori* discussions. But enough of this.

I would almost say that the concrete results are only of secondary significance for my goal. As I said before, I do not strive for systematic completeness. I will bring up only a small number of basic axioms. In the center lies the problem of balance, which from the standpoint of practical application of the theory is of negligible importance but it is fundamental for the science. In Germany, it has not received the attention it deserves but it is important to stress that it is the basis of our exact systems. The barter, price, and money theories and their most important application, the distribution, are based on it and therefore it will be discussed in length. These things form that part of economics, which is ripe to be discussed.

My presentation is based on the fundamental differentiation between "statics" and "dynamics" of the economy, a point that cannot be stressed enough. The methods of pure economics today are just good enough for the former and the most important results apply to them. "Dynamics" is totally different from "statics," in their methods and in content. Of course, the differentiation is not new … especially American theorists have stressed it. But in Germany it has been widely ignored and its implications have not been recognized in other countries either. We will see that it actually contains the key to the solutions to many controversies. It is so important that it cannot just be summarized in this preface but it will come up with almost all concrete problems. We will only deal with statics; the field of dynamics will just be mentioned in passing.

In this context, I want to mention a point close to my heart, and that is what you will read here about the problems of capital and interest. I apologize in advance that you will only read negative results of these problems. The most important axiom you will find here is that interest is not a "static" income but that it is more closely related to entrepreneur profit than to pay or income from property. I know very well that most theorists are of a different opinion. But I am convinced that that fact explains my dissatisfaction with all interest theories I am familiar with. But I had to stop with this result, so that my own interest theory would not be compromised by a premature discussion. I hope I will have the chance in the future to discuss this matter more completely than I can do it here. I do not like to call the existing theories insufficient… but I have to. To present a new interest theory—probably the 25th or the 39th—is not an enviable task. I did not look for it, it forced itself onto me.

I would have more to say in this preface of this book, for example I could write about the significance of the allocation problem; about something that I have called "variation method." These dry topics can only be of interest to the theorists of our field who actually might find them wanting. But it lies in the nature of the thing that in our science it is very difficult to satisfy both the theorist and those practical economists who nevertheless are interested in theoretical problems on the one hand, and on the other hand not to be too abstruse and too incorrect and at the same time trying to apply the scientific rigor of the exact sciences and not betray the peculiarities of our field. Probably the last part of this book will be of general interest.

One of my goals is to familiarize the German audience with a few things—terminology, axioms, and viewpoints. In Germany, the development of the theory has not been followed very closely; the German economist only knows vaguely what the "pure" theorist actually does. We want to teach to the German scientists the theories of other countries.

One of the most important points in this context is the question of the "mathematical method." Some readers might have not heard of it at all, others might have just heard general reasons in favor or against it. It would be unnecessary to discuss the general reasons, which tend to become ever more important in the English literature because of the rapid development of this approach. Furthermore, we do not want to present long mathematical deductions, because there is a lack of foundation among the readers and it would only scare them away. But we think if one wants to deal with theory, one has to do it as exactly as possible and that our way of thinking will totally absorb the thinking of higher-order mathematics. But we still are not saying that mathematics is absolutely necessary because our terminology is of quantitative nature or that complicated problems could only be solved through mathematical correctness. We are content with discussing the nature of exact reasoning in our field and to present a few points when our thinking becomes mathematical, whether we want it or not, and describe what happens in such a situation; what this process means and what can come of it. The reader then has to decide himself whether it is worth his effort to go into more detail and what to think of the criticism against this process. We will never go to a point where mathematical knowledge would be required. That would be detrimental to the goal of this book. And we hope to support tendencies and win people over instead of discussing generalities and criticizing the reader for not having enough background knowledge.

I am not a polemicist and I do not feel bitter. I have trust in the future of our discipline and do not regret anything about the past. With equal distance from authoritarianism and clinging to the old dogmas on the one hand and inconsiderate destructiveness on the other, from melancholic or complacent skepticism on the one hand and gushing hopes on the other, I calmly anticipate a new scientific day, which is about to dawn.

Cairo, March 2, 1908
J. Schumpeter

Acknowledgments

I would like to thank the Kauffman Foundation and especially Carl Schramm and Robert Strom for the generous financial support and encouragement in my efforts to complete the English translation of this book. I would like to thank Dr. Peter Kastner and Franziska Wilcox for their many efforts in the actual German to English translation. Also, I would most importantly like to thank my mentor, Professor J. Ron Stanfield, for continuing to encourage me to read the works of Joseph A. Schumpeter during and after my doctoral studies.

Introduction to the English Edition

At the young age of twenty-five, Joseph A. Schumpeter published his first book in 1908, *The Nature and Essence of Economic Theory*. Published in German, this book is little known and has not been acknowledged as a major accomplishment in that era in the field of economics. Given the detail, complexity and depth of this text, such an undertaking would not be attempted today by any but the most seasoned professional. Yet Schumpeter, in this book, undertook the overwhelming task of producing a coherent, formal, and complete analysis of market capitalism. At this early age, Schumpeter attempted to strongly differentiate between static and dynamic economic theory. An example of this dynamic analysis includes his attempt to show innovation as an ongoing integral part of economics and place the entrepreneur at the center of market capitalism. This book set the stage for his myriad of later works. More importantly most of his contributions, including his work on entrepreneurship and innovation as well as his concept of creative destruction can be traced to this original text.

Entrepreneurship and its activity, innovation in the form of new products and new production methods, according to this first Schumpeter book, would disturb the conditions of static economics and could only be fully understood and analyzed through the development of dynamic economic reasoning.

Schumpeter's work on general equilibrium analysis expands much of the early works of Leon Walras and is combined with his studies at the University of Vienna. In addition, through his travels to England and his personal discussions with Alfred Marshall, Schumpeter built his analysis on the base of classical and neoclassical economics but expanded his views with the incorporation of a vast array of works from economists and sociologists from the 1700s as well as the 1800s. These formulations in the book, comparing, contrasting and at times refuting a wide variety of economic and social thought from over a century ago, makes this original text from Schumpeter a most compelling read for professionals from a wide variety of fields.

As economists, sociologists, social scientists and other professionals look for solutions to the many social and economic problems facing society today, they are increasingly drawn back to the classical writers to search for forgotten or missed ideas from the past. One such source would appear to be Joseph A. Schumpeter's first text written in 1908. Since this book was originally published in German, this is the first opportunity for professionals to explore the original Schumpeter in the English language. This was Schumpeter‘s first attempt at a complete, comprehensive, integrated analysis of how economics becomes part of the social, political, and institutional structure of a nation. Schumpeter forms the foundations for much of his extensive social and economic thought in this first work. His later analysis of how society accomplishes economic growth, material advancement and income and wealth distribution and redistribution find their origins in this book. Schumpeter may be most recognized for his concept of creative destruction and although the phrase is not used in his original book, the ground work and conceptual frameworks for this concept is developed in this 1908 text.

As he attempts to develop a comprehensive general equilibrium analysis, he integrates much of the classical and neoclassical economic thought of that era. The book is at times tedious with lengthy and complex discussions and developments but remains an important contribution to the early attempts at understanding the discipline of economics and its relevance to society. He attempts to add to and further develop the works of economists such as Marshall, Pareto, Walras, and many others. In this process, he attempts to explain the many facets of economic analysis including moral, ethical, scientific, and theoretical as well as delineate the differences in each area. For example, he explains that entrepreneurial wage has "social justification" and therefore is not part of "scientific theory" in the economic sense.

Schumpeter viewed market capitalism as one of the few social structures that allowed social advancement through increases in income and wealth. He explained that while systems such as the aristocratic or the cast structure prohibits such advancement, market capitalism offered both economic as well as social advancement. Part of this upward mobility was defined by Schumpeter to be the result of the entrepreneurial efforts of members of society. Schumpeter proposed the concept that the negligence and complacency of the economically and socially powerful would allow an opportunity for the entrepreneur to profit and redirect income away from the more elite in society. He stated that this "upper-class" did not want change but the "less advantaged" were often if not always looking for entrepreneurial opportunity to better themselves. These opportunities would offer economic advancement first and then because of the individual freedoms of market capitalism, social advancement would follow.

The book is divided into five sections covering the methods and theoretical foundations of economic analysis. Schumpeter starts the book with a lengthy analysis of value and prices. Schumpeter writes the text in a style that constantly refers to previous explanations or suggests that a more complete discussion will occur later in the book. At times this proves quite difficult for the reader but this style was quite common one hundred years ago.

The second section develops the concept of equilibrium and Schumpeter states that this concept is essential for economic theory. The third section focuses on production and distribution and includes an analysis of rent, wage, and profit theories. Schumpeter goes to great length here to discuss and contrast static and dynamic economic analysis. The fourth section discusses the analysis of comparative statics. The fifth section attempts a long discussion of examples and methods to analyze the concepts set forth in the first four sections. Parts of this last section review and repeat earlier parts of the book. At the end of the book, in this last section, Schumpeter explains through many different examples how dynamic interactions between society, institutions, and government actions such as taxation work to bring about social as well as economic change continuously alters society. These interactions and the results are reasons that Schumpeter argues that economics is and must be a dynamic analysis and therefore cannot be fully explained with the static models of classical and neoclassical economics. According to Schumpeter, this process of dynamic interaction is an integral part of income and wealth creation as well as income and wealth distribution and redistribution.

The reader must be aware and recognize that over the past one hundred years, many economic concepts and terms have changed meanings. For example, Schumpeter in his original text uses the term redistribution of income to mean a redirection of income streams from the economically elite to the economically less advantaged. Today the term redistribution is usually associated with the government taking income from one group and awarding that income to another group. Schumpeter's use of the term redistribution referred to changes such as entrepreneurial activities to allow a redirection of future income flows away from one group to another group. He did not use the term, as it is used today, to represent a taking of existing incomes from one group and awarding that existing income to another group. Today this change in future income flows that Schumpeter discusses would be referred to as a redirection of future income.

This book offers much insight into the thought and economic depth of the young Schumpeter. This text was the academic start to an economic career that spanned over four decades, several countries, and many different appointments at both private and public institutions. Now in the English edition, hopefully the book will rekindle the interest in exploring the works of Joseph Schumpeter that are well deserved.

Part I

1

Introduction

I

Even those people who know our discipline just superficially, know about the multitude of approaches and the quarrels between their disciples. It might confuse, even deter, the beginner or the layman but it is neither special nor disturbing. Of course it is irritating that one cannot name *one* book that is widely recognized and that could summarize the position of the science so that one could recommend it to the public as general information about our field. The reason is not that the dichotomies were insurmountable; actually, I hope to be able to show the opposite in this book. Also, we cannot say that this dichotomy does not exist in other sciences as we will see shortly. The reason for this unpleasant situation is thank God a superficial one: The bitter quarrel is a rather recent phenomenon because each economist, instead of stressing what we have in common, seems to reject all positions that are not his and tries to pull the beginner to his side and make him into a warrior for his own position. So, these beginners are pulled into the controversy too early, way before they understand the problems. They often have an opinion before they have even started to work independently. Political or other tendencies that are outside the field are also to blame.

But, as I said before, the field of economics is not in any worse situation than other sciences. It would be wrong to conclude that the field needs useful methods, assured results, or even a clearly-delineated field of study, as understandable as it is that some people—tired of the constant infighting—may think that way. Since this declaration seems paradoxical considering the high noise level of our discussion about methods, we would like to briefly explain. We could name philosophy, political science, and other fields that can hardly be described as exact. In the field of psychology, for example, there are many different directions and we can safely state that in our field there is no difference bigger than between introspective and experimental psychology. Scientists coming out of totally different disciplines work in these subfields, of which the one tends towards philosophy, the other one towards psychology. Methods and findings of these two are hardly related and psychologists spend at least as much energy on the defense of their basic viewpoints as economists do. In the field of logic it is not any different: There are worlds between "categorical" and "modern" and these two areas have not been found together. But please do not confuse this dichotomy with controversies about single problems: Not a single question but rather whole approaches, whole systems with all their basic assumptions are at stake here.

It is even more significant that we also find this phenomenon in the exact sciences, which the laymen see as the quintessence of certainty and unity. The best example is chemistry: The exact and the experimental are represented by different people and they have little in common concerning their methods and their goals. They go their separate ways and only meet to quarrel.

And the same is true for the most exact of them all, the mechanics. That is especially peculiar since all the workers in this old traditional field have a remarkably similar training, career path, and opinions phenomena in their field. In addition, they pretty much agree on all concrete findings. But all of this still cannot create unity when it comes to methods and basic principles. Not only is the difference between classic and modern mechanics considerable—which is the natural result of scientific development – but there are also clearly distinct parties within modern mechanics that fight about more or less *everything*, the complete interpretation of nature and the values of the discipline. And as in our field, the practitioners do not seem to be interested in anything but what is of practical interest. Scanning the battlefield, it becomes apparent that today the foundation of this proud building is shaken and that there is a general feeling of dissatisfaction. Doesn't this show us that all sciences go through these quarrels, not just economics; that all systems have to make room for new ideas? And wouldn't it be wrong to be in despair over the fall of classic economics? One could actually interpret it as a sign of its capacity for development.

One could reply that the discussion about methods in our field is characterized by such a high level of intolerance towards the viewpoint of the opponent, that people do not even know their approaches and findings. But that is the case everywhere: The introspective psychologist feels misunderstood by the experimental, and the latter is inclined to deny the former any right to his way of thinking. The mathematical and exact chemist often disdains the experimental one and the latter, as I have experienced, sometimes does not even know the first one exists or what he does. And today the field of mechanics is in a similar situation, and even pure mathematics suffers from it.

We actually should not be too surprised since not only is the knowledge so vast but the methods also so varied that only a few people have a handle on *one* whole discipline with all its subfields. He chooses what is closest to him and his subfield is often such a large part of his personality that is as hard to shed as the moral character—especially for the best in their fields. The result is often the incapability to compromise. But compromises are a necessary result of scientific development and fighting them is as futile as trying to unify the world religions.

So, we do not take the inner strife of economics too seriously. We are pretty sure that the state of our field today will not lead to a destruction of our discipline in the future. We are supported in this by the observation that things have turned around recently and that a healthy "communis opinio" is developing. At least, that is a result of our discussion. On the other hand, we cannot and we do not want to deny that the situation is not completely satisfactory and that we will state here what we think the reason is.

Let me take the fight between the representatives of the abstract theory and of the historical school: Usually, both are right in their general assertions. But we do not look at their limitation that they often deal with different problems. Each method has its own field of application and fighting over generalizability does not get us anywhere. We will always stress that a discussion about methodological questions only makes sense in the framework of practical scientific research. Our viewpoint is that there is no contradiction between the historical and the abstract approach—their only difference is their interest in different problems. The pure price theory, for example, cannot be dealt with historically, the problem of the organization of an economy cannot be dealt with in an abstract way. And our discussions would not be as controversial, if we would have always kept that in mind (and some other things we will discuss later). People realize that more and more, although not all of them.

II

Here we want to give a short overview over the present important approaches. We follow a long tradition. Almost all economics books, especially the systematic ones, start with such an overview. This way the reader learns about the philosophy of the author and gets an introduction to the literature. We also have to do that, even if in this case the reader is expected to have prior knowledge of the topics we will discuss here. We have an additional reason: We see it as our task to contribute to a deeper appreciation of each approach, to demarcate them better, and hopefully put them into a more precise relationship to each other. To this end, several of them will be named here without going into any type of critiquing at this point but rather discuss them pretty generally. The reader will only be able to develop a yardstick out of the entirety of the discussion; we do not want to come to a judgment at the threshold of our discussion, as it so often happens. In this general information we will stress the points to which we ourselves can contribute. The general historic development of our science as well as what is usually written in this context—all this we expect the reader to already know. The intentions of our discussions are the excuse for their incompleteness and we mention names only in examples and as sparingly as possible, and only when non-mentioning of names could lead to confusion among the readers.

We will start out with the systems of classic authors, especially A. Smith, Ricardo, and their immediate successors, without analyzing how much they are dependent on previous authors. We have to do that for two reasons. First, they are the origin of most approaches and we have to discuss them in order to understand these approaches. Secondly, they are still alive and powerful, insofar as some economists still represent them. Let us now look at the first point, which presents a window to the development of our science.

Natura non fait saltum—Marshall prefaced his work with this sentence and it really captures its character very well. But I do want to contradict him: The development of human culture, and here especially that of knowledge, happens in spurts. Colossal rushes alternate with periods of stagnation, effusive hope alternates with bitter disappointments, and even if the new is based on the old, development is not a steady one. Our science can tell stories about that.

The works of the classic authors seem very fresh, still. That a cornucopia of facts and findings, of points of departure of which even today not all have been utilized, is offered by the "Wealth of Nations"! Scientists pushed forward without checking the reliability of the direction and exploited the break with the past. These new ideas broke through into wider circles—often misrepresented and *always* over-generalized. Disillusionment followed fast and we had a situation like an economic crisis: Exhaustion followed a period of productivity, exaggerated mistrust followed unconditional trust. What is characteristic in this situation is not the attitude of wider circles towards economics but rather its internal condition. Suddenly we have a standstill in its development, it looked as if the field had been exhausted and nothing could be extracted any more—and that in spite of obvious flaws that invited further work: No workers could be found. Only half built and already half dilapidated was the building of economics, when powerful opponents appeared. I cannot explain this strange standstill, these Hippocratic elements in our literature between 1830 and 1870. Most people with knowledge of the literature would probably support me if I said: The classic system was not destroyed by outside enemies but rather by internal paralysis (as the demise of societies cannot sufficiently be explained by the existence of outside enemies). The historical school stormed a fortress and only found a bunch of invalids in it. The works of the epigones would be of little value, even if a historic approach had never existed. We do not want to deny that *something* was achieved during that time: Almost every author contributed this or that detail. But the creative power was exhausted. That is especially true for J. St. Mill, as embarrassing as it is to judge an individual this quickly. There are also some beginnings that indicated promise but it is characteristic for the paralysis of the field of economics that they did not get any attention.

The impression I got from the literature at that time cannot be described any better than through the term "being stuck." Perhaps even Smith and Ricardo would not have known where to go next. That is definitely true for their successors. Their approach came to the end of its productivity, and there was no replacement. It makes sense that people generalized what was only true for one approach and thought that the whole field of economics would not have a shining future. Some thought the system was perfect and complete—something that is always a dubious symptom—others had a feeling of uneasiness without having a solution.

This situation became very clear during the celebration of the 100-year anniversary of the "Wealth of Nations" at the Political Economy Club in London. Actually, the year 1876 is already part of the new period. But the works of the new writers were still being ignored and our discipline seemed to be shrouded in the tranquility of death. Mr. Lowe who opened the debate expressed it perfectly: "I am not sanguine as to any very large or any very startling development of political economy. I observe that the triumphs which have been gained, have been rather in demolishing that which has been found to be undoubtedly bad and erroneous, than in establishing new truth; and imagine that, before we can attain new results, we must be furnished from without with new truths, to which our principles can be applied … the great work has been done." In other words, it means that the field of economics was "done," that nothing new and noteworthy could come out of it anymore and that one had to go beyond its confines to learn anything interesting. The only ones who showed self-confidence and initiative and were forward-looking were the "historians," especially Cliffe Leslie. And a newspaper expressed the impression of wider circles perfectly when it described the get-together as a "wake," not as an anniversary of economics.

With the loss of its internal power, our field also lost its external influence, especially since at the time of its upswing the field had gone out on a limb by tackling the area of practical problems and had given short and general answers to questions, which were too complex to solve on the first try. As the scientific building started disintegrating brick by brick (wage fund theory, population theory, etc.), one practical finding after the other came apart. And people had heard so much about economics, and the field was so pretentious, and the misuse of this science so evident, that people turned their backs on it.

This way the historical approach showed one huge success: The theory with which one could show everything or nothing, that became paralyzed in empty phrases, was thrown overboard and the field began to concentrate on collecting facts and practical problems of social and economic politics. But it was not a complete success. The discussion of current problems was still based on classical arguments and the free-trade party and the Manchester party still did not want to let go of their beloved theories. That alone, though, would not have had a big impact on the science. But many scientific economists also stuck with the theory. For a while there was the hope that these would be swept out after a short while. But that never happened. Instead, new activity sprouted in the ruins, and the flock of theorists began to regroup to grow and go on the attack again. The historians were not aware of the fact that they were faced by different opponents—they thought they were the remnants of the successors of the classical authors. But they were *new* warriors who picked up the same old quarrel about methods. It was a mistake to fight them with the arguments used against the classical authors. But they brought it on themselves by seeing themselves as grandchildren of those authors.

The reader knows which group of economists we are talking about: Menger, Jevons, Walras, and their successors. Their situation was difficult in the beginning. The period of being ignored was followed by being attacked and of many misunderstandings. The theory was put aside and people were not ready to accept it again. But the new approach weathered the storm, made progress, and today we can say we are on a theoretical upswing. The classical system did not benefit, though—quite the contrary: it suffered another attack, which totally shook it.

In order to fully understand this, we have to be clear on the nature and content of what we call the classic system. The first thing that is striking when one reads the classic literature in my mind is the fact that it consists of many different elements. It is astounding that this fact has basically been ignored, and we think the reason for that lack of results of the methodological discussion is the fact that these different elements were not sufficiently isolated and arguments that fit just one of them were over-generalized. The heritage of the classical literature consists of a scientific part and a political one. I do not think we go too far when saying that the big success and the devastating defeat of the classical system can be explained by the latter rather than the former. The attack of the historical and the newer socio-political approaches were directed against free laissez faire trade, the victorious catch words during the first half of the 19th century and against practical extremes of other theories. These circles had no interest in the real economic theory. Still, it was expected that this theory would fall if faced with those practical assertions and postulates. Those are not necessarily consequences of the pure scientific classical literature and can be separated from them. It is not difficult to prove that: For example, it is easy to see that the theoretical content in Ricardo's chapter on wage does not necessarily lead to what the author calls "poor laws." If one rejects the latter, the former can still be true. And we are only interested in the scientific heritage of the classical authors. But even that is not completely homogeneous. Yes, economics is its most important and most valuable part. But it also contains philosophies about the topic of individualism and collectivism, about the motives of people's actions, etc. That all that does not have anything to do with economics, we will show later. We can—and have to—admit that the attacks were legitimate in this point, too. But that is all; the pure economics of the classical authors, as paradoxical as it sounds, remained almost untouched. Attackers did not even get through to it and only charged it in general, in connection with everything around it. We can still observe this phenomenon in today's discussion.

It was the representatives of the new theory who investigated the classic economics. Did they destroy it and put something new in its place?

That is a question that is being answered in many different ways. We do not want to solve it here—the following discussions in their entirety will give an answer—but we do not want to hide our opinion: Yes, the system of the modern theory is mostly new and even those findings that concur with those of the classic system have been derived through a different method. Of course, we are indebted to the classical authors for the terminology and thought processes; sure, without the old one the new theory would not be possible but the former has become obsolete as the older literature in every other science. I regard this as very natural and is of equal distance to all extreme opinions we hear so often.

The preceding discussion builds the basis for a brief description of today's parties in our discipline. We already saw, and will see again soon, that we can trace back almost all directions of our field to the classical authors as their take-off point. It does not matter whether one followed their orbits and tried to substitute what was dismissed, whether adored or attacked—one always started with them. One might be inclined to deny that; each new direction tries to stand on its own feet and denies the impudence within older works; but it still exists. The historical school started from a criticism of classical findings. The classical authors provided its terminology, its systematic representation, and one finds classical thinking in this direction's work—whether it was uttered consciously or subconsciously. And that is, of course, even more true for the new theories.

So, we can see a clear development of our discipline, even if it has not been a straight, constant, and calm one. Like the branches of a river delta, the individual directions came from a common source and are closely related. One often hears that especially the German economists have lost contact with the classical authors: That is not true for the theory; as far as theory is being discussed in Germany, the classical authors are being stressed. But they are also very active outside the pure theory discussions—quietly but profoundly.

The economist who in his "introduction" discusses the different directions of economics, usually differentiates the pure theory—which he, depending on his viewpoint calls "exact," speculative," or "deductive"—then especially history of economics and description of economics and tries to characterize them with some general remarks. That is not sufficient because there are so many differences within the theory that a general judgment can only be made in very general terms. We therefore want to keep the different groups separate.

In our opinion, then, the classic systems are the common birthplace of all the approaches of economists, at least when we consider the pure scientific side of it. And with that we do it justice. Not *one* of its parts can be upheld today but *everybody* has contributed to today's state of our science. But the classical authors still are a vivid power today, more so than in any other science. Quite a few mathematicians have not read Newton or Laplace. That is not possible in our area: Many people even today go back to A. Smith and Ricardo. The reason is that people in our field are not sure what our classical authors can teach us today and how they have to be interpreted, while in other sciences the valuable parts of older works do live on in the new ones. But there is another reason: Wider circles who understand theories very well, nevertheless do not understand the modern system of theory because its scientific framework is much more difficult to grasp. On the other hand, these same people do not have any problem following the classical authors and get more satisfaction out of them because they can get brief answers to burning practical questions. So, both the laymen and the expert economists turn to the classical authors rather than the modern ones. After we now have shown the significance of the classics for the development of our field and, thus, for the present situation, we have to include them among our modern approaches: They are still alive today.

It is a strange phenomenon, the group of researchers that is still based on the classical authors. We do not want to try to judge; not to explain this phenomenon. Of course, the reasons we just discussed are not sufficient because we can find researchers whose *main interest* is in the pure theory. But we have to say that we cannot think of another science in which a group of scientists finds the development of its field of the last forty years foreign. The economists we are thinking about here are, for example, Professor Sumner from the U.S., Professors Nicholson and Cannon in England, Professor Dietzel and others in Germany. In a way, A. Wagner can be included in this list and there are many lesser-known disciples. According to them, the basics of the pure theory that was laid out by the classical authors, are still of use today and should be preferred over the new systems of theory, which is not fully accepted yet due to its newness and questionable value.

On the other side, there is a group of theorists, which we can call "modern." The founders of this direction we already have mentioned: St. Jevons, C. Menger, and L., Walras. They claimed to have put the exact economics on a new footing, which was not a development of the field but rather meant the destruction of the classic system. Indeed, their work was different in every aspect, in the demarcation of the field, the methodological means, the findings; in all these areas the classical authors stand in total contradiction to the authors of the present. We only want to mention briefly that it in itself is split: "The Austrian School" with its most prominent representatives Menger, v. Boehm-Bawerk, and von Wieser and many non-Austrian scientists – Wicksell, Pantaleoni, Smart, Pierson, for example—has a totally different character than the "American School"—J. B. Clark and his successors. In a still different group are v. Pareto and E. Barone—for a lot of different reasons.

A third group is formed by theorists around A. Marshall. St. Jevons did not have any disciples in England—as famous as he was. You can find his ideas in almost every book on theoretical economics but it does not very often receive praise without a lot of reservations. The theorists of this direction think that his criticism of the classical authors went too far and that his discussions are mere additions to prior knowledge. They think that there is not much of a difference between the two if one interprets the classical authors loyally and does not see brevity as a criminal act. They think that the new value theory is one-sided and in itself insufficient. So, this approach is characterized by a certain eclecticism; one might be of a different opinion but it has a lot support in our discipline. Marshall is the theorist who gets the most attention today, even from people who usually keep their distance from the theory. And there is really no other book from which one could learn as much as from this great work.

We can now contrast these "*theoretical*" directions with other directions. We already mentioned the economic historians. Here we have to think of the interesting phenomenon of the development of new theories based on historical materials. Probably the best example is the "Theory of Modern Capitalism" by W. Sambart. This direction seems to be on a fast upswing and will soon be written about a lot. But we cannot put it next to the "exact theory"; it actually is totally the opposite, both in its nature and its goals: It does not try to build an exact framework but poses hypotheses about concrete questions, hypotheses similar to the ones in the field of political history. They do not strive to be generally accepted but rather are related to single historical facts. There is almost never a connection between the two—extended thought processes do not occur. So, there are certain parallels to the hypotheses in biology, which also deal mostly with problems of development. The biggest difference to our static theory is that these new theories are anything but static. But perhaps theirs is the field of "dynamics"! We will see.

Another group of economists deals with the great problems of today, the development tendencies of the world economy, questions of currency politics, modern monopolies, etc. This approach differs from our theory in two areas: First, their work is predominantly practical; and secondly, it is based on concrete phenomena of reality, on collections of statistical facts. That is of course totally different from basing your work on abstract hypotheses and similar instruments of exact thinking. It also deals with the present instead of the past. Of course, we will have to make the connection between our theory and the findings of this type of work, but for us it is more important to stress that those two have to be kept separate.

Other economists have turned to social policies, some to a point that they are "economists" by name only. That is definitely the case in Germany. But of course it is not up to us to judge this direction. I do not want to give the impression that I do not recognize the validity of this direction by my musings from the standpoint of economic theory. The opposite is the case. But it has to be stressed that economic theory and social policies are totally separate fields, both in theory and content, and that the social politicians' opinion of the political problems and the theorists' opinion of social policy problems have to be a dichotomy.

But we find these encroachments a lot. A good example is the majority of French economists who mix different approaches. This direction, especially the academic economists, is the successor of the practical-political inheritance of the classical authors. Theory for them is not an end in itself but a platform for political tendencies. We have to appreciate their contribution to the theory but we do have to stress that we do not have anything in common with them. Among them are many economists who are interested in economic policies—not in theory—although they do not try to do without it.

And finally, we have to mention scientific socialism, which of course has its own theory. Although this theory does not go up or down with its practical postulates, it is still used by many non-socialists. But we have to be careful calling the latter "bourgeois." The exact theory as it is represented here is not partial and does not lead to any practical postulates. Very often, we find attacks against socialism in many theoretical works on the present distribution of production profit. It actually has to, since its theory proves that free competition leads to "profit maximation." We do not want to analyze this here. Not because we would be against socialism but because of theoretical reasons that do not have practical meaning.

This is all we have to say here. This book is purely theoretical. It tries to dissect as exactly as possible the basis, the methods, and the main findings of pure economics in order to gauge its nature, its value, and its potential for further development. This should be enough for an introduction; more remarks about the relationships of our narrow field will be found further into the book, especially in the second part and towards the end of the book.

Now we want to start our task and lay out the basics of our pure theory, as dry and plainly as possible in order to be as unassailable as possible.

2

The Point of Departure of Our Theory

I

We are faced with some problems at the threshold of our discipline, problems that seem to be based in its nature. Every discussion of economics starts out with many undoubtedly highly interesting and highly important problems. The motives for human activities, the fluctuating forces of society, the reasons for economic activities, etc.—scientists think they have to discuss all of this and much more before they can start to tackle the real problems of our science. They force upon us ready-made opinions on topics such as the types of human needs; how they can be explained and then satisfied; and how these different types should be evaluated. And everything that follows in their work seems to rise or fall with their opinions. Mostly they are general axioms, presented in a very authoritarian tone. And we do not care whether they are uttered overtly or can be read between the lines. Even the author who tries to ignore them, cannot do that if he analyzes what he actually says. A furious and confusing discussion is going on, and some scientists totally concentrate on it, to the point that some of our colleagues neither have the time nor the energy for constructive work. What is the driving force of an economy— the individual or "the society"? What guides the human being more—egotistic or altruistic motives? And it does not matter whether the one or the other is correct—are these motives mainly of economic nature or do others play a large, even decisive role, i.e., ambition, the will to dominate, love of country, etc.? Indeed, what is more natural than that these things are so important for economic questions is that they have to be answered before we can move on? One might even think that; that in itself is not even enough. Are the actions of humans simple and regular enough to be able to describe them scientifically or do they originate in a free will, which would not allow for an exact description? Are their motives based on natural laws, on measurable "powers," with which the natural sciences deal all the time? So, we are even slipping into the field of free will. But if we really want to tackle these problems, we have to admit that our field is in a grave position. We are forced to include all these things into our field and have to give up any clarity and independence in our discussions. We would give up clarity because the indicated problems exclude clear and precise solutions. Partly, they are in the area of metaphysics and this fact excludes any type of real exactness. Foggy metaphysics would shroud our discussions. And we would give up independence because some of those problems belong into other disciplines, like psychology, physiology, and biology. Since we are just dilettantes in these fields, we need constant help and so we lose our independence.

Indeed, in all these questions we are being attacked by enemies of our science. As a matter of fact, the sheer fact that we deal with these questions explain the mere existence of these enemies. We are embroiled in a quarrel that will not lead to any results and it will only end when everybody involved in it will just get tired. And as long as not everything is on the table, we will not come to an understanding and people will not develop trust in our discipline. But do we really have to wait until mankind has answered all these questions? In this case we would have to give up economics altogether because we will never run out of questions. So the question has to be posed, whether we really have to solve *all* problems, whether we have to blow up all hurdles instead of trying to navigate around them. Other disciplines do it, too. If the field of mechanics wanted to answer the question what "power," movement," and "mass" *really* are, the beautiful building that we admire today never would have been built. Wouldn't it be possible, then, in our field to also tackle problems without having to do all that groundwork that saps all our energy?

When we look over the arsenal of our findings, we observe something that shows us the correct path: The discussions that have provided us with the most valuable findings in our discipline are virtually free of all these controversies. For example, the person who asks what the interest on capital is and what its laws are, does not really care whether economic or artistic interests have greater power over the economic subjects. The same is true for the money theory and one could find many more examples. Questions like this should only play a role in introductions and very general discussions. In the real work environment, in the practical part of our science, they do not play a role. So, one can assume that they are a lot less important than it sometimes seems. This seems to be a path out of our quandary.

So, let us use this path! We neither want to strive for new ways to solve problems nor do we want to produce ammunition for any of the quarreling parties. I have started on a different path, one that avoids fruitless controversies, a path that does not add anything to the popularity of our field but can be recommended to anybody who is serious about scientific work, and who prefers precision and cognitive correctness instead of unclear phrases and colorful generalities.

It is the following: We look at a group of concrete findings, which are typically called pure economics, and ask ourselves how we can understand them with a minimum of background and axioms; we analyze which underpinnings we really have to know and use; and we refuse to comment on any problem unless it is necessary for our cause. In other words, we analyze which of them are necessary for our theory and, further, what economists want to do with them and what they do when they come up with these overgeneralizations. It is not important to us what these assertions generally mean or whether they are true but rather what they mean to *us* and whether they are useful for each of our cases. It becomes clear right away that the whole thing becomes clearer because it is more limited. In addition, it takes away from the aggressiveness of our quarrels because we do not try to solve the problems in general but rather in very limited cases.

We do not want to embellish the basis of our discussion but word it as boringly as possible. We want to say as little as possible about things that are not really part of our domain. Our introduction should be bland and formal but therefore as clear and correct as possible. It has to be purged of every word that is unnecessary for what follows. The less the reader has to digest the better. We especially will avoid getting too deep into questions that are not part of our domain and to try to *explain* our presuppositions: If we go into philosophical, sociological, physiological, and other underpinnings of certain phenomena, it appears that our discussions are dependent on their level of correctness, and thus could be refuted by philosophers, sociologists, physiologists, etc. I cannot stress enough, that that would be wrong.

We would like to contribute to a critique of our science in order to show what the exact content of the wordy presuppositions is that we meet at the threshold of our science and that we are given when we ask about the foundation of theoretical economics. We gladly sacrifice the interest in our field for scientific rigor. We put dry assumptions—which might not say anything interesting but there is no doubt about their sense—in the place of the most beautiful philosophies. Everybody can embellish them the way they want. As long as he accepts them we do not care what his reason might be. We will limit ourselves to a very small area because that allows us to control it.

What is, then, the result of this form of proceeding? Does it do what it is supposed to? The reader might want to judge that for himself but we want to mention in advance that we will accomplish want we wanted, in a quite surprising fashion: A whole bunch of controversies simply disappear. If one does not deal with them with general arguments but really analyzes what they really are about, one finds out that there really are no roadblocks but one can easily avoid them. All others—and I really think *all* of them—can be rewritten in such a way that the sticky points do not have be touched upon at all and can therefore be neutralized. All objections that I know of can be taken into consideration and anybody who appreciates the meaning of the exact discipline of human actions will be ready for a sacrifice that is necessary in every cleansing process.

In our work to purge everything unnecessary or compromising from the main questions of the exact economics, we get to the following statements which seem like bare skeletons—but that makes the delineations of our discipline so much clearer. That might seem strange to the economist—that is the reason for the preceding comments and for the fact that our discussion will be interrupted frequently for further commentaries. But everybody who is interested in the exact sciences will find in them well-known ideas. They will lead straight to the problems with which we will be dealing.

II

If we look at any economy, we will find that each subject owns a certain quantity of certain goods. At the basis of our discipline lies the realization that all these quantities, which we want to call "economic quantities" are in a state of interdependency, in a way that if one of them gets changed all of them change. That is a simple insight that is so obvious that it does not need any further explanation. We say that those quantities form the elements of a system. Even if they altogether are arbitrary and random, the individual ones in themselves cannot be random and independent.

Now, if we find there is such a connection, that each quantity of one element or a few of them relates to only one other one, we call this system unequivocally determined. We call this state the State of Equilibrium. The individual quantities in this state we call *normal* or *natural*.

When given any state of an economy, it is our task to deduce those changes of the quantities, which will happen in the near future if nothing unforeseeable happens. We call this deduction "explanation." We get there through a *description* of the interdependencies. We therefore define our task as the *description of our system and its tendencies of movement*. If that can be achieved unequivocally without having to use axioms of our field, then there is a *self-contained economic discipline*. Our descriptions are therefore "*economic laws*," as long as they are of high significance. In their entirety, they comprise the discipline of the "pure" or "theoretical" economy.

III

Let us halt here to discuss what we just wrote, especially the advantages of our method. Above all, it allows us a precise definition of our topic, free of any type of vagueness. Of course, it can only be fully appreciated at the very end of our discussions. In general, it is a characteristic of a strictly scientific approach that the reader or the listener only learns during the discussion which direction the author is taking and why he chose this specific organizing principle. Although they can be found in the very beginning, the first sentences are always the result of later discussions of what is necessary in preliminary deliberations to understand what follows. Just looking at some definitions shows us what economists in the past did not do but also how inadequate their definitions are. We do not want to talk about those who see economics as the science of the best means to reach economic well-being and, thus, strip our science of its scientific character; we are beyond that. But even the more correct approaches are very unsatisfactory. Some have described economics as the science of the satisfaction of needs. The satisfaction of need is a question of physiology or, looked at from a different angle, a question of engineering or, from yet another viewpoint, a question of cultural history. Such a definition creates all kinds of expectations, which will be disappointed but not those which would be justified. This definition does not indicate at all the nature of the pure theory nor its concrete problems. In addition, it does not delineate the field either. And finally, it infuses a lot of problems and vagueness into our science by using the term "satisfying needs."

The definition of economics as the science of economic activities does not fare any better because that would necessitate a full explanation in our discipline, which means some information on the nature of human activities (especially the economic one), how economic ideas and habits can be explained, etc. Biology covers these problems. This approach does not do the questions of pure economics justice. It does not fathom economic activities, it actually is not even related to them. Of course, prices are a result of "economic activities." But the important point is that we deal with them on the basis of certain formal assumptions but not on what they are based and therefore we do not have to even deal with human activities. And when we do not have to, we will not do it on the basis of "scientific economics." But that will become much clearer later on.

Another definition, the one of the "economic principle" goes too far, because this principle covers a very wide field and it is about the generalization of a logical rule.

While this definition is on the one hand too wide, on the other one it does not contain everything necessary: The economic principle by itself is not enough to solve our problems. We need more building blocks in order to erect the building of our science. At least this interpretation of economics is more correct than any other I know, especially the one that sees economics as a function of the egotism of the individual. This definition also is too wide because one can also act egotistically outside the area of economics. But aside from that, this definition creates a lot of problems for our field, which easily could be avoided because the element that it stresses the most does not even play a role in our problems.

I would like to mention yet another definition: One often calls economics the science of production, distribution, and consumption of goods. But theory does not deal with everything that is entailed in this "production," for example the technique of production. As far as "consumption" is concerned, we only look at certain elements such as consumption delay, meaning saving the money; in general it is behind the processes we are interested in. And we also do not deal with the distribution problem as thoroughly as necessary but just one side of it. We never say which parts of the three phenomena we are discussing—what is missing is the characteristic element.

All these definitions—perhaps even *all* that have ever been written—fail because they were written a priori. Instead of looking at the concrete problems, theorists have always tried to explain the name of their field (here we do not want to deal with definitions that encompass more than the pure science). And this name is "economics" or some such thing. Isn't it only natural that it is the task of an economic science to research economic actions? But that is not necessarily the case as other sciences show. For example, the field of psychology does not deal with the nature of the soul; it does not even comment on the question of its existence. So we can say without a problem that economic theory does not have anything to do with the nature of economic activity, that it does not even have to be defined. That is not a paradox at all. And when we then keep in mind that the scientific nomenclature is an inheritance of bygone periods and that the development of the science leads to a specialization of the disciplines and to a shift of their problems, we should not be too surprised when the terminology does not meet today's needs. But it is still a good idea to stick with it even if that might lead to misunderstandings and a skewed perception among people outside of our field.

We looked at the concrete problems of the pure theory and peeled off anything unnecessary and got to the dry but exact definition, which you read above. When evaluating it one has to keep two things in mind: First, we do not want to define the whole field that today is called "national economics" or "political economics" but rather the much smaller field of "pure economics." There are other theories dealing with economic problems which do not belong to this group so that, for terminological reasons, we have to differentiate here between the areas of "theoretical economics" and "economic theory." The latter is much wider than the former. The reason why we pick a group of economic theories instead of their totality is that that group forms a self-contained system. [We use the term "system" in two different ways: as a "scientific system of theorems" and a "system of connected quantities." I hope that does not lead to any confusion.] We definitely do not want to limit the field of economics. We just want to analyze a part of the field in its true form without any impurities.

Secondly, please do not forget that we want to give an exact definition, which only contains those and only those elements that are necessary for the following discussion and which really forms the basis for the following train of thought—but not a popular one. If we wanted to show which material theorems the reader can expect, a different one might have been more useful. We just want to work out the exact content of the known definitions and cannot deny that the beginner might not be able to work with ours.

IV

Let us proceed: Certain interdependencies and functional relationships are what we are interested in. The fact that the economic quantities are in such interdependencies justifies dealing with them separately, as long as they are accurate. The accuracy of a system of quantities is a very important scientific fact. It means that we—as long as certain data is known—have all necessary elements to "understand" the dimensions and movements of the quantities. In this case, a separate, independent discipline about such phenomena is possible and that is what we have to prove. Even if an equation system offers nothing but the proof of a clear-cut interdependency that is worth a lot: That is the basis of a scientific building. When we have proven its existence, we have as the first big result, that the economic quantities are not random numbers but are rather determined ones.

This axiom has often been misunderstood. But controversies about this point have almost always been about socio-political consequences. Nothing seems to be clearer as the fact that economic quantities are *not* unequivocally determined but rather determined by social power relationships, which can be manipulated. From a socio-political standpoint, this axiom has therefore been criticized continuously. Indeed it seems to judge all socio-political endeavor rather harshly. Especially the representatives of the workers always assume—and often rightly so—that there is always a political commentary behind them. Therefore I want to stress here right away, that for example the axiom that income is not determined haphazardly but in a certain sense determined by nature, does not mean anything but that it can be deduced from a certain set of data. We do not judge socio-political attempts to change the existing income distribution since nothing is being said about whether this data can be altered or not. But our sentence also seems to contradict everyday experience: For example, there can be a wage increase without any change in the financial situation of the company or without any other type of change in economic circumstances. We only mention this objection at this point—we will discuss it at a later point. There are other reasons, why one has a problem accepting terms such as "natural," "regular," and "normal" in this context. Partly at fault are the economists who only too often abuse these terms but partly it is of non-scientific nature. We do not want to discuss these questions at this point because it will become clear that we can avoid them altogether. What is important to us is to protect the words "natural" and "normal" against the suspicion that we in the end mean something different from what we said previously and push philosophical and political axioms. These terms only relate to the given condition of our systems of quantity of goods, which we do not want to judge. We do not care whether there are normal or abnormal, desirable or deplorable conditions or whether they all have the same relative justification. We will see that our discussions are totally independent of any concrete condition. We do not want to claim that the economic subject's ownership of goods—or as it is sometimes called, "the distribution of goods in the area of the researched area—could not be different. We also do not claim that the distribution, which is the basis of this theory, is the best one. Certainly a violent event could change it and one cannot claim that that would be bad for an economy; what we do claim, though, is that from a given distribution plus a few more certain data we can deduce another one if nothing unforeseen happens, like a violent intervention. Each economic quantity within a system has a certain given dimension. Now, if an economic subject receives a different amount of a certain good that is abnormal from the perspective of our theory. A different reasoning would have to be found. That does not mean we would not accept such a case nor that we see it as an abnormality or a temporary phenomenon. Perhaps the term "normal" and even more so the word "natural" suggest both; in this case both terms are misleading and we want to stress that we do not want to be associated with the group of economists who say that. For practical reasons we do stick to the terms but do not want to put any different meaning into them; thus we take away their controversial character. But the price for that is high: We relinquish every material assertion and demote this terminology to a harmless but meaningless means of scientific thinking. But in our area we only use it as that. In the following discussions we will see that these controversies, which play such a large role in our literature therefore are utterly superfluous, that our tight definition pulls the rug from under it. We got them out of our path.

Let me comment on the term "balance." It actually is not a very good term for the situation in which nothing changes as long as there are no outside interventions. The term reminds us that the field of mechanics and analogies with that field are not very popular and actually do have some problems. We again would like to stress that we do not want to draw any conclusions from such an analogy and that we want to stick with the term and we do not want to use it in any other form as the way we have defined it. The basis and the central problem of our theory is what is necessary to determine the balance of our interdependent system. Details will be discussed at a later point.

V

The description of the interdependency of the elements of our system in order to be able to interpret the different conditions of that system is the task of our discipline, as we have said. And we also have said that a scientific explanation of phenomena in the discipline is nothing but their description. So, for us the two terms "explanation" and "description" are synonyms, or in other words: We cannot and we do not want to contribute anything to the understanding of economic facts but their description.

It is not normal (and might even sound like a paradox) for a theorist to say that he only describes facts. Usually one sees explanation and description as opposites; theory is supposed to find "the reasons for the facts," the "forces," the "laws," which determine the facts. But when you look closely, you figure out quickly that the core of every theory is nothing but a statement about the functional relationships between certain dimensions. Everything else is just garnishing and not important. That is the most obvious in those sciences that do not speculate, especially in the exact natural sciences and here specifically in the famous definition of mechanics by Kirchhoff. We cannot find reasons here but we do not need them in order to get to concrete findings.

We now claim that that is also the case in our science: Everything worthwhile that has been written about pure economics is just a description of facts and that every time economists claim to do more they are wrong. At least they are wrong in how they express things. Often, axioms that look like speculation are in reality supported by facts; they really are description of facts. Then it is possible to hold on to them and defect any attacks simply by correct language and shedding of any speculation. But often people are simply wrong—and the findings have to be given up.

A good example for the first mistake is the axiom that "everybody strives for a most complete satisfaction of ones needs." It seems to be one of those important axioms which get heavily attacked by historians, and rightly so. For our axioms, though, only the observation is necessary that everybody wants to buy as cheaply as possible and sell as expensive as possible. This observation is the result of the description of processes of the market and it can be generalized to a large degree. An example for the second type would be the claim that individual freedom of the individual and of a society is always of the highest advantage. This axiom and all its consequences cannot be defended anymore, at least not in this generality.

We will show that in general the theorems of economics can be expressed correctly and are independent from axioms of this sort. But still one has to ask: How can we claim that economics only describes? How could we be so sure about our findings? Does the theoretical economist describe single acts of bartering, is there a history of prices? The answer to these questions contains the core of a cognition theory of pure economics.

If we want to understand any problem, we have to look at all individual facts that are related to the problem. This is the only way to perfect results. There is no other one—at least every other one would be speculation. And it also would not lead to the nature of things but just describes the relationships between them. But the attempt to walk this path would teach us two things: First, that it is impossible, and secondly that it is not necessary to have *all* facts. It is impossible because our materials will always be incomplete and even if they were complete, nobody could remember them all. And it is not even necessary in order to control all facts.

Despite its variety, we can observe certain similarities of the phenomena of a class. Each leave of a tree, each human of a race is different from all other leaves and all other humans, but overall number of similarities is much higher than the number of differences. In addition, we notice that we are not interested in all the facts to the same degree; we do not ask for reasons for these differences but they exist. And it is a fact that we are most interested in the phenomena that show the most similarities. And we see that for these reasons it is only necessary to know a rather small number of facts in order to get a good overview over the field. We soon reach a point at which the addition of new facts does not lead to more knowledge of the field. We can call this a law of diminishing profit: The first facts that we learn about a field teach us the most but the axioms that we deduce from them can mislead us so that it is of great advantage to continue with the observations. We do not learn very much new. The profit shrinks. But learning new facts is still advantageous because the picture we get becomes more usable and more exact. But we finally reach the spot where the picture is usable and exact and more "exactness" is not possible and would even become irritating. That is also true for our field. There are always surprises in human behavior but the reason is that the individual only knows very little. And the fact that we are surprised just shows that we expect a certain action. In addition, surprises usually happen in the small area of practical life.

But our science is interested in certain big phenomena and only in their most original forms, so there is little room for surprises. Why? One could say because of the existence of great laws, which soon leads to the problem of determinism. We do not say that, we just express the fact that generalizations usually work. We are aware that we can be proven wrong, but it is a fact that we do not want to prove but just state. Thus, we just stick to the facts and therefore we are seldom proven wrong. Human beings have the tendency to generalize facts they have experienced in their lives—and they are successful with this method. If a rational being, meaning somebody equipped with a logical apparatus, came down to earth and would meet a human for the first time, this being would make conclusions from this one for all others. From the perspective of the scholastic logic, that is false reasoning. We, on the other hand, think this is the healthiest method. We have to admit that our being comes to wrong conclusions but the number of correct conclusions clearly outweighs the wrong ones. The amount of facts differs with the motivations of the observers but for every motivation and for every observer there is—so to speak—a perfect level of knowledge with a certain amount of phenomena. It is like looking at a piece of art: There is a perfect distance between the piece and the viewer but this distance is different for each person and for each motivation to look at the piece.

That is why theory and description are so much more important. The "descriptive" economist or the historian does not undertake the impossible task of describing every fact, every source in his field and concedes that not all facts are equally interesting and also that even "unsupported" inductions usually prove to be correct so that even an incomplete description covers more than the facts alone. If that were not his hope, his work would only interest him for artistic reasons. In this case there is no *difference* between theory and history. Predicting phenomena definitely is the goal of both. And it is not correct to see them as opposites or to claim that they have different ideas about the nature of our science. The difference is the following: The "description" only catalogues facts, the "theory" changes them … not out of a specific motivation but just to get a better overview over them. It constructs a schema for them in order to briefly describe the unfathomable amount of facts and to make it possible to get a complete understanding of them in the shortest amount of time and at the same as completely possible. Their findings, of course, are probably not guaranteed since they are based on just a few of the many available facts. On the other hand, the findings of the "description" also are not sure—if you even try to get findings out of it. But, of course, that is what you want to do because facts alone would be boring.

But in our field, there is a big difference between theory and description; but this difference does not lie in the nature of the field but in the fact that theorists and historians deal with different problems and they differ in their selection of facts. No wonder, then, that the theorists and historians call the other approach worthless. Since description and theory use different approaches being embraced by people of different talents and thought processes, the dichotomy is easy to understand, especially when both go beyond the demarcation of our field in order to tackle the same practical questions.

VI

The explanation that our field offers is therefore a description of functional relationships between the elements of our system through short and generally accepted formulas. These formulas we call *laws*. The term "law" in economics is shrouded in a mist of misunderstandings and, as we already know, the target of criticism. The question whether there actually can be laws of human actions or whether there has to be a discussion about the problem of free will is being discussed constantly. Metaphysical and political hesitations for and against the term makes this discussion a messy one. We think that our definition of it avoids all those problems. According to that definition, economic laws are not postulates like moral directions. They do not represent an ideal but rather are an image of real processes. We do not claim that we want them to be generalizable nor do we want to base economic policies on them. Actually that was the philosophy of many economists and still is. Even when some authors claim to think like us, they often act differently and seem to support the notion of "free action" of these laws. It seems then that they are independent factors in the economic activities, as if they had eternal powers. Even if his might sometimes just be a less-than-perfect utterance of a correct thought, it is enough to contribute to the discrediting of economics.

Now, we do not have to stress that we do not want to find great causal connections, but we just want to describe visible processes. Not even historians could condemn speculations of any type more than we do. We do not philosophize what should be based on a certain necessity, but we describe *what* is. We expect that the same *might be* true in other cases that we do not analyze. We do not want to explain these expectations, but we find them nevertheless to a large extent. We could add a few words to our definition that expresses this fact; we could call our laws generalized observations. But we do not want to do that because we are not striving for a complete generalization in the sense that we exclude any possibility of an instantia contraria. Of course, we expect that our axioms are also true for facts that we did not observe, as every historian who has read thousands of sources about a certain law expects that the same will be applied at the same place and the same time. Otherwise we would not even come up with axioms. And we try to write them in a way that we can be *rationally calm* about. But we do not claim *in principle* that it has to be like this.

Too often "exact" laws are seen as the opposite of "static" ones. We see now, that that dichotomy does not exist. Both are based on observation of facts. The former often lacks the collection of facts that supports the latter. That is because they relate to such well-known phenomena that everybody knows from his own experiences that new statistics do not seem to be necessary. Everybody finds enough facts in his experience that is necessary in order to have the perfect number. Where that is not the case, as for example in the problems in the money theory, we simply have to collect more facts.

That all seems clear and simple to us so that there is no reason to describe our laws as "statements of tendencies," as A. Marshall did. All we want to say here is that different circumstances can lead to findings different from what our laws predicted. That is very logical and does not prove our formulas are wrong. Even every law in the natural sciences is subjected to eventualities. A rock on a table cannot fall to the floor. If somebody would therefore call the law of gravity "statement of tendencies," he could do that. There is no feature here that would be specifically applicable to *our* law.

On the other hand, we have not used our laws to their full extent. They are not deduced from facts but from systematizing them. Although that does not change their nature, the opposite *seems* to be true. We start with facts. But in order to abbreviate the description; to make it clearer; and to cut out elements we are not interested in, we come up with hypotheses that allow us to express them concisely. These hypotheses have been discussed a lot. They often seem to be big, general principles and lack sufficient proof from the facts. It therefore is sometimes seen as pure speculation. The "unproven hypothesis"—every theorist has heard this phrase and has tried to disprove it. Is the future of economics dependent on the acceptance of unproven theorems, or theorems that cannot be proven?

People have tried to proof the necessary hypotheses or they have just assumed that they are correct and that everything that follows is dependent on its truth. The latter is preferable because the former leads into other disciplines. That is obvious. But if you have to believe in some theorems to agree with yet another one, that is disquieting: One knows how controversial some of these hypotheses are. We do not want to discuss them here but just make our stance clear: Our hypotheses are as arbitrary as definitions. They are based on facts but we create them from our feeling of absolute powers. That is the reason they seem so certain. But we try to claim as little as possible, and where we claim we only do so to help our *descriptions* and do not pretend it is *understanding*. These two points make our hypotheses different from a priori speculation and therefore should calm down opposition. We will show our approach soon in some examples and will always come back to it. At this point we want to limit our discussion to the most necessary comments in order not to separate cognitive theory from practical work. Therefore we will just make a few more remarks.

What you just read does not form a big difference between exact and statistic laws. But even those have certain pre-conditions and when they do not stand out clearly it is usually due to a lack of clear language. And the historian also has to use hypotheses. As a matter of fact, each and every theorem makes sense under certain circumstances—regardless of the content. We do not want to suppress those but only to select and to express them in a way that it does not diminish the validity of our findings. The difference then between our description and the field of statistics is a more complicated instrument but in no way a difference in a priori axioms. It is based on facts the same way history is. Like history, we do not want to have anything to do with philosophies.

We even go so far as to avoid the terms "cause" and "effect." For higher precision, we do not want to talk about "causes" of phenomena but rather of functional relationships between them. The term "function," defined in detail by the field of mathematics, has a clear and unquestionable character—the term "cause" does not. We have to do that for general reasons but especially for our topic. We cannot follow down to the last detail what each single element of our system "is" and why it is the way it is and why a certain economic subject owns a certain amount of bread. We accept these elements as given and we will see that the concrete findings in our discipline are based on certain interrelations so that the term of function and not the term of cause seem to be more important. The clarity that it brings into the discussion helps us to overcome some difficulties and it is logical to use the term function since this way we make fewer claims than if we would use "cause and effect." This way we minimize the room for controversy.

So, theory offers us description and only description of certain interrelations. It would be wrong to think that it could do more. Often it would be a harmless mistake that would not affect our concrete results. But it would still confuse us when we think about the foundation of our discipline and it then could lead to opposition to economics in general.

Perhaps the whole quarrel about methods would never have grown to this point if the theorists would not have elevated theory to a religion. The claim that our theorems are more exact than experiences so that they can completely explain economic phenomena and their laws is responsible for so many attacks on our field. On the other hand, we have to admit that it was us who connected the fate of our discipline with that claim without enough scrutiny.

3

Barter Relations

If we now tackle the task to describe the interdependencies we talked about, we clearly see an already established relationship between economic quantities: the price or the *barter relation*. Almost all goods are in this relationship. In a complete economy, each good stands in a fixed barter relationship with any other good at any given time, or to express it differently: they are being bought and sold at a certain price. In this case it is clear that we can—with the assistance of barter relations—deduce all economic qualities from each element involved. For example, if we know the barter relations of labor to all other goods, we can deduce for each given worker the number of goods that he will buy. What is a constant is that the man works with a certain intensity, has a certain level of motivation to work, and has a certain taste, and that these variables do not change all of a sudden. We will get back to these variables later.

But there is not always a barter relation, not in an isolated economy and not in those elements of an isolated economy, which actually can also been found in a real economy. So, in order to not have to do without this available tool or the generalizability of our findings, we want to plug it in where it is missing by assuming that all economic activities are being defined as barter and assume that even where there is no barter relation, the economy functions as if there were one. That is not as paradoxical as it sounds. Please do not forget that every economic activity for us is nothing but a change of economic quantities. For example, whoever barters labor for bread, changes the amount of both goods he owns, and that is true for the hunter who barters the number of bullets and his labor for a growing amount of venison. In this way, we can use the principle of barter for each economic activity and even go further—we will get to that at a later point. And it is not new. It is an old thought to interpret production as a bartering of productive services. (That is the same thought that led Bishop Whately in his Introductory Lectures to call our science "Catalactics." His idea is very close to ours when he says that in economics human is a creature that barters and that he is only interesting for the science in this one point.) We find our approach correct when we keep in mind that that in describing the barter relations we do not use any assumptions that could not be used in an isolated economy; we furthermore know that these relations happen everywhere and we are happy when our findings work.

So, barter is the clamp that holds together the economic system or, to use a different metaphor, their wiring. Barter relation is pure economics, which becomes apparent from what we already have said, and it is true for the isolated system as well as the state. If we see any economic action as barter, and furthermore, if we see everything that is happening within our system as nothing but a change of economic quantities we call barter, we do not claim that any other method of treatment would be worse or wrong and we do not want to base any social consequences on this assumption. That has been done quite a bit—one example is the harmony economists—and to a large degree that is the base of the animosity against this assumption, which definitely exists. It has been seen as an attempt to blur social differences or paint them as innocuous. The harmonists as well as the classical authors in this point often took escapades into the world of social warfare and the other side often stressed that that the economic terminology does not fit the reality of social differences. But we do not want to claim anything like that. If we still do not get into these differences, as we will see in the distribution theory, we do not do that for any socio-political goals but only to express our opinion that the pure theory cannot deal with these goals with its means but they belong in different areas, which have a different character and different methods. We will always have to come back to the differences between our assumption and that of the older national economics. The latter had the hope to be able to understand the wheelwork of social life from the perspective of economics. The final consequence in this regard is the so-called economic historiography and everything in that area. We do not want to do that.

Today's economics usually works differently: It does deal with these questions but not based on the pure theory in the way former economics did it but rather more correctly based on new materials. This path definitely is defensible. But we do not take this path since I believe that a division of labor for fields so diverse is to be preferred. Those of you who are interested in exactly those problems should put down this book. But it would be unjust to call my belief outdated. It is absolutely in line with the modern beliefs about how to deal with social problems and when dealing with them is being excluded from pure economics, therein lies the same criticism of its one-sided interpretation in the typical fashion: exclude the problems or deal with them on a different basis—both of them mean the same for pure economics; in any case, the latter case has to make sure not to demand to have the last word and it also should not demand that from the theoretical side. We should not forget that when evaluating modern theory, one should not forget that it deals with a much smaller area than the older one. And we only want to deal with this smaller one.

We see it as our sole task to explain what "price" is and to deduce certain laws of movement. Of course this way we ignore everything that most people see as the most interesting and the price for the correctness of our axioms it is a large part of their value. What this value is we will try to explain in various parts of this book but we do not want to deny that people have a different opinion about it. But we do claim that this approach fits the narrowly defined problems best—better than the others. No big social results will come out of it. Nowhere does the difference in opinion become more apparent than in those "maximum problems," where we trade correct language and the general acceptability of our axioms with the interest in the problem of free market, free trade, laissez faire, of individualism. Another example is the value principle: We do not attach to it consequences as the ones Marx derives from the labor principle. Some theorists have done that, though—we will get back to that later. But for us, the value is simply an explanation principle that helps us to prove that our system is clear and unequivocal and to show more clearly the conditions of the equilibrium than the older theory did. As we said before, we do not deny that one could use social categories to analyze economic processes, and we even admit that in some respect that would result in valuable insights. One could, for example, start with the ideas generated by the term "price war" and do without what we call pure economics without feeling a void. The German science has been doing this for quite some time. The only support we can bring forth for our opinion is that that it leads to a clear, exact system, the only one that exists in the area of human sciences. Our interpretation that each economic activity is a form of barter *cannot be objectionable* and, as we have defined it, it does not only entail the so-called "Traffic [Trade?] Theory," but all pure economic theory is just an analysis of the barter problem. It has often been criticized that the theory reduces all economic activity to "dickering," and the term "stock exchange economy" was coined, with a side-glance at social and ethical doubts objections. This objection is probably based to a large degree on a misunderstanding of methodological means, even if such an objection is justified in some cases, especially where theorists try to tackle practical questions. In our opinion, which introduces barter even when there is no transfer, this term is just a synonym for "economic activity" or "economic deliberation about possible activity", or even better, the element of this barter is the core that lies in their words.

4

The Discussion of the Question, How the Barter Relation Can Be Grasped and Some Other Points

I

So, the barter relation defines our area. It jettisons from the body of facts everything that is not purely economic. We will see that everything that it does not entail either belongs to a different discipline or cannot be tackled by an exact treatment. We are looking now for a *principle* that will *describe* the barter relation. Each phrase that will give us the sought-after elements of our system when certain dimensions were plugged in, does qualify without having to ask whether if it in itself is a valuable finding or not. And since we cannot take into account all barter relations that exist, this principle has the character of an arbitrary hypothesis, which we can use as long as it does not become an inexplicable contradiction with the facts. Of course, we will, if we can, start with the observation of a fact, and, thus, this principle is not totally arbitrary. But we will also use it—in the process described above—also in other cases which we cannot observe, e.g., those that will happen in the future. We also will not be able to prove our hypothesis every time, but just build on it for right now. Therein lies the essence of scientific reasoning. When we have found such a principle, out of which we can deduce the barter relation and which allows us to determine dimension and the laws of movement of the economic quantities, our job is finished. The discussion of the laws of movement then is the complete pure economics.

The whole nature of our system, the image of our theoretical structure is dependent on the principle that we chose and depending on the various principles, the scientific images of one and the same reality can look different. Such a difference does not indicate that there are differences of opinions about the nature of economics or about practical questions, or that there is a principal difference between the authors of the images at all. If somebody takes the value the other one labor as the connecting link that does not necessarily mean a difference in the interpretation of social events. If in spite of the fact that the labor theory has a socialist tint, and most champions of the value theory seem to be anti-socialist, the reason for that fact is not the role that labor and value play in their respective systems, but rather that both parts grant their respective elements a status that goes beyond the role of a mere explanation principle. We do not do that because our findings would not be any better and because it is our principle to only discuss what is important for our findings. A certain explanation could be a circumstance that lies outside of our area and is of no interest for the social discussion. So, if we scan our field to find such a principle, we do not follow Marx's line of questioning, namely what do all goods have in common. We do not go that deep. We are not looking for any type of metaphysical similarity of certain characteristics; we do not ask ourselves how it is possible to compare things that are so different; we are content to know that such relations *exist*.

The best example to describe these relations is the "cost principle." It allows the deduction of quantities of goods to those of others and a number of barter relations to others. In a similar fashion, the number of goods is connected through the element of the amount of work, which—as we know—leads to a concept different from the cost principle. And finally, we have the value principle. Now, the selection between these principles does not depend on an a priori discussion of their correctness. In general, it is our maxim to not quarrel a priori about principles; and in addition, we would not be interested in their *correctness* but in their *usefulness*. We want to stress here again that we want to deal with the big controversies of our science. We want to avoid such *a priori* discussions and we want to get to our findings step by step without calling the one or the other approach right or wrong. We will use the value principle but not because we think it is the only correct way but because it is the most practical to get to our findings because it takes us the furthest. But we will not claim that all other approaches are "wrong" and could not lead to usable findings, as it is often said.

Of course it is apparent that in general the prices of goods are usually closely linked to their costs and that the barter relation can often be defined as the relations of costs. In these cases that is definitely not wrong and to say that the price is a function of the costs cannot be denied in most cases. If one says, though, that costs are the cause of the process, we will contradict because we want to totally eliminate the concept of causality, but if one says the only thing that is meant by it is that the price in a lot of cases can be deduced from the costs we do not have any problem with that.

It is the practical shortcomings, the shortcoming in the practical scientific work that makes us reject the cost principle. It fails especially in the case of non-increasable goods and in addition in the explanation of monopoly prices. Furthermore, it says nothing about the most interesting problems of our discipline. Because if we go through the deductions the cost principle allows us, we end up with labor and land as the final elements. But these stand in barter relations to other goods than the ones that produced certain quantities from them, meaning they have a price but we cannot subject them to the cost principle. That is not good because the pricing of labor and land is one of the most interesting problems in economics. Ricardo's systems show clearly, though, that this is the situation. Nothing is clearer than the fact that the cost principle is not able to present a theory of wages and ground-rent. Ricardo then has to look for other elements to fill this void. In the rent theory that is done through a totally new instrument, the law of the decreasing ground-rent. It is very clear and very logical that land actually should not have a price but since it does, the whole system should collapse if it is build upon the cost system. Ricardo goes the only correct path here that leads out of the cul-de-sac when he tries to eliminate the price of land in calling it a "plus." So, the rent is deduced without calling it a price. The fact that land actually does have a price is explained away in saying that this price is not a price.

Very similar is the case of the wage. When Ricardo starts his chapter on wage with the words that work is a ware that has a market price like everything else, we have to respond that when he does not want to see work as one of the non-reproducible goods like old paintings, he will either have to explain away wage as he did rent, or he will have to interpret work as a reproducible good and wage as equal to the reproduction costs. From the standpoint of the classic system, this latter theory is the only possible one. Outside of this system it has a totally different position and a much diminished meaning for the theory.

This is a nice example for the difference between the theoretical and the practical interests of a theory. Typically, the practitioner does not care for what motivates the theorists to come up with theories. For the theorist, of course, it is critical, whether a theory is essential for his system or is just based on an ad hoc element that one can drop again without doing harm to the rest of the system. Even for this case our axiom is a good example for how different a position one and the same theory can have within one and the same discipline on different developmental levels of this discipline. If the cost principle is accepted and made the basis of the theoretical system, it leads to the theory of the reproduction costs of wages. In a system of economics that is based on the value principle, no such theory can be deduced. The only way that such a theory can be advanced would be based on overwhelming facts. In the former case, it is just necessary that the theory is not being proven wrong. That leads me to the following comments.

First, such a theory can become a real legitimate criterion between two systems of one and the same science, legitimate because it is a system of a priori axioms and general basic principles. If we, on the basis of a system, get a deductive finding, as this theory, we have to check all other like findings in reality. The result of this reality check will contribute to our selection between two systems. If the finding is correct and valuable and if the same is not yielded by the second system, that fact supports the first one. If reality negates the finding, it seems to support a system that does not say anything about this point but we do not necessarily have to abandon our first system. Generally, we will not do that just because it fails in one point. Of course, it makes the whole system suspect because one has to expect to find more discrepancies with reality but if we have good reasons to stick with this system we will use an auxiliary hypothesis. Perhaps the best-known example for such proceedings in the history of science is the history of the Ptolemaic System: In the end the number of auxiliary hypotheses grows to a point that we turn away from such a patchwork as fast as possible and a new hypothesis takes its place, a more general one, simpler and more vigorous than the old one—which of course will have the same fate as soon as it has run its course. Nothing would be more wrong than to make fun of the old system and call it wrong. Besides the fact that it still can teach us quite a bit, one should not forget that there is nothing absolutely correct and perfect; that on various developmental steps one just has to believe in certain things; and the new system would never have come into being without the existence of the old one; and that we have to preserve the organic path of development. But it is not only fair to pay this respect to his predecessors but it is highly detrimental to science if one tries to build too much new and leaves the old too soon, and works with new devices ahead of their time. When the transition has to take place is a decision that requires a lot of tact.

Secondly, the thoughts of the classical authors have powered their way into the practical life. One can doubt whether that was to their advantage. They have been misunderstood a lot and they have been abused and of course the result was it was completely discredited. But especially neglected by the scientific economists was the interrelationship of their axioms. Of course, their system was not completely homogeneous—in several respects, especially not because it was not purely economic, as we already have indicated. But still, one cannot hold on to some parts and discard others, at least not when one operates in a purely economic sphere. But that has happened a lot; axioms which only make sense and can be understood within the whole system of the classics are often represented by people who stand on a totally different principle basis. The best example is the rent theory, which is nothing but the flipside of the cost principle and loses any justification when the other one has collapsed. But it is advisable to continue to discuss this problem in another context.

Now let us get back to what we talked about before. A stopgap for the missing determination of wages is, among others, the wage fund theory and the key to understand it lies in the basics of the classical systems. One should not assume from Ricardo's axiom that we cited that he wants to deduce the price of labor from supply and demand, in the sense of the modern theory. He did not want to do that at all and it is part of the benevolent misinterpretations of Ricardo in order to save him and deny the modernists their originality. But if Ricardo really would have looked for an explanation of wage in the value of labor, that would be a confirmation of our contention that here the cost principle fails (because supply and demand lead to the value, as we will see) and one has to look for a different tool. But, as we have said, that would not be too bad and we would be willing to go that way. But when we find a principle that does not require an auxiliary hypothesis and that produces a neat, pure, homogeneous system that generates many valuable findings, without having any disadvantages, it would simply be stupid to reject it, especially since we are free to formulate it in a way that in many cases would fit both conceptions. In addition, it would not help us a lot if we would attribute labor and land to other quanta of goods. Because if we would be able to dissolve labor and land in such a way, we would run in circles since those quanta of goods cannot be attributed to labor and land. So, we can never get to a complete analysis by using the cost principle.

What really convinces us the most, though, to stay away from the cost principle are not its problems in the description of our system but rather its incapability to supply us with the axioms, which are our most interesting findings. Nothing is easier to see than the fact that when we change one of the elements in the system, the cost principle is not able to grasp all resulting variations. After all, when something is being changed in the economic system, not only the costs but at least also the demand is a deciding factor—if we for a moment want to use a term that we have not been using enough. If there is more of a certain good—e.g., as the result of a good harvest season—our principle cannot tell us anything about the effect of that fact on the price. Whenever the classical authors and all those who stand on the same ground talk about movement axioms, they always use the element of demand or presume some type of its efficacy or use non-economic elements, e.g., the law of diminishing profits, certain axioms on population increases, etc.

What we have said about the cost principle we can easily say about the labor principle. It is, if not totally the same as the cost principle, nothing but a harsher wording of the same, or better: a step further into the same direction.

II

These shortcomings make us use the value principle. You see, we are not interested in a quarrel about principles. The only reason we prefer the value system is because it does better in the real world than the explanation attempt just discussed. But that was not the standpoint of those researchers who first represented it. They cared less about the pragmatic value than the truth of the value principle and tried to prove that it contained the "correct" conception of the economic processes. We do not want to follow them there, for two reasons. First and foremost, we are not concerned about the correctness of our hypotheses. They are not part of our results for which we have to vouch but they are just methodological means, the value of which we only recognize in their fruits. Their role is just a *formal* one and our laws do not gain any by knowing that they in themselves are truths. Secondly, by going this path one has become entangled in an a priori discussion which—being discussed in general reasoning and allegories—cannot easily lead to an agreement and which can be avoided easily by using the path I have shown.

Furthermore, the attempt to explain the value hypothesis leads into areas unknown to the economists—that is the fields of psychology and physiology. One starts with the needs and defines the economic goods as things from the outer world that stand in a causal connection to the satisfaction of needs. The barter relations are being deduced from the relative intensity of the barterer's needs, and to that end the laws of value are being determined on the basis of psychological observations. One says, for example, that with a continuation of satiation the need for more food decreases and therefore the satiated individual will pay less and less for more food. We have to say this about such an approach: Why is such an explanation given? The fact that what we see is only that the individual is offering a lower price; *why* he does that is initially not of any interest from the perspective of economics, and, besides, we just see that the individual acts that he gets satiated. We are, thus, faced with the following alternative: Either we admit that the only fact that allows us to fathom the feelings of the individual is his way of acting or we have to rely on the results of introspection.

Let us look a little closer at both possibilities. In the first case, the psychological deduction is just a tautology. When we say that somebody offers a higher price for something than somebody else because he sees in it a higher value does not explain anything because we simply conclude from the feeling for the value that he offers a higher price. So aside from the fact that we try to avoid a causal view, and that furthermore that definition has another objectionable point—that is, the term "things of the outer world" remind us of metaphysics—from the standpoint of the observer who cannot deal with the psyche of the observing individual nothing is won when one adds such a psychological axiom to a simple observation of economic activity. That the appearance is different, that one actually thinks one has gained something, can be explained by the inherited trust in causal relations. When one can combine two things by the word "because," one thinks to have gained an insight into their relationship. But here we only have—in addition of everything else—one link of a chain, the rest will not be explained through independent observations but rather deduced from the former. When we see that things are getting evaluated (and we see that by the fact that the individual does something to get it or to keep it) and say that happens because the thing stands in a causal relation to the satisfaction of the individual's needs, it does not happen because we could totally understand the act of evaluation. Therefore it is not a statement about facts like the one that the light comes on following certain electrical operations but rather it is a hypothesis about psychological processes of the individual, which we derive from his observable actions.

But even if we could *see* the evaluation processes or somehow else could become aware of them it would not help us very much. We would then have two sets of observations, one of them consisting of evaluation processes the other one of economic actions and could find out through experiments whether there are interconnections. But we would still not know anything about the *nature* of the latter. *How* the evaluation processes become economic activities and especially whether they are their "causes" would still be a problem about which one still could have different opinions. Only under the assumption of the existence of a free will that guides our actions without any determining influences the whole thing would be pretty simple. But this assumption would be shot down. The modern psychology and biology are of a different opinion and would hardly be willing to give the will that status. We cannot discuss this problem any further but we cannot ignore these things if we want to anchor economics in the problem of evaluations and wills. It is uncomfortable to admit that our science is dependent on an opinion of a different field, perhaps that it has certain metaphysical preconditions.

It is fairly simple to convince somebody that it is a good principle to stick with what one can see when one deals with problems of a natural scientific nature. That is different in our discipline. We are closer to our problems, we are right in the middle of things and scientific explanation seems to be able to go one step further. Because we are talking about ourselves and our actions, we think we can understand the processes better and in a different sense than those of nature. Everybody thinks that he understands his own actions, that he dominates them through his free will and judges the actions of others with a great deal of certainty. Very seldom does one admit how narrow the basis of this so-called understanding actually is. As we do not think about the very complex process of seeing, we just ignore these concerns in real life. But we are not allowed to accept this kind of vagueness in the foundation of a science.

We have another alternative, though, and that is inner perception. In the case of the introspection, things are absolutely clear. Here one could, if one wanted to, assume a causal relationship. Here one actually has two phenomena: I can directly observe my needs and my feeling for value. But that would not help me very much because not only my feeling for value is important but also that of all the other economic subjects. And since I cannot observe their psyche, I am where I was before, when I tried to do without introspection. But even if I wanted to use the findings based on introspection at all, I have to pose the hypothesis that the evaluation processes of all other people are similar to mine. If I would not pose this hypothesis, I would not understand them any better than before. In this case I would have to be willing to accept, for example, that the more food somebody has the more he values it. If I am determined to not accept such a possibility and build a hypothesis, I only continue in a formal, arbitrary way. Whichever words I might use to justify this hypothesis or even try to hide its hypothetical character, all of that is without any meaning for the pure economics and none of the metaphysical or any other type of explanations of my hypothesis can save it when the findings that are based on it collide with reality. Its only purpose is to come up with a schemata that is a fitting image of economic reality, and therefore it does not matter where it comes from and how it is decorated. It is very important to us to stress this point because only the highest level of rigorousness in this matter can show the nature and the architectonic forms of the theory clearly and graphically to friend and foe. In order to make our hypothesis plausible and clear, such discussions should be connected to it. Of course, its acceptance was helped by this. But one should not be fooled about its nature, as has happened a lot in the past.

III

So, what is its nature? What is left when we leave out everything dubious? Doesn't the value principle fall with the permissibility of its psychological justification? That last question has to be negated and it is what opponents of the psychological economics have overlooked. When in all our psychological deliberations we leave everything out that does not seem to have a solid footing, we still have something left: A formal assumption for methodological purposes. That is the essential thing, the exact core of those deliberations, that what is gained through them. We will do without the value hypothesis as a statement on realities but we do not want to do without it in general. Here again we seem to accept and to reject simply for general reasons: Only the detailed analysis shows us what is usable and what cannot be defended. We have to and we can forgo a theory of needs if we want to be very correct. Was that actually the starting point of our value theory? Even if that were so, we would not change our verdict; something can be very helpful as a heuristic tool even if it is not necessary for a deduction of the results. There is a difference between finding a theory and its description; not everything that led to it has to be absolutely tenable. There are a lot of examples for that in the history of the sciences and many ideas that have been of great importance for the development of a theory has to be dropped when one starts to look at the achievement critically. But that does not mean it is necessarily false or that the deduced results are necessarily unusable. It is a common experience that the path that actually led to valuable findings does not stand the test in the long run. And it happens especially often that something that in the beginning seemed to be solidly based on facts, in the end proves to be an arbitrary assumption. It seems to lie in the nature of things that the first conquerors of a new field do not look with fear at cognition-theoretical basics but rather leaves this work for future phases of the development. So this shows that the structure is not as solid as previously thought; one only realizes the audacity of this process when one looks back at the path taken and often one gets dizzy. The exact natural sciences are going through a process right now in which everything seems to get questioned. But that is not that bad. Yes, some basic assumptions that were deemed irrefutable have to be given up and some hopes have to go; one notices that one has gained less ground than one had thought and that one's work is really not that important; but the exact findings are not affected a great deal by any revolution in the basic principles: One could almost say that all of that just leads to a correction of the way everything gets expressed. And that is the case in our field, too. I think, though, that the foundations of our science are an excuse for the cognition theory; that one has to formulate it differently when one wants to be correct; that this wording stresses the hypothetical, arbitrary, also takes away the popularity and interest from economics and shows that its boundaries are narrow and that there is just a loose connection between economics and the big questions of human will and actions; but I also think that none of its fundamental findings really suffers when one gives up certain starting points after they have achieved what they were supposed to achieve.

But was the doctrine of the needs really the starting point of the value theory? Such questions are extremely important to us. Nothing is more instructive and nothing leads deeper into the understanding of this theory than this answer. But it is a difficult one and one can never be sure of it; but we always want to try to find out what was the source of the guiding ideas and we try to follow the originator's train of thought and at the same time this way we gain all elements necessary for its evaluation. This is the only way to actually own them so that we can continue building, so we know what we can expect from them. If one now asks the economic subjects what they are willing to give for a certain amount of a certain good rather than live without it, they will almost always have a certain answer. For each economic subject and for each amount of a good there will be another good that they are willing to give up while with a just a slightly higher "price" there is no barter any more. Of course, one could try to describe this price through the cost principle; for example, one could say that this price is the cost for the "buyer" to produce the good in question; but that would have the disadvantages described above. So let us throw out such an explanation attempt and just accept this price. And let us just ask these people at the same point in time what they are willing to give for another certain amount of the same good rather than live without it; we have to make sure, though, that that this other amount could not be used for anything else. Let us again note the answer. Let us repeat our question as often as possible. Let us assume that our economic subjects actually would act like this and always act like this under the same or at least similar circumstances—an assumption that probably not always but often enough matches reality.

Now we show for every economic subject the different amounts on the x-axis of a right-angled coordinate system and the prices, which he has given us on the y-axis. And finally we connect all the points in the system through interpolation to a continuous curve and *simulate* that the economic subject would within a certain interval give a certain price for a certain amount if he could not get it cheaper. The latter is simply fiction because in reality not every amount is a possibility because a lot of goods cannot simply be split and even the ones that can be split can sometimes only be traded in certain amounts. The function shown in such a curve now is the only thing we need and at the same time everything economists can do when they do value psychology. Any additional reasoning would not change its nature, it would only cloud it.

But why is this function called value function? That is not difficult to explain. The questioned economic subjects will say that to them a certain amount of a good is worth so much and not more than so much. If then asked why they are willing to pay a price for the good at all, they will say that they need the good. Indeed, one could not express the basic thought of value theory any more precisely and in a more popular way than through this sentence: Prices are being offered because the goods that are being paid for are needed. And that, now, is the starting point of the newer theory: It is in its nature, not to analyze but rather just accept a certain behavior of the buyer, or better because more precise, to just accept a certain scale of demand prices. What leads us to this method is the fact that an analysis of the quantities of goods, as we have seen, leads back to other quantities of goods, so that we would, if we would attempt such an analysis, run in circles: For this reason, we take a step back from our system of quantities of goods and from the outside build a superstructure of such functions over the quantity of goods, which should reflect for us the interdependencies between them.

This is our opinion. But the psychological economists also mean the same thing. We reach our conclusions through a different method, though. They also refuse to conduct the analysis with the help of the cost principle. They also start out with observable facts. But they express these facts through the term of "needing," the value, and they try to analyze this term by basing it on needs and their psychological and physiological bases. The latter is nice garnishing that is not necessary for the heuristic principle of our value hypothesis. But the term of needing is too broad and does not focus on the core of our problem, the observable configuration of a price; the term in itself is an attempt to justify our hypothesis and which is not very correct in a cognitive-theoretical way, even if it was very useful in the beginning stages.

The correction that we propose therefore is mainly one of language. The role of the value principle in the reality of scientific work will not be diminished—and that is what many of our opponents tend to overlook—when one has a different opinion about its nature. Let us therefore be precise in what the value principle really is: a hypothetical function, in itself unsound and arbitrary but that we have to get to through observations of facts. We have already said what of it is hypothetical and what is observation of facts.

The everyday diction makes us call our function the value function but it does not contain anything psychological or metaphysical as we will see—we always only looked at certain economic facts when we talk about it or grant it certain forms of characteristics. The latter is necessary. We could not do anything with our function if we could not comment on its form. We do not have to give its exact equation in order to be able to use it in our line of thinking. It was often said that it is worthless when we cannot do that and a rejection of the whole method was deduced from that. But everybody familiar with higher-level analysis knows that it contains the means to get the most theorems out of the given form characteristics of a curve even if they have not completely determined it. So, we do not have to establish every value function empirically in the way just discussed; that might be necessary at a later time but it is not necessary now and for the basic problems which we want to discuss. But we have to establish *something* when we want to work with our value function. But in the interest of scientific correctness we have to be careful to just concentrate on the necessary and nothing more.

It becomes clear now that just one characteristic of our curves is necessary and that beyond that they can do whatever they want to do, that is that they are negative towards the x-axis in our specific interval. That is the exact form of Gossens Law, the “law of satiable wants,” which is usually expressed like this: The intensity of the feelings of need diminish with the level of increased saturation. We do not want to discuss this law any further and just point to the well-known discussions of the value theorists. We just wanted to take for us the relevant core out of its psychological and physiological cloak. Thus, the real nature of the principle becomes apparent: For the field of economics it is not a “law”—although it might be for other sciences—but an assumption based on a generalization of certain scientific facts. As such it is always arbitrary: For example, nothing would stop us from coming up with the opposite assumption without being able to call it “wrong.” It is a fact that especially under the perspective of development the increase of demand and the increase of the amount offered go hand in hand so that over time it happens often that a larger amount of a good might fetch a higher price than a smaller one. Sure, this assumption would contradict others that we made above: for example, that our questioning of the economic subjects concerning the prices they are willing to give for different amounts would have to be conducted at the same point in time, etc. But these latter ones are only made to prevent our main assumption from colliding with reality. And from our perspective, psychological objections to such a method would be irrelevant. But it becomes apparent that our method is more useful for the description of the real observable barter transactions and therefore we adopt it.

I have spent so much time with this dry matter because it seems to be fundamentally important to me to show that the fundamentals of our discipline can be shown exactly and clearly and that they are unobjectionable. So much more should be said but I do not want to tire the reader and also for a lack of room do I have to omit a further discussion of the psychological value theory itself and additional details. I do want to stress, though, that a rather detailed knowledge of these things is absolutely necessary for the comprehension of what already has been discussed as well as what is going to follow.

This method is not just the only correct one and gets rid of some obstacles and vagueness in our path; it also clarifies very nicely the nature of our axioms. These discussions will contribute a lot to understanding its nature and specifically to the demarcation of economics and its position vis-à-vis other disciplines. We will get back to all of these points if necessitated by various reasons and the reader only gets a clear picture of our opinions by reading the whole book. Furthermore, we will be more specific about the nature and the value of our systems at a later point. But certain points will have to be discussed here.

5

More Remarks about Our Method

I

The path that we would like to go on and how we contrast it to other possible paths is what we mean by "exact." We describe such a path as an exact discipline. Its nature is that only those steps have be taken that are necessary to reach our goal. And the goal is to give an overview over a bunch of facts, not by simply describing them individually but by coming up with a schemata that not in itself but just its findings have to reflect reality. (What we mean by "not in itself but just in its findings" and that that is neither a fuzzy concept nor splitting of hairs, the reader knows and we do not have to further explain this.) The advantage of such a method is its brevity and simplicity and in the differentiation between the important from the unimportant; or to say it simply: to only use the necessary words and only those. Now it has become very clear that we want to stay as far away as possible from a priori speculation and a one-sided deductive method. We are not free of arbitrariness but that is only used for methodological reasons. So, this term "exact" is not offensive and even if it has a bad reputation for some economists, our version of the term should not raise any misgivings. We do not define it as the "exact philosophy" does; when we describe our method as "exact" we do not denigrate other directions of thought; and we do not sidle up to physics in an improper manner although we also do not see any reason why one would want to construe a different term of exactness for our science than for theirs. As we already discussed in the context of the law term, not everything in nature is "exact" either. If one pretends it is, it is nothing more than functional fiction.

The most important and most practical advantage of exact definitions of our starting points is we do not have to get into the psyche, the reasons, and the laws of economic activities as such. It is a sentence of fundamental importance that has never been stressed enough: Exact economics is not a philosophy of the economic actions of humans. Of course it is not a philosophy of human actions in general. Even that has been claimed; it has been said that human actions can be explained solely by economic motivations. We would like to stress now it is not a judgment whether that is correct or wrong but rather it makes no difference whatsoever for the bunch of facts we define as the subject matter of economics. Pure economics is not dependent on it and cannot say anything about it. It is not a theory of economic motives. Whether those play a large or a small role in the wants and the actions of people is not one of our problems. We do not ask which motives determine people. And that is the sole reason why we cannot include ethical motives. So, we are not principally against the so-called ethical school. We do not deny the meaning of ethical elements. Since "economic actions" are independent from the motives for these actions, ethics and economy are different types of dimensions and therefore no opposites. On the one hand, one can have economic motives but, let's say, out of clumsiness not act "economically"; on the other hand, one can have altruistic motivations and still act economically. For example, when you pull somebody out of the water that is considered to be an altruistic act. And still, basic economic fundamentals can be applied to this act: One swims to the person the shortest possible distance, grab him in the most useful fashion, and one tries to get back to the shore as quickly as possible and with the least expenditure of energy. The formal principle that we use for these acts we call the economic principle and put it in the place of the hypothesis of egotism. That is definitely progress, but we do not need a principle such as this any more, as we will show later.

We do not care about the rule of motivations, the realm of judgment. One could be tempted to combine all sciences that deal with human actions under one umbrella, under the perspective of value judgment. Then economics could be defined like a science of economic evaluation and ethics, esthetics, etc., in a similar way. But from the standpoint of economics we cannot allow such a summary because it gets us involved in things we do not want to get involved in. The problems of personality, of consciousness, of wants, etc., have been tackled by others with a lot of success, so that we do not want to get into opposition to the findings of those attempts. It also makes us be very careful in using the term "value," as physicists are with the terms "energy" and "mass." We have to point out again that this way we can banish all metaphysical vagueness from our path but only for the price of a large part of the interest of our discipline:

We separate it not only from all other forms of human actions but also from its original soil in which it seems rooted. It is clear that economists balk at this and of course we have to prove that the small field that is left over is of real value and an independent discipline. In my opinion, an analysis of human actions from the perspective of motivations has little to offer. Of course, this method makes understanding fairly easy especially in the early phase but it does not seem to have a great future and it does not seem useful to put so much emphasis on it, as, for example, Gabriel Tarde did. But even if it would not be this way, our discipline should stay away from it and it would definitely be possible that there could be another science of economic motives next to it. But it would not be able to contribute more to, let's say, the nature of branches of income and in general to pure economic problems as pure economics can. We got to a point that has not been dealt with clearly enough. Our exact method can contribute quite a bit to its enlightenment.

To act economically and to act according to economic motives therefore is not the same. The egotist, both the utilitarian and the voluntary cut his tree with the minimum amount of energy possible as would do the altruist. So, when both are planning to cut a tree, they might have different motives but their acting is the same. Even a special awareness of economic motives is not necessary here.

The older national economics assumed an individual egotism. In the eyes of its advocates that was a claim about the actual actions of people and at the same time a demand. In accordance with the philosophy of natural law of that time one looked for the key to understanding social life in the individual and the following sentence was promoted to an axiom—consciously and subconsciously: The free action of the individual creates state and society and is decisive for the economy. Then one tried to prove that the individual is guided—and should—only by egotistical motives because the free actions of the individual also advances the whole the most. Egotism and its development to its full freedom were propagated as the desirable goal. In the context of this individualism, free competition reached the level of a postulate, which led to some practical demands such as free trade, contract freedom, etc. A proud building was erected on this ground, half science and half practical program. It has often been stressed how the Zeitgeist determined this philosophy, which meaning it has in the history of the political ideas, and how and for what reasons a reaction against it followed. An "ethical" interpretation of the economic phenomena and a whole theory construction of the negation of egotism on the one side and historical fact research on the other were set against it, but the science did not win very much, as little as the exact natural sciences would win when one philosophical system would be substituted by another. But that is not the reaction, which from our standpoint seems necessary even if it was totally justified. We gladly give to our opponents the problems that are rather foreign to us and which cannot be dealt with using exact methods but it is more important to us to show that an exact discipline of pure economics is possible without endorsement, that such an endorsement actually would be against its nature and that can keep and develop what the classical authors had recognized as pure economic truths although its social philosophy lies in shambles.

The field of economics still has features that date back to this time and point to these things. I do not mean that each economics textbook discusses collectivism, individualism, egotism, and altruism, etc.—that can easily be separated from the economic content and are often included for didactic reasons. What is more dangerous is that terms and thoughts have snuck into the pure theory and especially into their foundations which might invite the same old criticism that is justified in case of the classical authors although the whole development of the newer economics tries to get away from that. Therefore it is important to stress that we do not claim: first, that economic activity is guided totally or to a large extent by egotism; and secondly, that it would lead to the best outcome for all involved; or thirdly, that there is a tendency to accentuate individual egotism more and more. What in the new economics reminds us of these things is something totally different than it was before: they are not claims or demands but rather just methodological tools. Right away, this interpretation clarifies our path and gets rid of any metaphysical fogginess. It allows us to hold our position, to connect a clear sense with every word to prevent fights over that sense. The price we pay: We give up a lot of interesting and gutsy claims. Even an opponent of the classical authors remarked that the deepest questions in economics "cannot be solved mathematically but only in connection with history and philosophy." But he was probably thinking especially of practical questions, especially in the area of social policy, etc.

Here we have to counter that these questions are not questions of the exact economics and that they do not have any scientific character if philosophy of any type starts playing a role. One example is the problems of the tax policies. If one asks what a tax does, this is an economic question and it can be solved economically and mathematical formulas are very helpful here. But if one asks whether a tax is "just," one has to say what one means by "just" before it can be answered. At this point, any type of scientific work stops. But if one agrees on this point, the scientific discussion can start. But we do not want to have anything to do with philosophies like the one about the justice ideal and turn our backs on the word cascades that under this name drown the economic discussion. Sure, such an analysis of economic facts is possible: As the multi-layered actions of humans lead to different opinions, they can be looked at from many different perspectives, scientifically or non-scientifically. But we just want to *describe* and nothing else. We do not condemn other opinions but we want to stray away from them.

II

Let us be more precise what we have to say about the element of egotism as the foundation of pure economics. That element is actually a hypothesis, which is more or less correct, more correct than its critics think, if one does not share our doubt about the motives as starting point. As it has to be stressed at this point, one could say egotistical action is an order of nature and ignoring it means the death sentence, and that therefore egotism is going to play a major role among the motives of humans. Therefore it definitely can partly explain human actions and that while the extent can be discussed it is considerable. Aside from that, it is interesting to observe conduct based on egotistical motives when one knows for sure that the human being does not act according to it; because he would always consider carefully his egotistic and his non-egotistic motives and try to find out what he gives up when he does not act egotistically. The ethical motives also have their law and are neither indefinite nor arbitrary but rather are in a solid relationship with the others. For this reason, the consequences of individual egotism are not as insignificant as some writers seem to think. But if we make the hypothesis if individual egotism is the foundation of our discipline, we cannot avoid the question in how far it really dominates and which goals guide it, although that would not be important for the correctness but just for the significance of our findings. One would always have to analyze, though, in how far that hypothesis is actually needed in order to limit a possible controversy to a very small area. It is clear that the human being does not only act according to egotistical motives and also that individual egotism is not only based on economic elements but others as well. The first insight destroys the theory that the human being is just an egotist but not when egotism is defined so widely that it also includes all acts out of altruism since it also satisfies a need—a statement that degrades the theory to a truism. The latter insight takes away from the individual egotism the simplicity and uniformity, which would make it an ideal explanation tool. Thirst for power, enjoyment of exertion and similar things make it necessary to differentiate between eudemonic, hedonistic and an energetic, voluntary egotism, and we cannot be criticized for not using this very simplistic tool, if we do not want to know anything about egotism, not even to speak of the criticism of historical and social nature of such a point of departure—whether this criticism is justified or not. Rather we can be happy that we do not need hedonistic or other hypotheses for the explanation of prices and if at any point anything like that would be necessary, it would be a good idea to limit one's assumptions to the minimum and to the concrete problem for which it is necessary.

We do not deem it necessary to construct a *homo oeconomicus*, sort of an embodiment of hedonistic egotism as has happened in the past. Not that we think that this would be wrong in principle; we totally understand that the authors of this construct have the correct thing in their mind but we think we can do without it and therefore avoid it. We also do not look a priori at a "homme moyen." Sometimes it can be useful to claim that the value functions of different individuals are similar. But we cannot prove that and a finding gotten this way definitely has to be supported by facts. It could happen that it proves to be correct, more than we had expected and it might be more true than its assumption and also that a finding based on a wide foundation and deduced from the surest presuppositions or induced from the richest observation can fail miserably due to any reason; but we will wait with this assumption until the opportune moment and limit it to the case at hand.

Finally, we do not find it necessary to limit our findings to the "ordinary business man" as A. Marshall does. Sure, this construct is related to our philosophy—because it is a construct although it seemingly is based on an observation of reality. But we do not want to look at the acting humans at all but rather only on the amounts of goods they own: We want to describe the changes, or better, a certain type of changes, as if they would happen automatically, without looking at the people who are responsible for those changes. For many ends of economics in their wider and usual sense this method might not be good enough or a different one would be better; from the standpoint of pure economics, though, it is the correct one in our mind. This method more pointedly stresses the nature of its axioms and it is nothing but the exact core of what the economists can tell us about motives—even at first sight it might not seem too promising.

So this is it what is left of this part of the older system of economics: Besides political, ethical, etc. objections in their various forms and if one limits oneself to the area of purely theoretical discussion, one can say that three different paths have developed through critical work on an uninterrupted development path, which represent achievements which are not without value and positively compare to methodological tools of sciences that are developed even higher: that with the help of homo oeconomicus—the hedonistic calculator—that of the "ordinary business man," and mine. All three are "correct," that means free of vagueness and flaws in their principles, and they have their roots in the beginnings of our science; but they are still very different. Homo oeconomicus is a construct whose hypothetical character has been noticed by now in which it differs from the economic existence of the former whose real existence was claimed. The "ordinary business man" represents the consideration of new perceptions of motives of people and the most loyal attempt to combine the teachings of the classical authors with these new perceptions. Our approach is definitely the most rigorous and most clear and in our minds superior when we try to define the nature of our discipline; but only there, in other cases people can choose between the other options.

6

The Methodological Individualism

Now we have gotten rid of the vagueness around the value hypothesis and the problem of the motives of human actions. What is left to do is to stress that we, too, start with the ownership of goods by the *individual*. We have to expect a lot of opposition because as everybody knows that the individual approach today is perceived as a failed one: The automism is one of the most popular points of attack by the theory's opponents. The reflections of the classical authors started with the individual and the new economics followed that more or less and thus was subjected to the same type of attacks, which were directed against the first ones initially. The opponents of the theory usually do not know that there is a difference and what the difference between the old and the new system is in this point and most of the times criticize both without a difference. The theorists gave their answer and now we have one of those controversies, which shows this lack of results, which we find in so many of the discussions dealing with the foundations of our discipline: Both parties whack each other with general arguments and defend them with a bitterness borne out of the assumed political and social importance of their argument. Of course, an understanding cannot be reached in such a manner and often it seems that is not even a goal. But that is exactly what would be necessary to solve the problem of which problems and goals the two diverging interpretations address. When one does that the fight loses it odious character and the difficulties disappear automatically. This is what we want to do without haste. First we want to look at the criticism of the theory's opponents against the individualistic interpretation of things and then the various tendencies *within* the theory itself, which follow the same goal.

What did the critics of the classical system want when they attacked its individualistic foundation? As almost all attacks against the classical system, it was directed against some practical extremes. Individualism is juxtaposed more or less to socialism and any type of social policy; the slogan of "free reign of the economic force," individual initiative and responsibility was used against other slogans. The political defeat of the individualistic liberalism also damaged the scientific reputation of those works in which individualistic postulates were set in a seeming connection with the foundations of pure economics. Those are all very well-known things. It is also known that the gigantic development of socio-political efforts in which the scientific circles are so interested led to a rejection of individualism for ethical and for political reasons. The individual was told that he owes his existence and his development to the society and that the fruit of his work belongs to not only him. But enough of that. One can safely claim that the animosity against the atomism in the field of economics came out of this direction to a large degree. We, on the other hand, have to say that there is absolutely no connection between individualistic science and political individualism. The attacks by historians and social politicians against individualistic social economists may be justified; some definitely, and when the historian criticizes the political statement of the theorist, he is right; such a statement would not be possible if the theorists would have paid more attention to history. But we would go to far to blame the field of social economics for that: The theory does talk a lot about of free competition, it does say to a certain extent that it would lead to the highest possible satisfaction of the economic subject; but this axiom loses everything objectionable and also any practical interest when it is posed correctly as we will see later. Out of the theory we cannot garner any arguments neither for or against political individualism. Whoever denies such a possibility is absolutely right and we agree with him when he opposes the misuse of the theory for a defense of indifference in the eye of social misery. But he is wrong when he therefore wants to throw out the theory because of it.

To summarize this part of our argument: We have to differentiate clearly between political and methodological individualism. Both have absolutely nothing in common. The first is based on general axioms, such as that freedom contributes more to the development of the individual and that of the society than anything else and makes a whole number of claims; the latter does not do anything, like that does not claim anything, and does not have any specific pre-condition. It only means that when describing certain economic actions, one has to base them on the acts of individuals. The question is now just whether this point of departure is useful and leads far enough or whether one should take the whole society as a starting point for some problems or even the whole field of social economics. But that is just a methodological question without any principal meaning. The socialist can answer it in the sense of methodological individualism, the political individualist can answer it in the sense of a social interpretation, without contradicting themselves. So, we have achieved something: We have taken away from our question the practical implications as well as the crown of thorns of the immediate interest. In the newer economics that already has happened to a fairly large degree already and this is a big, perhaps the biggest, difference between the modern and the older system. With the first, it is often difficult to separate pure theory from practical positions (although it is possible), the latter tries to stay free of digressions and many theorist have rejected any relationship with "Manchesterdom." This principle often gets violated, though, and here the opponents are right, but in general we can say that the science got rid of this drag.

Now we turn to the second part of our task. We have to say that here we cannot do much more than to show that we know the objections and what we think of them; an exhaustive answer to the whole question can only be given by this whole book.

To replace the individual approach by a social one or to at least stress it more is one of the most important requests, one that gets mentioned a lot. If somebody were asked what in his opinion is the most necessary reform in our field, this one among others would be mentioned without fail. But how should that happen and what would be the advantage?

It seems to us that the tendency mentioned grew to a large degree out of the one we just discussed. The social politician and the social economist are often one and the same person. While the first one stresses social elements, the second one probably does the same. We will show that it is not a necessary interrelationship. But we cannot simply ignore the scientific opinion of this group but rather have to look at it. In addition, we get ideas from the fields of biology and sociology that point us in the same direction. Some biologists talk about a "erreur individualiste," meaning one looks too closely at the individual itself while it is nothing but a link in a chain of a long development. In a similar vein, some economists think that the human being cannot live by itself and can only be understood in the context of his social environment, and that he furthermore is controlled by a thousand social influences, to a point that they cannot be studied at the individual level. Individualistic economics therefore is of no value; many sociologists are of a similar opinion. The influence of biology was even more direct especially through the medium of the so-called organic interpretation of the state, but we are not very interested in that at this point. The third element of the tendency discussed here is formed by some theorists who operate with the terms society and societal value also within the pure theory.

Let us look at it a little closer now. It would not be of great use to us to step into the general discussion, which is all too well-known. If we wanted to examine the nature of the social economics, for example, we would have to comment on the two interpretations, which are totally opposite of each other. Those are the interpretations of the economy as "organism" on the one hand, and on the other as "results of the economic activities and being of the individuals." Again, we see here that it would be easy to defend both interpretations with very general reasoning. Each mass manifestation of course consists of individual manifestations and one could assume that in order to understand the first, the latter have to be examined. And it is also clear that all members of an economy or a class of any type are connected through many more ties within their group than with members of other economies, so that economic (and other) effects and interdependencies, cooperation, and antagonisms play a big role, which do not necessarily show up in the individual. That leads to the consequence that one has to take a social group as a point of departure for ones train of thought and at the same time as its yardstick. The one party can always prove to the other one that the state is no animal body and that every machine consists of different parts like the first one, that humans never live alone and a machine is more then the sum of unconnected pieces of metal. We always stress that analogies and generalities do not lead anywhere: Only the detailed analysis can lead to valuable results; but here we talk about something different: What the economy actually *is* and whether the individual is the engine or something else is the engine is not important for us. In general, we would be happy to accept everything the social politician or the historian has to say about this point and we would not even deem any abstract construct, let's say, in the sense of a natural law worth discussing. We absolutely admit that social influences determine the actions of the individual and that the individual is a tiny factor but that does not matter here. We do not care how actually things act but rather how we have to stylize schematize them in order to reach our goals, and that means which interpretation (from the standpoint of the results of pure economics) is the most practical one.

That is a paradoxical and at the same time fundamental sentence: The economist should not care about the nature of an economy? We do not hesitate to answer this question with a "yes." We would even go further by saying that we do not even care about the nature of economic activity. We have to look at what we try to accomplish—in this case it is the price—and only mention what is absolutely necessary to get to our goal. Only then the shape of our thinking process and its meaning becomes precise and plastic. And we cannot say a priori what is necessary.

When we apply this to our question at hand, now we understand the nature of our approach, which we want to call "methodological individualism." We have already seen that it does not contain any demand or any moral or other judgment of various organizational forms of social economics and therefore cannot be hit with opposition in this category; we also see that it does not say anything about facts because we do not say anything about what determines people's actions. We want to describe certain economic activities and even that very narrowly. The deeper reasons for them might be interesting but they do not influence our findings. They belong to the field of sociology and therefore our results cannot be denied by the argument that one cannot explain what happens in an economy just by looking at the actions of an individual. When the economist cloaks his individualistic method with facts and claims, for example, that the individual is the pivot of all explanation, we cannot agree with them and stand on the side of their critics. But we should not forget that those claims usually do not have to be made without changing the pure economical part of the problem. In this case the criticism can easily go too far and being right or wrong are getting mixed up.

Finally, methodological individualism is no speculation of a philosophical nature, no model for the future, or some such thing. All that has been tacked to the theory, half of it has not justified the other half. Every impartial observer can see that our observations cannot be attacked by these slogans that have been repeated ad nauseam.

We only want to say that the individualistic approach in a short and useful way produces very usable results but also that within the pure theory a social approach does not provide any advantage and is therefore superfluous. Sure, as soon as we go beyond the limits of the pure theory, the whole thing looks different. For example, in the organization theory and in the sociology in general, individualism would not get us very far. We do not have to shed tears over this, though, when we think of the limitations of it as just a method.

Now, we have taken an additional step and eliminated some difficulties, which are often in our path but at the same time takes away from our question any scientific principal interest. We have not solved a problem but shown that we do not have to solve it. Automatically, it follows that those theoretical discussions, which work with the famous or infamous instrument of "Robinson" cannot be hit by the criticism that such could only exist in exceptional situations and not for very long. Here, the misunderstanding that we can find in many of these criticisms becomes especially clear.

There are no principal objections against "atomism" as we represent it. Objections that were brought forth in the past related to things, which seem to be directly related to it but can be separated. Of course, we are not interested in the individual process but they help us describe the mass phenomena in our field. The activities of an individual are so meaningless to us as the color of hair of an individual is to an ethnologist. But he cannot learn about the color of hair of a whole culture by looking at that whole culture but rather by looking at individuals and then construct a theory about the culture by synthesizing individual observations through a "typical" or "representative" statistical method. This example does not totally hold but it shows us that the individual method and social results are not always compatible.

We believe that even today the old individualistic method is still indispensable but only for pure theory in its most narrow sense. Our method only fits that and has produced useful results just in this area. It is both impossible and superfluous to leave it behind—for the group of problems that are being worked on these days. Perhaps that can happen at a later time as it is already happening outside the very small area. But for now and in the near future anything new would only hinder development. We cannot prove it here with general reasoning, though; only the reflection of the details of the pure theory can show that, it has to be analyzed through each of its individual axioms.

All we could do here was to react to some objections, to clarify misunderstandings, and to show the reader that we do not want to do anything that would create principle doubts. Only *that* can be discussed in general terms. So, we will not talk about social categories and show that the individualistic approach in our sense, stripped from any practical interest, has proven to be successful in our area and is sufficient. This second part of our proof is only created out of the entirety of the whole book. Everybody is free to invent economic vocabulary of a sociological category in order to discuss social or political problems, where it seems desirable. We stress over and over again that this is only true for the system of the theory in its purest form.

At this point the two most important groups of terminology should be mentioned, which were supposed to introduce a social element and which we want to reject for reasons we already have discussed. The first is characterized by the words "national income," "national wealth," and "social capital" and plays a big role especially in the German literature (Held, Wagner). Especially Stolzmann stressed the necessity to introduce it. But nothing supports our standpoint as much as the fact that he actually does not use it very much in his discussion of theoretical questions. Where he uses it, it only has an effect on the language but does not change the individualistic foundation of the theory.

When one builds the construct of our theory unencumbered by prejudices and any demands coming from the outside, then one will not even find this terminology. Therefore we will not even deal with them any more; if we would do it, it would become clear the amount of vagueness and problems attached to it, that they are closely related with a lot of skewed opinions, without leading to just *one* really important axiom.

The second group is anchored in the term of social value. Even in the earliest phase of the theory we find first hints, but it has reached principal significance today, in the "social value" of the American authors. Some of the terms in this context have no use at all, for example, the "value for mankind," which actually does not even have a precise meaning. (More about this in my article "on the Concept of Social Value" in the Quaterly [*sic*] Journal of Economics 1908.) But even this one we cannot discuss here, but rather just say that we can live without it and that when we reject it we only do so for methodological reasons.

Something else: We often find the terms "collective demand" and "collective supply." Those are not social categories but just combinations of individual ones. When we use them we do not do so out of consideration for social elements. That would mean we see social phenomena just as a sum of individual ones, a standpoint we reject emphatically. Those terms stand on a totally individual foundation.

7

About the Term Value

I

Although the full meaning of what we will talk about on this topic will not become apparent until later, and although it is our principle to discuss things where we use them, a few necessary remarks have to be summarized here. (They are not only of interest to the theorists.) Just when we ourselves are clear on the explanation principle we want to use we will go on to the study of the amount of goods, whose methodological superstructure are the value functions. Value functions and amounts of goods, that is all there is in our area of research, all that creates our image of reality. We only see the *latter*, the former we just create around them. Let us look closer. During the following discussion we will not avoid psychological terminology since it often easy and brief.

First, I want to mention that we do not differentiate between the terms "value" and "benefit" but rather see them as synonyms. Psychological value theorists have made that differentiation as far as we know—in two ways: First, they said that things get "evaluated" even if they are not "beneficial," for example alcoholic beverages, etc. It could be useful to express the subjectivity of the valuation linguistically. But there is neither anything absolutely "beneficial" nor anything absolutely "valuable." "Benefit" and "value" are both expressions of individual assessment and therefore we do not see a reason to differentiate between them. If one wanted to avoid misunderstandings through secondary meanings of our terminology, it would be best to create a new word, like Paretos "Ophelimity." But we do not want to do that. Here, where we assume that all elements are known, we do not expect any problems. We just want to touch upon it briefly and then quickly move on.

Furthermore, only those goods, which are fairly scarce were ascribed a value. Here, one followed the linguistic convention, which for example used the term "useless" under normal circumstances, although it is of course "valuable." "The benefit becomes value, when its non-existence becomes a possibility," one of those theorists said and thus expressed the beliefs of the whole group. Von Boehm-Bawerk said, "Benefit and scarcity have to come together to form a value" (Pos. Theory p.142). "A man is sitting at a bubbling spring with good drinking water. He has filled his cup and enough water to fill another hundred cups flow by him every minute. And now we imagine another man who travels through the desert. He is still another day away from the next oasis. And he is down to his last cup of water. In both cases it is beneficial to satisfy your need. And to the same degree" (Pos. Theory, p.140f). But it only has a "value" in the second case. We do not go overboard by calling this differentiation one of the most fruitful and most fundamental in all of our science. The proprietor does not care too much about goods that are just beneficial. Such goods equal zero for our welfare and only those have a value that provide us with a piece of satisfaction, welfare, quality of life, in other words, which are scarce compared to the demand.

We have to say a few things about this. Above all else, the difference between the two does not seem to be such a big one in our eyes. Goods, whose values have been minimized here are those, whose marginal benefit is close to zero. Well, the transition from a small marginal benefit to zero benefit is apparently a smooth one, not a sudden jump. In the same way, the boundary between free and commercial goods is also a fluid one.

But even more important is the following: Even free goods have value functions. One can see that when one makes it into a commercial one by making it scarce. Even to find out whether a certain good is "free" for a certain individual, we need the value function, since the zero-point of the marginal benefit is dependent on its form, or to say it in a more popular way: on its demand. So, there is no *big* difference between free and commercial goods, and for this reason value and benefit are synonyms for us.

II

That brings us to an important point, to the term aggregate value. There is a value function also for free goods, just its marginal benefit is zero. But what is the value of the *whole* amount of that good for an individual? Sometimes it has been said that this aggregate value also is zero (v. Wieser, recently F. A. Fetter). The train of thought that led to this result is simple: Each growth would have the value zero, even the last little part —it often gets overlooked that this claim is only true if the piece is very small—and because every small piece can be seen as "the last one" and that all pieces of a good—if available at the same time—have the same value, so one thinks that the aggregate value can only be zero because it is nothing but sum of the values of the parts. This train of thought is supported by the fact that the complete supply of free goods does not get more attention than the individual parts.

But this confirmation is deceptive. It is correct that these things do not get the attention they deserve. But a simple operation convinces us that that their aggregate values are not zero: If that were the case, the economic subject would have to be prepared to give up his whole stockpile of this good for a small advantage. But who wanted to live, for example, without water?

Just this thought shows that that reasoning cannot be correct. But we can really pinpoint where the problem is. Of course, one can see each part of the stockpile as the "last" one. But that only means that one can put each little part, as long as they are identical, in any order or pattern one wants to. If you add up their values, though, not all of them are the same. Only *one* has a marginal value, all others' values are higher. As long as all of them are there, each individual one has the value of the loss of the satisfaction of the need caused by its being missing but only if *its* missing under the presumption that the *others* will still be there. The values now cannot be added up, that is not too surprising. That the aggregate value is higher than the value of its parts is only a paradox as long as we give them the marginal value. The axiom becomes clear when one thinks of the sense of the different operations. If the value is the expression of the "meaning of a good for our welfare," it becomes clear that if one wants to find out the value of a whole stockpile of an individual, we cannot only look at the marginal value but rather at the progressive benefits of the pieces further out, i.e., one cannot multiply the whole amount with the marginal benefit but rather we have to multiply each part with the degree of the intensity of its position and then come up with the sum of these products, i.e., we have to integrate.

Then the paradox disappears that many of those goods we see as indispensable have "no value", like e.g., water. Of course they have an "accumulated value," just its marginal benefit is zero, meaning it does not have a price.

This approach is, first, more general and, secondly, it matches the facts much better. The term "accumulated value" has some problems, of which we want to discuss only the biggest ones in order to not bore our readers with details of the theory. The accumulated value of a lot of goods is very big and we should attach the symbol for "indefinite." That is the case with all things that are necessary to sustain the life of the economic subject, e.g., food. If we want to get a "finite" accumulated value with which we actually can work, we cannot take our integration all the way to those amounts whose value for the individual is large, i.e., not to integrate from zero but from a certain low margin, above which the life interests are not being taken into consideration anymore. We have to leave to the individual an existence minimum, so to speak, and can only find the amount of goods that goes beyond it.

That is a very important restriction but which should not surprise anybody who knows the function systems of other sciences or the functions theory in general. Actually, in the modern functions theory first the boundaries between those the function exist are analyzed before the function itself is being looked at. It is always just intervals in which we move around. We cannot be interested in anything outside of the boundaries.

We based our deliberations on free goods. But it is of course clear that the same is true for the economic ones, that their accumulated value also is not a product but an integral.

We want to point to another reason why theorists might have come up with the opinion just discussed. It is the wish to be able to deduce the actions in the economy from the value phenomena, to show that the normal prices are always the expression of the full values of the goods and that the economic actions do not effect the meaning of the goods, which they had in the isolated economy. The marginal benefit is important for the price. If it would not be important for the aggregate value, too, there would be a discrepancy between value sum and the price sum. Such a discrepancy actually does exist; it is wrong to think that the income problem has been solved when one has deduced the value phenomena, which are based on the prices from which incomes are derived, the "productive performance." Clark and his successors for example do this. We will come back to this later and see that the formation of the price leads to the situation that the person who barters a good usually does not receive the aggregate value.

III

We saw how important it is to differentiate between value and value *function*. While in the older economics vagueness and ambiguity of the term value created difficulties, which are very well-known by the beginners and which have not been overcome, the newer economics is in danger of creating misunderstandings in a different area, which are no less irritating and annoying and which have led to many obscurities. Therefore we want to spend a little more time here. It is the following: When one talks about the value of a certain amount of goods for a certain economic object, one always has to realize whether one means value function, aggregate value, or marginal benefit. The axiom "The value depends on the usefulness" is only correct when interpreted from the standpoint of value *function*. Of course, this is based on the needs of the individual, how they are expressed in their esteem. That is often called "intensity scale of the value." But this sentence refers to the aggregate value, it is clearly incomplete and even wrong. Only when the amount of goods is a constant, so that one can ignore it, is it correct in this sense. But if it varies, the aggregate value is dependent—as is the marginal benefit—on usefulness and on the circumstances, which determine these variations. These circumstances consist in part of value phenomena. If one reduces or buys a good, one has to weigh the benefit of those goods one has to spend on it. But there is one that is not a value phenomenon, and that is what A. Smith describes as "toil and trouble." And so in one sense—and we will get back to this later—one can say for sure that the "value" is determined by the benefit *and* by the "costs." The well-known allegories used by Professor Marshall and Professor Edgeworth used in clarifying these facts are in this sense absolutely on the mark and one can understand that the proponents of the cost principle cannot grasp how one can deny that. Indeed, the value discussion of the recent past has stressed the "value" too much and many times the arguments of the quarreling parties have missed each other. It seems to us that a solution to the controversy lies in that clear differentiation made possible by the mathematical illustration—and only by it. This solution is probably not the final one but we still would like to present it here:

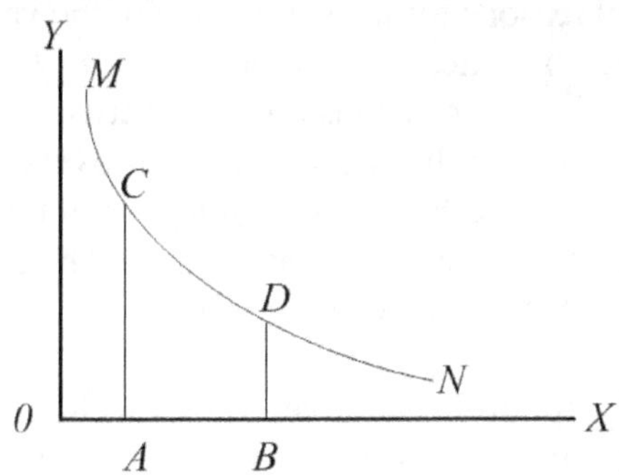

On the x-axis of a rectangular coordinate system, let us enter amount of goods owned by an individual and let us interpret the y-axis as the intensity of the value—as the marginal benefits of each amount if the individual would not own *more*—we get a curve —MN—of the intensities, that is of the value function. Its integral, i.e., the plane ACDB is our aggregate value. The two are totally different. (According to our earlier discussions, we exclude the amount OA, its benefits being indefinite, because the life of the individual depends on it.)

Our illustration also teaches us about the nature of the marginal benefit. This term also could mean two things: First, the value intensity [pg.107-original] of the last small part and, secondly, the value of it [original-pg. 108]. In the first case, it is shown by the line BD, in the latter by a small plane of the height BD. The usual definition of the marginal benefit as the "value of the last part" is therefore not very clear and unequivocal. One usually tries to illustrate the term by pointing to the loss an individual would endure in satisfaction of his needs if he would lose this last piece. Here one thinks of the *latter* meaning. That is old stuff for those who are even vaguely familiar with the literature of the "mathematical" economists. It seems necessary to me, though, to point this out to wider circle.

An agreement in the value controversy seems to become obvious through these differentiations. Where the classical authors talked about "value" and meant barter value, their analysis was not very clear and not complete but it was not wrong: The barter value is dependent on the marginal benefit and this marginal benefit is dependent not only on the value function but also on the amount of goods somebody has, and also on other elements than the value phenomenon. And where the modern proponents of the cost theory think of the value as the aggregate value, the same is true. But the latter are wrong when they think that that refutes the psychological theory. The other way around: The psychological value theorists are right with their general reasons for the supremacy of the value; but that is only correct as long as they mean the value *function*. Where they mean the aggregate value, their discussions are only partly correct.

One now could check the whole cost controversy and all arguments accordingly and find out their real meaning—both would go too far for us. Only the role of the value as we see it should be dealt with later more precisely. That will show the exact implications of the claims that both parties make.

It is especially apparent that even those authors who usually show a high level of carefulness and clarity and who stress this differentiation, are very careless in the cost controversy, as, for example, A. Marshall.

Also in another context we cannot any longer talk about "value" in general terms. Each value is dependent on a judging subject. After the introduction of the value functions, there cannot be an objective value any more but only a value for anybody and it is misleading to call price an objective value. It *only* seems to be objective on a large market and looked at from the standpoint of the individual who for practical purposes neglects his own influence on it. But even there it is not totally correct and it becomes *wrong* when the number of the dealers is small or if the influence of one individual for one reason or another becomes significant. The newer theory deserves praise for having come up with a much better understanding of the fluctuation of prices than the classical authors did. And it is only a simple consequence that the term "objective value" has become superfluous. So, we are not going to use it and do not want to waste more time on it because the topic has been discussed thoroughly enough by our predecessors.

But another term has to be discussed more thoroughly, that of the barter value. It has often been stated that the difference between commodity value and barter value is not as fundamental as formerly assumed, or better: that in the modern system it has lost the fundamental meaning it used to have in the system of the classical authors. But the term barter value has been kept around. If somebody sees the chance to barter a good he will evaluate it higher than before when he only looked at the commodity value. If he even thinks of bartering it, the good has to bring a higher benefit than the direct consumption of productive usage. But this value of this good is nothing original. It is nothing but the value of the goods to be bartered. Of course, this new value function of our good has its meaning. But it is not a new type of value but rather two types of commodity values—the one which the good represents directly and the one of the goods bartered for this good—which have to be weighed against each other.

This one has been called subjective barter value and we do not have anything against this construct. But then one started talking about an objective barter value, which just means the "buying power" of this good. This expression is definitely skewed and we will avoid it in the interest in the purity of our system. "Value" here is being used in a different sense as for example in "heating value," etc. But while the heating value of a type of coal, for example, is a fixed dimension based on certain chemical quality, the barter value does not have such clarity. In addition, the term invokes ideas of a long gone phase of our science, in which indeed it had a more solid meaning, and finally the term has totally lost its basis—that is crucial for me. If one claims, for example, that the barter value of a good equals the amount of work contained in it that is something solid, quantitatively determined. If one furthermore sees it as different from the commodity value, then that is of great significance. But when one leaves these interpretations, this term ought to be criticized.

If the amount of a good increases to the point that its marginal value is zero, the value curve starts to go below the x-axis—the value becomes negative. That values can become negative when they are not valued is a well-known phenomenon: water during floods, wood in the jungle, etc. are known examples. The psychological national economist feels uncomfortable with the goods in the situation just discussed. There are two things we have to say.

First: If one has a lot of a good, it does not mean it becomes worthless. As a good with a marginal value of zero still can have a substantial aggregate value, so it is with a good with a negative marginal benefit. We just have to subtract the plane below the x-axis from the positive aggregate value to get to the real aggregate value. Obviously it would be wrong to multiply the *whole* amount with the negative marginal benefit with the result that the economic subject does not want to have the good at all, which clearly would be wrong in most cases.

Secondly: We only see this loss, this feeling of aversion that sets in when we have too much of something as a "negative value" in the economic sense. Other things have been put into this category. We do not deal with this "aversion." We only care whether one longs for things or not. Everything else does not matter to us and the "hedonistic" or "utilitarian" philosophies of some economists are irrelevant to us. We only have to talk about a certain type of "aversion," the one triggered by work and consumption postponement. Some people even saw work as a negative value. Whether that is correct or not we will discuss later. At this point we only want to say that we reject that.

IV

We just want to touch upon the problem of measuring the value. It creates some of the most important objections to the "psychological direction" and the new system of economics in general. Right after it started to receive a lot of attention, a lively discussion started if measuring a psychological dimension, if an intensity dimension is at all possible. One was leaning to deny that and rather claimed that nobody could say what a certain delight would be worth. Furthermore, one doubted the existence of a unit for expressing that value. Finally it was said that a precise value system is an achievement of the modern economy and that it did not exist in primitive circumstances. The primitive person does not know the value of the possession of a good; he does not understand the barter possibilities.

The first objection is obviously wrong in light of the fact of psychological measurements and should not have been brought forth if one would have known the probability theory and just a little bit about modern psychology. It is not difficult to measure the expectation, something the probability theory does; the field of psychophysics provides us with methods, which show us the possibilities of measuring; it is correct that nobody could say how much something is worth to this person but that person could say whether something is worth to him more or less than something else; furthermore that we always look at marginal values—all that the reader will find being discussed in the works of proponents of this direction. It is beside the fact that one cannot notice a certain number of dimensions of the value—everybody who deals with these things knows that.

The non-existence of a unit also would not be a big problem. The example of the probability theory shows us that we do not have to have one where we are just dealing with relationships. Or, more correctly: Where we need a unit, we can just make one up. Therefore, the criticism hurled by von Cassel against the Austrian School—measurements that do not relate to a specific unit are useless—is null and void: Where we deal with comparisons of values, one of them can be taken as a unit and all the others can be described through it. And since we do not deal here with a certain unit but just the existence of *any* unit, one can just add this number to other numbers by other authors. This makes a lot of sense even if the authors do not always give this explanation. We find the same process in the field of mechanics: The mass of bodies are only relative numbers and can be expressed arbitrarily; but when *one* of them gets fixed, al others are automatically fixed, too.

Of course, I do not think that I have totally covered this very interesting cognitive-theoretic topic. But I limit myself to what I already have said; the only thing that we have to say in the fight about the psychological value measuring stick, is that it is superfluous and that from our standpoint of value hypothesis we do not have anything to do with the problems of measuring of psychological dimensions: it belongs to those that we do not have to solve but rather to weed out, to those economists who fight about without any reason. We see here that often things that seem to be stumbling blocks on our path, actually are not even on that path when we start to look closely. A tourist would not get very far if he thinks his path is getting lost between some rocks; when he walks on, he sees most of the times that the thing is much easier than he thought, that some rocks, which he thought he had to climb are actually not even on the path. But he can only see it there; from afar he could not see whether the path leads anywhere. We have to work the same way and when we do so, we see—perhaps not without astonishment—that we can float between philosophical rocks without stranding. Our path is the same as the one in the field of mechanics concerning the mass of bodies.

I would like to add just briefly one more thought: In the theoretical construction of our unit lies the *one* foundation of our money theory. As far as money is a measurement of value, its nature can be understood through our method.

The third objection, which we have mentioned is based on a misunderstanding: Everybody who acts at all has a certain value measuring stick because otherwise he could never choose between several eventualities. But we will talk about it in more detail later.

Part II

The Problem of the Static Equilibrium

Section I

1

Introduction to the Following Exposition

I

In the following part, we attempted to set aside or circle around some difficulties, which concern the foundation of our discipline. It is about showing that an exact discipline of the human economy is nothing absurd; that the demurs, which gave reason to these large circles, also turn away from it, but by taking a closer look are to be taken less seriously than one would like to believe at first glance.

We cleared our path, insofar as us being able to now take a step further. We want to now describe our exact system, which, according to our stand point, does not mean anything of the lesser than to expose the entire, pure economy. Although, in doing so, we cannot bring all the details of the theory, and especially not let ourselves get into all discussions that were ever held, but rather limit ourselves to the main characteristics of the structure, and to relatively few questions of vital meaning. For the epistemology, as for the material content of our science, as well as for the foundations, as for the concrete problems, we believe to be able to achieve quite a bit, and it lies in the interest of the exposition to not go too far into detail.

In the center of this part, stands the problem of the equilibrium. It would be beneficial to immediately say a few things about this for now, as an introduction.

From our perspective, the mutual reliance of the elements of our system has fundamental meaning. The state of their equilibrium can be said to be the problem of the static economy: the foundation of all our results is methodological, as well as material. However, to the reader, the arguments that will come out of this will be more important, and we will only briefly outline these. When we look at the elements of our system, the question especially arises of which of these should be chosen as points of departure and viewed as data of the problem. We will answer the question by stating that *all elements are given simultaneously and only their variations can be found* and don't surpass the fact of their state. However, usually one attempts that: every national economist brings forth certain arguments, which should explain the existence of all goods, so for example, the ones about the geographical and climatic relationships, about human nature, etc. We also have to concern ourselves with these things, although for another, merely negative reason, namely, in order to prove that these things demonstrate foreign elements in the economical system. This is the first point. From this an introduction of the methodologically important resource of the difference between static and dynamic can be gathered, whose meaning will, of course, only result from the entirety of our executions, and a further remark about the cost principle, which will reveal itself within this context.

Then we get closer to the price theory, which forms the core of the pure economy, and which first displays the strict evidence of the distinct determination of the state of equilibrium, and clarifies the nature of the correlation between the elements for us. We will only take a brief look at these, and also more at a few importantly seeming points, rather than emphasizing the systematic completion. However, before doing so we will say a few things about the liability problem, and also discuss the much argued questions of the free competition and the maximum theory. Within the price theory, one furthermore finds two sections of large, practical interest. One is the monetary theory, the other is that of economizing; the latter with a short remark about capital growth. These things do not let themselves be separated from the price theory, but rather come out of it themselves, which, as a side-remark, says much about the fertility of the value principle.

Herewith, we would like to point out the manner of our further research. The third section carries with it a further use of the pure price theory: the theory of distribution. Here one can also not argue of there being completeness and particularity. We all primarily say that, which we have to contribute ourselves, and generally leave it to the reader to complete the missing information from the expositions of the modern theorists. Here one can also go further, and find the opportunity to make methodological remarks. These and a few negative results about the interest theory expose the essential result.

The fourth part concerns itself with what I call the "variation method," as its practical usage then briefly glances over the pure tax and protective duty theory. These latter things only have the character of examples, in order to bring forth the previous generally-exposed foundations in a livelier manner, and they not only contain nothing new, with disregard to a view stimuli, but also remain far behind that, which can be said about these items nowadays. The only important thing is the method, from which the practical results are brought forth, which seems to pull the pure economy towards this direction, to be won, to be clearly deducted, and to demonstrate that it is the only thing that will lead to this goal.

The fifth section exposes a summary of the above-mentioned parts, in some regard; it doesn't put forth any further material results, but rather limits itself to giving a final verdict about the essence and value of the static economy, and a few things about the direction and the views in suggesting further work.

II

Let's take a look at the economy of any individual, or any individuals wherever and whenever. What is of interest to us from this standpoint of these tightly-circumscribed reasons that we are focusing on is, like we said, the fact that every economic subject in every given moment finds itself in the ownership of certain types and quantities of goods. This fact exists for every condition of the economy. May it be a priori dubious by the never-ending volume of the economy's forms, if that, which can be generally said has enough content, in order to make it worthy of attention; may every difficult economic emergence serve as those, which are void in the simpler sense; the economic condition of an individual, or a group always lets itself be characterized through their ownership of goods. It is the result of all moments, which can interest the observer in this connection, and the same ones let themselves be read off simultaneously from it. Furthermore, it is the starting point for the exact methods of the pure economy, represents its operation, in order to realize the problems of the economy.

Which goods, according to type and quantity, do the individual economic subjects have? How can exactly this ownership of goods and this behavior of the economic individuals be explained by this? In order to answer these questions, we should add something, according to some people's perspective, even everything.

No two economic subjects have the same ownership of goods; no two would behave in the same manner, even if this case were to occur.

Within their economic trade, all their relationships in life, personal and social, their entire history and that of their ancestors, no less the fiats of the surrounding nature, mirror themselves.

From the ground, which they control, from the climate, in which they live, in short, from the geographical milieu, each mental and physical habitat is more or less, but either way in a very high degree dependent upon the expression that one explains by the term "race-character." Ethnology, "ethnology" and, from the other perspective, biology also teaches us that like flora and fauna, as well as at the least many things about the human race and his trade and sorrows are to be understood from those influences, within themselves, in as far as they cannot be contrasted as being independent of each other. However, because once- acquired characteristics can also sustain themselves under other conditions, they do gain certain autonomy, and are able to be placed for many purposes next to those mentioned, as special declaration moments. Furthermore, since an impact on the geographical milieu on the part of the human race within certain boundaries is possible, one can speak of an interaction between the same and the nature of the human race, so that the milieu forms its human races, but also the races their milieu.

One can think about the question, to what extent one can explain the social organization from this perspective in different ways, and if the moments present which of these must be understood differently. But certainly it belongs to the part, under the influence of "nature and race." Then again, it is in a position, once available, to sustain even then for a period of time, if the forces that created it have ceased to have an effect. It gains an independent existence, a life of its own, and must be taking into consideration as a new factor, where it can be valid to explain concrete conditions. Herewith, even an impact on the development and the characteristics of race, and even on the external nature can be verified, so that one can even speak of an interaction here. We would have to reach back far, if we would delve ourselves deeper into these things. But for us, it only deals with one point. It should be emphasized how difficult it would be, to want to present a clear causal chain in detail. In fact, one would have to be violent with reality, if one were to insist on it. A general, mutual dependence exists in all these things, and it would be just as false or incomplete to speak of the causation of one through the other, as from the other through one, at least from the stand point of the sciences of the human trade.

On the other hand, the result of all these relationships is then entirely, or partially—the personality. It may more or less have that on its own characteristics, which cannot arise out of it, from itself, offhand. It can be better or worse, assessed in this way or the other way, an egoist or a friend of man, of strong or weak will, etc. Its position in social life, its destiny, experience, and relationships to others may arise from one or the other group of moments, and be interpreted and assessed in a very different manner. In any case, a strong impact from this perspective cannot be denied from anyone. Likewise, it retroacts on these moments, and must, be it, because it has unexplainable, idiosyncratic characteristics at its disposal, be it, because it also is a "continuous type," and, once formed, becomes an independent factor to a certain degree, in the abstract, regarded as an independent moment.

Therefore, the nature of the case does not offer us a comfortable operation, in order to describe all these things. Moreover, we have an infinite, complicated entanglement of effects and counter-effects ahead of us.

The economic condition and the behavior of the individual towards it arise from all of this. Both must be realized out of the totality of these conditions, but as they follow out of them, they also retroact on these things. Actually, it is nothing more than a universally-known, banal truth that has to be different from not only the economic trades of various people, according to the available ownership of goods, but rather also that the economic trade and the economic condition themselves influences personality and, finally, racial characteristics. It is clear that, for example, type and quantity of nutrition, influence the physical and even the character traits of the consumer; that the entire races can transform themselves mentally and physically through deficient supply. It is equally known that the type of activity of daily work stamps a person and leads to the acquisition of mental and physical traits, which can then play a large role in the further development of the individual and the nation. And also these things become independent forces, and the marks, which they leave behind within each person, do not suddenly and quickly disappear. Surely, the foundations of the economic trade may generally realize themselves from the milieu, and such a view will be sufficient for many purposes; although, in the national economy and its closely related disciplines we often have to be concerned with such singularities, and with such short periods that all these things can be viewed as independent, interacting factors from this stand point. For example, if one were to consider the coherence of the physical and moral habitat of the human race with the surrounding nature, one can also still agree with the claim that the first is completely explicable out of the last, with the only presumption that one can adequately explain the discrepancies through migrations. However, from our stand point, meaning through the explanation of a concrete, scientific emergence, it is completely indifferent if one can explicably acknowledge a specific character trait out of the milieu, which previously belonged to an individual. It is there once, and won an independent life.

Therefore, if one were to say that the economic condition and the economic trade is dependent upon the totality of all these relationships, then this would only be one half of the situation. The other is that both retroact on these. Just as that, which arises out of these that everyone acquires and devours, therefore, again, affects all surrounding relationships of what everyone acquires and devours. Therefore, the economic trade cannot be explained without the economic trade itself, and never the economic condition without the economic condition itself, or—more properly expressed—*among the moments, which one must gather for the explanation of the ownership of goods of the regarded individuals, also exists the former ownership of goods*. So if one were to follow the history of the human economy step by step, then out of each given condition, one would indeed be able to read off the former, but one will never reach the point of restoring one or more of the explanation moments to others, rather, one will always find the same.

The effect and interaction of these moments on one another is the actual matter of scientific observation on a social area. It is of utmost importance to acknowledge that, since through this, light can be shed on many fruitless disputes, and a deeper understanding into the social events can be reached. But we want to no longer dwell on these thoughts. Mainly, we only wanted to mention an example of a large system of interdependent moments before, we will now demonstrate that something similar exists in regards to the pure economy.

Within these large movements, lies the small area, to which our attention counts. Of course, all its emergences are dependent upon the large things, which we just mentioned, but we would like to see if the movements upon it cannot let themselves be described in general sentences that are shorter and simpler, as it would be possible if one would want to take all of this into consideration. Evidently, it is a vast field that one would have to govern, in order to thoroughly understand each concrete condition of an economy; and it carries this with it, that one can only say few things in general about it, moreover, that such general sentences would only have little content. The problem therefore is to see whether one could not, without elaborating on all these things that can be described in our field as observant regularities, quasi on themselves, and without searching for deeper reason. For this purpose, counted our exact fundamentals, which we presented in the first part, and this is also why we have attempted to eliminate the term of the economic trade that immediately pulls us into those things. If we would not or could not do this, then our discipline would be in a grave situation. The historical school tells us nothing new, when it points out that each economic emergence is a result of polymorphic forces, and complicated processes; but the demand to yield to all this, means a relinquishment of an economic science. In the attempt to obviate these difficulties, lies no renunciation of their existence, rather only a methodological operation. And this, not the general arguments of the theorists, one can point out to the historians.

III

However it may be, every economic subject always has certain quantities of goods. And we have to describe the changes, that it performs on the same subject, that it gains, and from which it expresses itself. We are sooner to look at how the meal is prepared, not how it is consumed, and we adhere to the amounts of goods *before* the act of consumption, just as we also do not have to be concerned with the technical production processes, but rather with its pure economical condition.

The economic subjects can get their goods in very different ways, exchange them, or produce them themselves. However, we want to understand all of this, as explained earlier, according to the trade's point of view, and we also want to not differentiate in regards to this, for the purposes of this overview.

The first thing we can think of is that the individuals have, in no way, all those goods, nor have they undertaken all those changes on them, which lie in the area of possibility. To arrive at this, they could just as well own other types of goods and quantities.[1] Certainly, they furthermore own and reach also the goods, whose ownership really carries the character of contingency: They like to receive something unprovided as a present, to capture it, to find it, but in general, we see that the changes of the individual types of goods and quantities do not "planlessly" occur, but rather firstly acquire a type of good, and then at a certain point it is passed to the acquisition of another, and so forth. And in any case, we can—so to say—capture a type of ideal condition, onto which the truth more or less attaches itself. The regarded economic subjects cultivate a certain floor space, work with a certain energy in a certain direction for a certain amount of time, and use the remainder[2] of their types of goods in a certain manner. All those relationships that we mentioned earlier, express themselves within these things. In order to explain each individual case, we had to depict that broad area in particular. In every cultural condition, in every place, in every race all of this shapes itself differently; however, especially important is the circumstance that we can, by no means, contrast the individual as such with the remaining things, meaning to perhaps regard the human race and nature as the data of our problem. Since, firstly, neither of both things is independent, and secondly, their spheres of influence are not to be separated; when we view the amounts of goods that an individual owns, it follows *that nothing whatsoever is merely dependent on nature, and nothing whatsoever is merely dependent on human trade*. This even applies from the ground. But we just do not want to exhaustively explain each individual case, but rather we suffice ourselves with the observation that those changes within the *available types of goods and quantities regularly* occur.

It is of fundamental meaning to us that, generally, within consecutive economic periods the same types of goods are *firstly* produced and consumed. Surely this changes in the course of the development; although, only slowly and gradually, and *if one only regards short periods*, one will see that the outstanding, vast majority of the types of goods continually surfaces, and it only occurs relatively rarely that one of the same disappears, or that a new one occurs. The large mass is very constant. And *secondly*, it is fundamental to us that also the quantities, which the individual economic subjects acquire in consecutive periods from these goods, also under the *equal assumption*, are constant in a remarkable way, and changes in the same partially strive to balance themselves. These are two *facts* that we will still discuss in the fifth part of this work.

However, in order to be able to utilize them as the foundation of our system, we have to, so to speak, hew them / trim them through both of the following *assumptions*. The first is that the types—and qualities—as well as the application types of the goods do *not at all* change, and the second that those "most common" quantities of the same, as a matter of fact always and exactly expose themselves in a way that no tendency for change exists. These are *assumptions*, or better yet *fictions*; surely, they do not exactly agree with the truth. In as far as they do this, and what the significance of the results that are built on these is, we will also have to carefully examine in the fifth part of this work.

This is now nothing different than a new deduction of that, which we earlier named the condition of equilibrium. One could name both of those facts themselves the *empirical* facts, and name both of them bound together with the two mentioned assumptions the *exact* condition of equilibrium.

IV

We already said that we cannot exhaustively explain neither the concrete trade, nor the concrete economic condition of an individual, and that it must be our only endeavor to see, if we cannot, regardless of this, be in a position to find any sentences, which can of course only be of formal and general content; in a similar way, just as mechanics describe movements, without further fathoming them and the other characteristics of the moving bodies. We cannot justify why a specific individual has a specific quantity of a specific good (product); we do not know anything about the individual or the good. For example, if the latter is nourishment, than the physiologist can say something about its meaning of the former, and the biologist can say something about its type, and how the trade of the individual regarding the good is connected with that meaning. The cultural historian may interest himself with the notion of whether clothing or jewelry seems more important for the human race. And we equally do not concern ourselves with the technical process of production. In short, we are not concerned with goods themselves, but rather only with the *relationships* between the same, and also not with the relationships between *specific* goods, but rather we only concern ourselves *anyhow* with such between goods, or—even better—with *quantities* of goods.

We are therefore not examining onto which type of goods the first, and onto which then the second choice is made, etc. But we *note* that whichever good may be produced first, always stopped at a certain quantity, and will be passed to the acquisition of another, etc. *The point at which the acquisition of each good stops for each economic subject* is therefore of fundamental meaning to us: in the position of all these points to one another, the relationship expresses itself between the quantities *of the* goods that were acquired *from the* economic subject, and *a certain relationship*, and based on that, which was said, one will understand if we further say that in this *system of limiting points of the acquisition of goods* simply lies this formal moment, which we can handle without concerning ourselves with concrete types of goods, and concrete individuals.

What we need are therefore not theories about the reasons of the economic trade, but rather formal assumptions, which submit these boundary points to us in a short, simple, and formal manner, and *functions*, which *express the requirement that further acquisition of a good stops when its quantity is in a certain relationship to the amounts of the other goods* that lie in the economical area of the economic subject. These functions may or may not sensualize something really in existence, this "something" we can call whatever we want, all this is irrelevant. The only essential thing is that they have certain characteristics, and whatever the economists may have to say about it is secondary.

And now a short, mathematical remark, whose meaning will immediately become clear: that the increase of the amounts of goods disappear on those boundary points means that the differential quotients of our function, concerning these quantities have to be zero immediately. Let us measure all goods with one and the same unit, for example, in money,[3] and let *qa*, *qb*, *qc*, etc., be the quantities of the goods *A, B, C*, etc., so we come to the equation:

$$\frac{d\varphi}{dq_a} dq_a + \frac{d\varphi}{dq_b} dq_b + \frac{d\varphi}{dq_c} dq_c + \ldots = \ominus \ldots 1.$$

This function (symbol from above equation) is nothing different than a type of total value function of the ownership of goods of our economic subject, and this equation expresses a state of equilibrium and maximum. With your help, we can also reach this relationship between the quantities of the goods that the individual owns simultaneously. Since namely the "price sum" of the "sold," and the price sum of the "bought" goods have to be identical, then we have the equation, when we indicate the prices of the units of the particular types of goods with *pa*, *pb*, *pc*, etc.:

$$p_a\, dq_a + p_b\, dq_b + p_c\, dq_c + \ldots = \ominus \ldots 2.$$

Out of which, and in connection with equation 1 follows:

$$\frac{1\ d\varphi\ \ 1\ d\varphi}{p_a dq_a p_a dq_a} = \frac{1\ d\varphi\ \ 1\ d\varphi}{p_b\ dq_b p_b\ dq_b} = \frac{1\ d\varphi\ \ 1\ d\varphi}{p_c dq_c p_c dq_c} \ \ldots 3.$$

Which equation expresses the fundamental *law of the marginal utility niveau.*

In the diction of the "psychological" theory, this means that each good is being acquired in such a quantity *that the lastly-acquired sub-quantities satisfy all identically-intensive necessity movements.* It is this universally-known theorem that we also differentiated. It is nothing other than equation 3, it is only made bite-sized, and decorated with all kinds of ingredients. Whoever does not take offense at the same, and finds this deduction too dry, can always adhere to *this* diction. I only wanted to demonstrate that the root of the matter lets itself be captured strictly exact and sound, and that scientific correctness, in terms of the physicist, is also not an impossibility in our field. However, regarding the practical results no difference exists between us and the psychologists. Nothing different is intended and reached with all the psychological discussions, than what we also intend and reach with our stricter action. It is also to be noted that within the things said, there lies a somewhat different deduction of the worth function, as the one that was presented in the first part. We will not look at the same any further, since this would lead into theoretical details, which lie outside of this work's framework.

Therefore, the equation system 3 delineates everything that we retrieve out of the lively truth, the section that contains the pure economy. *Not the economized individuals, also not the individual concrete goods, but rather certain processes or relationships*, schematized in this expression, are the substrate of our discussions. It is a structure of our arbitrariness, but not just made up, it is a conception of the researcher, but not without relation to the truth. For whom, who understood that, there are no longer any doubts about the foundations of the economy, and the controversies about this resolves themselves; however, we want to come back to these things later, and no longer dwell on them here.

A belt of equations limits the economical sphere of influence of the individual. One can image the same as a circle, within whose center stands the latter part, and on whose peripheral lie the marginal points of the acquisition of goods. They are all relatively similar to the individual. Psychologically speaking, all limiting quantities are, when expressed in the same unit, *worth* the same to it, so that none of the same would tend to quit for a commensurate increase on another good, however else its economic trade may shape itself. And this—and only this—proves the phrase that the individual in the state of equilibrium reaches a maximum of the requirement satisfaction.

In the said things now lies the exact foundation of the economy, according to my perception, and it must be understood if one wants to understand the essence of our discipline. I do know well that my rushed exposition stands in the way of this comprehension; I alone could not have been more thorough. Each sentence has meaning. The reader, whom these things interest, is asked to dedicate some thought to them. Another lecture of this explanation may also be advisable. I regret not being able to recommend a repeat of this chapter, since it is absolutely essential. On the way to precision and to true correctness, our discipline must naturally distance itself from popularity. This is not my fault, even if my explanation may be very incondite. Even the most popular debate contains the same thoughts; only, it deceives so that the difficulties cannot be seen. If one wants true satisfaction, then one cannot avoid them.

I would like to mention something else: even the older economists are not completely alienated from our cognition. We find our law of the marginal utility niveau already by Ricardo, in the law of uniformity of the profit rates. Moreover, almost every economist has recognized a larger or smaller part of the matter. The new one lies in presenting, in detail, the root of the same, the "interdependence" in its universality, and fundamental meaning; one often finds *sections* from it, and individual ones of coherence, which we indicated, have already been handled in an isolated manner. One of the same also shapes the content of the cost principle, by which one is easily assured through some reflection. However, let us move on and discuss some more things that may contribute to a closer explanation of the said things.

V

Our law of the marginal utility niveau, and our state of equilibrium counts for each economic subject, it may be an isolated one, or stand in relations to others. Certainly, both cases differ from one another, namely more and more complicated possibilities for the economic process exist in the latter, but the process is essentially the same in both. The marginal points of the acquisition of goods of an individual are always dependent on one another; only, in the second case it is added that they are also dependent on the analog marginal points of the acquisition of goods of all other individuals. Therefore, one can easily move forth, and assume an unequivocal, certain marginal utility niveau for even the political economy. The simplest way to clarify the existence of such is by regarding the political economy as an economic subject—"John Bull & Co.," for example—and by sensualizing the same, by means of a "representative company," according to the process of A. Marshall. The image alone is inadequate, and obscures the essential character traits of the commerce economy; it is only completely suitable for the "closed" economy, without commerce. For the first, the construction can only supply a preliminary image, destined for fixating a first perception of the matter; but otherwise, one better speak of a system of marginal utility niveaus within the political economy. Nevertheless, it is a grand truth that unequivocally determines, even in the political economy, as the entirety of all types of goods and quantities, and with it also the "politically economical" marginal values of all acquisitions of goods that are dependent on one another; only, one has to understand this accurately; in the *commerce economy* this condition is not induced through a central, social action, and the effect of "social" needs, such as each image of the representative company could suggest, but it is rather the result of the interactions of the individual marginal utility niveaus on one another.

Therefore, in any case, again, our law achieves a dual function equally for the isolated, or closed, as well as for the political economy. It differentiates the relationships that are to be described by the economy from the others, and it does so both from other ethical, social relationships between the economic subjects, and from other, technical, etc. relationships between the goods. And so then it delivers us the basic law of these relationships, out of which everything further follows, it describes the relations of the quantities of goods to each other, which occur under certain assumptions, and will maintain themselves; it provides us, by using another term, the *production and consumption combination* of our individuals that follow from their idiosyncrasy, etc., and from their economic possibilities. It is a problem of *economical efficiency* that solved there is a logic of economical things that are being achieved there. This problem must be separated from that of the *technical efficiency* with which especially its first part—the production combination—can be easily mistaken, but is *methodologically* analog to it. The following views may now be recommended for the attention of the reader.

All appearances or conscious matter that constitute the "world," are interrelated and are mutually dependent on one another. If one were to comprehend a part of the same as a given, in order to derive another part from it, then this is always merely a methodological aide that may be useful or even necessary for certain aims, but never contains the entire truth. The scientific worldview that offers us the exact sciences is nothing other than a great system of magnitudes, which determine each other, and whose relationships are to be indicated by, and is the task of, science. In a smaller degree, each individual discipline also represents such a system, and describes the dependency relations between any data, but into which "being" it is not in a position to penetrate; and, also in this manner the pure economy.

All quantities of goods in the areas under investigation are given to us, and the question with which we have to occupy ourselves is always: how do the same change, if one of them is changed? Or: In what relation must they be to one another, so that no change occurs? This is all that we can examine by our method. Then again, this is not a theory of the economy, but it is all that is of real value in the works of the "theorists."

We can't describe all changes that go on within the quantities of goods, but rather only a group of the same, namely that, which is characterized by the exchange relation. It is not anymore astonishing that the chemical, etc. effects are inaccessible by us. But there are also others that are caused by the economic trade, and that we still cannot explain. An intervention of the law-making brutality among others may lead to vast changes in our system, without us having to say much about it. We have to comfort ourselves by explaining certain economical effects of the same, which is at least something.

Any quantity of goods undergoes an increase; how does that affect all others? All other goods and prices are affected by this. It may be that some of these effects, namely if the increase is not great, or occurs in a less important good, are so scarce that one may not be in a position to recognize them, and can neglect them, and they will often only exist in tendencies. Then it appears as if the inter-relations between the quantities of goods would not be complete, and would not span the entire area under investigation. As a matter of fact, only one or few of the inter-relations will almost always be important and noticeable. And this, as a rule, also leads the economists to only place emphasis on these, and to establish certain, simple chains of causation. But even if this is sufficient for many purposes, it must not be forgotten that one neglects other effects by doing so, which not only exist "in principle," but are also occasionally of practical meaning.

In order to put forth an example: if for any reason the quantity of granary at hand increases, then it is clear that, in general, the monetary income of those economic subjects, which now have more granary to sell, increases. But is not necessary; it may be that the price, as a result of the greater offer sinks to such a degree that the proceeds can be even lesser than before. Assuming that the first would be the case, then the sellers of the granary will develop a greater demand for other goods; this will affect their prices, and also their production, in general. However, then the prices of their productive goods will increase; for example, the wages of the workers that are occupied in their production, which, on one hand, has the consequence that an increased demand of various goods follows from this perspective, and on the other hand, that other workers will turn towards those branches of industry, which will increase the wage in general, etc. However, if the price of granary sinks considerably, then its consumers will benefit, so that, based on this perspective, effects of the same kind, as the ones mentioned will then fall out. A truly obvious entanglement of effects and counter-effects across the entire political economy follow from this one change, and if some of the same are hardly recognizable, then one could still say that it would rather be the task of theory to locate the more concealed ones, than those which everyone can easily see. Our conception is now much more equitable to these relationships, than the usual, and this is the practical moment that recommends the same to us, next to the theoretical, which infers that it is also more accurate scientifically. Through examining, for example, the effects of a toll or a tax on a certain good, one is easily led the wrong way, if one overlooks the general interdependencies of the economic quantities. The popular claim that, for example, a tax would have to fall onto the consumer, is rooted here: one finds that the costs of production of the unit are simply increased around the amount of tax, and assumes this and everything else—offer and demand—as certain. The fact that the offered and demanded quantity of the good can change themselves as a result of tax, which means nothing else than that costs and distribution are variables that are dependent on one another, leads to a somewhat deeper cognition of our system. But all effects of tax that go beyond this foster to be neglected, and if such a further effect once presents itself, then it appears to be a special discovery to emphasize it.

Our conception has a special, theoretical interest in the clarification of the cost discussion. We have already emphasized this in the first part of this work: however, from the psychologist's stand point, the value is the dominant principle of the economy and, even for the purposes of the economy it will be shown that no autonomous principle lies in the "costs." But the total value of a certain quantity of cost goods, and the total value of a certain quantity of consumption goods are variables that are dependent on one another, and are connected with each other in a reversible, functional relationship, which does not contradict the statement in the least, which is to be comprehended as the foundation of the psychological theory of value, namely that the same principle—that of value—underlies both. We will come back to this again. We only want to point out here that the setting up of a chain of causation between the two will only obscure the issue. The statement: "The value of the consumption goods is the cause of the value of cost goods" is in itself not more accurate, if it should mean something other than that the production of consumption goods is the goal of the economy, than the opposite: "The value of the cost goods is the cause of the value of the consumption goods." Both statements, in a particular case, may be suitable for explaining the change of one of both magnitudes. If the value and price of a cost good increases then the general consequence will be that the value and price of those consumption goods increases, and the same is necessary for its production. And, in order to describe this case, it is permissible to regard the first magnitude as being an independent, and the latter as being a dependent, variable; therefore, the latter statement is accepted. In the case to the contrary, the opposite counts. However, the entire truth never lies in it; it is, in reality, rather indicated through the recognition of the general interdependence. For each such chain of causation, another lets itself be opposed, and in general, one will find suitable examples for both; to argue for its prevalence is idle.

The same counts for the instrument of the "marginal productivity." It is not incorrect that the yield of the lastly expended "dose" of a production means "determines" its total value. However, one has the same right to say that the value of a production means determines how much of it will be expended, and what the yield of this last small portion that will be the marginal productivity is. All of these statements are correct as establishments of functional relationships between the elements of our system, and they are all contained in our conception. But their absolute value is scarce. They were useful as points of departure of the scientific train of thought, and depicted discoveries of a part of the system of interdependent economic quantities; they may further be sufficient in describing special cases. However, in general, and where one is concerned about being strictly accurate, they are no longer permissible, and they depict an evidently incomplete, even primitive, conception. It is to be regarded as vanquished through the recognition of the complete generality of the effects and counter-effects within our system, or better, through the recognition of the existence of such a system of elements that are determined by one another.

One sees that we attribute a fundamental meaning to this recognition—that fundamentally contains nothing more than a rather banal truth. We are not hesitating to say that it is the largest progress of the newer economy, and it exposes its most essential difference from the older economy. It is perfectly characteristic of the classical economists, namely of Ricardo, and of its followers that they only mark individual parts from it out of the system, and attend to it with each other, without organic coherence; and it seems that within this lies the most important *theoretical* deficiency of the same. Our recognition places the entire theory onto a new foundation, it gives it a clearer, more accurate form, and shows us its essence and its task in a new light. We gain a uniform method, and cohesion, and a connection between our results, and finally a firm stand point for the judgment of nearly all purely economical disputes and special theories. Everything follows more or less directly out of what our theory can accomplish, and where its boundaries lie.

The national economists, who first and fully recognized this issue, are L. Walras, v. Wieser, and A. Marshall. They did this in an original manner, and by using different points of departure; Walras through his admirable system of equations, v. Wieser through his liability problem, and A. Marshall through further development of the foundations of the classical economists. The latter circumstance explains that Marshalls exposition still adheres to much of the older exposition, and the same does not attain the purity and the uniformity of Walras' work. Especially in the question of cost, his generosity towards the classical economists causes him to not place sufficient emphasis on the fact that the reform of the economy does not lose meaning by the value theorists through this, and that one deprives Jevon's chain of causation of an absolute worth: This does by no means hinder, as we explained that the introduction of the value functions places the entire theory onto a new foundation. Otherwise, he even retains more of the classical system than my consideration justifies, and it needs deeper insight, in order to recognize that even his system in its essence is completely modern. In any case, his numerous successors—and he is the only one out of those three, who really attended school—have mostly overlooked it. This is why even today the overwhelming majority of the economists hold a stand point that must be considered as being obsolete.

VI

Let us sum up a part of our argument. The ownership of goods of an economic subject and its behavior towards the same is the product of infinitely complicated relationships, the product of an obvious entanglement of effects and counter-effects of various types, and different in each individual case. Why, of all things, does this or that economic subject have these types and quantities of goods, and why does it behave in this manner but not another towards it? According to our conception and in opposition to the typical (conceptions) it is in no way the founding question of the economy. Not much less than the entire field of knowledge, the entire host of disciplines that the human mind created, would have to be gathered, in order to answer it; fundamentally, this is not more than being self-evident, and we believe to have emphasized it sufficiently in the former. And even then it would be questionable if the answer to this question that sounds so simple, but is still so extraordinarily immodest, could turn out to be sufficient. Our entire endeavor is much more focused on "switching over" from the plentitude of life of the occurrences, into the clear and simple field of certain formal relations between the same, without doing violence to the first, without analyzing it, and without saying anything material about it. We *can* not go into the details of its explanation, because this leads far into fields that are foreign to us; we do not *need* to do this, because, as shown through closer examination, arguments about it doe not contribute to the completion of those small groups of results, which we would like to gain, and we do not *want* it, in order to make the recognition of our discipline not dependent on statements, which only other disciplines can judge, in order to not involve them in their foreign controversies, and finally, in order to not take its exact character, and its methodological and textual uniformity. And our problem is much more narrow and modest: namely, as explained earlier, the description of certain relationships between the quantities of goods in the study area. I believe that this rationale of "raisonnement" of the economy is not suspended from those demurs that foster to become ascertained against the typical (demurs). We do not explain everything that lies outside of our field as being meaningless; we also do not claim that it is governed by economical laws; we demarcate our discipline, without running into any principle view about these things.

Race, cultural background, social status, upbringing, personality of the economic subjects, all of these determine its economic trade, and all of these moments affect one another; the possibilities of the surrounding nature and social organization, and the own work of the economic subjects determine their ownership of goods; both groups of influences are dependent on one another; and even economic trade and ownership of goods determine each other. However, all this presents an abundance of problems, and also an abundance of possible views of one and the same phenomenon, especially that of the economy; we are attempting to appropriate *one*, and believe that it also has its warranty. Fundamentally, it has no exclusive right to the title "economic." There are also other ways that are possible and useful in dealing with the economical emergences, for some purposes perhaps better than ours that nowhere leads into the essence of the things, as the "driven forces" attempt to show. Only for reasons of the terminological expedience do we retain the designation "pure economical" for it. However, we believe indeed that it is best suited to find especially those formal statements, wherein our interest lies.

Figuratively, one can sensualize our processes in approximately the following manner: We are capturing so to speak moment photography of the political economy. The image shows all processes in a certain stage, and in seeming quiescence. However, we realize that in reality, lively movement exists, and we wish to describe some of it. This description should put us in the position—that is its only purpose—the momentary image that would offer us the truth in the next moment, and to divert us from the first, without taking a new picture—however, not to explain something about the picture in every detail, and to penetrate into the "essence" of the processes. On the other hand, our construction of the new momentary image should limit itself to the changes within the quantities of goods that find themselves in the ownership of the individual economic subjects. Only this is the purpose of the economy, and the assumptions and construction-aids, with which it confronts the emergences, serve only this purpose. The epistemologically most accurate definition of the pure economy would therefore be: The same has the quantities of goods that are located in the ownership of the individual economic subjects in any point of time, to lead back to those that previously owned a "moment," and on the shortest way at that, which is that of the formal assumption.

This cannot alienate. Similar things could be said about all the exact disciplines. The purpose of the exact science is to extrapolate the world of appearances, how it presents itself in a given point in time through the description of relationships that exist between them, or that are assumed to exist, from the immediately preceding condition. And the purpose of each special discipline is to render this work for certain emergences, and certain relationships between these. We can no longer dwell on this; even if this may seem unsatisfactory to some—the modern epistemological theorist will be satisfied with it.

Thereby is a point of special meaning. We derive the ownership of goods of the individuals from another that immediately precedes it, in terms of time. This latter one is therefore a datum of our problems. All quantities of goods are in every moment dependent on everything, and determine one another. Even if only one element of our system were to be different than it is, then all would be different. And, according to our conception, they are definitely determined only when they are all together. This was already explained. We always reduce an ownership of goods to the other; we never explain the advent of things. We even find the same categories, generally speaking. One can always—with practically irrelevant exceptions—group the ownership of goods of an economic subject into land, work, tools, raw materials, and consumption goods. And we find in the ownership of goods, which we derive from this with the help of our assumptions, then again the same categories of goods.

We even find similar, only few different quantities, and in any case, the same *types* of goods.

According to our conception, we can therefore not derive the one category of goods from the other, but rather only all from all of them. For example, we cannot gain the types and quantities of the consumption goods alone from the types and quantities of the productive goods. We will return to this again later. However, it is already very apparent here that the economic process and its results are not only dependent on the ownership of the productive goods, but rather that both can still shape themselves very differently from one and the same ration of such, depending on the type and quantity of consumption goods that the economic subjects own at its beginning. Only the *entire* ownership of goods of an economic subject characterizes its economic sphere of influence, and allows the derivation of another. *All* quantities and types of goods must be given *simultaneously*, if our "raisonnement" should even be possible. And we therefore did not place any emphasis in our basis on the difference between the consumption and productive goods, but rather only spoke of quantities of goods, in general.

Notes

1. So that their ownership of goods looked at from the stand point of the physical possibilities, appears as "coincidental" (Schumpeter, 1908, pg. 126).
2. As one can see, we are regarding the work as an economic good. We have not defined the term of the economic good, and have not set up claims about the characteristics, which are necessary, in order to make something into an economic good; we simply regard *everything that, as an economic good, onto which our view as the element of our exact system* is unforcedly applicable. But this cannot teach us a speculation, but rather only an *attempt*. We make such an attempt regarding work. Nothing is being predicated of its "being" by this (Schumpeter, 1908, pg. 127).
3. Without having already introduced the "money", we are here making use of a moment, whose usefulness lies in ones hands and is easy to understand without elaborating on theoretical difficulties of the matter (pg. 130).

2

Critique of the Common Exposition and Its Relation to Ours

I

Our process is not common. Namely its last-mentioned consequences seem to be essentially different from the common ones, and surely also less satisfactory than these. We must therefore stop, and will argue in this chapter what economists really do by introducing their "raisonnement," and what its purpose is. We want to examine and learn more profoundly everything that typically occurs in its methodological and contextual meaning. Through this, two things will show: firstly, one will clearly and precisely see which value will approach on the arguments in question, and secondly, wherein the difference towards our exposition lies. We are less concerned about the general statements themselves that one maintains to say for the sake of the argument for and against; it should rather be indicated what the typical point of departure actually achieves for us. Already here, it may be noted that it will arise that our exposition is nothing other than a refinement of that which all economists do, only cleansed of all coefficients. Nevertheless, a new exposition of some parts of the economic teaching edifice follows out of it, which, in my opinion is suitable to set aside quite a number of controversies, and to place seemingly conflicting theories into the right relationship to one another. I herewith hope to show that, and why my exposition is the more accurate one, and to "brush our discipline clean" of many things that do not belong in it, and to demarcate them against some matters of a different essence, which do not seem to find complete expression in their frame work after all, and to further contribute to the understanding and to the better judgment of a part of our science.

As a rule, one really does raise this immense problem of which we spoke, namely to explain the economic trade of the human race and its supply of goods. But how does one redeem the promise that lies in it?

By doing this, one runs above all into the problems of the humanly trade. One wishes to gain certain statements about it, from which one can originate. The same can be regarded as familiar and undisputable, that they do not need a further rationale, or one can attempt one of such. The lesson of demand, mediations about a never-changing scientific nature of the human race and the like, serves the latter more. Even if one were of one or the other conception, it remains entirely the same for the pure theory, and these statements, as shown earlier, are always only *assumptions* for it, in whichever form they shape themselves, even then when they display themselves as assertions about facts. The questions of the human nature and the humanly trade with its motivations and its development can never be understood in a purely economical sense, however much one may have to say about it. They can only be eliminated, and so to speak summarized in a bundle, and put aside. The construction of the "homo oeconomicus" and all philosophies of the economists about it serve this purpose that the human race, on each cultural level, and in all conditions trades according to essentially the same principles. Here one can see the methodological function of these discussions, and the reason why they are being so energetically interlaced.

The humanly trade should be explained, or that, which one cannot be explained should be proven as a constant datum of our problems, in order to secure our actual field from disturbances, coming from this side. However, a real theory of the humanly trade will never be reached this way. But we already spoke about this. The human race, or better, a certain behavior of the same is and must be accepted as a given, which, as stated, amounts to our procedure of the formal assumptions, if one wants to accurately express it.

But even if the humanly trade were to be crystal clear and coherent, and would offer no problems—which is, in fact, the stand point of many economists, without wanting to reproach them because of it—the economists could not explain everything that is to be explained about the economy, because the supply of goods clearly depends on relationships that the human race is not in a position to change, in short, (it depends) on the surrounding nature and its possibilities. These therefore form a second "bundle" that must be disconnected from our explanation, and whose content presents itself as a *datum* for the explanation of a certain economic condition. On the other hand, it is irrelevant if one accepts the same "sans phrase," or contemplates it. We will make some remarks about the latter very soon.

According to this, if one analyzes the bases, on which the teaching structure of the economy lies in this regard, then one finds two groups of data, which let themselves be characterized by the words "human and nature." They form its boundary and cornerstone, and lie outside of the actual theory. We saw that one cannot simply contrast the two with one another, since a mutual dependence exists between the two, but also that one could, for certain purposes of the theory, refrain from the same, and regard both as independent of one another. In this case, the problem of the economy would restrict itself to explaining those emergences of the economic life, which were called forth by the humanly trade in a given milieu of the outer nature, and on the strength of certain assumptions about the humanly trade after all. And the restrictions contained in it would surely be generally recognized, and would not be further noticeable.

These data alone are by no means sufficient. For example, it is clear that a certain technological standing position must be given, in order to explain a certain condition of the economy, and similar things can be said about this, just as about both of the other groups of data. The national economy could tell us little about the development of technology, since same is in fact partially dependent on circumstances, which detract themselves from strictly scientific treatment, because they do not present remarkable regularities from discoveries, etc. Finally, one also regards that the organization for the concrete formation of the economy that exists among the economic subject is of vital importance, and it is certainly also a merit of the historical school to have emphasized this. It is therefore currently typical that every systematic work brings longer or shorter arguments about this topic. We will still have to talk about this. However, with that, which we called pure theory, the same has a right to do little, and from the stand point of the first, this must also be regarded as a datum that must be disconnected, and cannot be thoroughly explained. The analysis of the economic teaching system therefore leads us to severely stinting its problem, and to show us this questioning, which we regarded as being typical, is much too far.

This is not however the only demur against the same. We have already numerously pointed out that absolutely nothing from the economy is solely dependent on "nature," and absolutely nothing is completely independent of it, and with it the mentioned contrast does not appear to have a purpose. For example, undiscovered ore deposits, or those that are not accessible through the technological resources of a certain cultural level are economical not available, and therefore it can easily and generally be shown that nature is not authoritative to the economy in a bad way, but rather that what the human race does with it. How much ground will be cultivated, and in what manner certainly does not solely depend on its physical state alone, it will, in any case, not be definitely determined by the same. Conversely, it is evident that the economic trade is never and nowhere entirely independent of the relationships of the surrounding nature, which is almost too banal to have to be said aloud.

But can one not at least deter the ownership of consumption goods from any data, so that its explanation becomes a problem of the economy? This is in fact the goal, and the typical apparatus of our discipline is configured to attain it. And one could also be satisfied with it. After all, the acquisition of consumption goods is the purpose of the economy, and the supply condition of the political economy is characterized in it, at every point in time. Therefore, the just mentioned moments that one suitably called "development conditions of the political economy" are given for any political economy, and the same is furthermore equipped with certain productive goods; then the problem of the economy would therefore be to find all prices, incomes, and the quantities of the consumptions goods that are being produced from it—they types of the latter are already given by the moments "human nature" and "cultural level" or "technology." Those productive goods are grouped into the categories land, labor, and capital, and a discussion is devoted to each of the same, which can easily disguise the fact that they are accepted by the theory, as being data that cannot be further analyzed.

The function of the teaching of the production factors land, capital, and labor, among those can also be counted one or some of the "conditions of development" —for example, from Marshall the organization—in the organism of our economy is a double. For now, it should communicate a certain amount of knowledge to us—we will still talk about this—and secondly, it should form the point of departure of the actual theory, quasi the anchorage ground of the "raisonnement." The moments, which the pure theory cannot explain by itself, are being grouped around those three terms, however, their results rest on them. One must have certain quantities of goods, if certain prices should be deterred, and the same may not change themselves arbitrarily, because these prices would then immediately no longer count. As long as we do not have a guarantee against this eventuality, our structure is up in the air, and our train of thought has no steering. Since it does this we must somehow stabilize our system, we need, so to speak, ballast for the same. One does not want to accept *all* quantities of goods as being given, because it surely sounds paradoxical, if the science of the economy would have to ascribe the results of the economy, and the goods to its *data*. Hence, one accepts *some* quantities of goods as given, namely—due to easily apparent reasons—the productive goods, with which the economic process starts, and then does flatter itself by being able to explain this latter. This realization and the practice that follows from it, to put the teaching from the production factors at the top of the teaching system, is surely a progress, even if its deeper theoretical meaning is mostly not recognized or emphasized. As a rule, it appears as if this section and the later following pure theory would not have much to do with the other at all, and the first would only stand in its place out of favor to its material content: Its indispensability for the typical teaching structure does not occur at all to most of the authors.

Looked at it this way, the teaching of the production factors emerges in a new light. We will still come back to this. For now we would only like to point out that an important admission lies in this acceptance of the production factors as data of our problem, which helps us to transfer this conception into ours, and to show that the first is only a lesser imperfect form of the first, namely the admission that not all quantities of goods let themselves be found with the help of the theory, that at least some of them must be given.

What can now be thought of this "modus procedendi?" Is everything alright? It really seems this way at first glance. The consumption goods consist of production goods, economically speaking. If it works to restore the quantities of the first that find themselves in the ownership of the considered economic subjects, to the quantities of the productive goods that owned the same, then we feel satisfied, our work is done, our curiosity is stanched, and we have, as economists, nothing more to ask. Our system seems to be restored to those data, upon which it is naturally dependent.

By watching more closely alone, the satisfactory appearance of the matter disappears.

If the available quantities of land, capital, and labor would be soundly given, or would in fact be independent variables, than much could let itself be said about one being supposed to use them as points of departure. But this is not the case. They are subjected to changes, and stand in dependence to one another, and to the quantities and values of the consumption goods, as we already said, and as one easily sees. And these relationships are being obscured by the standing conception in question. The same paralyzes and tears the general interdependence between the elements of our system to pieces. I believe I have already said enough in regards to this matter. However, it leads over to another.

Entirely as well as—or as little as—one can find the quantities of the consumption goods out of the productive goods, one can also conversely deter the first from the latter: It must be possible to gain those productive goods that one must have had, from the quantities of the consumption goods that someone acquired, and it is not understood why the one process should have more warranty than the other. Just as the quantities of the productive goods, one could accept those of the consumption goods as being soundly given; it is a fiction, as we saw, (that) the one is like the other. It surely appears that if we regard the consumption goods as unknowns, after solving the problem it is "causa finita," while the deduction of the quantities of the productive goods does not really satisfy us, since it opens a door to new problems. Then in particular the question is raised, why our economic subjects own just these, and no other quantities of land, capital, and labor. This difference is only specious, and this satisfaction is illusory. Because this question also remains open-ended in the first case, it only forces itself on us in a lesser apparent manner. What we gain is essentially the same in both cases, namely quantities of goods from other quantities of goods, and however we may grasp the matter, an unexplained remnant always remains, just as it cannot be different after what was said earlier.

The third demur that we have to bring forward, however, is vital. Certain quantities of land, capital, and labor are not sufficient at all, in order to find the quantities of the remaining goods, even not in the association with the remaining data, of which we spoke. It is clear, as also explained earlier, that the supply of productive goods is not solely vital for the formation of the economic process and its results, but also for the quantities of the already available consumption goods. And therefore one must still have to add a fourth to those three production factors, namely the always available consumption goods. In fact, this is not worse than the assumption of a certain quantity of capital. Because, however one may define this term, it always encompasses produced goods of any type, and its rank among the necessary data therefore excludes any economic processes from the explanation. That, and why this is the way it is, will later be explained even closer. But we can respond to all arguments that one may make for us against our *fourth* production factor—other authors, for example Jevons, have already recognized it through the action, even though they have not explicitly done so—that it is just as necessary as the "capital," which then again cannot be concededly done without—at least the majority of the economists admit this.

There are therefore no elements of our system from which we could say that they determine the others, or rather *all* belong in this category. And herewith we have then again arrived at our own conception, and have justified the claim that the typical is nothing else: a primitive form of the same. One only needs to congruously think further, starting from the usual foundations, in order to arrive at that, which was previously explained. In the introduction of this fourth production factor, in the foregoing of accepting certain elements of our system as given, in the further foregoing of a thorough discussion of the things that do not belong in our system—therein lie the main differences. And I believe to be able to say that this small reform, whose statements then again also showed us the meaning of our system of interdependent quantities, would be germane to the purity and accuracy of our theory.

II

After we have stated the principle position and methodological function of those moments, for which we would like to suggest the expression "system-determined facts," it is now still spared to say some words about the knowledge matter itself that economical works foster to convey to us, in the teaching of the "developmental conditions" and "production factors." It is the chapters about land, labor, and capital, and then therefore the generally recognized additions of today in regards to organization and human nature, which we mean.

A not very pleasant image presents itself. These sections represent so to speak hybrid disciplines that show no progress, and cannot live and cannot die: inadequate and incoherent statements about things, which are only thoroughly developed in other disciplines, and therefore cannot contribute anything to the credit of our science, as they are. Nothing is clearer than that the economist must always be an amateur here, and that which he says must be underdeveloped and unsatisfactory. We will see that we will not forgo anything especially valuable, when we eliminate these things from our discipline, and that really the only thing left to criticize, is that, which we also want to grasp—the assumption of the permanence of these facts. Our discussion will therefore serve to justify our boundary of the economy, according to these views, to raise its being, and to clear it from these strange parts of continuance, and to unify, and finally, to support *our claim for the division of labor* in the sciences of the humanly trade. Other results will also arise only through the discussion of capital.

We have already said so much about the moment of the "human nature" that we want to pass over it, after a short remark. Philosophies about the motivations, examinations of it, and conclusions of the diversity of human nature, according to place and time, and the teaching of necessity of the psychological national economists, these are three points, which we have our eye on. We saw that we do not need these things, and that the purely economical results from it are independent. We would now still like to add that only the psychologist, ethnologist, biologist, and finally, the cultural historic can say something noteworthy about it, and that we must turn ourselves to the latter for *everything* that should surpass the circle of banalities, without actually being in a position to follow all these disciplines individually. Since our discussions are therefore not necessary for our purposes on the one hand, but on the other hand they are also not autonomous and of little value themselves, therefore the conclusion follows for us that we better eliminate them from our field, and furthermore, that this loss is not grave.

Now to the "teaching of organization": The teaching of the forms of government, etc., does not solely belong there, but also rather secondly, that of the forms of law, and the remaining social relations and structures, and thirdly, that of the economical organization in its actual sense, on the one hand, division of labor, etc., on the other hand, cartelization, worker groups, etc. Now these things can be regarded from very different stand points, and for very different purposes, which we want to realize for the overview via two gradations that cross each other.

The first is the following: One can consider all these types of organization, but especially the former two from the *religiously-legal* stand point. It is the oldest and important for the political discussion, even still today. However one may think about it alone, it is certain that it does not fall into the field of strict science. The latter can entirely describe its existing views and follow its development, but never give *judgments* of another type about it. This is very evident and should hardly run into opposition. However, less generally accepted is that the same counts for the *teleological* stand point. In reality, most systematic works of the national economy bring discussions about the "expediency" of the law of succession, of ownership, or even of individual forms of government. And still it is not hard to see that the concepts of the desirability, the way things should be, however they may be defined, gravitate toward metaphysics, and are inaccessible to the exact acquisition, that the latter can only confine itself to a reporting history of development of the affected ideas, if it wants to avoid controversies that are only silenced by humanity. Anyhow, teleology and science are oppositions, (and) will always be. And something further: How infinitely banal these discussions mostly are! What sense does it make to carefully explain that division of labor enables a larger technical readiness, but is not beneficial to the personal development? Can one hold it against someone, if he or she does not value a science that conveys such things to him or her, and namely as a valuable result in itself, not as a cornerstone of far-reaching thoughts? What do we gain by discussing the pros and cons of the republic form of government? Even if we would want to *evaluate*, we would have to now say that *each* form of government can be good or bad; this does not depend on general arguments, but rather on concrete relationships. Did not even this realization become common property?

The third stand point—and we cannot but consider it the *scientific* one—is that of simple description, as well as of the facts of the organization forms, as those legal and teleological ideas of the human race about the same. Only it can come into consideration, when we are speaking of science; we can eventually include only it into the national economy, if it should be (considered) a science. Mind you, no judgment about the principle position of the national economy in these questions lies in it; its meaning within the history of the political ideas will not be diminished; surely the same is vast—especially that of the German national economists. Only, this moment must be separated from the scientific. This promotes the life-interest of impartial research.

The other grouping of the stand points that are of importance to us here is that into practical and theoretical. The first belong to the social politic. However one may think about the relationships between science and politics, and which conception of the social politics may arise from it, the essential difference between practical suggestions and theoretical interest of arising description is unmistakable. If both should be able to find complete expression, and if misunderstandings should be avoided, then one must separate them. With the social politics—then again: whose meaning we certainly do not want to diminish—we are not dealing with, but rather only with the description, with which we revert to the just mentioned "third stand point."

This now belongs to two disciplines, to history and to sociology. But is this not merely a question of words? What hinders us from accepting it into the national economy? Principally nothing at all; in the beginning of the social sciences, it was absolutely sound and practical to work on all these things together; each one by itself would have offered too little content, and would not have filled out its character. Furthermore, it would certainly not be a logical mistake to combine chemistry and biology, for example. All we claim is that both pure economy and the teaching of organization *can* be separated; that they are independent of one another, and mutually contribute nothing to their concrete results; that it is a mistake to believe that everything that influences the economizing would have to necessarily also belong to the economy—geology would then be able to belong to it as well, or the entire field of technology; furthermore, that it is recommendable to separate them if it depends on the day that *one* man can no longer contain the field of both, which now appears to us, to be the case here; finally, that it damages the clarity and the development of both disciplines, if they are not regarded as being clearly parted and separated—this obscures the views about its essence, and deprives them of the advantage to gain a specialized, for their purposes educated and goal-oriented, staff of workers.

This now leads us to concede this field to it, since there is once a form of sociology—and also a teaching of management—whose primary task is a theory of the organization forms, and which mandates its own methods, its own workers, and its own audience. That does not mean that any "national economist" should relinquish the same; only the "national economy" should do this, but each one may regard himself as a sociologist, and be careful in his judgment about the questions of the theoretical economy. This also does not mean that the practice to work on both fields together, in textbooks and councils should immediately stop; this would didactically not be easily possible; but one should not obscure, but rather emphasize the diversity of the fields, and make oneself understood with other pretenders, for the field of the teaching of organization—teachings of constitutional law, etc.—instead of tearing it to pieces.

That is all; it is only of importance to us to grasp that our theory forms a self-contained, individual system that stands methodically, as well as contextually opposite of the teaching of organization. Let us now go on.

Wherefrom do we take the justification to say something about the land, and the remaining relationships of the geographical milieu? Are we climatologists or geologists? The consequence of our pretension is not forthcoming: if we do not want to say anything false, without having to become geologists, etc., then we must restrict ourselves to the common places of the saddest kind, especially to the *fact* that the land relationships, etc. are of more relevant importance for the economy. We can say that the temperature of the North Pole is not very beneficial to the viticulture, that the demand for clothing is lesser on the equator, than in Greenland. And whoever reads this—what will he think of our discipline? For us, a further argument follows out of it, for eliminating these discussions—the first and most important was that we do not need these things to attain our results. Only when it is not of concern to explain concrete economic conditions will they become important for their "general laws," but if they are voiced in a meaningless and general manner, they lose all interest as well.

The matter is not quite the same in the chapter of the production factor "labor force." Namely, because there we find a theory that seems to have gained a civil right within the national economy, and one will not easily forgo it. It is the one that carries the name Malthus'. Should it also be "eliminated?" Now, it is obvious that it lies outside of our pure system. The interaction between the margin of nourishments and the population number is not economical at all, or rather not purely economical. It surely partially belongs into the field of biology. We can concededly ask ourselves a question, which lies in this direction and is purely economical, namely: How does an increase of the labor supply affect the remaining quantities of our system? Here, the increase in population is one of those interference causes, whose effect we can examine to a certain degree, with the appropriation of the theory, and so far, this topic belongs to us. But apart from the fact that this question cannot find an answer that somehow leads deep into the social happenings, but rather leads to a very particular result regarding the facts of the wage indexation, it is not one that is first and foremost taken into account. This is much more the opposite question, namely the one of how a certain supply condition affects the increase in population. And as economists, we cannot say anything about this, even then when we want to agree with the assumption that the measurement of the latter lets itself be comprehended by economic moments. Only then could we bring them into our schema, if we want to go as far as treating people according to analogies of machines, and letting supply and demand be deciding factors in their reproduction. Even if one is only of the opinion that this cannot be done, then one must forgo an economic theory of the reproduction of population. On the other hand, it must be emphasized that by far not everything that is somehow connected to economic moments is accessible to the acquisition by means of the exact economy. But wherever this is not the case, the economic moments become mere banalities, since we are then robbed of the possibility, of building longer trains of thought on it. These reasons that are also supported by the fact that the other aspect of the Malthusian Theory, namely the for it necessary hypotheses about the future development of the margin of nourishments, have nothing to do with the economic theory, and therefore dispose us to eliminate that theoretical construction from the economy, or at least to emphasize that both are independent of one another, and do not form an organic whole.

If our stand point is correct, then one cannot promise oneself a brilliant success from the population theory. It now appears to us to very much speak on our behalf, (when stating) that it actually finds itself in a sad state. Not the slightest progress is noticeable. In reality, one limits oneself to continually discussing the pros and cons of the one Malthusian thought with always the same arguments. Nothing of a continuance in construction, a development is seen: an only half scientific controversy is being lead about this unscientific theory, and if something came out of it, then it is the realization of the small load capacity of the construction. However, since we cannot put anything else in its place—is it not better to abandon even this constituent part of the national economy, which brings it neither methodologically, nor contextually a constructive ornament? However, then nothing of the economic population theory remains.

I hope that the reader will be under the impression that the nature of the matter, and not narrow-minded shoptalk, brings me to my approach in all the questions, over which I grazed in this chapter. Again, if these topics would be *adequately* treated, then I would still, in the interest of clarity, stand up for not having one throw it together with the pure theory of the economy, but apart from that, to gladly accept each effort. Surely, a national economist can also be an ethnologist, for example, Professor Ripley wrote the "Races of Europe." But then he must also be organized about it, and, if he does not already measure craniums himself, he should at least familiarize himself with the literature on these things. It is however impermissible to voice assumptions about it that lie hundreds of years behind the modern stand point of those disciplines—and namely to construct theories based on it, as it happens from time to time. An earnest renouncement, which is in fact absolutely possible, is better.

It can also by no means be denied that new, fruitful cognitions will once let themselves be won out of the combination of ethnological, economical results, etc. Only, one must here also require that one proceeds with experience, and does not mix these fields. It seems to me today that the next and most important thing is to perform a separation, and especially to process our field of activity free of foreign elements, and without rambling outside of its boundaries. Only by doing this, can one figure out the same, and what it can perform. And what one forgoes through this is, at least today, not much yet.

III

Our task is a rather different one, in relation to the third production factor, to the capital. What is fostered to be said about it lets itself be characterized through the words: discussion of the term, assumption of the capital, as an individual production factor, and finally, discussion of capital growth. And we also have some things to say about these points. But we want to attend to the third in another passage later, and we already spoke about the second, so that only the first remains. We now, by no means, wish to further continue the well-known, long discussion of the term; also not, for us to decide on the one or other; this could occur in one sentence; but we would like to contribute something to the better understanding of some capital terms, because it seems to us that various things can be mentioned for most of them, and that by taking a closer look, many an obsolete conception has a better effect than one would like to believe—that the older economists were more conscious about this, what they did, and there is more to their statements, which seem like definitions and word-battles, as it appears. Surely we cannot present the entire, long row of capital terms; we must rather assume them as being well-known in their essence. Only a few points that we will contribute to the discussion should be mentioned here. Apart from that, the reader is referred to the analyses of v. Boehm-Bawerks, J. B. Clarks, and to a row of articles in the *Economic Journal*, and finally, to the work of Irving Fisher, "Capital and Income."

It is decisive to the judgment of the role and the meaning of a term, to know the purpose that the creator of the same has in mind. Since the scientific concept formation is naturally arbitrary, it makes no sense to argue about "correctness" or "falseness" of a term. One also cannot juxtapose the terms that carry the same name in advance, and want to once and for all decide on one that is connected with the latter; in reality, it is absolutely possible to choose one for one purpose, and another for another (purpose), and all that one can require of every theoretic regarding this is firstly, not to create confusion, and secondly, not to reveal anything about the content of any of these ideas that does not pertain to it. This principal highhandedness explains the numerousness of the available capital terms, without seeing something so very deplorable in itself—the matter also has another aspect. Let us immediately say how we want to proceed with the capital term. We will avoid it as much as possible, and simply say what we mean everywhere that it applies, for example, tools, etc. This has the advantage of clarity, and also another, at which we will soon glance. But even where we need the word, we will by no means cling to *one* definition; however, we only do this when no doubt can exist about its meaning.

What are the purposes now that the capital term serves in the economical literature? It is the merit of v. Boehm-Bawerk to have separated two entirely independent ones. "In the Systems of the Political Economy," he says in the introduction to the "Positive Theory of the Capital," "one encounters the name and the theory of the capital regularly twice, in two separate fields; the first time, in the teaching of the production, the second time, in the teaching of the distribution of goods. The first time, the capital is represented to us as a factor or tool of the production, as a lever, who serves the human race, in order to wrest forms of goods from nature, with that much great success. The second time, it appears as a source of income or annuity fund; it is shown to us here how it functions as a magnet that pulls a part of the national product towards itself, and hands down to its owner as annuity, for the social controversies about the jointly created product: it appears with one word as the source of the interest on capital."

This separation of two roles of capital, and two groups of capital terms that follow out of it, seem, in fact, of essence to us, and we also want to make it. However, we would like to comment on two things about it. Once, we must remind ourselves of what we said about the role of the production factors in the system of the national economy. It exists in quasi stabilizing the same, eliminating things, and to explain those, which we cannot explain again ourselves, using our resources, as data of the train of thought; to characterize the niveau (level) of the economy, from which we must go out—but not *in completing a separated chapter about the "production"*: One of such does not exist for us. Now, this role of the term of capital will teach us to understand many of its definitions. But then, however, a further—third—moment, a third role of the term of capital that one can consider the "characteristic of the capitalistic economy" must be pointed out. In fact, the economists want to also make a contribution with their terms of capital—and maybe above all—a contribution to the analysis of "capitalism", to the understanding of the capitalistic economic processes and to the social happenings. This gives occasion to the following remarks.

Firstly, this moment by no means already lies in the other two. Which supply of goods must be presumed, in order to characterize the economic niveau, which supply of goods that must be *given*, we should depart from a pure theoretical question, or better, a methodological question that has nothing to do with the one that is the characteristic of the emergence that is described as "capitalism." We can solve the first, without even knowing or wanting to know wherein the essence of capitalism exists. But just as independent of it is the question, where interest comes from. We can by no means a priori say that it only appears in the capitalistic economy; it may be appear to be this way to it, but it is not necessary. For example, the claim that interest follows from the "battering of the advantageous production detours," and the one, that claims that the essential characteristic of capitalism lies within it, are absolutely independent of one another, and do not necessarily stand and fall at the same time. We will therefore have a third group of terms of capital, or of the same types, or, even better, of elements within the terms of capital to differentiate; for example, Marx' term will be attributed to it.

Secondly, one cannot go wrong in believing to see the main role, or even the occasion of the formation of the term of capital within the just-mentioned. The word "capital" is entirely superfluous, if we want nothing more than to characterize our "economic niveau." Its use saves us the recital of categories of goods, which belong to it in this sense, the same can in no way and any further occur so briefly that that terminus hardly offers us an advantage. One will not as easily admit this for capital as a carrier of income. And still, the matter behaves exactly the same here. However, capital and interest are well-knowingly related in the linguistic usage; if one just examines where interest comes from, for the purposes of science, and finds that it is reducible to, for example, the productive output of the tools, then one could in fact say that the capital exists, in this popular acceptation, in tools, but one could not say offhand that the essence of that, *which another* popular acceptation denotes as "capitalism", lies in the use of tools; however, if one cannot say this, then the terms "capital" and "tools" are merely synonyms, when answering the problem of interest, and the first is dispensable. The only place that the term of capital is in "its element," the only place it is not dispensable, is where it deals with the analysis of capitalism—and only therefore, because the theorists also want to achieve something for this, do they introduce this terminus. However, only the first two points matter to us, and therefore we actually do not need term of capital at all, which is the second reason that causes us to avoid it at all costs.

Thirdly, it is now distinctly shown that through this latter role of capital, as a characteristic of capitalism, we are not dealing with a mere definition, but rather with a problem, when we ask for the "essence of capital," and that discussions about words and "adaptation of terms" are not completely futile, just as one would otherwise often find in our discipline, moreover that by doing this, one does not argue about words, but rather about theories. Therefore, when we said that the concept formation is arbitrary, then this only applies to *one* aspect of the matter; this does not apply, in so far as answers to the problem already lie in the terms/concepts, and the affected controversies gain meaning and interest—only become explicable at all—however abortive the method of the argument about the meanings of words may be.

This leads (us) further. The same applies to the other two roles of the term of capital, and theories express themselves within its fixation. And then we recognize that these very boring disputes, namely (those) of the elder economists about their conception formations, contain much more than one could believe. Let us now explicitly pose ourselves the three problems, which correspond to the three roles of the terms of capital, and hide themselves behind their definitions: Which types of goods, aside from land and labor, must be presumed as given, in order to make the development of our theories possible? From which source does interest flow? What is the characteristic of the capitalistic economy? All three questions can be answered by the term "capital"; this alone, would not speak for itself, the actual answer appears in the form of the definition of capital. We do not agree with this method, and also want to eliminate the term of capital from the first two problems, but here, where we are only concerned with contributing to the understanding of the common teaching system of economy and the capital controversy, we can appropriate this view.

Above all, it must be emphasized that only the first two questions surely belong to the domain of the theoretical economy, in our case. The third does *not* belong to its system in its simplest form, already not, because the same should apply to all forms of economy, while one cannot easily speak of the phenomenon of capitalism, whatever else its essence may be, in the economy of a Bedouin or an austral Negro. However, it is still to be added that maybe—we do not want to make a final verdict—the same is characterized much more by ethnical, social, and other moments, than by economical, furthermore it is characterized more by concrete moments—for example, availability of entirely unpropertied economic subjects on one hand, and very wealthy ones on the other—rather than by general, abstract ones. This is one thing: separation of the moment of capitalism from the pure theoretical applications of the term of capital, and recognition of the fact that this emergence does not belong in the empire of this "economic logic," as what one could describe our system to be. The other, which renders us this cognition, is the understanding of some arguments in the term of capital conflict. One fought against includes the labor in the capital. This happened with different motives, however, we are only concerned with one here: one says that by doing this, one turns the worker into a capitalist. What does this do? It is very secondary for the pure theory. The difference between the worker and capitalist class that one does not want to see blurred, is very important for the social view, its contrast is an essential moment to the understanding of the social event; but to us, what is its place in the theory? Here we have an example of a modus procedendi in front of us that already wreaked havoc in the economy, and led to many a discussion with no results; to discuss each tendency, concepts, and theories with general reasons, without considering that the purpose does not only hallow the theoretical instruments, but also makes it foremost understandable that what can be useful and right for one class of problems, is wrong and inexpedient for another.

Now to the second "role," before we turn to the first, which is most important here. Why does Jevons define capital as supply of consumption goods, why do many theorists name nonperishable goods, with the exception of land, why other tools, and even other tools, and raw materials "capital?" Simply because they derive interest from it, and hereby want to remain in conformity with the popular contiguity between capital and interest. Capital is by now means to be understood as the soul of capitalism there; if some theorists believe to have killed two birds with one stone, so to speak, through their procedures, then this is a mistake, a beautiful illusion. But there, the term of capital is also no mere, entirely arbitrary definition; rather, an interest theory will be set up to begin with, and then the "interest stock" will be called capital—and this is the moment that is crucial to the judgment of these terms; of course we considered it better to simply speak of an "interest stock"; only, this illusion hinders it, *otherwise* there would be no given reason against it. But if one already used the terminus capital, then one may not condemn it in itself and in general, but rather only based on the interest theory itself that the terminus serves. Otherwise, it is impossible that something will come out of this. That there finally must almost—not entirely[1]—be as many terms of capital, as interest theories is thereafter no longer self-evident, and the effort of some theorists to aim at one convention about the content of the term of capital, without taking the interest problem into consideration, must necessarily remain without a result, as long as and in so far as capital and interest are independently associated.

After all, based on our previous constructions, we also see that even in those definitions of capital that were neither constructed with regard to interest, nor with regard to the phenomenon of capitalism, lies a healthy, methodological core, and more than a mere definition. The "relation to the acquisition and to the production," which, according to v. Boehm-Bawerk's happy expression, characterizes so many definitions of capital—almost all—what purpose does it have? The theorist knows that he cannot derive all produced types of goods and quantities by means of the theory, from the data of the "nature relations." Therefore, he wants to at least derive the consumption goods of the economic subjects, whose acquisition is indeed also the goal of the economizing, and places the production supply of goods as a datum, as another production factor, next to this. A much healthier understanding lies in this, than in the implicitness that this supply is not given by nature, but must rather be produced itself. This does little to help us, if we must acknowledge its production as lying outside of our system. Furthermore, some economists saw that the differentiation of production goods that must exist, and consumption goods that are supposed to be produced by them, are not completely suitable and sufficient. In the period that we are regarding and whose processes we can derive, production goods are also manufactured, and consumption goods out of the previous, which substantially influences the course of the economy. In addition, not only its ownership of production and consumption goods is vital to that, which each individual can and will consume, but rather also that, which it can exchange for it. For some economic subjects, even consumption goods only also come into consideration in this regard, and the supply of goods, by means of which they provide their livelihood, can also consist of consumption goods. This explains the term of "acquisition capital" as a "production factor" to us, and the inclusion of consumption goods into the term of capital. In a sense, we ourselves stand up for the latter measure, as the reader saw.

And finally, something can also be said from this stand point, for those "exorbitantly far" seaming terms of capital that can presently be regarded as being obsolete, for those, which, for example, also include the nation, etc. The organization relations, etc., must certainly be given and grasped in an unaltered way. It is nonessential if one now considers them as developmental requirements or as production factors, and if one, in the latter case then again, sees them as individual production factors or sees them together with other data, meaning therefore with capital. This may be unpractical; but this drawback disappears next to the considerable merit, the healthy, methodological understanding that lies in the production of these things among the data of the economic thought process.

Let us content ourselves with these insinuations that let themselves be easily explained and demonstrated on all the individual terms of capital of this group—a task that would go too far here, and that I would like to leave up to the reader. Perhaps the few things that we said, together with that, which we noticed about the other types of terms of capital are suitable to let the discussion of capital appear in a new light, and to introduce a new moment into it, which can contribute to a better understanding of this chapter of our theory. Let us summarize the last part of our argument once again. What caused the national economists to array this third production factor—perhaps better: the factor of the economic process—was the realization or the feeling that the system of the pure theory does not manage with the other two, in fact, yet another group of data—existing in given supplies of produced goods—is necessary for the description of the economic process. And this realization or this feeling was very accurate. The collective core of all these constructions lies in it, and this core is healthy. Of course, one had different opinions about the type of these even *further* necessary data; sometimes one believed through the assumption of a supply of imperishable goods—"standing capital"—sometimes through being able to manage with one of such of productive goods, sometimes one went even further; only seldom did one construct the thought to its end, and went as far as we are. But in looking at the whole picture, always the same—and in its essence the right—methodological measure exists here.[2]

Something else comes out of these discussions, namely a verdict of the frequently undertaken "dissolution of capital in labor and land" or even, only in labor. One particularly—from time to time, not without a side glance on social political moments—defended himself against placing the capital, as an independent production factor, next to labor and land. Alone by doing this, one merely obeys a methodological necessity that, as we have already seen and will still see, entails that a theory of the formation of capital stands outside of the pure system of the theory, and forces us to originate in given quantities of goods. Therefore, nothing shocking can lay within it, as the attempt to steadfastly support the demand of the owners of capital for income, and to place "capital" importance on the independent role of an independent factor, in their interest. We certainly condemn the same, but this does not lay in this "methodological measure" in itself. We do not deny that the capital "exists" as labor, or from work and land performance, only, we are of the opinion that we *can* not describe the process of its development from these elements in the framework of the exact system—that the pure exchange theory does not readily lend us a hand, rather its apparatus eliminates this problem—and also that we do not *need* to describe it for the small group of results, which we will later term as the content of the "static economy."

We could still undertake this dissolution perhaps this actually has its advantages. Except that, in place of the present datum "capital" we would then have to adopt another one, namely a given quantity of "previously done" labor and "previously accomplished" land performance, a type of "labor" and "land performance jelly." We could not have examined how this supply was accumulated; our "static" methods would fail at doing so; it would have to be given, even if not in exact goods, but *as an abstract stock of productive power*. We could possibly explain how it is used, the relation of quantities of the productive goods, which were produced from it, to one another, but not its existence, the fact that these labor and land performances were subserviently made for the future and the development, and not for the present, because this lets itself be explained from moments that do not show themselves in the state of equilibrium—and our system today suits only this one in a sufficient way. Nothing stands in the way of the assumption of such a stock. We do not need the same, since we are simply regarding all types of goods and quantities as given, and only regarding the relations of the latter to one another, and the variations of the same that lead to the equilibrium. But we do not have any objections to it in principle—we do, however, object to every differently-natured "dissolution" of capital in land and labor for the purposes of our field.

Every connoisseur of the new theory now knows that we just now defended and learned to understand a construction, which gave occasion to the lively discussions in the present, namely Professor J. B. Clark's term of capital. In these discussions, however, other points than those that interest us were emphasized, namely the question, whether or not something in reality corresponds to this construction. For this reason, let it be allowed that I briefly note several things in this matter. The reader is referred to Clark's and v. Boehm-Bawerk's articles for this controversy; the matter should not be exhausted here, the arguments of both authors should also not be elaborated. To us, the following is involved.

Professor Clark differentiates between capital and capital goods. The latter term encompasses raw materials and production tools, therefore that, which v. Boehm-Bawerk's term encompasses which is used more and more, and besides this, the land with all objective production factors, a summary that well emphasizes its essentially equal position from the stand point of the pure theory. However, capital is something different, according to him. It is a constant, permanent stock of production capability. In each given moment, it coincides with the embodiment of the available, concrete capital goods, but otherwise, it differentiates itself from the same, because, like it, it is usually not destroyed through the production, but rather continues to exist. Clark points out the fact—or he regards it as a completely undisputable and simply fact—that the capitalist keeps his capital throughout all production periods. The capital goods perish or, as one can express from the economic stand point in partial opposition to the physical one, they merge into consumption goods, others step—according to Clark, entirely by themselves—into their place, however, the capital as such remains. He strives for the expression of this thought with numerous images, in newer and newer variations. Just as a river always remains a river, even though other water droplets always compile it, just as a human being will always remain the same human being, even though all tissues in his body regenerate themselves, so is capital also, despite the unhesitating change of its concrete components.

Now to our comment on this: this capital fund represents a *fiction*, but a practical one, and from Clark's stand point, a necessary one. However he may fulfill his task as a source of interest, to serve it as a departure point of the economic raisonnement, as a production factor, etc., it truly has a purpose. Herein, we are different from both authors; from Clark, for the reason that we do not assert its reality, like he does, and we also comprehend it, as a fund of piled up labor and land performances, somewhat differently; from v. Boehm-Bawerk, due to the reason that we do not deprive it of a healthy sense and utilization. So then we understand in what sense one, along with Clark, adjudges this fund of complete movement, and to be able to say about it that it could move freely from one industry to the other. Of course in reality we only see formed, concrete goods, from which this abstract production power does not let itself be easily extracted; however, if one would want to explain the availability of precisely *these* goods in *these* quantities, then one could proceed in the manner that one equips each economic subject with a certain quantity of such production power "a limine," and now quasi observes, if it uses the same, out of which must arise analog mediations, those actually available goods and the limiting value, with the help of our law of the limiting value niveau. Furthermore—thirdly—Professor Clark says that his term of capital corresponds to that of the business practice. I do not believe that this is correct, moreover that an illusion of certain external similarities exists here. However, this is not of interest to us here, and we want to content ourselves by stating that this point is irrelevant to the theoretical usefulness of the Clarkian fiction. Finally—fourthly—Clark assumes that this capital fund will always be maintained, and will not perish in the production. Certainly this is the most alarming fiction of all. But which economist is completely unfettered by the idea that the reserve of the consumed "capital" goes on quasi self-evidently, more or less automatically? Almost no one; and then one is not far from stepping into the Clarkian conception. The same will hardly let itself be avoided, if one wants to stay within the framework of our system.

There would be many other points to still be discussed here; we would only be able to offer a small contribution to the resolution of the questions here at hand. We must be content, when our discussions justify our previously developed stand point, and in addition, show the reader how much there is still to do in this field.

Notes

1. Because not every interest theory is based on a term of capital, as is the case, for example, with the seniors. (Scumpeter, 1908, pg. 168)
2. However, it is of course a grave mistake, as v. Boehm-Bawerk emphasized, if one "blinded by the symmetry between the three production factors and the three branches of income" then believes offhand that this "capital" must have to carry interest. (Schumpeter, 1908, pg. 171)

3

Static and Dynamic

I

We now come to the topic that is of great methodological meaning, and that the majority of the German national economists did not pay adequate attention to. Our most well-known methodological works ignore it, and indeed, its importance only becomes clear to us from concrete work and not from general discussions about the principal questions. However, it touches virtually every economical work, and one can say that clarity about it is necessary to actual understanding.

As we saw, our train of thought originates in a certain ownership of goods of the economic subject. By doing this, we emphasized that these quantities of goods exist in a certain point in time, and said that our results, if our theory were to ever come so far as to supply concrete, numerical results, will only count for this point in time, or for a neighboring one. Concededly, our theories are universally valid in themselves, therefore, independent of certain regional or temporal relations; but, they are also just formal, and do not reveal anything about its concrete state; and even then, when we therefore do not refer to such, we thought it necessary to state that our arbitrary—although SOME HOW obtained—data do not change beneath our hands, so to speak. Why have we done this?

Likewise, as we retrieved the value function, the economic subjects, so to speak, or better, as we determined or accepted them, we emphasized that all their parts should refer to one and the same point in time, and one and the same geographical, social, cultural, etc., milieu. We took the same care, when we spoke of the exchange relation. The assumption especially played a role in the discussion of the teaching of the production factors, that our system should be stable in essential points, and should only present very specific changes. And therefore, we also carried out such restrictions in other places. This is best illustrated by the allegory of our "moment photography," whose purpose it just is to show us a state of quiescence; even if we then lift this ban, and revive a portion of the image, we still adhere this state of quiescence to another—and by far greater—one.

It is immediately noted that our adherence to one and the same point in time or to very short time periods only has this purpose; by doing so, we aim at retaining certain portions of our image of reality unchanged. If we would observe longer periods, then this ascertainment would conflict too much with the facts, since, as one easily sees, unpreventable events would arise in the same, which would change our entire system, and compared with those, the processes, with which we concern ourselves, would entirely disappear. We will come back to this in a later part of this book.

Are all these suppositions that adhere to all our phrases now just sayings that one might as well omit? Of course, the answer is negating. We are not proceeding in this manner out of temper or arbitrariness, but rather simply because we cannot do otherwise. And not only we cannot proceed otherwise and see ourselves compelled to recognize an important constraint of our methods here, but rather each theorist, in the narrow sense, is in this position, whether he may acknowledge it, or not. If Ricardo speaks of the influence of the introduction of machines, then his statements originate in a given condition of the political economy, a specific capital, a specific extent of employment of the workers. Malthus' population-theoretical results assume a specific technique, or even a specific developmental process of the same, a specific organization of the political government, and a specific population increase as given—and probably other circumstances as well. And these suppositions are essential for the understanding of his theory, and for the assessment of its results. One moment, v. Thünen's raisonnement has given quantities of labor, the next, such ones of capital, etc., for assumption. It is hardly necessary, especially after the previously said things, to cite more examples. No one, who deals with a purely theoretical topic can evade these ascertainments, which are of course, only rarely formulated in an explicit manner. But they already exist then, when someone speaks offhand, in the course of his train of thought, of the "available land," "capital," etc., or eliminates any moments by means of the "ceteris paribus."

This latter resource—I would like to call it the motto of the isolation method—is certainly indispensable, not only for us, but also for each discipline, as well as for the isolation method itself. It is surely clear that one can never put an emergence in the proper perspective and understand it completely, if one does not describe them *for himself*, and eliminate moments, which would tarnish the image. Therefore, we often make use of it. Even in our field: If I want to describe the cost movement of a commodity, then it would be mostly recommendable, at least for a first approach, to abstain from the accompanying changes in the value of money. But I do not mean this here. In the mentioned case, I am at liberty—and this actually forms a portion of my task—to later introduce those variations of the value of money into the problem, or to regard them on their part, so that only a temporary restriction of our results lies in this procedure. *Here* the matter is a definitive one—a definitive one, at least for the pure economy—and in addition, a very serious one.

We already saw that there are many things that, even though they are of vital importance to the *economizing*, still lie outside the field of the *economy*. Then again, we do not want to enumerate them again. That we cannot say anything about the same ones in themselves is neither astonishing, nor regrettable. But we must also assume them as being *unchangeable*, and this is more serious, since such an assumption, as I said, does not, only for very brief periods, destroy the usability of our results. However, this being so, one readily sees that those things are actually not allowed to change themselves. A change in human nature, in the geographical milieu, in technology, the social organization changes our entire system. Our given supply of goods, from which we go out, loses its current meaning, even if it was not materially affected by this; if, for example, the value functions change themselves, then the production process will be different than it was up to this point, and therefore, changes in the quantities of goods—and *types* of goods—will eventuate, which we powerlessly face and, which we cannot say anything about. Certainly, our formal laws are also valid then; but they lose all interest, in regards to those changes in the foundation of the political economy. Our equilibrium system is interrupted; a new equilibrium will presumably manufacture itself, but we cannot say what it looks like, and by which processes it is caused. Eventually, we can make only a few, small contributions towards it. Subsequently, great problems escape us, for example, so that, of the tendencies of the distribution of income, and even all, for which those things play the main role.

But this is not all. Indeed, the economists also go by certain, given quantities of goods. However, we do not, as explained, assume any quantities of goods as unchangeable, but rather allow *all* variations; however, *all* must be therefore given to us, even if just for that moment, which serves as the point of departure for us. However, its existence is certainly a problem, and one can not avoid regarding the same as an economical one. Nevertheless, we cannot solve it. Even if we wanted to comprehend land, as simply given by nature, we would not be able to do the same regarding the accomplished labor, and the available capital: we could presumably construct for both special theories, but from the stand point of the exact theory, in the proper meaning of the word, nothing is won by this—it remains true that these things cannot be explained by and of themselves, but must rather be accepted as data. The matter appears to be especially unfavorable, if one completely accepts our conception, since, according to it, *all* goods figure under the data after all; however, we demonstrated that the common conception merges into ours by itself, and is not sustainable by itself.

Since this is a point of fundamental importance, we want to once again make clear why such an explanation of the creation of capital and even the existence of all produced goods in the framework of our system can actually not be found, and the same *data*, and not *problems* must be for the latter. This standpoint differs so much from the common one, and is so essential to the true understanding of our field that I can hardly emphasize it enough. We can certainly—and this is our only task—extrapolate a condition of our system from another, and it will then appear as if we could trace the sequence of consecutive conditions back to the most primitive conditions of the economy. But this is not possible; especially due to the mentioned reason, namely because during the course of our derivations, we would very soon run into circumstances that destroy the continuity of the same ones, and shock our system by its foundation. But if this were also to not be the case, we could have never gone back farther, when we found the same types of goods. We could never lead the modern house back to the pile-dwelling, the Armstrong revolver canon back to a shillelagh, etc., because if the human being *completely* dismisses the acquisition of a type of goods, in order to merge into another, then our systems of equations immediately fail, in order to make entirely different room, and we are able to say nothing about why the transition succeeds, and what its—at least very complicated—effects are. Yes, we will see, when we later return to this matter, that not even all changes in the quantities of goods, but rather only *not too great ones* can fall into the circle of our views. And basically, this is only self-evident. Wherever the entire value system of an economic subject, wherever really *everything* regarding its economy changes, or wherever even the same one becomes considerably different, just as little about exact things can be said there, as about the effects of the eruption of a volcano.

The same also applies to capital. May one also dissolve the consumption goods into their production factors then there will always be goods among the same ones that are produced, and may one continue the dissolution until then, then one will still always run into other elements of capital. But one cannot infinitely continue this dissolution within the system from the stated reasons, and even if one could do this, and the construction of an economy without capital that has been attempted by quite some authors is in a position to introduce itself in our system, a bridge to the "capitalistic" economy would not be available, since all concrete magnitudes that are irrespective of the consubstantiality of the processes, behave differently here. One cannot consider an economy free of capital, and then introduce a specific quantity into the same, in order to see what happens. By doing this, *everything* would be changed: The values of *all* goods—some would receive a new role, others would be devalued—their quantities, all value functions, even the human being would change and mature, as far as it can come into consideration economically. All that we can do, even for capital, is to describe the variations of its quantities under the influence of the data and elements of the system, and the effect of independent—not too great—variations of its own quantity, onto the other elements.

Now, these restrictions are important enough. Therefore, there are also, without a doubt, economical problems that the pure theory, which is contained in itself and independent from other disciplines, is not able to solve. So then the field of the study of economy molders into two parts, into our exact system, and into those problems that are strictly "economical" without being able to be discussed in the first one. This is not a bauble of a logician, who is addicted to classification, but rather arises naturally from the essence of the matter.

If our statements perhaps partially appear to be strange, then it is due to the fact that we strive to be precise, clear, and distinct; there is just as little new about the differentiation, and even the essence of the stated things, as our conception of the study of the production factors. We only said what more or less everyone acknowledges, at least through the act.

In more modern times, one is also principally mindful of the matter, and gave the names "static" and "dynamic" to those two groups of problems, into which our science molders, a terminology that we want to retain out of comfort, even though it is quite unfortunate in my opinion.

This differentiation is fundamental. Static and dynamic are completely separate fields, they not only have to deal with different problems, but also with different methods and different material. They are not two chapters of one and the same theoretical structure, but rather two completely independent structures. Only static has been dealt with somewhat sufficiently up to now, and in this book, we will only concern ourselves with it in essence. Dynamic is still in its beginnings, it is a "land of the future."

Not only were both fields not always sufficiently limited, and even their diversity was not always accurately comprehended and appreciated in their meaning, one also often overlooked them. And this often became very noticeable, especially through controversies, one can say, that the main cause for some result-less controversies lies in the circumstance that the arguing parties reproached each other indiscriminatingly with static and dynamic arguments, or better, did not recognize the static or dynamic character of the same. We have already mentioned examples of this, and will still get to know others later on, among them is the practical, and most important by far free trade controversy. Our differentiation is therefore by no means merely a matter of principal importance, but is rather also very essential to the character and the value of concrete results. Really, the first question that one must ask oneself, in order to be able to thoroughly understand and analyze a theory, is whether or not it is meant "statically." And our judgment of it will often depend on this question. For a theory to be "static" means to be won with this apparatus of conditions and data that characterizes static; such a theory can only be understood through the foundation of our system, and only has sense and meaning in the same. It then stands in unsolvable connection with all other theorems of the same, and cannot be accepted or rejected for itself alone. And one forgets this time and again, wedges different claims into our system, or judges a statement of the same without any regard for the coherences, in which it must be understood; and furthermore forgets, among others, that only he can judge a statement of our system, who himself knows this exactly, that if this requirement is not applied, then something can very easily appear to be quite plainly false, or even ludicrous, which serves a good purpose in this milieu.

The very real meaning of the demand to keep static and dynamic apart also shows itself in another manner. Their neglect particularly explains the insufficient stand of some parts of our economy; based on the biased opinion that the economical theory must be able to cope with all economical problems, and in the belief that static contains the entire economy one often attempts to apply their methods to materials, which react against such a treatment. Then one contents oneself with quite some exiguous statements about it, and even quite some "workings of terms" that one cannot pass over and that have been repeated since the classical authors without having made any progress. I am thinking of the theories of the development of capital or assets, for example, of the economizing theory, the massive problem of the economical progress, and more of the same. As the most important example of a stunted theory through this wedging into our system, we will get to know that of interest. It is ruled out of having vital importance for all these problems, to be freed of this strait jacket that becomes the apparatus of static for it. Only then can it become the adequate treatment for them, to which, as already may have been emphasized here, the supply of new factual materials most of all belongs. Here lie the points, where the criticism of the "historians" is often far too entitled—much more than towards our system in general. However, this separation is only possible through the precise knowledge of the essence of our exact raisonnement and its foundations.

What is now the precise limit of static compared to dynamic? We will mind ourselves to generally answer this, and to give an unyielding rule at the outset. This would go entirely against our principals. If we want to stay true to the same, then we can only proceed in the following manner: we will develop our exact system, and consider all its parts, and continue to use our method as long as it can be unforcedly done so, and we believe that the results, which will come out of this will be worth the effort, and will become at least just as complete as those that we could also win in another manner. A group of uses will arise from this, which we can be sensibly calm about, but unfortunately we will run into problems too soon that we cannot say enough about; we will just concede these to "dynamic." However, a field exists between this that is methodologically and epistemologically highly interesting; namely this field, in which it is *advisable* to apply our methods, even though their conditions do not, strictly speaking, exist, because they lead to de facto, useful results, and where, on the other hand, it happens that we prefer another method, even though we could apply ours, because "too little comes out" of the latter. It requires tact and judgment to proceed correctly from here, I would almost like to say "instinct," and here we encounter perhaps the most attracting question of epistemology. We will speak of this field in another place; here, we only want to say few words about the two "unequivocal" ones.

Generally speaking, we must take two opposite considerations into account, by limiting the scope of our method. We must be aware of its limits, and make the necessary reserves, everywhere we want to permit ourselves a deviation from the strictest correctness. However, this may not misguide us in being too afraid and too nervous to prove whether we are really standing on solid ground. Because by doing this, we would surely come to the point of limiting ourselves to very few and moreover meaningless statements. Then it would be of advantage not to establish the conditions of the method for all our purposes once and for all, but rather to adapt it to each of the same, and to be as liberal as possible wherever exemption clauses appear to be proper. Malthus' population theory, for example, we would surely term "static," if we would want to include it in our view, though we are not doing this, even though we usually assume the population number as being constant in static. But this theory captures so many moments as being constant, and loses so much of its meaning, if one takes the economic development and its possibilities, as well as possible changes in the habits of the human race that are explainable in another way than by the margin of nourishment, that it is obviously most likely suitable for static relations. And we would also usually be ready to make such concessions, even if no further occasion to do so will arise here. The cost theory and its most important applications, namely the monetary theory, distribution theory, etc., are *secured*. The methods of static are sufficient for this, and these problems form its actual domain. And not everything is accessible to it that is connected with the phenomenon of *development*. Yes—the development and everything that belongs to it evades our view; the pure economical system is essentially without development. We will still speak of this limitation again, which is the most painful of all, but it arises naturally and inevitably from the essence of our system. Completely different moments are decisive for this great problem, than those that expose our system, and the complexity of the relationships that come into question will still rule out an exact approach for a long time to come. And yet, one cannot misjudge that the development is the most important one of all phenomena, whose explanation we strive for. We would anyway also state how unsatisfactory the image of reality is that static reveals. However, its scientific meaning is in fact great, and therefore it surely earns careful processing.

Part II

The Problem of the Static Equilibrium

Section II

1

Preliminary Questions of the Cost Theory

I

We will now turn to the derivation of the trade relations, in and of whose laws of motion the entire pure economy lies, as we explained. We believe to have sufficiently countered the demurs that can be raised against this conception of the latter; but even if one joins the same, one can also face the problem of cost in a very different manner. Even if one were to accept everything that we said about the purely economical, about the derivation of the study of organization, etc., if one has willingly followed us here and is now ready to study the trade relations themselves, entirely descriptive as we recommend, then one could still accuse us of one-sidedly limiting ourselves to *one* way of dealing with the matter, apart from the fact that this way is perhaps not the most complete, and even partially wrong. The data of our problem are the quantities of goods in possession of the individual economic subjects and the value functions that belong to them. We ask for the cost of all goods, and arrive at their assignation through a formal process that we give general validity. One could now say that the formation of cost in general happens in a very different manner, and also very often does not happen how our image indicates it. Even if one had overcome those demurs that keep some national economists from placing the manner, in which the savage trades, next to the processes at a modern stock market, and had one even recognized or admitted the consubstantiality of both, then still enough remains for one to go mad, due to our method of treatment. Very many costs are for now not at all determined by the participating parties. Such a case that often plays a large role in history, and also plays a specific role is that of the authoritarian taxes of costs. If it is also added here that the seller *must* offer a specific quantity of the concerning good, so that he cannot freely regulate his supply, as, for example, the cabby, who must stand in his place for a certain period of time and accept every ride, or that the buyer must take a specific quantity, which was the case, for example, of salt in the ancien régime of France; therefore, the rules that we want to eliminate are really completely or nearly completely checkmated. The influences that determine the cost here are others from those that we are regarding. May they now be of economical and non-economical nature—both are possible, it was the case for both, without this difference being of importance to us—a contemplation of the appearance of cost, which originates in the social power factors, and is in a position to grasp this case fairly well, while ours seems to utterly fail at the same. Of course we can say that we can do two things for such taxes of cost: firstly, we can introduce them into our system, where they will then form data, and secondly, we can examine the effect of such a tax of cost on the income formation of the participants, and that leaves more or less to do, depending on whether the authoritative establishment leaves more or less leeway for commerce. Furthermore, the tax of cost will mostly not differ too far from the cost of our theory, and finally will always be compared to the latter; however, it still remains true that our theory only plays a secondary role here. A very important case of this type just now emerged in the present; it is that of the cost politics of great ventures. The first example was provided by trains, on whose tariffs the governments secured their influence, and also other groups of interest gained interest. These influences were validated in very different ways, in any case, it is certain that the cost appointments that would have been expected according to our theory, would have been increasingly modified through this, without us having a means by which we could work on these influences with the method of our system. In the present, the formation of cartels and trusts has stretched the field of these emergences more and more. The cost politic of the same has very soon directed the public's attention onto itself, and on the other hand, governments, parties, groups of interest, public opinion, etc., have influenced the same in a very different manner. Already the far-reaching interests of such powerful organizations and their rulers implicate that such simple functions, which are how we need them to be, can be difficultly constructed, and the cost formation is much more under the influence of national and political relations elsewhere, so that completely different things are going to become determinant and interesting for the observer. We included that we would also have to search for the explanation of the cost formation, at least partially, in moments that are not purely economical, and it actually appears that our exact approach will be applicable. Some national economists have drawn very interesting consequences from this. This is how G. Cohn brought up the analogy with the taxation for handling the train tariffs, because by having regarded this principle, to him, the same appeared to have the ability of being explained more easily, and Acworth has partially agreed with it lately. Even though we cannot share this conception, it must be admitted that in such instances, the cost formation is, so to speak, placed into our system from the outside, and cannot be explained offhand by the same. We will still say more about this point later-on. In addition to all these difficulties, it is still added that the cost formation becomes monopolistic here, which already makes our problem more difficult for itself alone, as we will see. Furthermore, through such great emergences, our *interest* is greatly occupied by other points of social nature, development-theoretical nature, etc., rather than by the formal laws of the cost formation, that the former still receive little attention, even if their results are more adequate. Therefore, the view point of the social power factors seems to completely suppress our view here.

But besides this, there are still other moments that make our approach more difficult. The costs display certain hairiness, namely even then when, according to our laws, a change would have to follow. This teaches us above all that other moments, for example, habit, custom, etc., than the ones that are regarded here have an effect. It is often the case that one adheres to certain costs, even though all relations change themselves. The costs are much less sensitive in the retail business than in the wholesale trade. Another cause of disturbance is that for some goods, a portion of the cost is paid in the form of a present, which the seller counts on, and without the cost being a different one. These component parts of the cost now have great permanence. It would be redundant to mention further examples of these universally-known facts.

We further learn from these facts that at the same time and under the same conditions, different costs are in fact possible for one and the same good, and they permanently maintain themselves. However, it is now of fundamental importance to our theory, which will still be discussed later on, and has already been said, that it is in a position to derivate an *unequivocal*, specific cost. Nevertheless, a cost will maintain itself just as well in the usual practice within oftentimes considerable limits, as another. This teaches us that the margin is not as scarce, as the theory portrays it. One summarizes these things under the name "friction resistors," and it is then alleged that these things are of no principal importance.

However, one can now say that it surely does not involve magnitudes of a higher order that one could so easily neglect. Moreover, it much more involves important, constant moments here that substantially influence the course of the economy, and bring about important results.

However, we finally observe that the cost formation, if all of this were to be correct, does not simply happen in the manner in which the theory indicates. One very easily convinces oneself of this, if one looks at the usual manner of the theoretical derivation. One says, for example, that an increase in cost happens in the manner that the weakest sellers are omitted, the supply is thereby decreased, and the competition among the buyers therefore becomes sharper, whereupon an eventual increase in cost emerges. In reality, we almost always see that the costs increase, because the sellers simply raise them if a reason to do so exists, and often more so than this reason warrants. This is the conception of everyday life, whose *weaknesses* are too obvious to require special explanation; but we do not want to deny that a very small grain of *truth* lies in it. It is the moment of the "cost battle," on which adversaries of the theory place emphasis here; and it cannot be denied that the same element contains those that escape the instruments of our theory, and that these elements are suitable for explaining many emergences that apply to the cost, yes, that could deliver the basis for a substantially different cost theory.

If one asks us: What use is it to derive rules that always suffer exceptions, and namely those that are constant and important, and in themselves interesting, occasionally more interesting than those rules themselves? Therefore, we cannot but award a right to this question. Some theorists that have answered responded to it by stating that the theory contrasts an ideal state with reality, and also that the economical development strives for such a state. If this were the case, then it would be fine indeed. But it should *not* be this way. We are not regarding the image that the theory conceptualizes as an ideal one—it would surely be difficult to prove that it is one of such—and we also do not risk to claim that it represents the goal of the development; we have already explained to a great degree that such questions are better to be eliminated entirely.

Wherefore are we then replacing the view of reality with such an unsatisfactory theory? All that we can say to this is only that we, despite all this, believe that its results have *sufficiently great* importance, that they cover a *considerable*, even very considerable portion of the depicted field, and prove themselves, within limits that one must never lose sight of, quite well. And this cannot, in my opinion, be denied.

II

All the demurs that we just discussed, express themselves in so far that the "free competition" that is assumed by the theorists, is almost always lacking in reality. We are hereby touching on a point that played a significant role in the history of the national economy, and from which the difference between our exact system and that of the classical authors clearly emerges.

Certainly, we also usually assume free competition. We will still determine the closer context of this assumption more exact. However, for now we only mean by it that we want and can determine the cost only there, where it is not fixated by other influences, than the ones regarded here. For now, we are not concerned with the matter as to what extent this is the case.

However, the matter appears to be in a completely different light for the classical authors. The main emphasis is placed on an entirely different emergence, namely on the "free game of the economical powers." Mutual undercutting—"competition"—the loss of others as economical motives, responsibility for oneself, etc., is set as the normal state that the development strives for. That implies a specific state of the political economy, a specific mental habitus of the economizing people.

And one now takes a step further, and considers this as being desirable. The thought process that leads to the demand of the laissez faire, to the free trade, etc., from there is clear. Then free competition becomes a postulate that a party crowds around, and then the economy is brought to the socialism of every slant, in a contrast to every type of regulating encroachments. It is claimed that competition leads to the best satisfaction of all needs, to an ideal state. At the maximal problem, we will get on to a point, which we are skipping here. However, the reader must be explicitly told here that we are not following in these footsteps. The "laws of nature of the economy" by no means require free competition, and have *no* tendency *to induce it*. One may discuss the pros and cons of economical freedom by using other arguments; for example, one could say that it forces the same to give its best, and one may respond to it by using other, just as well-known arguments. But the pure economy has no part in it. It does not "require" anything, it does not give a criterion for the evaluation of the usefulness of any organization form. One cannot any better contrast our *hypothesis* with this *requirement*, than if one were to call on the pronouncement of an outstanding representative of this group of national economists, who stayed true to the science, as well as the politics of this old stand point, the economists of the "institute": "… le monde économique est gouverné … par des lois immuables qui y maintiennent l'ordre et en assurent l'existence et le progress … les obstacles, il faut les lever, détruire les monopoles naturels, n'en pas créer d'artificiels et laisser faire." An entire program of social and economical politics lies in these words. We do not have anything to do with it. We are aware that one could respond to those arguments that, furthermore, the development seems to run in the opposite direction. And we do not wish for or regret this. Our laws do not have the higher blessing that was often given to them. Surely, they are in a sense inalterable, but namely in a *different* way; the purely economical processes always let themselves indeed be described in always the same formulas, and to explain these is the subject-matter of our study but the concrete results of the same are determined by the circumstances, as well as its value judgment.

In view of the fact that most of the modern theorists also cannot refuse to surrender themselves to still adding something to the hypothesis, it is above all important to emphasize that one *can* separate it in the form, which is how it is really necessary for our results, from all the rest that it gets blended with. In fact, the pure theoretical results are not being altered if one simply lets these things away; they disappear entirely by themselves, if we, being true to our practice ask ourselves what is the core of that, which the theorists do; if we now keep the essential points, then we see that nothing, which would lead to these other problems, lies in them.

It would perhaps be better to entirely avoid the term "free competition" that immediately awakens political and social, ethical and historical perceptions, and instantly makes some suspicious. It unnecessarily carries a difficulty in our way. Nevertheless, one must remain aware that we only want to link this entirely different, limited meaning to it.

Do we really forego much when we enforce such a renunciation upon ourselves? Above all, we forego an examination of the development of the organization forms and the "driving forces" of the political economy. However, this is indeed a field that is closed off to our methods anyway, which we already explained and do not want to repeat. Thereupon we turn to the discussion of the pros and cons of free competition as a social economical form. Now, is it really so difficult to forego those never-changing pros and cons arguments that do not permit an exact approach at all, whose evaluation as "a matter of opinion" about the rapprochement is as good as eliminated, because surely every man adheres to that, which corresponds to his conception, his social and economical position? It seems that this belongs to those things that one can let go of, due to their worthlessness, even though their practical meaning may be great.

The suppression of the weaker, damage of the social interest through careless "filthy competition," etc., on one hand, advantages of unrestricted operation on the other—certainly, all of this is obvious. A *general* discussion about this can hardly convey more than banalities. That, which is of importance to *us*, what *we* alone need is solely this *assumption* as a *methodological aid. Only this is the role of the free competition in the pure economical system of the future*. If this point of view would gain ground, then very many judgments about our science would be to the contrary, and many adversaries, who are currently still absolutely in the right with their opposition, would become silent.

We would like to make one more remark: the *hypothesis* of free competition by no means covers only processes in a developing commerce economy. Of course, it is also never fully realized here; however, by observing some of the processes, it can also be used in economies, whose organization seems to involve the exact opposite of free competition. When farmers traded apples for nuts on a soccage farm—I do not know if this was also forbidden of them—then free competition exists between them to a certain degree. And even in the economy of a *robinson*, one can say that something similar exists between the possible uses of a good, just as "free competition." The principle that lies in it is also not completely checkmated in an economy without commerce, perhaps communistic, that would not be surprising and lose everything paradoxical, if one limits it to its exact content, and detaches it from the circle of associations, in which it tends to emerge.

Strictly speaking, the same means none other than the loss of moments, *which would* paralyze *our system or attract our attention so much* that its results would lose its interest towards it. Its function in the organism of the pure theory is therefore a predominantly negative one: It does not claim nor require anything, it only eliminates what does not belong in it. Therefore it is only an isolation apparatus thus far, and this is just about everything that remains from its former meaning.

III

We now want to remove another stumbling block that lies in the way of the pure theory, in a very similar manner, as it just occurred in regards to the hypothesis of "free competition." We are referring to the well-known and notorious *maximum theorem*. The theorist, found guilty of the crime, will have claimed that the "free game of the economical powers" would lead to the greatest benefit and use to all limbs of the political economy, while it is nevertheless responsible for so many unpleasant emergences of the modern competition battle; furthermore, that every intrusion in the same that it moreover covers up by its "harmonistic" conception is damaging and all attempts to remedy the social destitution are necessarily powerless and, yes, only worsen the evil. If this accusation is correct, then this is very alarming. Because despite the question of whether the theorist is right about the claims or not, our science will be wrapped up in a boundless discussion, is necessary in order to take a stand on the arguments of the social parties, and is suspended from the unscientific misuse on one hand, and lively hate on the other. And it *is* surely partially *correct*. We could deny this, when faced with the clear statements of numerous national economists, who do not allow any doubt? The rescue does not, however, lie in the evidence of the truth of the same, rather, I would like to emphasize above all that I am completely convinced of its falsity and take the view that a great benefit and a gain for science, such as politics, lies in its combating by historians and social politicians. If our theory should collapse, then it must be freed from this gangrenous limb; therefore, it must either be ascertained that the maximum theorem is not essential, and that it can be omitted without damaging the rest, or that it can be formulated in such a way that it does not claim all that, which we indicated. The first is not possible—we cannot do without the maximum theorem, which we will soon see—but probably the latter. Our theory itself innocently emerges from the process that was made for it, may many—most—of its advocates also make this verdict.

Thereby, we see again—as so *often*, even though not *always*—that the criticism of the theory's opponents goes too far. It almost always adjusts itself according to their circles of interests, above all against certain practical consequences, and does not penetrate into the actual theory at all, rather, thinks to have disproved the same unanimously with the first, without examining whether the bridge between theory and practice really is this solid. However, this means taking far too drastic measures, and mostly leads to passing general judgments, which the theorists can easily counter. However, on their part, these misjudge or ignore the true element of the criticism, and fail to emphasize the autonomy of the theory towards those conclusions. Therefore, it is often difficult to separate right and wrong, which are to be found on both sides. However, if one does this carefully, then the matter solves itself with ease. Of course, it also becomes apparent here that much must be thereby abandoned. Even our maximum theorem is completely flawless in itself, and as far as the theory needs it, as everyone will admit after the following explanation. But its practical content, its social slant, and great, scientific importance thereby vanishes—it is *methodologically* important to us, but what it *reveals* is nothing more than a banal implicitness.

The problem of the economy is describing the state of equilibrium to the economic quantities—and certain variations of the same. All acts of exchange tend to realize it, therefore realizing a state, in which a change of quantities no longer takes place, that therefore strives to maintain itself, and is hence especially interesting. And in this state, in which the acts of exchange stop, our functions, whose sole purpose is to simply describe the changes, must result in the value zero for *further* changes. The state of equilibrium is thereby defined, and that is why it is called that. And the differential calculus teaches us that at this point, where certain differential quotients, which represent the measurement of changes, are equal to zero, *disappear*, certain functions—these are the value functions in our case—assume a *maximum value*. This is the fact that is dependent on every interpretation of these functions: The cessation of further acts of exchange, therefore changes in the economic quantities, and the functions becoming the maximum is *synonymic*, and the state of equilibrium can be characterized by the first, as well as by the latter moment. In the first case, we can characterize it as the resting state, and the latter as the maximum state: both terms convey the same / are synonymic. *This is our principal*; everything else only serves its exemplification.

The exact content of the maximum theorem, the core of all that, which has ever been said about this very controversial problem, is therefore none other than this phrase: *No tendency for further changes exists in the state of equilibrium*. And the role that this phrase plays in the theory is to solely *define* the state of equilibrium, which is our primary task to examine, and thereupon *help* us *in the ascertainment of that cost*, which must exist if an equilibrium should prevail.

However, our theorem is indispensable for this latter purpose. We could not ascertain the state of equilibrium without the same. The one requirement for its existence is that the bought and sold quantities of a good are equal to one another. But it applies to every cost. In order to single out the *equilibrium* cost that interests us from the infinitely many *possible* ones, we must now express that it and the distribution of goods that emerges under its control strive to maintain themselves, therefore, that the further changes to the expressed symbol become zero. Under which requirements the latter occurs, and whether one or more of such equilibrium costs can exist in a given point in time and for a given good are then further questions that do not concern us here.

We have therewith answered the question that has engaged us: The maximum theorem expresses the loss of tendencies for changes in our system, and is essentially an *ascertainment equation* for the specification of the state of equilibrium of the same. *Everything else about it is irrelevant to the theory* and the deep social problem that is therewith associated, does not concern the same.

Above all, we want to make our result clearer for ourselves by helping ourselves to a popular diction. When we speak of an economy, we say that it is balanced when its subject does not undertake any further bartering acts—let us remind ourselves that we conceive every economic act among it, and *among it* in turn, only wanted changes of the *quantities* of good that are in its possession, whereby we interpret labor performances as attenuations of the ownership of labor—because it could not increase its position or its satisfaction of needs through such. And we are interested in this state, because everyone sensibly *seeks* it—indeed, we are not bound to strict accuracy at this point—and therefore this state can generally be attained and will strive to maintain itself, if nothing unusual happens, while all other states can be regarded as mere intermediary stages on the way to this one, and display no such tendency for hairiness. The economic subjects therefore barter, because they need the goods that they barter more than those, which they have to give away for this, and they therefore have an advantage from this barter. But everyone knows that sooner or later the point is reached where one no *longer* demands new purchases, finds it painful as a further deficit, consequently, the barter no longer offers an advantage, perhaps even a disadvantage, and one therefore ceases to barter, meaning this "equilibrium" is attained. By observing the bartering individuals, then we can ask ourselves two questions. If the cost that someone barters with is somehow fixed, then we will ask how much the individual will barter. The same will answer: I will buy such a quantity, as "my money suits" me. Our further task lies in determining which quantity this is, but we now do this by continually singling out more and more quantities, and confronting the individual every time: "does this quantity still suit your money?" And as soon as the answer we receive is no, our curiosity will be satisfied, and it is only still spared if we can construct a general rule, *when* the individuals *care* to state that they are satisfied—always: *At this given cost*. The refusal of the individuals to make a further purchase, which signifies the attainment of the state of equilibrium, therefore helps us to unanimously determine this state and the requirements of its eventuation. If the cost however is not fixed, but rather produces itself only on the market, then our interest will naturally first serve the question, what cost this will be: If we have answered it, then this case is lead back to the first. Now, if this cost should be worthy of interest, then it must display some hairiness, and it can only do this if no one can underbid or overbid it under the given circumstances, without harming himself—at least directly; the further causes may certainly be advantageous to him, but do not concern us here—therefore, without either paying more for a good than it is "worth" to him, or receiving less than it is worth to him. Furthermore, it is that this cost, at which also no one can refrain from the barter solely *for the disadvantage of another*, without *oneself*—again: directly—suffering a disadvantage. This is the equilibrium cost. But which one of all the costs, at those one would even trade, is it? Again, we cannot proceed in any other manner than to see at which cost this is the case, and which one allows to barter such quantities with an advantage, that no one is inclined to increase it through further demand or suppress it through further supply. One has said that this is the one, at which the demand equals the supply, more precisely the demanded and the offered quantity of a good are equal to one another. But this would suffice only if we would already know something about these two values, otherwise this is an equation between two unknowns. Only the *available* quantity of the goods is given to us and it must be found how much of it and of economic subjects, who possess nothing or not enough of it, will be demanded. The mere equality of both quantities does not suffice for this purpose. And the missing ascertainment now gives the maximum theorem: firstly, those quantities must be equal, and secondly, no further demand and no further supply are allowed to emerge, if they are bartered at this cost. The equilibrium cost must make just as much turnover appear to be advantageous that "buyers" and "sellers" stand by it: it precisely differentiates itself from the other costs thereby, and this is the content of our theorem. In order to prevent misunderstandings, we want to explicitly say that we in no way believe to have added an essential correction to the formula "supply equals demand" with it. Surely, J. St. Mill meant exactly the same as we do, when he constructed it, and only did not explicitly separate the two requirements that are necessary for the equilibrium. This probably appeared to be redundant to him, but he *meant* both with this formula. Also, this diction is absolutely adequate in general, but it has the disadvantage to not highlighting the connection of the equilibrium problem with the maximum theorem, and thereby barricades the way that leads to a clear understanding of both.

One can acquire another explanation of the maximum theory's essence and role, if its essence and its role are viewed in other disciplines. Of course, this only carries weight in its formal nature, and does not have anything to do with a material dependence on the same. This also does not mean that the maximum theorem is an instrument that is lugged in from foreign fields of knowledge that could possibly not fit into our field; we want to solely raise an explanatory example. We are choosing that of mechanics for it, but not because the same is related to the economy in any way, but rather because it is elaborated the most. Even if a "biological equilibrium" were to have more to do with our science—a question that we neither discuss, nor predetermine here—then we could permit this for ourselves, just as one can demonstrate a logical rule in general, in a desired field.

Now, a body is in equilibrium when it does not move itself in any direction—or not in relation to any other. This phrase, as little of value and as self-evident it appears to be, is of substantial significance, and its mathematical expression not only *defines*, but also *determines* the state of equilibrium. Translated from the language of symbols, this expression says that the sum of all gains of movements, or of all accelerations in the state of equilibrium equal zero. And this in turn means that at this point, all these movements assume a maximum value for the describing functions, popularly called "forces." If this is the case, then *nothing* happens to the field or in the system of point masses that one observes: they are in a state of rest. As long as a new acceleration is not somehow administered to them, they *remain* in a state of rest, no tendency for any type of interruption of this state, of a change in state, lies within themselves. Every system of point masses "strives toward such a state," and its examination and the specification of requirements of its emergence is therefore of special interest. Yes, the entire world of emergences has such a "striving for a specific state" and therefore one can place all processes under an all-embracing formula that expresses the existence of such. I think of Machs expression $f(x, y, z \ldots) = 0$. The position and the essential meaning of the maximum theory is the same everywhere, and its mathematical expression is identical—it is always an ascertainment equation, whose content is an implicitness and lacks interest in itself, although, it is indispensable as a link in the chain of the scientific thought process.

However, we are not finished with that, which we have to say. We did certainly say that we do not want to have anything to do with the maximum theory in the sense of the individualists and harmonists, and displayed wherein the exact content and that, which is essential to the theory exists, also, that this is surely irreproachable. However, does a bridge between the two really not exist? One of such certainly seems to exist, and the reader may have probably noticed it in the course of what was said: however, we do not make improper use of our theorem, do not pass a value judgment about the state of equilibrium, above all, do not think of characterizing it as "desirable" or demand its bringing about; we also avoid going into the psyche of man, his needs and motives, etc.: the reader can indeed rest assured that a transgression on our part is not to be feared in this direction; but are we not in fact speaking of maximum? When we emphasized that the essence of it is the loss of changes—characterization of the state of rest—then this still changes nothing that, as we, ourselves emphasized, this state of rest with a maximum value of our functions causes. Of course, we said that the character of the latter is solely a formal one, and it is indifferent to its essence how we interpret it, but in fact, we did indeed call them value functions, if they are identical to the value scales of the psychological economist, according to their gestalt, and all our epistemological barricades will not protect us against the fact that one will express our maximum theorem in the following manner: In the state of equilibrium, every barterer receives a maximum of value or probably even of "gratification." And this is that formulation that one can consider as being the usual. I will now forego on insisting on my principal stand point all the more, as I wish to continue to demonstrate that also the psychological formulation of the theorem, meaning that form of the same that one encounters in modern, theoretical literature—very distinguishable from that of the harmonist group—in the here-discussed relation is irreproachable in itself, which does not however, rule out that some strings that are attached to it would like to surpass the field of pure theory, and are unsustainable so far. The role of the theory's theorem is not changed by this formulation, so that we in turn did nothing more than specifying its exact core, which *all* modern economists do.

So where does the matter actually stand, if we accept this formulation of our theorem? Do we not in fact therewith claim that this equilibrium that occurs through free competition, leads to the maximal use for all limbs of the political economy?

Above all, it can be said that value and satisfaction of needs in the sense of psychologists is indeed not the same, and the maxima of both can very well fall apart. Maximum of value does not imply maximum of economic well-being. The leaders of the psychological direction adequately explained this, and since we do not completely agree with this view, we will not dwell upon this argument.

But another consideration can—also only prima vista and preliminarily—be replied to this question. Let us assume that some power deliberately fixes the "cost" of a good, and namely in a way that it cannot be coextensive with the equilibrium cost. Even then, a state of equilibrium will emerge after a certain number of bartering acts, if one would even barter according to this cost. And this one also corresponds to a maximum, in the sense of what was said earlier. We can imagine that the cost is fixed in one for all or a highly unfavorable way for a portion of the barterers, but we will still speak of a "maximum of satisfaction." It is clear here that we do not regard this state as being ideal and in what sense this "maximum" is meant: this degree of satisfaction of needs *that is possible at this cost* will be attained, and this is nothing more than self-evident, and also nothing *more* than we said earlier, namely the characterization of the state of rest. Our theorem is certainly not saved by this, since the claim that the equilibrium cost permits a greater, an *absolute*, maximum of satisfaction would still be possible. But we only see the point that matters for everything, namely the conditions, under which the coming about of this maximum state is alleged. And now, the main point.

Let us first regard an isolated economic subject. Its economy will strive for a state of equilibrium, in which the limiting quantities of its goods will be in strong relation to one another, which we can call "costs" in our sense. And since no tendency for a change exists in this state, we will say that a maximum of value exists. The psychological national economist, who believes to be able to see into the soul of our subject will state that the same distributes his productive means in the "most advantageous" way, and has achieved the greatest possible satisfaction. We do not know anything more specific about this maximum that varies according to race, cultural level, and individual conception, and is attained in various ways. However, the fact that a maximum exists is certain, if the economic plan has not failed: because then our man would seek to change his economic situation. But is this maximum an "absolute" one? Is this satisfaction, for which the individual is even capable, reached? Certainly not; the obvious limitation is given in the data of our system: the highest possible satisfaction is certainly attained, but only the one that is possible *under the given conditions*. These are, as known: external nature, technology, supply of goods at the beginning of the economic process, and more of the same. All that our theorem requires is therefore that every man organizes himself as well as possible according to his taste, as the conditions allow. This is certainly an irreproachable phrase that we can incidentally formulate even more accurately and more irreproachably from our special stand point. But enough of it: The usual form of the maximum theory also does not contain anything false, and I do not believe that a difference of opinion exists about the same. For the economist, who is free from our epistemological demurs, the matter is clear, yes, self-evident, even through this formulation.

The doubts first begin in the political economy. Every bartering act that indeed continually comes about through free agreement, certainly also contributes to the increase of "satisfaction" of all parts here; otherwise it would simply not come about. And it is stopped—the state of equilibrium emerges—because both parties that face one another believe that a continuation of bartering would not give them an advantage at this cost, and this means that they believe to have attained all attainable advantages, that the latter is a maximum. But after what was said, it is not difficult to indicate the true sense and the limitations of this phrase, where all doubts vanish by themselves.

Indeed, it only counts among obvious conditions. We can surely also speak for the commerce economy—among well-known reserves—that every man can establish himself in various ways, under given conditions, which lead to various great "satisfactions", and under which the one that corresponds to the state of equilibrium leads to the *greatest*; likewise, that in general, every man *seeks* to establish himself as well as possible under given conditions, and a tendency therefore exists to cause this state of equilibrium. But what obstacles does this aspiration encounter? Above all, the same as in the isolated economy, of course: the limitation of the natural possibilities—no one will want to question this. Here, however, we then have that, which was not necessary there; to assume a given, social organization, and that this one also forms a supposition, in regards to which our theorem must be understood, was admittedly not often emphasized, but will also not be contested, at least not today. However, there is still a third supposition, namely the cost, the equilibrium cost itself: Every man can evidently only attain the type of satisfaction that is possible at this cost—bartering conditions.

Now this is less generally accepted. The reason for it, why this moment seems to escape the majority of the national economists, should lie in the circumstances that this cost, a product of the general aspiration towards the maximum of satisfaction, indeed offers the guarantee in a way that it also realizes the same.

Although, it can be above all countered that every man only strives for the maximum *of his* satisfaction—let us adopt this view for a moment, which, as the reader knows, is not completely ours, but certainly practically that of all other national economists—and therefore the result of these individual aspirations is by no means *necessarily* the most advantageous for *all*. It is not clear in one's mind that the latter would first require special proof. But many a thing could be answered to it. So let us go somewhat deeper. What does that cost depend on? Certainly partially on the "scales of need"; but just as certain, on the quantities of goods that every man possesses and has to offer prior to bartering: The limiting uses, from which the costs arise, are, as we know, the result of the value function, as well as of the possessed quantity. *And there we are at the crux of the matter*: the maximum that is realized by the state of equilibrium is dependent on the previous distribution of all consumption, as well as production goods, which must be *given* to us; only *that* maximum can be attained, that, based on the same, can be attained through free barter.

This now immediately sheds light onto certain doubtful points, which have never been adequately gone into, as large as the role that they played in the discussion was. A "hunger wage" is supposed to potentially be the maximum of satisfaction that a laborer can attain? If one of such corresponds to the state of equilibrium, then the laborer is never supposed to be allowed to hope for something different? How often one has held this against the theory! But the answer is simple: Certainly, through free barter and due to the given distribution of goods, our laborer will attain no more than what corresponds to the state of equilibrium, and that, which he attains, even though it hardly protects him from starvation, gives him that maximum of satisfaction, is the best that he can attain—*in this manner and under those conditions*. The claim, which one so often identifies as being nonsense, loses everything paradoxical. Of course, much more was often meant by it, and that conditionality was overlooked, often then when important conclusions for the practice were extracted from it: Now, this is unsustainable and those conclusions are false—the opponents are right in this regard.

And every infringement on that state of equilibrium is supposed to be damaging and reducing to the total satisfaction? The answer is affirmative—*under those conditions*: the price of a good, for example, without anything else changing, especially without a development of any sort being caused by it, is increased by, for example, a tax about the equilibrium cost; it is therefore certain that the only actual, economical consequence is that a row of bartering acts is prevented, which could be advantageously negotiated, and it can be shown exactly that this disadvantage and that, which the "buyers," who also buy at a higher cost, suffer from is greater than the profit that the "sellers" make from the sold quantity at a higher profit. In this sense, for example, the specification of a maximal work-day is "damaging." But the same may be a necessity for the development of race, it may lead to technological advances, it may effectuate that just as much and more is accomplished in the shortest amount of time than in the longer one. All of this does not contradict the maximum theorem at all, if one would only comprehend it correctly. It refrains from the external-economical moments, and it does not regard the developmental possibilities. One can say that these are exactly the determining factors, and our theorem therefore loses that *practical* meaning; but we are already saying this, and above, we have grappled with wherein its *theoretical* (meaning) exists. One can probably also justify it another way, for example, with the hypothesis that free operation leads to the highest performance, etc., and then it gains higher meaning; but it then falls out of the field of the theory that is neither in a position to justify such claims, nor to further realize its own results.

Therefore, our theorem is also "right" for the "commerce economy," even basically self-evident; *one can say that it is right in so far as it is self-evident*. And this is then also the result that we have to state: *one trusts the maximum theory so far as it is plainly true and does not say anything particularly interesting—but one mistrusts it where it claims more, where it wants to be more than an ascertainment equation*! We are gaining something by this realization, as melancholy as it may sound: it teaches us that the structure of the economy is free of deficiency, which many considered to be deadly. And with it, we are by no means foregoing much; what would it benefit to continue economizing with an imaginary abundance? All the social philosophy that was built on the maximum theorem is certainly worth little, after all.

We are at then end of our effectuations; we only want to make two more remarks.

To begin with, we are now more in a position to specify the difference between those two conceptions of the maximum theorem very poignantly. Despite other conditions, the same is based on the assumption of a specific, primordial state of distribution *of all goods*—also that of consumption goods, since, as one was easily convinced and as was already explained, the results of the economic process itself can still be very different for given quantities and a given state of distribution, according to type, quantity, and distribution of the consumption goods that are available at its beginning and during its process. However, whether this distribution, which forms a datum of our problem, then again, materialized itself under the control of any maximum requirement is an entirely different question, and then, a further question is of what nature the same is, when available. While one formerly believed to have now thrown together and solved these two different maximum theorems, when one had solved the first, we now strictly separate them and refrain from an examination of the latter, which leads into sociology and history. *We believe that this separation solves our controversy* and suffices for a clear judgment of the arguments of both parties. It puts an end to the partially, downright ridiculous misunderstandings that the theory encounters, and to the partially just as downright ridiculous pretensions of some theorists, and lets the demarcation line between right and wrong clearly stand out on both sides.

Finally, one last point must be pointed out: it is the strictly static character of our theorem. We have seen all that it requires, in order to be right, and especially emphasized that it fails at emergences of the development, as we mentioned the example of the maximal work day. It only makes sense in the static system and on the basis of a constant economic state that is static in all essential points. But understand me correctly. I do not claim that a "dynamic" equilibrium is impossible. In reality, one of such is perhaps also given by the facts, what we meanwhile do not want to pursue here. Only, its requirements will be different ones. The maximum theorem that was really elaborated alone so far, and that is necessary for the pure theory alone, insofar as it currently has claim to general acceptance, is *essentially static*. One may say that a "biological equilibrium," as well as a version of the maximum theorem that is considerate of the development, is more suitable for the economic truth; maybe, but we currently have little use for one of such scientifically, and for the purposes that concern us here. In fact, the rudiments that find themselves by some economists in regards to this also do not go beyond the demand itself and some universalities. Since it is our policy to no sooner forge scientific instruments then until we need them, and to abide by that, which we can satisfyingly work out, without making phrases, which could reveal unavoidable deficiencies of our methods without improving them; we therefore limit ourselves to what has been said. At a later point, we want to emphasize how important a "more" would be here and at other points.

2

The Liability Problem and the Questions That Are Attached to It

I

Before we present the derivation of the cost relations, we must take care of some principle questions that we have not yet clarified enough. We said that "a belt of equations" limits the economical sphere of influence of every economic subject, and it is the exact expression of the same. These equations say that the equilibrium prevails in the system if the barter relation of each good to every other one equals the reciprocal value of its marginal utility relation. If this is the case, then no tendency will exist to change the barter relations and that state of the quantities of goods which exposes itself under their control. Each of these equations approximately looks like this:

$$\frac{\text{Grenznutzen des Gutes } A}{\text{Grenznutzen des Gutes } B} = \frac{1}{\text{Tauschrelation oder Preis von } B \text{ in } A}.$$

Let the cost of good A therefore be expressed in units of good B, for example, equal to three, let someone therefore be inclined to buy units of good A per three units of good B on the market, *but not for more*, or let an isolated landlord be inclined to spend three units of good B for the attainment (meaning production) of one unit of good A, *but not more*, then the above marginal utility relation equals three. Popularly expressed, these equations only prove that every man will produce as long as, or barter as much of one good, as it seems advantageous to him. And since all of his economizing expresses itself in it, we therefore said that those systems of equations characterize the same, and represent its exact-scientific mirror image. They are the core and the foundation of the pure economy, its alpha and omega, and contain the entire pure theory in a nutshell.

Let us now make a simple transformation to our equation: let us multiply both sides of the same with the denominator of the left one. Then we have:

$$\text{Grenznutzen des Gutes } A = \text{Grenznutzen des Gutes } B \times \frac{1}{\text{Preis von } B \text{ in } A}\cdot$$

Let us assume the equilibrium cost for the time being—let it again be *three* units of *B* for one unit of *A*—as being given, which, of course, it usually is not, then it would yield that the marginal utility of good *B* is equal to one third of the marginal utility of good *A*. The economical trading of the individual or, more accurately, the changes that we notice in the quantities of both goods are therefore described by an equation between the marginal utilities of the same. Again, popularly speaking, our economic subject will behave in a way that he will make such bartering acts, so that he is ultimately indifferent to whether he acquires another unit of *A* with the expenditure of three units of *B*, or keeps these latter ones. Morally, it *costs* him the same to forego another unit of *A*, just as another three units of *B*—and he therefore calls it quits with the bartering acts. If one "barters," one abandons one value for another, namely the same for production, as well as for the commerce-economical barter. If one wanted to express that one expresses good *A* and would have to forego a portion of it, in order to acquire and savor some of good *B*, then one can do this by saying that the first or more accurately, its *value forms the cost of the latter*. This diction indicates which good is the one out of the two that one foregoes. *But nothing else*, and strictly speaking, one could say the opposite. Therefore, one can also express our transformed equation as follows:

$$\text{Marginal Utility of Good } A = \text{Marginal Costs of Good } A.$$

This is now that form of our equation, in which it was first constructed. As you know, one did not derivate it in the manner that is represented, but rather constructed it based on conspicuous observations, and entirely different interpretation. Entirely different conceptions and ways of thinking adhered to it, and as the new value theory arose, it appeared as if one had wanted to construct a different definition of equilibrium cost. This is however, as we saw, incorrect: the difference can only lie in the interpretation. The equation of marginal utility and marginal costs itself, along with mutual dependence of both moments must certainly be acknowledged by both parties that face each other, because the new cost derivation also leads to it.

This is now that, which we want to further conduct here, in order to also say a few words about the various possible interpretations then. We also want to forget *our* derivation for now and regard this equation in itself, which, in turn, leads into the discussion of costs. One sees that those economists, who abominate this controversy and do not consider it worthwhile are in the wrong. Objections can certainly be made against the manner in which it was introduced, but it is by all means fundamental. We are not seeking it, and do not want to intentionally approach it anywhere, but it always gets in our way; we, so to speak, trip over it all the time.

Now, what does our equation, marginal costs = marginal utility, actually say when we take a deeper look? What should it accomplish? We must not search for the answer to these questions in clear expressions or in general discussions of the national economists. It is seldom that one bluntly says what one does and why one does it, yes, I believe that one mostly does not even realize it. We must much more look at what is *actually* attained, and ask ourselves what is necessary for the attainment of the concrete results. I believe to have already done this, and can be brief here. Let us therefore say that the purpose of the pure theory is to describe the "pure economical" processes, and to therefore above all examine the state of the economy that the same tend to cause by themselves, the state of equilibrium. This one is, as we know, defined and characterized by the following: when it exists, then there is no tendency toward a further change. Now, let us consider a manufacturer in a commerce economy, and let us adhere to the observations and the expression of the daily routine. When will "no tendency" be present for the man to make changes, meaning to continue to produce? When the proceeds that he can expect from the sale of further products no longer displays an excess over the costs, which this further production caused, meaning, when the marginal proceeds equal the marginal costs. And we hereby have the origin of our equation. But one can comprehend the matter even more generally. One could indeed reply to this formulation that due to various economical and externally economical reasons both more and less can be produced. In addition, it only suits the commerce economy. Let us therefore simply say that the state of equilibrium is that, where the tendencies, which work towards a further acquisition of a good—may it be "money" or different one—balance those, who operate in the opposite direction. This now expresses our equation; this is its most intrinsic content. It is indubitable that such an equation can be constructed, since it of course only speaks of implicitness. We therefore see that our equation is in itself entirely independent of what we call these "influences" or "forces," whose equilibrium it expresses. Yes, it also *always* presents a maximum state of the same, as we exposed earlier. This has nothing noticeable, if one stays current that, in fact, only the consequence of a mathematical rule as an entirely formal moment lies in it.

To begin with, we do not find ourselves on controversial ground because of this. We want to express the existence of a state of equilibrium that is recognized by all theorists. One can do this very formally, without thinking about the nature of those "forces" that cause it. We have explained that the description of the economic equilibrium and those movements in the economic quantities, which lead to it, is our goal, and that we must construct certain formal functions, may they be value scales or something else, for it. The decisive factor is its *form*; if one agrees on the same, then one will reach the same results. As far as this is the case, there is little occasion to sputter about its *nature*. And this is the case in our theory to a certain degree. One only demands few form characters of our functions, and no doubt can exist about the same. Because of this, the concrete results of the "value theorist" define so little of those of the "cost theorist," and their exact expression is often identical. If one has understood the truth that the essence of each exact discipline exists in the describing of processes based on formal assumptions, and if one is aware that the latter are only methodic aids that owe their existence to our arbitrariness, then one will not see anything disconcerting in what was said.

If one measures both sides of our equation with a common measurement, for example in money, which is of course necessary, then an expression arises that every man recognizes under certain reserves, and it is indifferent to its existence what the marginal proceeds and the marginal costs are "made of." One equally knows that the greater the produced quantity becomes, the more the marginal proceeds decrease and the marginal costs increase, and this suffices in presenting both moments as two intersecting curves in the known manner, and to conceive an entire row of cost movements. Of course, all of this is not as simple as it appears to be, and by taking a closer look, quite a few not so uncomplicated questions present themselves. Yet, an important truth does lie in it, which not only expresses many—innumerable—experiences in everyday life, but is also sufficient for many theoretical results. If one, for example, asks for the effect of a tax that is placed on the unit of a good, on the cost of the same, then one simply allocates its amount to its unit costs, and observes how the equilibrium consequently shifts. And the result is independent of what those unit costs "are." The national economist, who concerns himself with such a question, justifiably does not go into the problem of value and costs.

But we still must occasionally do this. This is above all offered with regards to the future of our economy: If one later needs *more* form characters of our curves, in order to arrive at complicated and concrete results, and especially if one will proceed with processes that actually count on the basis of our theory, then the question of whether we can manage with those that we called value functions, or must also construct others, is very decisive. However, the cost controversy is then essential to the examination of all exchange relationships between the quantities of all goods, and namely to the distribution theory, whose entire construction is dependent on it, as it has already been explained in the first part of this work.

II

Then what are the moments, which the two curves, as are well-known as the supply and the demand curves, that determine—what do the two limbs of our equation mean?

No difference of opinion exists in the demand curve and the sum of money that stands on the left side of our equation. The demand curve is simply the value function,[1] and the marginal proceeds measure a marginal profit. The classical authors would also not have argued against this; they did in fact not express it as clearly as the modern authors, but nevertheless meant it. And the so prevalent dictum of today that they did not voice, only because it appeared to be self-evident to them, give us—right or not—in case, the right to regard the matter res judicata, and to disregard further elaboration.

But what are the costs? What are the moments that are sensualized by the supply curve? Different views of this are possible. The decisive difference is the following: the sum of money, which stands on the right side of our equation, surely is an equivalent of something; and namely either for the values of expended goods, or for a different kind of expenditure. In the first case, we only have a principle for the explanation of cost in front of us; in the latter, two independent ones. The first one is the answer of the "marginal utility theorists," the latter, that of the "cost theorists."

So now, what is this independent principle of cost? As is generally known, one answers: labor difficulty and consumption delay. The prices, which the sum of costs consists of, are supposed to be equivalents, not for values of goods, but rather for the trouble that the production of these goods causes.

For us, the question of which view of the two we are supposed to choose now exists. We are standing here in front of crux of the value controversy. Our earlier discussions about it have hopefully cleared up a portion of the same, and shown what is to be thought of a group of the arguments that were brought forth. Its essential progeny is that we now, after we can differentiate between total value and value function, and understand the sense, point of departure, and methodological meaning of the controversy, proceed from a precise questioning and the entire situation, on which salient points have focused, in our opinion. We have thereby also shown our readiness to let the meaning of our cost theory of the price in the development of our science, and its relative justification befall justice, and to make some concessions to the stand point of the cost theorists anyway. But the main point is still spared. However, in the course of the discussion, that, which we declare to be the main point is not always stated, namely that decision about the theory of the labor efforts and the consumption delay in the center of interest, above all, not in the earlier stages of the controversy. But this is indeed the case today. We are aware—and we completely agree with v. Boehm-Bahwerk here—that the cost theory formerly had a different purpose, and the modern form of the same—let us call the same the theory of "disutility"—was not the form of the classical authors, even if the representatives of the disutility theory are inclined to smudge the differences and to impute the classical others their new conception: It is in fact a success of the discussion that the disposition of the cost theorists had to be concentrated around the theory of disutility, and tapered off with the mentioned question. Of course, only its most advanced representatives did this, and there are still followers of the classical conception. We have also made concessions towards them, but also explained that we consider the marginal profit theory to be more complete. Although, one could altogether say that the disutility theory represents the modern form of the cost theory, and the latter only plays a role in this form today. This role is significant. The greatest portion of the English-American theory takes this view.

Its most important representatives in England are Professor Marshall and Edgeworth, and in America Mc Vane, his most important opponent is v. Boehm-Bawerk. The articles of the latter that represent a sample of well thought out criticism are suited the best as information about the matter. We must assume them to be well-known, and cannot reproduce their content here, if the framework of this work should not be transcended. One only finds my own conception of the matter, and a briefing of the problem that is uncommon otherwise, and a derivation of the results. But I would not have presented it, if I did not believe that it suffices for the assessment, and contributes something to the common approach.

Avoiding general arguments about the sole "correctness" of one or the other stand point again, we want to ask ourselves two questions: Firstly—what did those theorists want from the disutility theory? And secondly—what can the latter achieve?

What a theorist wants from a theory is a question that is always very determining for the understanding of the same. We are not getting tired of emphasizing that every theory is a creature of arbitrariness—artificially produced for some purposes—and it is clear that it can only be completely understood from the stand point of these purposes. Now, nobody can argue bona fide that the theory of disutility, even though it is fundamentally different from the former cost theory, still emerged from it, and has the purpose to enlarge it and thereby maintain it. And if it can be proved that the fundamental idea became another in the process, then this was certainly not intended, which is clearly seen by that fact that it is being contested. The great traits of the matter's developments are simple: As the marginal profit theorists arose with the claim that *both* limbs of the formula "supply equals demand" are controlled by the value principle, therefore to be understood from the "demand side" and in the "costs," which the classical authors solely attached great importance to, lies no independent explanation principle—that "the costs are value appearances," so as to repeat a superb word—one contested this in this manner to begin with. This was even more possible as we saw that the marginal profit theorists often did not correctly and never entirely precisely express themselves, yes, occasionally said things that were downright wrong. But eventually this stance became unsustainable and there was no other choice than capitulation or withdrawal into the stronghold of such an independent principle for the "supply." And one did also follow this latter path. In the search of such a principle, A.

Smith's famous saying presented itself above all: "That, which a good actually costs someone, is the effort and endeavor to acquire the same." This phrase, as A. Smith means it, is not only true, but even self-evident. Of course, every good must be "worthwhile" if someone should strive for its possession, and for the contemplation, whether it should be acquired, this "effort" will certainly play the same role as the profit that one expects from it. Alone in this form, it is so vague that one cannot do anything with it. One must be clear about the form of the "toil and trouble," the form of the function that should sensualize it, if this moment should be introduced into the economical train of thought. So then, wherein does this "effort and endeavor" exist? In labor? This does in fact depend on the next thing. But the demurs against this conception are too apparent, as that one would have had a desire for the same. Above all, the analysis of the cost goods would never only be ascribed to labor—but rather at least *also* to land, which would be extremely fatal to this theory—and therefore, the questions would then arise, whether the disinclination that is associated with labor would in fact be the defining moment or not perhaps its *value*, which latter possibility would approach the necessity of a capitulation in front of the marginal profit theory dangerously close. We will see, whether one escapes the same; at any rate, one tried. The example of the socialistic value theory may still offer a base, but the same did not in fact lie in terms of those theorists. Rather, it answered that the moment of the "toil and trouble" exists in labor effort and in sacrifices, in effort and sacrifice. This formula now is very unfortunate, because what does "sacrifice" mean? None other than the surrender of goods for the purpose of acquiring others. And the amount of sacrifice can only exist in the value of those goods that are to be surrendered in production or bartering. If they would not have some kind of value, then their surrender would not be a "sacrifice," and it only is one, in so far as they have one of such. All that one therefore achieves from this expression is that one separates one good out of the complex of the cost goods, namely labor, and explains that not its value, but rather its disinclination that is connected with its expenditure comes into consideration for it. More about this later on. Here, still more about the moment of "sacrifice." If one wants to avoid this dead end, then a replacement for the moment of value must also be sought for the goods that are to be surrendered. To disperse them in labor is, as mentioned, out of the question. So then one thought of the consumption delay, waiting or abstinence, and hurried to mate this moment with that of labor efforts. Even though it is nothing new—it is known to originate some time ago—it was nevertheless new in this context, and in the English theory, its introduction is often considered to be a progress towards the former conception, a necessary correction of the former disutility theory, which only attached importance to the labor effort; which is what it is: The recognition that this moment does not suffice, it is a too narrow of a basis for the cost emergence, this is certainly an advantage. But what is to be thought of this instrument? One disperses the consumption goods into labor, land, and "capital"—here we are passing over our objections as a matter of principle, against this operation—and constructs the supply of consumption goods from these three elements. The term sacrifice or waiting—both amount to the same if one does not want to blunder into the marginal profit theory by means of the first—therefore stands in the place of value of land and "capital," or only of "capital" if one eliminates land by means of the classical bonds theory. And what this means is that the value of the productive goods that form "capital" is not determinant for the price formation of the consumption goods, but rather the extent of the feeling of disinclination, which causes the owner of capital to let his "capital work productively" instead of immediately consuming it, or better, that the value of the capital goods simply is based on this feeling of disinclination. But wherein does this latter exist? Certainly only in "disinclination," which causes the renunciation of a satisfaction, and the extent of the same is, according to its definition, really none other than the value of goods, whose consumption is being "delayed." With this, we have again arrived at an emergence of value, and this demur seems so battered to us that we will skip a row of others, which can be used against this conception. Therefore, nothing will come of this dualistic disutility. *If one cannot get by with the moment of labor effort*, then one will find no rescue in the moment of the consumption delay; the same is solely another expression for one emergence of value. And admittedly, one can *not* do it.

Let us now move on to our second question. What should the disutility theory achieve? The answer can be no other than the following: it should explain the gestalt of the supply curve. We need a supply curve that must firstly be useful to our purposes, and is secondly never allowed to collide with the facts. This is all, and this does not yet mean, as one will be convinced by closer consideration that it corresponds to something in reality, but rather only that it must have certain form characteristics. The same can be said for the demand function, as was explained earlier: its psychological rationale only serves the purpose of determining such form characteristics and to eliminate certain economical emergences, with which we just do not want to concern ourselves in this context. If a new use would be possible for a good if, for example, its quantity has reached a certain amount, which expresses itself in the sudden increase, rather than decrease of its value, then the demand curve would no longer decrease, but rather increase. But then, it could happen that it does not cross over the supply curve at all, and no state of equilibrium, or even more would emerge. If this should not occur, then this possibility must be eliminated, and this psychological law is just suitable to do this. The matter concerning the supply function is very similar. It must show the opposite form characteristics, namely to increase with the price and the available quantity of a good for the dual purpose, because this is necessary in order to assure the intersecting with the demand curve, and therefore the image of the state of equilibrium, and thereupon, in order to express those economical facts of the supply's increase under the stated requirements. Let us look at the matter.

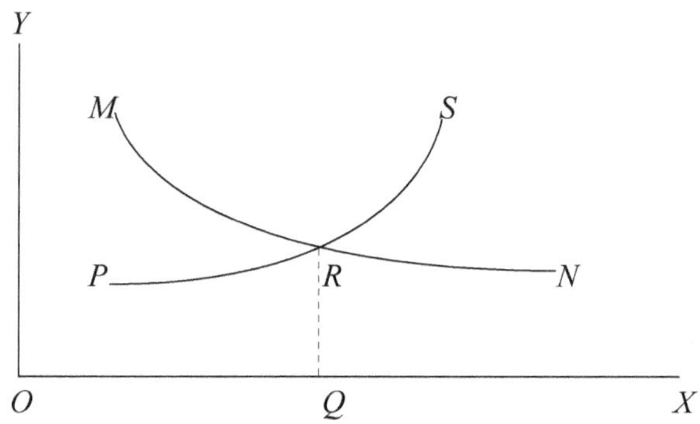

Let us spread out all possible prices of a good on the y-axis of a right-angled coordinate system, and the quantities of the same that are offered and demanded at these prices on the x-axis, then a "demand curve" of the gestalt M N and a "supply curve" of the gestalt PS arises. The intersecting point R indicates the state of equilibrium, R Q sensualizes the equilibrium price, and O Q the quantity that is turned over at this price. None of the two curves may have turnaround points, if our simple image is not supposed to be tarnished, and for this reason we are making a row of assumptions that are not supposed to be exposed any further here. We are generally far away from vindicating completeness or strict correctness for this exposition. We are aware that we are brushing many theoretical, detailed questions aside, and are letting the theorist be excused of some things. But we must not overload our work with details, and are satisfied to say the necessary things for our argument.

At this point, one had sought after a hypothesis in order to explain this gestalt of the supply curve. However, we must above all remark that a difference in opinion about such only makes sense if something will be changed on the results by doing so. Otherwise, every argument about it is idle and without practical value.

It now appears at first glance that the supply curve, formally regarded, is none other than an inverted value curve. What kind of value curve could this be? Well, simply one of those goods, which must be relinquished to the acquisition of that, which is being talked about, so either that of a "cost good" or that of the production goods that are to be expended by the production of the first. Not only does this view simultaneously encompass the cases of bartering, as well as of production, it also has another advantage. That is to say, if it is successful to relate the supply curve that is conceived as a value function to the value functions of the consumption goods, so that one can derivate them from the latter, then the possibility arises to significantly limit the number of our underlying assumptions; *one then only needs* to inquire the individuals of *the value of the consumption goods*, and consequentially gains all others. This would put us in a position to describe the interaction of the values of the consumption and production goods in the abstract and by means of our system, without referring back to further factual observations, whereas such a relationship does not exist at all, if the supply curve is based on an independent principle. As already mentioned, this is especially important to the distribution theory: If the productive goods' measurement of money, that "equivalent" that is on the right-hand side of our equation, lets itself be explained by value functions, then the distribution problem is therewith ascribed to the bartering problem, and one can say that it is herewith already principally resolved. And this is possible; the supply curve can in fact be understood as a value curve, as we saw. Then the "psychologist" does not want to further justify it after all, we want to thereby leave it at that. The matter is alright to such an extent that there is hardly anything left to wish for, and the reason as to why we derivate an ulterior cost theory, is simply because *no* reason exists for seeking one of such.

Surely one can also explain the gestalt of the supply curve in a different manner. This is no further surprising, since we indeed only know—and need—so few general characteristics. But it is redundant to bring up other hypotheses. This is our *own* argument, and we only put emphasis on it. For all the others that are introduced in this context, we refer to other expositions, and mention some of them only on occasion. The matter of fact, which the supply curve sensualizes can be expressed in two different ways: If the offered price of a good increases, then the offered quantity increases under otherwise the same circumstances. Or: If the offered quantity increases, then the offered price increases. Both sentences say the same thing, even then, when one replaces the "if" with a "because" in both. A "because" probably seems to say more than an "if"; however, if it is clear in one's mind that a phrase that is expressed in the language of causal relation also only basically describes facts, then one knows that this is an illusion, and will never think of wanting to prove that one of the two phrases is more right than the other.

Both can be explained just as easily by means of our conception of the matter, and this also counts for the formulation: *Because* the offered quantity of a good increases, its offered price increases just the same. However, the same was the point of departure of other hypotheses. In a similar manner to how the physicists of earlier times imputed a "horror vacui" on water, in order to explain its increase in a vacuum tube, the national economists have also sought after a special force, in order to justify this increase of the supply curve. And it would not be our purpose to consider the method of both as being "false." The "horror vacui" is certainly suitable to describe that occurrence, and the *progress that lies in the contemporary conception solely exists in the fact that one can describe the same with means that can also be used for other purposes*, that one does not need to refer back to a special explanation, but rather subsume the occurrence under a large category, and can be conceived in one and the same formula with many other things. Therefore, those hypotheses of the economists are not "false." They are those, which one calls "law of the diminishing returns" and "disutility." They can be covered with facts, and overall achieve what they are supposed to. But if one can replace them with our value functions, then we will regard this as progress, and will be happy about the great unity and purity that our system gains from it.

This is our main argument, as we said. But other deficiencies adhere to those aids as well. They are very plausible in themselves: The wants of the human being that aspire after the satisfaction of needs as *one* of the determining forces to conceive economizing, and the limitation of nature's physical possibilities—the law of diminishing returns thereupon comes to light—or the physical possibilities of labor effort—this is the core of the disutility theory—as the *other* is certainly logically permissible. The wants of the human being and the ability of nature, satisfaction of needs and burden of effort, are those not just as bounteous, as well as justifiable points of departure? By taking a closer look alone, it appears that one cannot go as far with them, as one is supposed to believe.

The law of diminishing returns was initially constructed for the agricultural production, and then expanded to every type of production. It can certainly be considered as a purely static state if carefully formulated. One can certainly say that every economical production cannot exceed a certain product quantity without the costs of the unit of output increasing, if one does not make improvements to the productive apparatus, a stipulation, which the law of *rising* returns is supposed to eliminate. In this form, the law of diminishing returns certainly plays an important role in English-American literature. While one formerly divided all productions into three groups, as is generally known, into such that follow a law of diminishing returns, such that follow a law of rising returns, and such that follow a law of steady returns, it has currently become common for static to acknowledge solely the first-mentioned, and we do not want to deny that significant progress lies therein. No great interest will be placed on the case of the steady returns that can be conceived as a marginal case of each of the two other "laws." But the acknowledgement that a rising return is impossible within the assumptions of static is certainly not without importance. If one now acknowledges the universality of the law of diminishing returns in static, then the same is suitable to explain the constant rise of the supply curve. But we do not need it, or better, we already have such a law of diminishing returns: The more that is "bartered" from a good, the more the seller must deprive it of more important needs, or the more important uses must be deprived of the pertaining productive goods, and then the "utility return" of the sale or of production would diminish even then, when the growth of satisfaction that is expected from further acquisition remained constant, and only would be possible at an increased "price." If the physical production return were to also decline now, then that growth of satisfaction would diminish even faster, as if this were not the case, but we do not need this moment only to acquire our supply curve. But something else: The mere fact of the decrease of the physical production return with the increase of the produced quantity would never suffice alone in determining the price of supply. A supply curve that only sensualizes this fact would be incommensurable with the demand curve that is indeed at least based on the value hypothesis, and we could never juxtapose the two. The value of the quantities of goods that are sensualized in the supply curve would still have to be known if this is supposed to be possible, and an explicit determining point of intersection is supposed to be found. We will still come to speak of this moment when we talk about the pension theory. So while the *value theoretical* law of the diminishing returns is in a position to completely replace the *physical* one—it would be an easy thing to consider the latter in the gestalt of the value curve, which forms our supply function—it is not the case for the opposite, and one could never get by with the physical diminishing law alone. Since we also do not need the same for our pension theory, as we will see, we therefore simply have no use for it—its role in the modern system of the national economy has ended. It does not interest us more than other production technological facts, which indeed also have an influence on the type and quantity of the goods that are to be produced, without being components of the pure economy as a result. We place great emphasis on this division of the *physical* and the *value theoretical* law of the diminishing returns. It is not always clearly recognized; but it is very important to the evaluation of the newer American literature, among others.

Not quite the same can be said of the disutility theory. Certainly, the labor effort—it is the only thing that we still concern ourselves with here, after we have already covered the other element of disutility—generally rises with the progression of labor time disproportional to the latter, and finally till the intolerable, so that this moment can also explain the gestalt of the supply curve. And here we will say above all that we do not need it, and therefore have to disregard it, according to the principle of the "thought economy." But here, we cannot utilize our second objection that we raised against the explanation of the supply curve's gestalt through the law of diminishing returns, namely that the latter does not replace the law of value; at least not quite in the same sense: However, something similar will arise here also.

So what does the disutility theory tell us? This is expressed in the equation:

$$\text{marginal utility} = \text{marginal affliction}$$

which means that equilibrium eventuates there, where the demand curve that is to be explained through the value function intersects the supply curve that is to be explained through a disinclination curve, so simply by that quantity of goods where the utility of further growth balances the "damage" of further labor efforts and consumption delays. Although, we saw that we can simply conceive the consumption delays as being the surrender of values of goods, so that our equation can be expressed in the following manner:

marginal utility = marginal labor effort + marginal utility of the goods that are to be expended, in order to bring out the moment of the labor effort that will from now on be the only one to come into consideration.

Marginal utility of the product - marginal utility of the goods that are to be expended = marginal labor effort. In order to be frank, let us call the expression that is located on the left side of this equation "marginal utility of the labor product." The disutility theory would boil down to interpreting the supply curve of labor differently than that of all other goods, or more correct, that of the other *productive* goods, and simply to call a limb of an equation of the system that describes the state of equilibrium of the economy. But what for? The exact expression of this one limb differentiates itself through nothing from those of the others, the curve that sensualizes the same is the same or a similar one as that, which sensualize the others. So why not also have an integrative interpretation? What do our results gain from it? One could say that the disutility is simply a "determining force"; may or may not be; it would not be anything conspicuous, if the situation would arise that it does not show itself in our exact *image* of the economy.

It would certainly be solely *possible* to explain the supply curve from the disutility, and contrast it with the value curve. One could say that psychologically-speaking, inclination and disinclination are commensurable values, and the disutility function can therefore be constructed without intervention of the value function. While I must first put the facts of the law of diminishing returns into the language of the calculation of value, and put the physical unity of goods into relation with the chosen unity of value for this purpose, this is not necessary here; value and disutility can readily be measured with any common measurement. And even there, one can still not do without the help of the value. This was already emphasized from a different angle, and should only be briefly and popularly mentioned here. If an isolated value only produces one single good with its labor, then the interpretation that is expressed in the equation "marginal utility = marginal affliction" certainly applies. It is unnecessary to explain that it will produce as long as further utility growth no longer balances out further labor effort. However, if it uses its labor if only for the production of *two* goods, then the situation is somewhat different. Then, it will probably also work up until this equation is realized. But it does not tell us how much of the labor time determined in this manner will be used for one good, and how much for the other good. This relationship that is in fact decisive for the quantities, which are produced from each of the two goods, is obviously dependent on their values. And what lies closer now than regarding the supply curve of labor from the stand point of each of the goods as the reverse value function of the other?

It is very similar in the commerce economy. The laborers who only have *one* labor opportunity available to them will also behave in the same manner as the isolated landlord. But if more are available to them, then the wages will be decisive for the manner of how they divide themselves into the same, consequently for the supply of labor in each of the same, and if the same have a tendency to balance themselves, then this is the cause of those movements, which the *value* brings about, better, *describes*.

Therefore the equation: marginal costs = marginal proceeds certainly holds true in general, and it sparsely comes down to the interpretation of both values in principle, if one agrees on their laws of movement. But the interpretation of the "costs" as "disinclination" would only find independent meaning in labor, and would also only lead to the same laws of movement in certain special cases, as it fails in others as "value"; and so we therefore dismiss it.

But does it give us something anyway, which the value cannot give us, namely a determination for the entire labor quantity that is actually accomplished, an independent moment for the available quantity of the good "labor"? Yes, certainly—*more* labor can never be accomplished, at least not by free laborers, as is balanced out by the result of the same. But this moment is absolutely analog the technological characteristics of the other production factors. That labor quantity is a given in every given state of the economy, and one economizes with it, as well as one economizes with the given land that can of course be utilized very differently. It is dependent on population number, race, climate, the entire social order, etc. One could certainly attempt to justify it further. The delimitations that we are making do not in fact lie in the things themselves, they are moreover arbitrary. But we could only accept the disutility into our closed system, if *in place* of value we put it into labor, if we said that labor has no value, but rather only disutility. Because our equilibrium system is absolutely determined: We already have as many equations as unknowns, and can therefore not concede labor with value *and* disutility, since our problem would be over-determined by doing so. So we must *choose*. No one knows this better than a mathematician like Marshall, and he therefore *replaces* the value of labor through its disutility. This cannot be done, as we see; we can also not do without value in regards to labor—so we must now simply forego disutility and enqueue it in those moments that stand *behind* our system so to speak. The necessity is only a methodological one, but never the less imperative. One may consider this to be a flaw of our methods, but it has many of such. If one believes anyhow that it is of use for many purposes, then one must befriend oneself with it. And we constantly regard pointing this out as one of our main tasks. The non-mathematician does not see the content matter as clearly and at the most, feels vague that the moment of disutility causes difficulties. He then either operates patiently with it, or seeks to prove its insignificance. But one can never come to clarity be doing so. In the innermost essence of our system lies the key to understanding. But enough of this.

Our result is that we are forced to regard the supply scale as a value curve. There are therefore *two demand* curves that intersect, and not a demand curve and a supply curve that is different in substance. At least we believe that this conception preserves itself the best and most likely puts itself forward in its entirety and by weighing the pros and cons for all causes. If one believes to be able to justify them even more in-depth, it is all the better; it is more important for our purposes to emphasize that a moment of arbitrariness lies in this arrangement, and to show that both of the curves are substantially independent of differences in opinion about their nature. Cognitions of this kind may seem to have a depressing effect on laymen, but true understandings can only be won with their help.

Conceptions that touch on ours are not entirely foreign to theorists who stand outside the circle of the marginal utility theory. Mill has already said that in every demand lies a supply, and in every supply a demand, and many statements of similar kind can be quoted, from past and modern time; this may please those, who even still today strive to stand up for the classical authors, and something gratifying does indeed lie in it. Such isolated statements alone only have limited meaning; the essence is what one *does* with them. A remark, an aperçu is soon made, but the decisive action is only taken if it becomes a foundation of a greater whole. This also applies here. Despite all the examining of the recognition that the former view is incomplete, one still adheres to the dualism of supply and demand today, and despite the admission that it is not admissible to reclusively base demand on value and supply on the costs, which we find in advanced ones, everything will remain unaffected. The dictum that supply and demand influences one another in all regards and are contingent upon one another also does not change anything, even though such a profound truth lies in it. So what is the point of: "all right, all right, we also know this, this is of course self-evident," which the arguments of the value theorists are always greeted by? In fact, one is *not* certain just how the matter actually behaves. We have just attempted to expose those points that matter.

III

But not all is said yet. We want to interpret the supply curve as an inverted demand curve, as a value curve of the production goods. As we said, we could be satisfied by inquiring the economic subjects about the marginal price scales of the latter in a similar manner as we did with the value curve of the consumption goods, and then we could leave it as that, which would lead the economic subjects to their answers. Namely, we could interpret the same in the sense of the marginal utility theory, as well as the disutility theory. But we choose the first alternative from the mentioned reasons and assume the value functions of the production goods arise from the ones of the consumption goods, for whose production one can use them. We therefore consider *the production goods as potential consumption goods*, which is as descriptively as one could perhaps express it. We conventionalize or schematize the production process of a good for our purposes as an exchange of production goods against that good, whereby the former simply appear as potential consumption goods. Or even more explicit: For every production, one exchanges quantities of consumption goods that one could *otherwise* also produce with certain quantities of production goods, for a quantity of a specific consumption good, namely one that one *actually* produces. In every production, lies an abandonment of *otherwise* possible uses; that to the benefit of the necessary productive good of the same, *one* of the possible uses. This conception helps us in using the moment of barter for the derivation of the "prices" of the productive goods—which yield the static branches of income—to therefore base the distribution theory on the value curves, but in addition to also describe all changes in prices and quantities of goods that can happen within the static assumption with its help.

This conception is therefore extraordinarily important. But it is essential for its understanding and its evaluation to be clear that it is an *assumption*, a *principally arbitrary ascertainment*. We cannot prove it, just as little as we *prove* that the value function of a consumption good rests on the psychological law of the satiation of needs. The psychological economists may attempt this; it is indeed plausible, it also greatly contributes to the popularization of the theory. But if one agrees with that, which was said in the first part of this work, then one will also readily verify the presence of a new hypothesis here. The same is useful and valuable, and does not collide with the truth anywhere, but other hypotheses are in principle just as possible and "justified." The criterion between the possible hypotheses only lies in the results and one can then say that ours is the most fruitful by far. Their introduction—made generally known by v. Wieser—is therefore a scientific deed of great importance, yes, it would not be wrong to first date the existence of a uniform, satisfactory system of the pure economy back to it. This changes nothing on its character alone.

But now the question is raised of how our assumption of the closer one is to be carried into effect. The supply curve a good gives us, *is* the value function of the production goods, and this one is the value function of those consumption goods, which could otherwise by produced with the latter. But there are usually a large number of these consumption goods. If we let it be enough with the functions of such and want to derivate the ones of the productive goods from this, then a new problem arises: only if solely *one* other use of the production goods of the regarded consumption good would be possible, the matter would be very simple. In this case, the supply curve would be the inverted value curve simply of that other way of use. But in general, this is not the case. Especially if one categorizes all production goods into the three categories labor, capital, and land performances, as it is typical and necessary in regards to certain purposes, one must acknowledge that these three production goods are simply used in all productions, so that in the supply curve, one of every good of the value curves of all other goods must somehow be expressed.

In fact, this is not more than self-evident. In a "closed," for example "communistic," economy their performance can only then give a specific production from certain quantities of those three production factors, if it is convinced that no needs that are more important to the commonwealth are to be satisfied with the first—whereby it is of course indifferent for our purpose to determine how something is a "need of the common wealth" and furthermore, the most important of these needs—and this conviction can only be won through the observation of the entire, remaining supply of goods. For every economical expenditure this performance will be under the pressure of the values of all other possible uses, and this "pressure" will have a specific influence on the magnitude of the first—it is indeed none other than the consequence of the limitation of the provisions of goods and the desire to make the best of them. Our theory of the supply curve—and basically all our theories—now expresses the fact that both of these moments suffice in forcing a specific line of action under given conditions, and especially in very noticeably translating the arbitrariness for the quantity of the supply for each individual good. And it also makes us aware that only all of those elements combined, from which it takes its point of departure—value functions and quantities of all goods—are sufficient for the determination of each of the same.

The matter is principally exactly the same in the commerce economy: the supply of a good will be dependent on the given price of the three production goods' prices, and the more one produces of it, the higher these will rise, thereby putting an end to production at a specific point; and for the same reason as earlier, namely because they must be revoked of more and more important, other uses. So then the values and prices of the production goods in all other uses will also have a say in the supply of each individual consumption good here, and so then the influence of *all* consumption good values and prices will also make itself noticeable for each individual one here. If one wanted to ignore the same, then it would continuously amount to a specific quantity of "money" or another measurement of value, which would then measure the "damage" that was made; and namely in the commerce-less, as well as in the commerce economy. If one wanted to popularly express oneself and look past the fact that this diction has epistemological, as well as other deficiencies, then one could say that the main problem of the economy lies in describing certain necessities that force the limitation of the quantities of goods onto the economical trade—the concrete forms and other relationships of the economy may always exist and be everywhere—and to derivate their consequences. Our proceeding from the quantities of goods therefore appears in a "deeper" meaning here, in a somewhat different light than earlier.

This now has an important consequence for our supply curve. It explains to us why the best theorists never speak of a supply of a product, but rather always of the supply of *productive goods*. In principle, nothing would withhold us from bringing the demand of a good face to face with its supply. If we were to do only this, then we would only have an excerpt of the truth in front of us that only suffices in bringing useful results for some, not for all cases. If I look at the supply of a good by itself, as if it were only dependent on the value and the other ratios of this one good and without regard for the values of the others, then this may be sufficient in demonstrating certain truths—it is also not correct there—but it is certainly incomplete, since this supply is indeed under the influence of the quantities and values of all other goods. And these latter simply function through the values of the productive goods. So if I do not want to disregard this effect that is in fact the primary lever for the adjustment of all values and quantities, and to capture the supply of every good in its interaction with all other supplies, then I may not construct an individual supply curve for every good, but would rather do better by speaking of a supply of production means, which is of course assembled differently for every good. Within the value curve that is interpreted this way, the total value *of all* goods and the mutual dependency of the same are expressed. In every given state of the economy there are, in regards to all productions that happen within the same, distinct determining supplies of production means for each of the same, which contain all decisive moments. The latter would however not let themselves be read off from the supply curves of the individual products. If this remark is enough to show the reader that there is a row of theoretical detail-questions here, whose careful answer is absolutely necessary for a representation of the theory that suffices for higher demands. The actual, practical interest of the same is scarce, and this explains why most of the national economists—and also theorists—do not pay attention to them, and rather ad infinitum accept certain ambiguities and falsities. However, we want to no longer dwell on the discussion of such questions, whose comprehension—and interest—requires a long engagement with theory.[2]

We must therefore derivate the supply curves from countless value curves. But when we have done this, we have still not reached everything yet. Though we then have the value curves of combinations of the production means, but not yet the ones of the latter themselves. If the same combination of production factors—proportional quantities of labor, land, and capital—were necessary for all productions, then one could derivate those of this combination of production goods from the value curves of all products. But then, one would still have to win the value curves of the three productive goods from the latter. However, those combinations are in fact not equal, and this path is therefore impassable anyway. Our problem is therefore direct: We must derivate the value functions of the individual productive goods from those of the individual products. And if we still need another term, we say that we "attribute" the values of the production goods to those of the products, and have to find the rules of this "attribution," we have thus *reached* v. Wieser's problem.

One can popularly express its content in approximately the following manner: It assumes that the productive goods have value, because one *needs* them, that wage, pension, and interest get paid, and land and capital things are also economical welfare and economical considerations in the closed economy, because they lead to the acquisition of consumption goods. And the value of the latter is simply assumed as the measurement of this "need," the magnitude of the satisfaction of needs that is dependent on the latter. Satisfaction of needs only directly give consumption goods, therefore, the value "originates" within them. And this value reverberates so to speak on the productive goods, as the light of a luminary onto a "dark" wall. The question now raises itself of how this value reverberates on the productive goods, and how much value they receive through it.

We have already presented the methodological importance and the essence of this conception. We presented those dry statements only for this reason, and in order to put them into the right relationship to other possible conceptions. Whoever all the grazed-upon problems do not interest can be satisfied with what was just said. But one would then have no right to complain about unsatisfactory and unclear points in the theory. Surely, the deeper analysis that we attempted is perhaps not worthwhile; but then one would do better in abandoning the theory altogether. If one does not want this, then one must just go deeper than general argumentations for or against free trade, etc., permit. And since I am under the impression that many a person wishes this today, and, being tired of arguments about principles, wants to expand on the matter, so I hope that one will excuse my statements, as abstruse as they may seem to be. Of course, they are not fascinating lectures, but I believe that because of this, one will have an actual benefit, and will better understand now what the theorists actually plague themselves with.

IV

It only still spares to *solve* the attribution problem, to therefore actually derivate the individual productive goods. In order for us not to have to be even drier than it is anyhow necessary, as we have up to now not always strictly held on to that diction that we view as the more accurate one, we also want to continue to draw on the same freedom, where it appears to be possible without any damage. But everyone who finds this important can be easily convinced that psychological dictions, etc. are never essential to us and can be easily corrected.

Actual solutions to the attribution problem are only offered by the "Austrian School." These are not exactly the same. However, it lies in the essence of the matter that such differences do not have any further reaching consequences. The only thing we want and can do is show that productive goods also have value functions, and are of the same type as consumption goods, and that the ones of the first let themselves be derivated from those of the latter. The first point only serves the interpretation of the supply curve, and the second spares us from having to empirically determine the same, and gives us that relation, which the theory of the income formation, therefore the value and price formation of the production goods is based on. This alone is everything that is necessary. If one is in agreement about this and about the solvability of the problem, then all conclusions from the attribution theory will be identical, even though the solutions to the problem may be different. Since we do not execute concrete computations, but are rather satisfied with the mentioned general moments, then such differences cannot lead to differences in, for example, the distribution theory or otherwise have any ramifications. Namely, an incorrect solution will also by no means influence the further results, and even the lack of a concrete solution will not make itself very noticeable if the solvability itself is not in question. This fact explains why this fundamental problem was dealt with so late and so little. One can say that authors simply regarded it as being solved, and operated just as surely with the values of the productive goods, than with those of the consumption goods. All of those, who asked themselves what the "share" of the individual productive goods, perhaps labor or land, is for the productive effect did this.

For example, Thünen's theory is certainly an attempt of an attribution theory in this respect, and one can without a doubt also understand the modern works about the distribution problem under this title. What other than an attribution theory is J. B. Clark's system? Yes, even many executions of the classical authors can be interpreted this way. Our problem is therefore nothing new, according to its essence, which of course does not rule out that it was just recently consciously formulated and recognized in its fundamental meaning. Up until then, a deep gap existed in the system of our economy; and even though it was mostly overlooked, and this, as we said, does not make a progress impossible, it did nevertheless exist, and every deeper analysis had to lead to it.

We only want to occupy ourselves briefly with the solution of the problem and not discuss other solutions. Even then, the matter is still rather complicated. By the way, we want to simplify it for ourselves at all costs. Since we, as we said, cannot think about dealing with concrete cases from reality and must be satisfied with showing how the matter behaves in principle, nothing therefore keeps us from choosing our examples as easily as possible.

For now in preparation, a few illustrative cases: I would like to take a business trip, from which I will earn, let's say, 1,000 marks. For this purpose, I whistle at a cabby, in order to take me to the train station. If I cannot get to the train station in another way, namely another cabby is also not available, so that my business is absolutely dependent on him and his willingness to take me to the train station, what would I be ready to pay him in the most extreme case? That, which I am left with must certainly not only compensate me for my other costs in money—train ticket, etc.—but also for my labor, to namely generate as much for me, as my occupation would have otherwise generated for me in this amount of time and through this use of energy. Let this be 500 marks. But I will possibly be inclined to give away the other 500 marks—if really only purely-economical motives guide me—up to a minimum that must stay with me, in order to even still motivate me in making the decision of *this* action. Nothing paradoxical lies in this. If the 500 marks do not really sufficiently compensate for costs, labor, and discomfort of the trip and the business, and the other 500 represent a type of "pure win," then this ride is actually "worth" 500 marks to me. But in reality, I will only give the man his "tax" and a more or less generous tip, and he will generally also be satisfied with a very small portion, approximately one hundredth of that sum. Did I therefore "exploit" him? Our example shows us the pointlessness of this question within the economy. However, we will talk about the fact that our attribution theory is not in a position to say anything about the "justice" or "injustice" of the distribution of an economical success on the contributing factors, at a later point. It should already be remarked here that despite the fact that a moral value judgment does not belong to the domain of an exact, describing discipline, entirely different moments than those of the productive performance would have to prevail for one of such if it should make sense practically: one must not lose sight that the productive performance of a production *factor* does not yet justify the allocation of its entire return to its *owner*, that furthermore, actual *suffering* of a portion of the economic subjects must be avoided above all others, with complete disregard to the value of the production means that they command, and that the moral judgment reacts much more to this moment than to any other.

But other questions interest us here. Especially—is our example perhaps senseless? What is the purpose of saying that the cabby is performing a service for me that is worth 500 marks, if he neither gets that much, nor *should* he get that much, nor a tendency also exists to allocate him that much. As a matter of fact, no joy would come cheaper than to ridicule our representation of the case. Exactly the same can be said indeed of all other cost elements of my business trip. Would it not follow that all of them together are worth much more than their success itself? And yet, nothing senseless lies in it. If the cabby would be aware of his advantages, then he could actually get more than his tax, namely 500 marks in the extreme case. One can of course say the same of all other people whose assistance I need for my business, and all of them together cannot get more than that sum. But from the start, everyone measured the same candidature for it from them and everyone's highest gain and the value of everyone's performance was measured, in my eyes, by the 500 marks.

Our example is nevertheless unfortunate. Such simple cases are always a double-edged sword, and we would like to advise all theorists to resist the attempt of constructing such cases. They are meant well and are absolutely irreproachable in themselves, but they often run into misunderstandings, and make a downright strange impression on the non-theorist who does not grasp their deeper meaning. Examples from a great framework have a much better effect and are much more conducive to the character of the theory, as attractive as it may appear to demonstrate the great laws of economic life with small examples of every-day experience, and therefore proving that the same formulas are adequate for all processes. So let us choose another: various groups of interest participate in a venture, for example the construction of a railway. Everyone's contribution is indispensable so that the success, measured in money of the "pure win," is dependent on each of the same. Each one must get so much that its "costs" will be replaced, therefore, as much as it could get for its expenditure elsewhere, otherwise it will generally not make a contribution. Other reasons may probably cause it to do this regardless, it may for example, put emphasis on this undertaking gaining influence and also be ready to sacrifice for this purpose; but moments of this nature will not smudge the lines of the processes, as essential as they may be to the understanding of a concrete case. But then a surplus remains whose attainment is the *actual* economic reason of the undertaking, and this surplus can be monopolized by each of the contributing groups. They will have greater or lesser success, depending on their energy, organization, and the representation of publicists and parliaments, but each of the same can hope for the *entire* success from the start; at any rate, the *entire* success is dependent on their contribution, *consequently attributing it to it*. If it involves foregoing their contribution, then as an example, another opportunity for acquisition opens itself to it, which eliminates its assistance in the construction of the railway; the other participants thus seek to prevent the transition to the same, possibly with the sacrifice of almost the entire surplus. Thus, nothing counterproductive lies in striking the value of the contribution of all individual ones with the total value that the undertaking realizes. But on the other hand, the groups must share in the earnings, not everyone can get everything.

This is now the big crux of the distribution theory. Laborers, capitalists, and land owners, all of them, or really the productive goods that they own, are indispensable to every production. It is easy to show that the productive success of all three categories is dependent in the same manner, and that there is no criterion that would be suitable in singling out the one production factor from the other in this relation. Of course, one occasionally went this far only with labor, by attributing it the entire value of the products that are produced with its help. But the same can be proved just as easily *from a pure economical stand point* for the other production factors. This view therefore does not seem to lead very far. At any rate, it does not give us a distribution scale for each surplus of value that we measure here with money and consider to be net income or for that surplus about the value of the individual production means in other usages. It certainly has a meaning for reality and is no figment of the imagination without backing of the facts; because one of the three production means *can* actually have the potential of carrying the entire surplus away. But it is nevertheless insufficient. One has sought to withdraw himself from these difficulties in a different manner. We want to pursue the following path. *In principle, the values of all of those products should be attributed to each production good whose production it takes an active part in, or rather, the value functions of all of those products should appear in the value functions of the production good.* However, this has the consequence that the value scales of the first ones are not summable. But what does this do? What purpose would such a summation be necessary for? If one always stays aware of what our value curves actually signify, then one will find nothing conspicuous in it. And these value curves will give us actual laws of exchange: Always when an element that is necessary for a specific production combination should be given away, the owner will simply glance at the entire success that becomes impossible through this, and not on a portion of the same. The exchange relation will then give us the scale for the distribution of that surplus, which the value attribution cannot give us by itself.

We also find a similar thing for the value functions of the consumption goods. If several consumption goods collaborate for a specific advantage, so that all are necessary for its attainment, then this advantage must appear in the value functions of *all*. Otherwise it could happen that, apart from everything else, one or all of the same would have no value functions at all, depending on whether or not it also allows other uses. And this would lead to the absurd result that they do not obtain a price. One tends to call goods that stand in this relation to one another complementary, and our solution to the attribution problem refers to this case, as well as that of the productive goods. One can therefore define it a bit further as *the problem of the derivation of value functions of goods, which only cause an advantage from the value function of this latter*.

It could also appear in the case of the complementary consumption goods that we are making a double-calculation, that we appoint one and the same value several times. We are in fact doing this, and one must exercise caution when using our approach. It would actually be manqué if, for example, one wants to evaluate the total value of the ownership of goods of an economic subject due to the same. It expresses that each of the complementary goods must mete out to that economical problem that corresponds to the entire advantage, since it is dependent on each one of the same, that namely the entire advantage always comes into consideration in the exchange of a good that belongs to such a combination. And this is why we choose this conception; a summation of total values of such goods that come about in this manner would not make sense, it would give a value sum that would be greater than the value of the entire advantage.

The difficulty that we spoke of only exists as long as one wants to make this summation and holds on to the idea that the value of a product must scatter into the productive goods of the same, like the warmth of a body onto a wall that is illuminated by it. If one abandons the first and continuously reminds oneself what our curves signify and what we want to do with them, then the latter disappears.

In the explained cases however, a moment was missing that seems to be suitable to give the missing determination of the value attribution. It is that of competition. Going back to our example of the construction of a railway, if the laborers, capitalists, and land owners do not form three groups like we said, but rather under-bid one another amongst each other, then their portion will become *determined*; during completely free competition, from which it would arise that other railways would also be built immediately if the first one gives such a "surplus" of the "costs"[3]; this surplus that should be divided up would furthermore have to have a tendency to disappear. What happens now? Certainly, the shares of the productive goods for the proceeds from one production are only absolutely determined in the case of "free competition," as we have yet to see in the price theory. If this one does not exist, then our conception also does not suffice for an absolute determination of this share. Its advantage solely exists in the fact that it makes the use of the laws of exchange possible for us. *But the result is not absolute*.

Let us further differentiate alone. That, which is only absolutely determined in the case of free competition—and not otherwise—is none other than the *price* of the productive goods and furthermore their final *marginal utility*. According to our conception, their *value functions* are also completely certain otherwise. Here, it is a question of whether these ones can also attain a determination through the moment of competition, which they are otherwise lacking, according to some theorists. And the competition of other economic subjects does not come into question here, but rather another type of competition indeed, namely that of other possible uses. One could also argue in this manner: If productive goods only have a specific use, are only suited for the production of one good, then the value function of each one of the same is no longer determined. But for example, if one of them also has another use, so that it can be pulled out from this, then the entire value that the first use realized is not dependent on a concrete quantity of the same, but rather only on that from which one must forego if one pulls it out from the latter that must necessarily be of lower value if the entire process is even supposed to happen. This productive good could only be struck with this lower value, and we would be in a position to set it into our calculation with a specific, namely this lower, value and would only have to distribute the surplus onto the remaining production goods. But since almost all of them allow more uses, then the same specific values would also arise for others, and it lies in the sense of this conception to get to a place where our surplus can only be attributed to one of the contributing factors, whereby the same seems to be attained as through our conception: namely the determination of the values of all productive goods.

In our examples, the value of the performance of the cabby would therefore only amount to as much as that of the ride, which he could have otherwise done, the value of the performance of our laborers in the construction of a railway only as much as that of that labor, which they could have otherwise attained, etc. And this conception would surely be more plausible than ours in many aspects.

Alone the following concerns seem to make it impossible for me. Above all, it does not solve the problem, but rather only moves it a step back. So where does the value in those other uses come from? Either there is *still* another, or not. In the latter case, we are facing the exact same problem, and the first must also sooner or later be traced to a final type of use with the lowest value, whose value is then lacking for the explanation. So then we do come back to those difficulties that lead to our conception. So then, what happens if *all* the cooperative goods have such a lower value, which one should the surplus be attributed to? Such a case is absolutely possible, and when it occurs, this surplus of value is completely in limbo. And this must not happen; the *entire* value of the product must be placed in the value functions of the productive goods, if we are supposed to regard our problem as being solved.

Both of these demurs lead to the third: This conception overlooks something, namely the appreciation value, which is the cause of a new possible use for a productive good. The reason why it overlooks this lies in the mixing up of value function and total value, which we have been blamed for repeatedly. When a new advantageous use of a good becomes possible, then its value increases from two causes: Mainly because a lower quantity remains for the previous uses. But not only because of this, but also due to its *value function* getting altered. Because the economical requirements for our construction of the railway are given, the labor becomes a more valuable good than it previously was, and this higher value is expressed in its value function. So if one says that replaceable goods retain that value function, which befits them in their lower value uses, and we also previously drew on a similar manner of expression, so that we did not have to make reserves, which would have not been understood yet in those parts, then this is not entirely true. We will immediately discuss the elements of truth that nevertheless lie in it. But it is final that in the construction of the value function of a productive good one must always look at all the products whose production it contributes to, and has no right to discard the value of one or some of the same from it.[4]

Those "elements of truth" are the following: they also let us understand the origin of this conception. If it is a matter of foregoing a specific quantity of a consumption good or even a good, then one deprives the "last," least important stirring of need of this quantity, as is known. By doing this, one therefore popularly foregoes, even if it is not correctly stated, the marginal utility. We only take the marginal utility into consideration for our considerations of the marginal utility in every exchange, or else for a renunciation of a small quantity of a good. And the psychological economists tell us that the value of a good is simply characterized by the loss of satisfaction that the abandonment of one of such marginal quantities causes. Now, it also applies to productive goods as far as this is *even* true. But since their marginal utility is certainly none other than their utility in the uses with the lowest value that are in fact still dealt with, and that it is certainly being taken "from the margin" for necessary quantities of a productive good for a new use, then it appears as if only the use with the lowest value must actually still determine the value of our productive good. But this is not entirely true, or better, this only counts under the assumption that the value function does not change. But since it does this, this conception is inapplicable. However, only as far as one bears in mind the total value and the value function. The marginal utility of our productive means is in fact determined by the value function of the use with the lowest value. And if the quantity that is necessary for the new use is so small that one and the same use has the lowest value before and after, then the marginal utility will only be little indeed, this means that only so much is changed as is caused by the decrease of the quantity in the same. Because furthermore, the marginal utility is crucial to the price; it can therefore happen that the new use will hardly exert influence in the same, for example, our construction of the railway no longer increases the wages of the laborers, which can be explained by the decrease of the labor supply in the lowest-paying occupation. But this does not generally apply—even though it does as a rule "in praxi"—and not in principle. And it never applies to *all* parts of the value scale of the productive good and its total value. Then again, we see how important it is to separate the value function from the marginal utility. The first one is that, which we want to derivate.[5]

The other element of truth in the conception in question is the following: When a good's new type of use that was not previously possible suddenly becomes possible, then one can, however, if one wants to decide whether and in how far it is supposed to be made, only proceed by contrasting the value that is realized through it with the one that was previously realized in the other uses. In this regard, if one were to already include the value function of the productive good in the first one, then this would be very wrong and would lead to the result that *no* growth in utility will be achieved. One can view *each* of the possible types of use from this point of view and say in this sense that each good has as many value functions as types of use. If it is a matter of determining the economical meaning of a type of use, meaning to calculate the marginal gain that is produced by it, then one can in fact proceed no differently. Certainly this fact has primarily lead to this conception. Alone, when all of the regarded uses are regularly carried out and their results are completely foreknown, then the values of all will show themselves in the value functions of the pertaining goods, *must* show themselves if no "surpluses" are supposed to be present, with which we would know nothing to do. And this is our case. We must assume the value functions as constant in the static state, because they are necessary data of our problems. No surprise, no progress of new productions is allowed to occur, since our system would change this from the ground up. All productions must continue exactly this way and with the exact success that one anticipated, and all production and consumption combinations must be fixed once and for all. They are again reflected in the value functions, which our results are based on, as well as all the facts of the needs, tendency, of the surrounding nature, etc.

Let us still add that all acts of exchange must also be foreseen and the system of the value functions must be adjusted according to them, thus, all is said; for the theorist who specializes in this subject area. We do not want to further go into these dry questions, but rather only briefly present our solution to the problem whose leading principles we just explained. This can also be skipped over, without causing damage to the understanding of the following. I do not claim to have touched upon all points that are necessary for the solving, I am rather absolutely aware of the incompleteness of my executions about this difficult problem.[6] But it is not possible to offer more in the framework of this work.

The solution that we recommend is therefore in essence the following.

If a good only has one use, can therefore, for example, only a consumption good be produced from a production mean, and if there is no substitution for the same, then its value function is simply that of that use, of that consumption good. Its supply function then is this value curve, only just "inverted." We do not always want to repeat the latter, but rather be content to derivate the *value functions*, namely the value functions of the *production means*, even though this also applies to the consumption goods with several uses.

A consumption good has several production goods that cannot be used for anything else and cannot be replaced. The value functions of this latter are then identical to the value function of the first, each in itself, whereby one must only be mindful of the fact that such units must be chosen for the x-coordinates of the production goods' value curves, which correspond to the quantity of these goods that are necessary for the production of the product's unit. Let this be mentioned once and for all here as well.

A product has a productive good that is "irreplaceable" but useful otherwise. The value function of the latter is a type of value function of the group of goods, whose production it is necessary for. It is composed of those parts of these goods' value functions that currently have the greatest ordinates. Let us explain this in psychological terms: First, the use that yields the greatest utility will be adopted. As long as one stays with the same, and for every piece of the x-axis the value curve, which this quantity of the good that is dedicated to this use sensualized, simply gives the value curve of that use. If the regarded economic subject were to only have *this* quantity, then the other uses would be out of the question, and only the value function of *this* use would pertain to our good. However, if the economic subject has more of the same, and first adds this "more" to another, then a third use, and so on and so forth, then the value functions of these uses would apply to those quantities of our productive means that are dedicated to the individual ones, whereby it lies in the nature of the matter that the individual pieces, which the value functions of the productive means are therefore composed of, join one another; because the value function of one must touch that of the other at the point of transfer from one use to another, since at this point, the first, coming from above, sinks underneath the latter. Through this, it can happen that the value function of a use, after having sunk underneath another once, later becomes once again determining, due to the *faster* sinking of the other, therefore, that a use, which is already abandoned for the benefit of others will later be admitted again. This changes nothing on the principle, which we can express in this manner: For the individual parts of the value function of a good, which is suitable for various uses, but is indispensable for this, the value functions, which *correspond to the actual uses of its individual parts* continuously come into consideration.

Furthermore, if a productive good is now suitable for several uses and is substitutable in all of them, then it has a value function that is based on a similar principle, only that the functions of its substitutes in those uses come into consideration for their pieces, which would have to be foregone in the case calling upon them. The second fundamental principle of our problem-solving lies in it.

Furthermore, a product has two productive goods, from which one is otherwise useful, but the other is not. Both are irreplaceable. The current rules only apply to the one that is otherwise useful, one must be mindful of the fact that for the other one, if one wants to realize its value, one must forego another—that of the other uses of the productive means that is also useful otherwise. The value function of the latter can therefore not be that of the product, rather, their ordinates must be shortened for an amount that is suitable to this circumstance. But let it be emphasized again that the value function of the otherwise useful factor is not only composed of the ones of these other uses, but rather also contains those of our product.

When a product has *several productive goods*, which are irreplaceable but otherwise useful, then each of the same has the value function that arises from its uses in the manner that was explained, but its ordinates are to be shortened according to the values of the *other* productive goods in their other uses.

But if these productive goods are in addition also substitutable, then a new principle is not necessary and one can take care of the case in which such productive goods concur with irreplaceable and otherwise not useful ones. These problems can only interest the specialist, and we are hurrying to end these statements, which are so dry.

Everything that is to be adhered to is only the principal possibility of the solution to the problem of attribution. The same is already proven by the fact that we adjudge specific values to production goods with the same certainty as consumption goods. Furthermore, let one not forget that we only derivate *value functions* and not *total values* by means of the attribution theory, and furthermore, that the same does construct the basis of the price and distribution theory, but does not actually solve their problems, as many theorists currently believe. Namely, it does not yet give us a scale in itself for a "fair" distribution. After solving the problem of attribution, the moral demands of concurrent producers for parts of the product are as inextricable as before.

Notes

1. Meanwhile, one could make the following distinction between the two that would perhaps not be unpractical: The value function could be constructed *without* consideration for the variations in the estimate of a good, whose marginal profit submits the unit of measurement, in order to solely present the value scale of the regarded good. The demand function could conceive these variations with it, so that it would also express how the greater sacrifice of the cost good that is necessary as a result of the purchase of greater quantities of the first, or as a result of higher costs of the same, influences demand (page 219).
2. Only, let it be remarked that our conception bypasses all the difficulties that we would encounter by the interpretation of the supply curve by means of the law of diminishing returns; difficulties that are not unsurpassable, but are also not irrelevant (Schumpeter, 1908, pg. 241).

3. The reader hopefully understands the meaning of our terminology; for example, the term is called "costs" here: value in money that is realized in other uses. The brevity of our discussion makes complete accuracy in the manner of expression impossible, and I am making a point in warning the reader of possible misunderstandings (Schumpeter, 1908, pg. 250).
4. This point constructs the main difference between v. Boehm-Bawerk's solution and ours (Schumpeter, 1908, pg. 253).
5. This is the main difference between our solution and Prof. v. Wieser's (Schumpeter, 1908, page 254).
6. A bit more information about some points that belong here in my "Bemerkungen über das Zurechnungsproblem" (Remarks about the Problem of Attribution). *Zeitschrift für Volkswirtschaft, Sozialpolitik, und Verwaltung* (*Magazine for National Economics, Social Politics, and Administration*). Wien (Vienna) 1908 (page 256).

3

Elements of the Price Theory

I

We finally now come to the price theory. It is almost superfluous to tell the reader that it is a delusion to believe that the same should not achieve anything else for us than the explanation of *one*, but very important, emergence of the commerce economy. This impression is only generated through incomplete depictions. But it is certainly clear by now that the foundations of the price theory are also applicable to the pure-economical processes of the isolated economy without commerce; thereupon, they represent *a system of logic and of economical things*, so that they and their uses can even encompass the entire static economy. But what is further overlooked in the non-mathematical depictions is not only and not mainly an entire quantity of attainable results, but namely the circumstance, in which the main interest of the price theory for science is anchored; the circumstance that it brings the exact proof that our premises are in essence, therefore meaning the moments that our system is based on, sufficient in irrefutably determining the prices of goods and the quantities of the same, which the individuals will acquire and abandon, and to recognize a distinct interaction between all prices and quantities; that therefore, on the one hand, our system is self-contained and contains all elements that are necessary in completely "understanding" the processes, whose description it was made for, at least from *one* point of view, and that, on the other hand, there *are* normal variables of these prices and quantities in a specific sense—a logic of economical things.

The problem of the price theory is therefore generally the following:

GIVEN: *m* Individuals A, B, C .... and their value functions for *n* goods I, II..., thereupon their ownership of these goods

$$q_{a1}, q_{a2} \dots q_{b1}, q_{b2} \dots$$

WANTED: The exchange relations...$p_1 p_1, p_2 p_2$ ...., through which the exchanges will occur and the—positive or negative—growth ... which those given ownership of goods will thereby experience.

$$dq_{a1}, dq_{a2} \dots dq_{b1}, dq_{b2} \dots,$$

This is the main problem, which allows for numerous variations and enrichments, and whose importance is a very fundamental one. Its development and the discussion of its results determines the entire pure economy, if understood correctly, therefore, that discipline, which is self-*contained*, self-*sufficient*, and methodologically and contextually uniform, which we speak of here. We cannot think about studying it further here, or even just presenting it, as much as it is already exploited. This would lead us far outside of the framework of this work. The only thing that we want is to show this theory in its meaning, to touch on several important points, which do not sufficiently or not at all emerge in depictions that disdain the thought forms of the higher analysis, and invite the reader to familiarize himself with the literature of this thing, before he judges the essence and value of the theoretical economy, and especially to show him the great master of the exact theory, Léon Walras.

We mainly have to prove the distinct determination of the prices and growth of the goods within that main problem. This happens by us showing that we are in a position to construct just as many determination equations as we have unknowns. Now, the number of the latter is obviously equal to the number of the prices of goods that are to be determined—therefore *n - 1*[1] plus the number of those growths of the economical quantities—that is in turn equal to the number of the available economic subjects multiplied by the number of the available goods, therefore *m.n* -, thus equals *n (m + 1) - 1.* Our determination equations fall into two groups. Firstly, our law of the marginal utility niveau must be realized after the completion of the exchange acts for everyone—this yields equations of the number of the individuals—*m*—multiplied by the number of the goods minus one, as one can easily see: thus, *m (n - 1)*; *m + n - 1* equations are therefore still missing. This gives us another group; let us express that the sold and bought quantities of every good in our market are equal to one another, cancel each other out, thus their sums must equal zero: this yields n equations; and let us furthermore express that for every individual, "proceeds" and "expenditures" must balance one another, we therefore obtain even more m equations. Therefore seemingly one too many; alone the sum of the last named one results from the analogousness of the sold and bought quantities of all goods, so that the number of our equations reduces itself to one, meaning to one number of the unknowns.

With regards to that, which was said earlier, this demonstration hardly requires a further explanation. It encompasses exchange in a stricter sense, as well as production and the formation of income. We will still come to thoroughly speak about the third point, but we would like to still remark about the second that the possibility of an important enrichment of our system of equations offers itself there. Because nothing hinders us from introducing the production coefficients of the individual products into the same, meaning *to allow for the quantities of the productive goods, which are technically necessary for the production of the individual products*. But we do not want to go into this any further.

Our solution of the problem therefore firstly exists in the proof of its distinct determination, and secondly, in the mutual dependency of all prices, values, and quantities, from which various laws of motion of the same arise, which we will come back to. However, we cannot achieve more. But we *could* indeed, if the value functions and quantities of goods were to be given to us concretely, derivate the prices and the changes of these quantities that will result from it; but as long as this is not the case, the proof of the distinct determination and the existence of a state of equilibrium, furthermore the clear and correct depiction of the economical exchange relations between the elements of the goods is all that the theory has to offer us.

II

The next thing that offers us the same is a depiction of the formation of prices in the event of a monopoly. What we understand by this is the complete control of either the demand of one or of the supply of one good through an individual or a combination of such, if the latter entails a mutual pricing policy and eliminates every competition between its members. This case differentiates itself from the one that was presented in an essential point. Those equations that we summarized as our "second group" also apply here, as is easily seen: That, which is bought of the monopolized good must be equal to that, which is sold of it, and the "proceeds" of everyone, including the monopolist must likewise be equal to the "expenditures" expressed in any mutual measurement. But the equations of the first group do not apply here in quite the same manner. The law of the marginal utility niveau must indeed eventually be realized for the monopolist, as well as for his competing opponent; however, not quite the same relationship exists between the one of the first and that of the latter, as in the case of free competition. Why should the monopolist agree to a price that only corresponds to its reciprocal marginal utility relation for monopoly and price goods if it can receive *more*? We already saw earlier that competing individuals only do this because they would otherwise be undercut. But the monopolist cannot be undercut, and therefore that price that corresponds to free competition only forms one lower limit for it, which it will not sink below, but by no means also simultaneously the maximum limit, which it cannot exceed. Is the monopoly price thus not distinctly determined? In reality, our system of equations as it is fails; one could easily give a maximum limit of our monopoly price: It would be represented by that price at which no one wants to purchase anymore; but infinite prices and infinite magnitudes of the offset quantities are possible between both of these limits.

Fortunately, we can however call on a moment that enables us a distinct determination of the monopoly price; and with its help, an exact theory of the monopolistic formation of prices has developed itself even in spite of this circumstance, yes, it showed itself to be especially fruitful and allows for the application of exact methods and the gain of exact results, even to a greater extent than the theory of the competition price; it was even correctly depicted much earlier than this one. The reader is to be directed especially to A. Marshall's depiction. Let us grasp the matter in the following manner: It is very clear that we, if the monopoly price, the price that the monopolist actually wants to demand, would be given to us, derivate the quantities of the monopoly good that would be offset at this price with the help of our system of equations, could respectively prove its distinct determination. So if we have it, then everything is all right; in the worst case, we could therefore still then say something about these processes, if we had to regard the monopoly price as a datum; the performance of our system of equations reduces itself to this "something," but it does not *completely* fail: How much every individual will acquire at that price of the monopoly good and how the marginal utility niveaus of all individuals—including that of the monopolist—would form themselves, could still be said, and I make it a point to emphasize that this is by no means *nothing*.

However, as we said, we can also, with the help of a hypothesis derivate a monopoly *price* itself that distinguishes itself among all *possible* monopoly prices that are strictly speaking for the purpose of our system of equations, in that it actually will frequently exist, and even more frequently will be sought after, and that it, even if the monopolist were to decide on another for some reason, will always be the one that one compares every other one to, and that one regards as *the* monopoly price.

χατ' ἐξοχήν

This hypothesis is that the monopolist seeks to turn his "proceeds" into a maximum. One must be mindful that we by no means claim that this striving is "natural" or the rule. This would entirely contradict our principles. We only allow this tendency both of the mentioned characteristics, and only go on to say that they are sufficient in fixating one and only one monopoly price from them. The first should indeed be sustainable, and we will immediately prove the latter. One therefore sees that we in no way misjudge the fact that ethical moments, encroachments of the authority of the state, and considerations for the future could cause the monopolist to demand another price, but at the same time, that such influences also do not take every meaning from our raisonnement. It must be emphasized after all that a *new* hypothesis lies here, since this is often overlooked: the parties concerned can only go under the competitive price if they want to conceive to sustain a *loss*—the monopolist could reduce his "monopoly price," if he only wants to make do with a *lesser gain*; and the fact that he does not do this is a continuing hypothesis, which effectuates that the results are far off from reality and are more difficult to verify than the ones of our first system of equations; the competitive price cannot be *exceeded* because no one would pay a higher one—the monopolist *can* exceed that "monopoly price," although this causes him damage.

However, if one makes this hypothesis, then one can derivate a distinctly determining price. This can easily be shown, even without higher mathematics, although the same becomes indispensable for further conclusions from it. But we do not want to elaborate on this, and want to content ourselves with the evidence in its simplest form. It should hereby for further simplification also be assumed that the monopoly good costs the monopolist nothing, is therefore a "gift" of nature, such as a mineral spring. Incidentally, such a simplification by no means voids our results, but rather only serves to let a principle come forth clearly and simply, wherefore it makes little sense to smile about such constructions of the theorists or to consider them to be practically meaningless. The Robinson, the meteor, our mineral spring, these are only embodiments of methodological measures, which ease the understanding and solely represent an accommodation towards those laymen, which are then the most suitable to scoff at it.

Now, there is surely always a price for our monopoly good that is exactly so high that the demand for it stops. If the monopolist could offset his good or even just a portion of the same at this price, then he would make a large gain; but as it stands, he would offset nothing, and his proceed is therefore zero. If he would demand *no* price at all, meaning the price is zero, then he would perhaps become free of his entire inventory, which would be quite good in itself and if he were to get *something* for it, but under the given circumstances, it would again lead to the proceed being zero. A continuous line of decreasing prices and another of increasing sales now leads from the first price to the second. The reduction of the gain of the unit and the increase of the number of offset units are two reasons for the determination of the proceeds that counteract one another, which is always given by the price of the product multiplied by the sales. The decreasing of the price from that highest level will initially increase this product; but if one continues with this then it will eventually sink. And a maximum value of the same therefore lies between it, a maximum of proceeds. If this should not seem convincing, then it can, however, only be proven with the help of Rollesch's phrase, but we want to content ourselves with it.

This evidence shapes itself entirely analogously for the case that the production of the monopoly good carries a fixed price, not with the quantity of the product varying sum of costs, and *similarly*, when the costs are a function of the produced quantities of the same. However, we do not want to elaborate on this, and also not examine this interesting case that is present when there are still "small" competing sellers next to a large monopolist (as for example the Standard Oil Co.), a case that has a special, practical meaning lying ahead of it. Finally, let it additionally be remarked that everything that has been said also applies mutatis mutandis for the purchasing monopoly.

In this sense, there is therefore also a distinct determining *monopoly* price. But one cannot forget that this sense is different from the one in which we speak of a distinct determining competitive price. One sees this especially clearly when one considers that we could still make other hypotheses in place of ours, for example, according to Marshall's process, the one that the monopolist wants to make his profits to a maximum and other things more to that of the "buyers." All these hypotheses would lead to different and also distinct determining process, without one of the same being able to claim advantages. The force of the facts pulsates stronger in our derivation of the competitive price, something arbitrary undeniably clings to the monopoly price. However, there is much to be said for the hypothesis that was adopted by us; with the same picture, one could say that one feels the pulse of the economic life better in it than in the others; and we certainly believe that one can content oneself in it on the whole. We put so much emphasis on this aspect of the matter only because it is important to us here to go forth entirely certain, and to critically light our path step by step. But of course, one will not be allowed to overestimate that, which our hypothesis can achieve. Since it is still to be added that because of the social meaning that befits many monopolists, encroachments of the political force and also other "interrupting" moments play a greater role here than for the economy of one of many competing individuals, which is but a drop of water in a sea. It also brings the magnitude, power, and secured position, furthermore, also the far-seeing, more capable administration of many monopolies—especially those of the modern trusts, etc.—with it, that the future and conscious maneuvering in its pricing policy stands out much more than in a large quantity of competitors who only do what they must to a higher degree, follow the flow of events to a higher degree, and whose trading is forced more by the circumstances—is pushed more than it pushes—which of course facilitates its description. All of this is different for large monopolists, although one must be aware of fearing this moment too much. But then the pure, static theory will very often accept the *actual* monopoly price as a datum, will have to forego its explanation, and it is beneficial for it that even then, as mentioned, we are still in a position to allow an interest, which, even though it is lesser, it is still relevant.

III

But we must unfortunately still go further: Also in the case of *limited* competition, meaning when there is in fact more than one, but only few "dominators" of an article that are independent of each other, the matter is principally the same or even worse for the theory, as is the case for the monopoly. And this is now something completely new to most economists; even the mathematicians among them misunderstood this, especially their great Pionier Cournot. Nothing is more typical than one already speaking of free competition if for example only two sellers appear on the tarpaulin. And in fact, must they not limit themselves to the compensation of their costs through mutual underbidding? One answers this by stating that this would be handled very clumsily, since they, even if they do *not* do this and do not arrange to meet, could secure the advantages of the monopolist position—which would however spread onto them. It is therefore not so self-evident that they will so readily underbid each other up until that point. But such a tendency will surely exist, since everyone will seek to rob another of his clientele. But they will presumably become aware of the lost profit much sooner, before this effect has occurred, and if no prospect or intent exists to destroy the competitor, even stopping without any agreement or to even seeking back. And this is why there will be no resting point, no more than a momentary, "labile" equilibrium. This explains some very strange side leaps of many prices to us, which, before Professor Edgeworth [1] clarified this point, seemed to mock every theoretical ascertainment. But if this is an enrichment of our knowledge, then it does also show us that there are prices that are simply *not* distinctly determined. And this lies in the matter here, not in the deficiencies of our picture—which is of course a comfort in a certain sense—so that no helping hypothesis can bring us any further.

There are also other similar cases. The exchange between two monopolists or two isolated economic subjects belongs here. Their estimates of the goods that are to be exchanged form <u>*limits*</u> for this price within the same, but it is indeterminate. This is also often misunderstood, but not as often as the just mentioned facts. Since no one can underbid the opponents, no reason exists as to why the "reciprocal marginal utility relationship" should be determinant of the price. *This* price would of course make the profit of both a maximum, and if one puts the mutual advantage above the individual one, then the price would be distinctly determined. If we wanted to assume this, then this would however represent a further hypothesis, namely a much bolder one than the one that helped us to determine a monopoly price. One could not say that it suits *frequent* processes, but it would rather practically always assume a far-reaching altruism on *one* side—if we would like to make use of this expression—or—if we want to be more concrete—only describe exceptions. But if we do not make this or a similar hypothesis, then our problem is so to speak twofold indeterminate as opposed to the problem of the monopoly price, where at least an under or overbid occurred on one side.

The same applies in essence if more than two opponents confront each other. The limits within the ones where the price must be then become narrower—more and more narrow, the more opponents emerge—but it is therefore still not distinctly determined. There the question is raised: What is actually necessary so that "free competition" exists? In one sense, we said in a previous spot that it already exists when only a few or even only two individuals unaffectedly barter. But this was only one side of the matter—it affected the lack of "cause for interruption." In this sense, one could also speak of free competition in the economy *of one* individual.[2] But its further assumptions are, conceived very precisely, the following.

Firstly: The number of opponents must be very large, strictly speaking, our "*m*" must immediately be infinite. Because the interval in which the price must lie only then becomes so small that it can be considered as a point.

Secondly: all goods must be indefinitely divisible, and no current market quantities may exist which cannot be bartered.

Thirdly: *every* individual must be able to barter with everyone, otherwise submarkets would form within the market, which would have to make our first assumption illusionary; and no individual may be so powerful that he, even if others have the same good to offer or to demand, can pursue monopoly policy.

It is self-evident that no agreement between the economic subjects may exist; however, the lack of considerations of others, etc., and total awareness of the economic interest, as well as the will to only promote them is not necessary: With regard to the latter point, we believe, as opposed to most authors, that these things can be partially included in the demand function, partially—as misapprehension, etc.—can simply be disregarded, without significantly influencing the usefulness of our picture.

The result that we reach is in some degree surprising: not only does free competition never and nowhere exist; it *can* not exist at all, conceived in the sense of the theory. What do we want to think of this now? However, the matter is not as bad as it appears to be. It just also shows itself in our field, which also applies to *all* exact sciences, that our exact system, correctly depicted and thoroughly thought through, is just an unrealistic entity. This does not hinder that it nevertheless goes well with reality. Our knowledge may estrange further circles and also repel many comrades of our discipline. But whoever loves and knows exact science will hardly wonder about this, nor therefore also doubt the economy. It is my task to state the weak points more precisely and to place special emphasis on them; but this does not hinder me from trusting our science.

One must certainly warn about the thin areas in a sheet of ice where we amuse ourselves, but it would be absurd to give up ice skating on their account. That, which is said is a memento for some theorists, to not feel too safe and to give up a warning, the illusion that the theory is dead certain, so to speak. But it does not justify the position of their opponents. Yes, we can say that our conceptions concerning this matter are more epistemologically interesting than they are of practical meaning; they do not change the fact that despite everything, our system is based on a wide base, and despite everything, it is an admirable construction that proves itself to a broad degree.

This is all that we would like to say about the foundations of the pure price theory. It is only a little. But we cannot offer more, and this "more" would have to also only primarily be a presentation. Rather exact knowledge of the accomplished things is necessary for the understanding of this paragraph; only he who is familiar with the modern price theory will be able to overcome the concerns that are highlighted by us. We only want to mention one more point before we leave this field, which would be so worthy of a deeper study.

IV

This point is the following: We have said that the price must be equal to the reciprocal value of the marginal utility relationship of the exchanged goods for every economic subject and every good, at least generally speaking. However, something else must still be added in order for our marginal utility niveau to emerge. It does not suffice that that formula is realized for every individual good; in fact, the prices *of all* individual goods must furthermore stand in a certain relation to one another, namely also behave just as the marginal utility of the goods to which they apply. This in itself does by no means already lie in that of the first sentence if one states it as we just did, but rather forms a further requirement of the state of equilibrium. Of course up until now, we have meant *both* things when we spoke of the marginal utility niveau, but we want to now emphasize that strictly speaking, both requirements are to be separated. One easily sees this if one observes the changes in quantities of each good: If an economic subject first exchanges a good *A* for a good *B*, and then a good *C* for a good *D*, then the exchange relation of *A* and *B*, and that of *C* and *D* must certainly be equal to the reciprocal value of the marginal utility relation of *A* and *B* in the first case, and of *C* and *D* in the second case. But a correlation between these two exchange relations does prima vista not appear to exist. One of such only then emerges when we use one and the same measurement for both cases. If we do this in the manner that we assume that our individual only exchanges one good, for example *A*, for *B* and *D*—then both cases can be compared. If *one* unit of *B* "costs" him *three* units of *A*, and *one* unit of *D four* units of *A*, so if the price of *B* in *A* is equal to three, the one of *D* in *A* equal to four, so then, if these are supposed to be equilibrium prices, the marginal utility relation of A and B must be equal to one third, that of *A* and *D* equal to one fourth. But one also sees that the prices of *B* and *D* in *A*, three and four, must behave in the same way as the marginal utility of *B* and *D*, therefore also as three to four. Otherwise, a resting state would not eventuate. In fact, let us assume that the prices of *B* and *D* do not behave this way, but rather for example, as three to six, while the marginal utility relation of *B* and *D* remains without change equal to three quarters, and let us see what will happen. If our individual only sells one unit of *D*, then it will be able to obtain two units of *B* for one "proceed" of *A*, consequently make a larger profit then if it had kept that unit of *D*. It will therefore do this, and will not satisfice itself until such a profit is no longer able to be made, therefore that relation between the prices of both goods is realized.

Now the question is raised: can such a case even occur, can it happen that for the attainment of the maximum utility that is possible under the given conditions such an *acquisition of goods* becomes necessary *solely for the purpose of further exchange*? Certainly. Why should it not be able to happen that the prices of the good *B* and *D* determine themselves with "*3 A*" and "*6 A*" on the market, while there are individuals whose marginal utility relation between the goods *B* and *D* are equal to three quarters? And all these individuals, furthermore all who find themselves in ANALOGOUS cases will then be in a position to advance to that state, which our law of the marginal utility niveau portrays, through the direct exchange of goods that they own for those that they wish to acquire. They must and will in fact acquire quantities of goods that they do not need, solely in order to exchange them for those that they actually need. That relation between the prices, which is required for the existence of our maximum utility, can only be attained through this process. We readily see that this case must be an extraordinarily more frequent one and the indirect exchange must therefore be a necessary element of the mechanism of every market, in which more than two goods are exchanged. One could say that no free competition could be in such a market without indirect exchange, that it necessarily belongs to its existence. *In most cases by far, there must therefore be a demand for goods—one or more—which does not explain itself through "needs," but rather more specifically through the technical necessities of the market's mechanism.*

This result is extremely important, not only because it illuminates an essential moment of the exchange processes, but also because it allows for a very meaningful use. We now come to this latter one in the next chapter. The circumstance that that, which was said of my knowledge was only explained in front of us in the price theory by one theorist, namely v. Walras, who incidentally did not make this decisive implementation, explains so many a weak point in the economic teaching system of the present.

Notes

1. Teoria pura del Monopolio. Giornali degli Economisti 1897 (page 269).
2. It should be clear as to why all quantities of goods and "exchange relations" are determined in the case of the *isolated* individual. For further clarification, look at that, which is said about the law of the marginal utility niveau (Schumpeter, 1908, pg. 271).

4

Foundations of the Monetary Theory

I

Let us ask ourselves how that, which we just derivated corresponds to reality, then the answer is: the phenomenon of money. Now, this is not insignificant. The steep paths of the theory have in fact led us to a nice viewpoint there.

If we never conceal weak points of the theory, but rather continually guide the reader's attention to its deficiencies, then we are probably also allowed to point to a significant and valuable result of the same with satisfaction. And the matter could really hardly be more satisfying here from the theorist's standpoint. Our system yields entirely by itself, without every gimmick and without attracting new moments, an exhausting and satisfying explanation of an important economic emergence, which is so appropriate and clear that there is hardly anything left to ask about, of an emergence, which was the item of many speculations, yes, is perhaps the oldest component of the economy, without one having been able to come to secured results. It gives us all the same necessary moments for understanding, permits a large number of derivations from it, and spreads a bright light over the controversies that are here. All of this deductively arises from its foundations, and even though observations from reality for the verification, as well as for solving practical problems are of course necessary, the fundaments of the matter do immediately arise from our price theory; *even though the latter was by no means constructed with regards to the extraction of a monetary theory.*

This moment is especially important now. Had we initially contemplated the monetary theory and constructed assumptions for the purpose of observations from the field of finance, then it would have been no special achievement if statements about money would have arisen from it. One often said that exact theories and namely mathematical deductions only basically offer tautologies. This is *true* to a certain extent—even though a misunderstanding is partially in it, which we however do not want to further discuss—because the exact apparatus is surely only in a position to principally derivate the consequences from that, which one *gives* it. It is in a position to process its data, to present them in a new form, and new knowledge may lie in it *in one sense*; but in *another*, it is the data alone that contain the knowledge. One sees this in, for example, the price theory, and we therefore placed emphasis on describing the same solely as the method of the description of facts. It presents an abundance of facts that we must know in order to be able to construe it in a shorter and more correct way than direct description is able to do, but this is all for now. As to the monetary theory, we however see that this method can accomplish even more, can offer results that amount to or still come close to new discoveries, even if they are certainly only a consequence of observing facts in the last place.

In fact, the proof that indirect exchange/barter is something necessary, leads to the fact that there must be goods that one does not exchange for their own sake, but rather only to use them for further exchanging, consequently to the phenomenon of money. If we were to know nothing, have never heard that this phenomenon existed, then we could discover it by means of our theory. We could come to the result, solely due to theoretical contemplations, solely through discussing the equations of the exchange theory that something of that nature *would have to* exist. And we could also find the fundamental laws of the emergence, without glancing at the gearing mechanism of the monetary economy.

But since we are de facto very familiar with the fact of money, one could think that our "discovery" just is not great. But a bit of contemplation would show the superficiality of such a conception. Above all, this circumstance does not touch on the side of the matter in principle. It would still be a great success of the theory, still a nice piece of evidence for the value and the usefulness of the conception of our system, even if only something universally known were to come from it. The meaning of the same would in principle not be affected, and that "achievement" would always remain a meaningful moment for some opponents of the theory and a confutation of some well-known arguments of the same. Precisely the banality of a result is in the sciences of the trading of humans, whose task is the description and explanation of many things that are accustomed to everyday life, and do not seem to cause the "practice" problems, are in no way a demur of sweeping importance, but rather often simply an advantage than a criterion of reality for a result: the accent is placed on simply not extracting the same from everyday life, but rather derivating it from deeper, hidden sources. If it conforms so much to reality that it seems banal, then this is only evidence that truth flows from those sources. *Nevertheless*, because of this result we could say that our theory, even if not according to the level of development, but according to the essence, stands next to the system of mathematical physics whose representatives indeed also regard it as their proudest achievement when their theory immediately yields an emergence of reality that they did *not* have in mind when establishing the fundamentals. The best accomplishment of a theory always lies in an enrichment of knowledge through a reduction of an "unknown" to a "known," may the "unknown" also be very well "known" to everyday life in the scientific sense. An accomplishment of this nature makes an impression on further circles especially when—actually *only* when—a theory is validated through an emergence for which the latter is not the case, namely therefore when a "prophecy" is accomplished. Therefore the sensation that, for example, Leverrier's discovery made. The layman only then has the feeling that there really is "something behind" the abstruse equations of the exact sciences. However, this moment is irrelevant in principle and for science, as well as the question whether or not a scientific theorem allows technical uses. Although our result may now only be a modest one, it is in fact of similar type as the best achievements of the exact natural sciences, and the theorist certainly has very good reason to be very happy about his.

But it is then by no means self-evident, banal, or irrelevant, because it gives us, popularly speaking, the "essence" and the laws of motion of the money's value, and is the cornerstone of a valuable and viable theory of the first and only useful monetary theory—and therefore also an important argument for the benefit of our system of the pure economy altogether.

Therefore according to our conception, the monetary theory forms an integrating component of the system of the pure economy altogether, in the sense that it one cannot separate from the remaining parts of the same. That is to say that on one hand, it emerges from the price theory. The latter is essential for its understanding, and if one wants to write a monetary theory, then one cannot avoid first presenting the entire foundations of our system, not only in the same sense, in which one likes to say that one can never understand a theorem in itself and without the coherencies in which it stands, but rather in a much more direct one: it is simply impossible to cover the monetary theory "in itself." But on the other hand, the same is also *essential* to the understanding of the processes in a commerce economy. A very significant difference of the same compared to the isolated one lies in it. We cannot possibly completely understand it without the emergence of the indirect exchange/barter, since the processes would shape themselves in an entirely different way without it. So we do not have a choice of whether or not we want to cover the monetary theory here, rather, we *must* do it. This can, however, happen very briefly; only a few basic principles are supposed to be exposed, since a more complete explanation would lead us far outside of this work's framework. We only want to state a few questions about principles and point out the foundations and outlines of the monetary theory, more to show where our monetary theory differentiates itself from the common one, and how suitable it is in letting us understand the essence of the matter and putting us in a position to pass judgment on other theories, rather than saying everything that it allows us to say.

II

We want to first glance at the current stand of the monetary theory. The chapters that tend to convey this title in systematic statements, and also the monographic works about this topic that have lately accumulated in an almost conspicuous quantity in no way offer a pleasant view and everyone who thinks of this literature will surely be somewhat surprised, when we claim that the monetary theory represents such a great achievement of the theoretical economy. We then also hurry to explain that this does not apply to the usual approach to this field, but rather only to that, which the theory *could* be and certainly *will* soon be, to that, which the *economy* offers and not to that, which its *representatives* write. But this verdict does not hinder us in acknowledging that very many valuable accomplishments lie in the enormous literature about the monetary phenomenon. It is just that the same refer more to the solution of concrete questions of the monetary policy, etc. as we will soon see, and not to the theoretical foundations of the matter. And our criticism primarily has to do with the latter, whose brevity will hopefully not be construed as superficiality.

Above all, the monetary theory, as it is stated, forms nothing less than an integral component of the price theory. In fact, it has become typical to approach it entirely by itself, and to remove the "monetary veil" that encases the economical processes in pure-theoretical discussions. The latter is even regarded as a progress of the scientific view compared to that of the practical landlord. In fact, this approach has its advantages: certain basic principles can actually be quite good and presented much simpler if one disregards money, and it is also true that the opposite modus procedendi lead to several mistakes. But this changes nothing about the fact that a complete understanding of all processes cannot be attained in this way, and this view is only then strictly correct when one limits oneself to the "commerce-less" economy. The reason as to why one overlooked this is solely because one did not clearly recognize or did not adequately appreciate the fact of the indirect exchange, what was first reserved for the "mathematical method." Because of this, the anchor was missing that tied the monetary theory to the price theory, and it was therefore natural that the first seemed to be rather independent. Another disadvantage also came out of this and explained itself from it. One constantly explained the "introduction" of money out of convenience and said that "money" is produced in order to "facilitate" exchanging/bartering, in order to overstrain the exchangers of incommodity, to look for someone who is just in need *of the* good that they have to offer, and owns and wants to exchange just *that*, which they wish to acquire. The decisive point does not lie in it. Even if everyone could run into a suitable opponent without any difficulty, money, meaning indirect exchange would still be necessary. It depends on the *indispensability*, not the bare *convenience* of a monetary good for the mechanism of the market, and the key to understanding lies in it. This knowledge can not even be expressively found by L. Walras. Jevons had furthermore certainly introduced his monetary theory with an exchange theory, but he did not place emphasis on the decisive point. And the same applies to many accusations of our theory, which one can find here and there. Precisely that important point, that, as we saw, is also epistemologically as interesting and places the monetary theory into the correct relation to the price theory, is always missing to my knowledge.

So then the monetary theory only emerges as an annex of the remaining structure of our science, as a special theory about an emergence that must be explained, because it is also an economical one, but needs special aides in order to do this. So what is actually written in these independent monetary theories? They fall into two distinctly distinguishable components, into a fundament and discussions of practical questions. So what does the first contain?

The answer cannot be gratifying. We have here one of those chapters in front of us that do not bring honor to the national economy. In my opinion, the critic could not fail to have the impression that he learns rather little of value from it, and I believe not to profess too much when I say that his verdict can only be: a science that does not offer *more* is not worth the effort. And that of the theory will divert and lead him to the "study of facts" more effectively than all demurs in principle of the historians—without being able to tell him that he is wrong. The state of common place, the complete indifference that is a mark of that, which is offered—apart from the discussion of several practical questions—is a characteristic of monetary theoretical works, is an indisputable fact that is not made right by its authors occasionally emphasizing the difficulty and profoundness of the problems that they are dealing with.

But to the point! Most interpretations gush about the austere elements of theory that they bring to encase. The most comprehensive chapter by far in Jevon's "Money" is dedicated to the recital and discussion of all of those substances, from which "money" was ever produced. Such implementations must be deprived of any meaning, except for a certain culture-historical interest. What is supposed to be accomplished by this? Could one not just as well also discuss the different types of food and their advantages and disadvantages in the theory? Such things are however in every monetary theory, in Walker's, Helfferich's, de Foville's, Laughlin's, etc., just to name a few more modern ones. And not this alone. The same applies to impartations about technology of the character, and more about others. Which scientific knowledge is supposed to come out of this? At least the economical theory—I do not know whether another discipline—could not thereby gain the least, however. And with a regularity that one painfully misses for some fundamental theories, a point maintains to recur that I never hear or read about without sensing a lively feeling of humiliation; it is the discussion of advantages, through which the precious metals distinguish themselves and through which they especially put themselves forward as material of money. Yes certainly, they are very divisible, small quantities have large value, they do not change—but is it really our task to make statements of that kind, mind you, not as starting points of an exact thought process, but rather as interesting truths in themselves? If this were the case, then one could only draw that consequence from it, which the historians have already drawn. Jevons considered it useful to generally construct the desirable characteristics of the material of money: divisibility, probability, etc. We do not want to sneer at it out of respect for this brilliant theorist. But one can only regret such elements in our theory—this type of monetary theory is unfortunately not without analogies in other parts of the national economy—and one must hurry to say that they are foreign bodies that can be easily removed from it, basically do not belong into it at all and are without any connection to the rest.

Thereupon, a history of development of money maintains to be given to us, as to replace the missing explanation. How, where, and when the money was produced is very indifferent to the purpose of the theory from our standpoint, according to which the same deductively arises; but if one does not have such a derivation, then one must indeed examine those facts in order to come to an answer of the main questions through their observation. But one generally did not do this, rather, that, which claims itself to be a statement of fact, is a *hypothesis* that is supposed to simultaneously yield the monetary theory. No doubt can exist about it. If we hear that, when the exchange traffic began to develop itself more, "one resorted to reference means"… etc. in the well-known manner, then surely no result of prehistoric studies lies in it. Rather, we have one of those claims in front of us there, whose period of prosperity was *before* the occurrence of such studies, and which—incidentally more in that field, which one can call sociology than in the actual national economy—played a large and not always credible role, and almost reminds one of Rousseau. We of course are of the opinion that the criticism of such theories went way too far, namely overlooked the fact that many things, which were expressed in the language of the presentation of facts, are not to be understood as such, but certainly there is also much that is true in their demurs, and the demand of careful study of sources is not unwarranted. In any case, the meaning of such a hypothetical history of development reduces itself to an attempt to generally and convincingly define the essence and the role of money at all costs.

Then these are the definitions that remain when one removes all that is foreign and all that is a limine unsustainable from the current monetary theory. It and the discussions that link themselves to it constitute their true foundation. One debates the question subsequent to them of what is to be regarded as money and whether "valueless" money is possible, which are its role and its surrogate. Only one more thing is added, which is however something very important. It is the quantum theory, which forms the only constituent part of the monetary theory that—whether true or false—really says something. One has not come out above it. Reasons for and against the same accumulated more and more, but one has not yet come to solving the questions that it poses, and especially to a new theory, which could replace it. The matter is as many other ones in our field: no one is satisfied with the existing one, but no one knows how to improve it, and a discussion whose defectiveness is actually perceived by everyone drags itself away without an end.[1] Many are of the opinion that the quantum theory has been overcome, but one could not cut oneself off from it after all, and a reaction in its favor has been introduced especially in most recent times. Its opponents ("credit theory of money" among others) and some attempts in most recent time were much less fortunate, which we do not want to go into. But be that as it may, no one has ever claimed that the quantum theory contains a complete explanation of the phenomenon of money, and one can therefore say, without having to fear much opposition, that the national economy neither commands a monetary theory, nor has it ever commanded one.

III

We only want to briefly indicate the direction in which one of such in our opinion must be sought, whereby we will also come to still speak of some of the common theories here. There are only a few fundamental statements through which, as we hope, the monetary theory can be placed onto new and viable foundations.

As we said, the indirect exchange is the corner stone of the explanation. As soon as more than two goods are supposed to be exchanged between more than two individuals, acts of exchange will take place whose purpose is the acquisition of goods for further complete or partial exchange. Every good that is a thing of such an act of exchange is in so far money, therefore fulfills a solely technical function in the service of the market's mechanism, meaning the one that is currently and since a considerable time fulfilled by "money" in the popular sense of the word.

It is now in our option to limit the scientific content of this term to the latter, so therefore to current money that is mostly minted by the state anyway, and a discussion about it would just be a debate. This would surely not change anything about the essential connection of this government/public money with the emergence that we just spoke of, but it does recommend our terminology to us. However, to only place importance on this formal moment for the scientific explanation would obviously be so superficial that we would not have uttered a word about it, if it had not actually happened. But regardless, there is still no occasion for a special "rebuttal." Rather, we will see that something can be said for this opinion from another standpoint, which of course does not justify the fact that the essential point is thereby overlooked.

So we stated the first fundamental principle of the monetary theory in which the explanation of the phenomenon of money's essence lies. The laws of the value of goods that serve as money follow directly from it. The possibility of exchange altogether alters the value functions of one of every good, as was formerly presented. It does indeed represent a special use of the same from the owner's standpoint. It is also easy to see *how* the value functions are thereby altered. One must introduce the values of those goods that *can* be exchanged for the pertaining goods and from these again those that are actually *being* exchanged into the value functions of the first, in the manner as we have shown.

The same applies to a good that not only determines the exchange, but has rather already been acquired for this purpose to a much higher degree. The indirect exchange therefore causes a further alteration of the goods' value functions, which are used for its implementation; the reader can explain to himself in what manner this is done. However, the indirect exchange also influences the values in another way, this time not only the value *functions* of those goods. You see, the tendency lies in it to strip the same ones from their use, which they are directly suited to serve. When there are of course many of such goods, this will occur less; however, if the practice to only use one or only a few goods for the implementation of the indirect exchange exists, then relatively large quantities can be constantly stripped from the actual use of the same, as *is* the current case for the precious metals and surely WAS the case for all goods that typically served as "money." This has the consequence, as does every limitation of a good's quantity, of increasing its marginal utility.

Both moments are equally important, even though only the latter cherishes to be emphasized. Both show themselves most clearly when only one single good is used as money, although they have the same effect in principle. In this case, the value functions of all goods, including the ones of its own use, are so to speak reflected in the value functions of the same, and the one that is quantity that serves as money can be distinguished from it at every given moment, although in constant interaction with the one that serves the direct use. The entire monetary theory lies in nuce in these sentences, and a simple discussion and development of the same gives us a rich harvest of knowledge of the phenomenon of money.

Of course, we can only say little here. But before we do that, something else must be said, something that we can in a certain sense consider being the other corner stone of the monetary theory.

You see, we need a measurement of value in order to be able to compare variables of value. The possibility in principle of one of such was stated in the first part of this work. There, it was also said how we exactly determine our value functions: namely in the manner that we "retrieve" it from each of the individuals. The answers will be given to us, expressed in "quantities of another good" so that the unit of this—arbitrary—good served us as a measure of value. The good that now serves as "money" is suited for this role just as well as any other, yes, it recommends itself for obviously practical reasons in choosing the same for doing this. It is reclusively infinitely important, and I think it is important to recommend this truth warmly to the reader, in spite of its brevity in which I mention it, that both, the function of a good as a means of exchange and the function as a scale for value *are to be strictly separated: Both functions are completely different according to their essence, do not have anything to do with one another in principle, and are completely separable in particular*. We can use "money" as a means of exchange, and nevertheless all goods, let us say to value them in apples, without this having any difficulty in principle. In fact, both are occasionally separated: if a specific good has a special meaning to someone, then he will be inclined to value every other one in units of the first, even though the money good is another one. The poor father occasionally expresses his valuations in units of bread, the theater enthusiast in theater tickets. As scarce as the practical meaning of these cases may be, they do show that such a separation is possible.

To me, this knowledge now seems to be of fundamental importance for the correct understanding of the phenomenon of money, and its deficiency to be the cause of some misunderstandings. One needs the term "money" occasionally for one, occasionally for the other of both functions, and mostly for both. It thereby happens that one uses sentences that are correct for one for the other; at any rate, a really clear conception is not possible, as long as one throws both together. We only want to get to know some of the cases where this distinction is *practically* important in the following.

The monetary theory as a scale of value and the monetary theory as a means of exchange are two completely separate things. Here first a few sentences about the first one: the fact that a good is chosen to be a scale of value does not have—as opposed to it's choice of means of exchange—the slightest influence on its "value." If I, psychologically-speaking, assume the enjoyment as a unit of my valuations that the consumption of an apple per day under *otherwise given* conditions provides me with, namely therefore for a soundly given consumption and production combination, if I, according to this, set up all goods that I own or can acquire in "values of apples," then this does not change anything about the magnitude of enjoyment.

The following is to be thereby considered: I may say that a quantity of any good, for example one thousand of such "values of apples" is equal to me. Perhaps I do not even own one thousand apples. And *if* I were to own them, then I would value every one of them far less than *one* of them, so that my measurement of value would thereby change. On account of the marginal utility that one apple would *then* provide me with, I would have to appraise that quantity of goods at perhaps 1 million apples, etc. But my earlier appraisal did have a good purpose. Of course, if one were to express it in the following manner: "That quantity of goods is worth one thousand apples to me," then this could lead to misunderstandings, in any case to ambiguities. But I just cannot express myself in this manner, if I want to say only *that*, which is talked about here. But if I say: "The enjoyment that the consumption of the quantities of goods provides me with is one thousand times as big as that, which the consumption of the one apple per day provides"; or "In the extreme case, I would give ONE THOUSAND TIMES THAT APPLE for that quantity of goods," then the matter is all right and does not require a further statement. The reader is now in a position to make another correction to our construction of the value functions, which we would abstain from doing in your position, so that our exposition is not burdened with a moment that could have not been stated there yet.

Let us go on. It has become common, especially in English literature, to differentiate four functions of money. The same are characterized by four words: means of exchange, scale of value, and two that I better leave translated, namely store of value and standard of deferred payments. We are now in a position to evaluate the same. We have just discussed the first two; they are of fundamental importance, but of completely different essence. Only the first one *necessarily* fulfills money, the latter probably does as a rule, but not always. How are the other two? One can surely also store wealth in another way than in money. Every good that is not subjected to perdition is in principle suitable for it. Another explanation is hardly necessary to see that this function is not an essential one. However, an important moment for the value of money lies in it, insofar as money actually fulfills it. Because by "storing," hoarding the money good, its available quantity gets lessened for circulation and other uses. This is certainly not without meaning; it is not of importance in principle for the foundations of the theory. The fourth function finally also does not contain an independent moment, but rather only highlights one of the cases for which a measurement of value is necessary.

We want to now lay two important questions before us through which we can show the fruitfulness of our theory. They are firstly, the question of whether "money" can consist of a substance that has no "value of use," and secondly, the one of how a multiplication of money affects its value. These questions have placed a significant role in the history of the monetary theory and have an obviously practical significance, so that one can virtually consider the answer to them as being a direct touchstone of a monetary theory. Yes, one could say that solving them forms the primary task of the theory. The problems of paper money and the causes of the price movements are, as is known, the practical pinnacles of the same; problems, about which there is an entire set of literature that is partially of theoretical and partially of "descriptive" nature. Can our theory say something general about it, or can only the study of facts lead us to realization? We will see. But it is already clear from the start that we would also need *concrete* data for the analysis of *concrete* cases. This should not surprise us and is the same in all fields. It will only be able to involve a contribution to the general understanding of such problems altogether, and at the most, will be able to involve a theoretical foundation for the observation of concrete cases. Statistics and history must achieve everything else—and one can very well argue that precisely this "else" is the best part of the matter.

To begin with, a clear formulation of the matter due to what was said already suffices for the solving of that, which pertains to the first question. Above all, it must be emphasized that we do not speak of "credit money" *here*. A document that contains a promise of a specific sum of "money" can in general if its encashment is secured circulate just as well as "money" itself. We do not conceive them as "money of valueless substance," but rather only as actual money, therefore things, which fulfill the role of money simultaneously through their own power and without backing up their value on other things for which they represent a payment slip.

Let us clearly distinguish between money as a means of exchange and money as a scale of value again. Surely only something that has value itself can serve as a scale of value. This is almost too obvious to require an explanation. In order to be able to compare the different goods with one another, one must bring them down to a common denominator; a unit of value is necessary for it; and whatever one chooses this unit of value to be, it must always be a value. In order to remain in the psychological manner of expression: it would be possible for me to choose any feeling of value of a specific intensity for the unit of value of my goods, only if I am able to adequately hold on to the same, in order to constantly have it at present. The same would not have to be adequate for any economic good, but could have been taken from anywhere. So I can therefore also exactly measure the ordinates of my value functions *somehow*, without the gestalt of the latter changing because of it, because only the relationship of the ordinates to one another matters. Yes, even simple ratios could provide this for me, as we have already seen, but their unit will constantly represent a specific, although arbitrary value. So if one calls the scale of value "money," then *this* money cannot lack a foundation of value.

Now money as a means of exchange can also not do without one of such; because it could otherwise not stand in specific exchange relations to other goods. But this only means that the conception of something "of value" combines itself with it, but not that the substance, which it consists of and that actually circulates, must itself have value. A piece of paper with which the conception of the value of a sheep is associated can in itself, provided the necessary requirements, circulate just as well as the "sheep" itself if only these papers are not available in a larger amount as the real sheep. Then one will as a rule, if it concerns the use of the sheep for indirect exchange, acquire those papers instead of real sheep. And in it—in this differentiation between *value of substance* of money and *relation to value*—lies the answer to our problems. It is hereby clear that any regulatory power must watch over it, that many of such papers are not arbitrarily produced, and in this sense, one can say that money of such nature can only exist within the state. The popular question of whether paper money is "money" can therefore be affirmed.

And now to the second problem that we want to solve: how does the multiplication of money affect its value? The distinction between measurement of value and means of exchange is even more important here.

If my ownership of that good increases whose marginal utility serves me as a measurement of value, how does that affect the latter? Very simple: this marginal utility will sink, and my measurement of value will therefore become insofar smaller, the expressions of numbers of my estimates will become insofar larger, but not in every relationship that would be expected according to the quantum theory, namely proportionally to the growth that my ownership of that good experiences, but probably in another that is given by my marginal utility scale.

But we can also adopt a question that leads us to the answer to the quantum theory. I can measure my ownership of goods by means of an arbitrary unit of value. Now, if I, for example double the number of the same, what I am indeed at liberty to do, and do not change anything essential on my estimates whose purpose only exists in fixations of relationships, then my unit of value will naturally sink to half of its former size, and the expression of numbers of my estimates will double. And this is now the right core of the quantum theory; a final verdict about it readily arises or nevertheless the principle of a final verdict—other moments would still be necessary for an exhausting evaluation, which we cannot go into here: It is correct in its most inner being, and in the manner which z. B. J. S. Mill meant; but also self-evident and no further interesting; that, which it furthermore says does not have to necessarily be *wrong*, but it still is nevertheless incomplete and must be treated with great care. It could certainly be that that correct core maintains itself better in practice than one would like to believe, and furthermore, that it *seems* to maintain itself *even* better than it actually does; and the latter applies to the quantum theory in my opinion. But the objections that it is purely extrinsic and superficial and does not trace back to the foundations of the price theory, furthermore, that it, in at least its rigorous form, maintains itself in only one—and of little importance—relationship, should hardly be refuted.

How does the multiplication of the *means of exchange* of "money" affect its value? Here we must again differentiate between the increase of the good's quantity that the foundation of value of the means of exchange delivers and its potential "money character" *without* such of the good that they refer to. We have two types of effects before us in the first case. Firstly, the value and price of that good will sink, therefore, the prices that are expressed in the units of the latter increase, namely for the demand scales that exist for this good. Thus far, the change of the price niveau will be solely nominal. But secondly, another effect will still emerge. You see, if the increase occurs imbalanced, for example, only occurs for a portion of our economic subjects, which must be the most common case by far, then at least a displacement in the buying power of the same will first occur. All of those who command a steady income will at first be at a disadvantage, and production as well as consumption will seek to pursue a different path. However, a reaction against this process will soon arrive, but until this happens, such fundamental changes of the national economy's former state could already have occurred, so that a return to the same is impossible.

Let us now look at another case. In order to stay with our example, new pieces of paper will be emitted, which should embody the value of individual sheep, whereas up until now, only as many were available, as there were real sheep. What will the effects be? For now, we will look at both of the ones that were mentioned, so that this "emission" functions insofar as an increase of the available sheep. The price of the sheep will sink. The price that determined itself for the same, as only so much units of paper money circulated as there are sheep was already smaller than that, which would have existed if there would not have been paper money, but the sheep would indeed have been means of exchange; because this function would have partially deprived them of another use. But now, after the quantity of paper money was increased even further, it will happen even less that sheep will be used as a means of exchange, wherefore the quantity that was available for other purposes of the same will increase and its value and price will therefore sink. *The emission of paper money therefore diminishes the value of the good in which the same is made out*, and with it, we have worked out one of the reasons of its devaluated effect on "money" altogether—including paper money itself. This effect also pertains to credit money of all sorts, including book credit, insofar as it is not "fully covered."

The second cause of the devaluation, which also applies to "credit money," as different this position in other relations may be, lies in the following moment. The increase of buying power, which those economic subjects, who profit directly or indirectly from that emission of paper money, experience, naturally—this would at least have to be this way in an otherwise static state, whereby we readily admit that we can only conceive such processes within static to the slightest degree—allocated lesser and lesser intensity to the satisfaction of needs, from which a further sinking of money's marginal utility follows in a very obvious way that is of course accompanied by an increase of this marginal utility for those economic subjects who do not take part in this advantage. It can hereby occur that the value of one unit of paper money also sinks under the value of the good's unit that it refers to, without the intermediating of the moment of mistrust in paper money, which we disregard, however important it may be in practice: The latter will then completely disappear from circulation and will solely be added to its other uses, but the value of paper money will be completely independent in this case.

We will incidentally not be surprised if a money good has a much higher value than it would befit from the value of the substance that it is made of. In this case, the entire supply of this good will be brought into the service of circulation and the value will only be measured accordingly, a case that has probably never occurred in this form, but was able to be repeatedly observed in another—you see, if a gathering of further quantities of a money good from other uses was not possible, meaning by "cessation of free coinage."

We want to be satisfied with this. I do not believe to claim too much when I say that all necessary elements for a natural, as well as clear, solution to all problems that pertain to the phenomenon of money lie in these executions. Of course, not all difficulties in the few remarks that allowed me to make these limitations that are in this work could be eliminated. But the way in which one must search for their elimination, in which one will also run into a solution to the problem of the bimetallism, should nevertheless be clarified. And if this is the case, then this cannot remain without influence on the evaluation of our exact system. The historian as well as the practitioner must actuate theory more than just anywhere in the field of money. The slightest assumption about the effect of this or that monetary rule of measurement more or less, unavoidably involves "theory." It lies in the nature of the matter to, even in the driest presentation of facts of the history of money, in the meaning that is adjudicated to this or that emergence, that there must be hypotheses that one can neither let go of without also letting go of the pertaining section itself, nor being able to specify and justify accordingly without consciously or subconsciously, openly or enveloped stating one's position in the questions of the monetary theory. A serious warning follows from it.

Note

1. The reasons against it always remain the same, while the positive statements of the quantum theory, especially in England, show some progress in formulation and advocacy. An attempt—or rather three—was also made in examining it in the facts, it was done—of course, with a negative result; a verification of the manner that was attempted *had to* fail (Schumpeter, 1908, pg. 285).

5

The Theory of Economizing

I

We would like to go another step further and attempt to introduce an emergence into our system that greatly occupies the national economists, namely economizing. The very first thing that we want to direct the attention of the reader to is again our way of proceeding. And we thereby claim, again as usual, that not only something of our own lies in the same, something that would only have meaning for this book and would only be determined through our own methodological conceptions, but rather that our modus procedendi lies in the essence of the matter and is solely expressed in it, which *all* do. We only specify the common method and attempt to show what its true nature is, free from obscurities and embroidery. This should help us in gaining a verdict about it, what is to be thought of it, what it achieves or can achieve, and where the limitations and requirements of its usefulness lie. We want to see what the static economy can do for this problem and how it can do it, and which value pertains to that, which maintains to be written about it in theoretical works.

In my opinion, an interesting contribution to the epistemology of our discipline and to the understanding of its essence and its results thereby arises, yes, a contribution to the knowledge of the essence of all theory altogether. We always emphasize indeed that it makes little sense to discuss the same in general, but can rather only lead the work of concrete problems to a realization of actual value. Only *this one* can lead us to actually understanding something about the matter, and one only gains a verdict *in retrospect to theoretical experience*, if one may so express oneself, that makes sense. The same then attunes by itself as one of the fruits of labor, and no longer requires general justifications; it is not as plain and simple as all the generally accepted ones maintain to be, and cannot be made as easily plausible to the layman; but it also *otherwise* outclasses them that the same only look like supplemental "apercus" next to it, where that, which is true and false can be seen as clearly as oil and water in a glass.

That point that is so methodological interesting for our current topic is the following. We have seen an example of a deductive—and nevertheless very valuable—knowledge in the monetary theory, and have therefore found it in practice and not through a priori statements, that could possibly lead to new, meaning not already contained in their assumptions, truths that are in the best position to show us a study of facts. We will now get to know an example of a theory that is in fact exact, but is also of an entirely different nature, that can be so to speak inductively introduced into our system from the outside, at least to a certain degree, due to new facts. Once it is introduced into the system, once these facts are stylized in a way that this is possible, then this type of theory does not differ from the other one at all, and the fleeting observer can easily overlook the difference between the two. This is practically also not a great misfortune, but here, where we want to thoroughly look at the theory, the same is fundamental. And in my opinion, it is a very fortunate coincidence that two instances for two entirely different accomplishments of our theory succeed one another here.

What do the national economists tell us about the phenomenon of economizing? Only a few[1] give an actual theory of the same; we want to immediately indicate wherein the same exists. Most tell us two things. Firstly, that it is well and good to economize, and that it is recommendable for everyone not to spend his entire income. The economical meaning of economizing is great, depends on the moral characteristics of the population, and so forth. Statistical data often complete these statements, which belong to those that we imperatively would like to be eliminated in the interest of our discipline's reputation. Secondly, one tells us—at least many national economists do this—that the economizing explains the formation of capital or of assets. This is certainly very important, and we have yet to prove this statement. One can say altogether that the theory of economizing forms one of the weakest points of the economy.

But we want to first develop the pure theory of economizing. Pay attention to how we thereby go about it. Economizing is surely an economic emergence of greater or lesser importance. We will therefore be desirous of allowing them into our system, *if this is possible*. It does not *have to be* possible by any means, and it can be accomplished in a very different way, if it can even be accomplished; because it does not enable us to assume from the start that our formal assumptions must suit every economical emergence, that each one of the same can be brought into our schema. This is in fact, also not the case for a row of important economical facts, and we have already been forced to admit that static only exhausts the *theory* of economics. Now, it could also be the case here that our approach is inapplicable. We would therefore not yet abolish the same, mindful of the services, which it is still in a position to give us, but to rather first regulate the fact of economizing to dynamic, and to disregard it in static. But even if it turns out that our static methods do not fail here, it will not follow from it that they necessarily cover the entire emergence and all their consequences. They can offer to tell us *something* about it and to fail *at other points*. Whether or not we will approach economizing in static in this case depends on the magnitude of this "something." We must thereby guard against two opposing mistakes. On the one hand, we cannot shy away from every difficulty that can perhaps be eliminated by a small artifice, but on the other hand, we cannot harm the facts: we cannot light-heartedly explain that economizing is for this or that reason not an emergence of the static economy, when we can indeed arrive at useful theorems. But we must also not insist on pressing an emergence into a schema, if it thereby loses its essential characteristics, if it cannot so to speak, live it up to the fullest even if we, in doing so, do nothing that is logically wrong. One sins in both ways. One often approaches emergences with methods whose assumptions barricade precisely the essence of the matter—we will come across an example in the theory of interest—and with which one only gains banalities or directly wrong results. And in the same manner, one probably simply explains that this or that emergence of the theory is unapproachable, whereby an attempt to use it would in fact be quite successful. There are no general rules for when one or the other is in place; this is a matter of discretion for the scientific competence. Just as the statesman must first proceed with an iron fist, then with a velvet glove, and an essential criterion of his talent lies in the right choice of one or the other proceeding, the theorist must also first safeguard his authority towards the facts, must master them to a certain degree, and must not let himself be overpowered by them, which, let us openly admit it can never happen without any arbitrariness—*no theory completely lacks arbitrariness*—he then must carefully and gently take its details into account. And also in both cases, the justification for the chosen way lies in the success, not in the general rules.

All that we can therefore do is attempt to see whether we can use our methods for the phenomenon of economizing and what comes out of it. So we want to do this. "To use our theories" means none other to use the *schema of exchange*. Can we do this? What is necessary for this purpose? The answer is simple: firstly, a "good," and secondly, a value function of the same characteristics as all the others. Regarding the first point, we must create and assume for our purpose a new "economical quantity," a new type of our system's elements, that our economic subjects also own "economizing funds" next to the goods that serve production and consumption, which can of course also be equal to zero—just as the quantities of each of their remaining goods. These economizing funds can exist in any goods; we will suitably comprehend them as sums of money. One immediately sees that this has no difficulties, and that we can so far place these new elements next to the old ones, without being modest. But the second point, the value functions of this new type of goods may cause a problem. The psychological national economist who bases the value functions on satisfaction of needs will have to establish an essential difference, since the economizing fund should not serve the enjoyment, which is at first revoked from it. One can therefore only explain its value by the satisfaction of current stirring of needs, if one does not want to speak of a special need of economizing. However, both ways are absolutely possible and make sense. Yet, we want to proceed in the same manner as we did for the construction of the other value functions, meaning we also want to retrieve the estimates of the individuals here for different large economizing funds, constantly proceeding from zero, and see whether the function attained in this manner also looks like all the others. It is clear that the first one is possible and the latter is the case. We do not want to bother with showing the closest one that also applies to the economizing money as a law of diminishing marginal utility, that every further increase is also estimated lower here than the one that is directly preceding and of the same magnitude, and that our individuals stop economizing at certain points under the same assumptions, which we have to make for other goods.

We can therefore conceive our economizing fund for our purposes in exactly the same way as other goods, and the economizing thus appears as an economic use of the available means, just as every other acquisition of goods. From that follows how easily one sees that we also stretch our law of the marginal utility niveau to economizing, and can speak of an exact exchange relation of the economizing fund to all other goods, therefore virtually of a price of the same. This will hopefully not cause any misunderstandings, even if we deny ourselves of elaborating on it. The essential result that arises from it is the distinct determination of the economizing fund of every economic subject. The mentioned moments do in fact suffice in exactly proving that the "economizing money" is available in a distinctly determining quantity within the national economy under given conditions and in every point in time, and is distributed among the individual economic subjects in a distinctly determining manner, and is also in an exact interaction with the quantities of all other goods through which it is determined and which it participates with, and contains a certain—"normal" or "necessary"—relationship to them.

That is all; the entire, pure, static theory of economizing lies in it. Is it worth something; is it especially worth the effort? It is certainly not without meaning, and one could highlight the same through a complete representation in a much more impressive manner than we are able to do here. The realization of the distinct determination of the economizing fund, its contingency through the other elements of our system, even the possibility itself to conceive it as a good as all the others—all of this is not without scientific value. Due to our theory, we could furthermore eliminate certain laws of motion of the economizing fund that are of the same nature as the other quantities of goods. But here in turn it must be admitted that we do not have *more* to offer, namely cannot make broad uses of our theory, which we still get to. We will have to again characterize it as a "matter of taste," whether one wants to think about it favorably or unfavorably. To have a preference or an aversion for exact reasoning will thereby play the primary role and whomever the one eventuality lets to be chosen for a conception or course of education and a circle of interest will have to remain conscious of the fact that his verdict, as all verdicts, only has subjective worth, even if it *insofar* certainly always is entitled to receiving attention. We will again emphasize this in summary at the end of this book.

Let us additionally remark that one could use the exact same process for other things and could also speak of a benefaction fund and suchlike. And the same relative interest and the same modest but not completely illusionary value of realization would also pertain to such theories, such as that of economizing. A possibility for the expansion of the field of the exact economy opens itself here, a view of further development. But we certainly do not think very highly of it. But let it be mentioned that the theory of economizing differentiates itself from these latter things through a moment that makes it *necessary* for the system of the pure economy, at least then, when the same is supposed to be sufficient for all requirements: Because in certain, more complicated cases it is seen that the economizing fund is necessary for distinct determination of the state of equilibrium. This belongs to the details of the mathematical theory, and we do not want to go into it here. But furthermore, we occasionally need the economizing fund when we study the effects of price movements, and will talk about this in the fourth part of this work.

But does the theory of economizing not have a use of upmost importance; does it not explain the formation of capital? Now, as far as our exact theory of economizing comes into consideration, the answer can only be flatly in the negative. We can already not explain how the economizing funds develop, we must rather assume them as being given and limit ourselves to examining, respectively proving their distinct determination in the state of equilibrium and their variations. And for the same reason as for all other goods: Because our static apparatus necessitates this. A transition from one state in which it would not be economized to one of such where this happens or where there is just a larger disposition to economizing in principle, presupposes a change in human nature, thus in *all* value functions, and is therefore just as unascertainable to us, as the transition to the production of goods that were unknown up to now, or to new economic methods. All of this must *be certain*, cannot change, as we have explained it. We cannot completely examine the uses of the economizing fund for the creation of means of production, etc. This would indeed result in a *development* to work towards a new cultural state in which everything is different. Our methods fail them, and even insofar as they do not, other things thereby come into the fore of interest, which are better suited for the other approaches. Only the saving of small sums, at least relatively smaller, whose investment is not considered and which do not essentially impact the course of the economy are possible in principle[1] in the static economy, otherwise it ceases to be static. Particularly the emergence of new "capitals"—and this applies to all meanings that this word can have—is such an essential "dynamic" moment, can only be approached in connection with the problem of the development to this extent that every attempt to press it into the framework of static can only deplorably fail. This is strikingly proven by the pure theoretical theories of capital formation, which are so undeniably unsatisfactory and give the historian so much to excuse himself for. *We* at least do not dare to take this step, even though our theory of economizing thereby unfortunately becomes restricted. We would rather like to admit that it only covers the economizing money "in the stocking," than to risk a fall into the water when fishing for problems of dynamic from the static shore. At least the little thing that remains for us is then irreproachable. And we are in fact left with *something*. The constant balance that we have in the open account of our bank—but not that, which we have in the deposit account, even if it is not invested at the moment—belongs here,[2] and many similar examples can be found. This differentiation is in itself also not with interest, and we must be thankful for our methods in leading us to the same one. But we cannot go any *further*.

A Note about the Theory of Capital Formation

Here we want to say a few words about the question of whether the emergence of economizing explains the capital formation. A theory of the latter is surely not possible in the framework of static and our remarks can therefore not actually be counted towards the subject matter of this book. But to calm ourselves down about the fact that we do not forego easily attainable realizations when we force this constraint upon ourselves, and furthermore in order to show the reader that static and dynamic do in fact sharply contrast one another and their differentiation is by no means a theoretical mood, in order to therefore also give that, which was said an undertone that is absolutely necessary for its complete understanding—we want to allow ourselves a brief digression for these reasons, and say quite a bit about a topic with which one could fill volumes. The brevity that is offered to us does not allow for meticulous correctness of expression and can easily cause criticism that would not have to fear a more complete representation. Here we invoke the generosity of the hopefully "suitable" reader.

In order to avoid the aggravating difficulties that lie around the term of capital, we want to split our question into two others: Does economizing explain the formation of "assets" in the popular sense of the word?; and does economizing explain the formation of capital, capital being understood as "produced means of production"? Only the consideration of facts can teach us this; especially for the first question. How do "assets" come into existence? Or where do those sums of money come from that one considers as "his assets" in usual life? One can fearfully especially answer, without opposition or having to give a long explanation, at least to the theorist of the discipline: These sums represent capitalistic income of constant sources of income. It is indifferent to our purpose, how this capitalization takes place and where the sources of income come from—whether they were acquired in a scientific or non-scientific way, for example through the giving of land. What interests us is the fact that such an asset was surely not "saved." Even if the source of income can be produced and can itself be ascribed to savings activity in some way; the sum that represents the asset is secured, not piled up through economizing; it has its origin in the mentioned process of capitalization.

A large, very large, number of assets surely emerged in this manner. By contrast, who could ever acquire a somewhat significant asset by saving a part of his daily expenses? Who even saves in this manner? The latter question is the more important one, since it is not useful to us in constructing a general rule about it, of who "can" economize, when the ones who it pertains to actually do not economize. We can at most give ourselves good teachings. Now, this question must be answered on the basis of observing facts. Here, I cannot present those materials that bring me to my answer, but I must rather limit myself to giving this one myself. However, I mean that it will sooner run into agreement than into opposition. You see, I believe that those people who have the greatest incomes do not "economize," but much rather the workers and mainly the middle classes. If the savings activity were to be a simple function of the size of income, then this would probably be different, although a point would also enter here for a very large income where the economizing would stop considering the indifference of acquisition, although the savings activity of the size of the income would also then surely not be proportional to other values—as is also well-known the case for other goods that the acquisition does not keep up with the growth of the acquirer's means. However, the savings activity is undeniably *no* such function of income. The moments of the social position, of the "obligations," of the demands of life, habits, etc., in short, the diversity of the assets of mankind and their social milieus hinder this, namely to an extent that does not make an abstraction from it *impossible*, but indeed *valueless*. To me, the facts of the case now seem to be—and we are currently not without static, as well as not without monographs about it, even though "more" would be desperately wished-for—that a high position and luxurious habits—a high standard of life—mostly do more than to balance the size of the incomes, and people with a large income, also apart from the pure theoretical moment of the sinking marginal value of the economizing fund, economize less intensively than those with a small one, yes, most often or in a very significant amount of all cases, *not at all*. And to me, it arose out of observations and considerations of this nature that economizing has a significantly lesser importance than a social emergence and than a principle of explanation of economic problems—even though it does still have a large one—than most of the economists care to accept. I can prove this just as little here, as I am able to present the rather far-reaching consequences of this point of view. I would like to rather remark that for me, new elements for a theory of capital formation, and even beyond this, for a type of theory of the economic development have emerged in this connection. And if this standpoint is right, will the methods of static, which teach us modesty and protect us from mistakes not prove themselves surprisingly well? Do we not discover unexpected agreement of the theoretical picture with reality?

But do assets not also emerge in a different way than through "capitalization"? Certainly, another important cause for their emergence is the trading profits. I use this expression here in the popular sense of the word and do not only understand coincidental and speculation profits by it in the narrowest meaning, but rather those "entrepreneurial profits" of every kind, from foundations, etc., which are knowingly much more significant than the pure theory would like to lead us to believe—especially because the competition is as good as never "free"—and which are the substance of many assets in a reachable manner. It is none of our business here of how they explain themselves, we will still speak of this in another part. They are here, and this should suffice for now. But now the question arises of whether economizing does in fact play a very essential role for the explanation of the formation of assets from these elements. As a matter of fact, one has claimed this. While a part of the theorists explained the formation of assets—actually the formation of *capital*, but this, as we will see shortly, amounts to the same thing for our purpose—from productive operation—industry—another has stressed economizing here and even others have united both moments. Nothing seems simpler than proving all three theories. If assets are supposed to emerge in this manner—therefore not through capitalization—then it must somehow be "produced"; of course, the "product" is likewise not allowed to be immediately consumed if assets are supposed to emerge; and it is therefore also ultimately self-evident that both—producing and not-consuming—must collaborate.

But is this "non-consuming" equivalent to "economizing"? One can certainly *call* it that, but the question is whether it is the same emergence, which we came across *here* and which we have approached in the *text*. The answer can only be in the negative. *There* we dealt with a saving of the usual income that the foundation of the standard of life forms the person concerned, *here* lays a profit that is outside of the usual budget and was never regarded as an actual element of income. *There* it dealt with the generation of a small reserve fund; *here* it deals with the generation of the foundation for new productions and consumptions, of a new approach to life. This differentiation is essential and I only regret not being able to present it more in depth. If one calls both processes "economizing," then one must say that the same has two different roles. But the moment of "economizing" only tells us something interesting in *one* case: It shows us a certain type of application of income; but only a banality in the *other* one: That no one or as good as no one immediately consumes his industrial profit. In this latter case lies all that is important in the moment of the acquirer: Such an earning is outside of the income, so to speak outside of the marginal utility niveau of that, which is earned, and its consumption, which would change the entire approach to life is mostly quite out of the question. It is not possible in static, in which everything is designated and free competition presses all profits down onto the costs; it is essentially a phenomenon of development. It is attained by extraordinary efforts, by an energy that wants to move forward and does not scrupulously search for a hedonistic equilibrium—we express ourselves so incorrectly because of the brevity—and which often obey other motives as an eudemonistic egoism. It is mostly self-evident that it is not "consumed." It was hardly ever acquired for this purpose. On the contrary, for the *static* income it is not self-evident at all that something is economized; because it is initially there for immediate satisfaction of needs.

We will now immediately evaluate the first of the three mentioned theories of capital formation more favorably. It really stresses the defining moment, and in it lies a much deeper knowledge as one should believe. The second theory, the "theory of economizing" of the formation of assets is also by no means banal. But it is wrong, as we will now see. But the third theory presents itself most unfavorably. We also see among other things why an "economizing Rothschild," whom we occasional run across in theory, so humorously affects us. It is admittedly possible that a millionaire also develops a savings activity in our sense, namely puts something aside from that, which he considers to be his constantly secured income. But one can never explain his millions from it.

I actively regret that I cannot dwell on these things any longer and must hand them over in a public form that is incomplete in so many regards. Maybe I am able to later show how important that differentiation that has never been made between those two types of economizing is, and how the said things can be used for a correct definition of income, how it is an important link of a chain from which interesting new realizations depend on, which can lead to the regenerating of some very unsatisfactory parts of the national economy.

Let us come to an end: the formation of assets is not a static process and can furthermore not be explained through the moment of economizing. Entirely the same can be repeated for the generation of capital in the sense of produced means of production: The same do not emerge from "economizing," that is certain. They are also acquirements of efforts that destroy our state of equilibrium and have insofar never been satisfactorily approached by the national economy, as the same has not yet thrived beyond static. And not only these efforts, but also their fruits change the entire "system." But we will still deal with this later, and we therefore close here. But one sees that we certainly have reason to remain within static and can hardly gripe about the limitations that this inflicts on us. But if one does attempt to go beyond it before the weapons are forged for it, then one builds where there is no solid ground—and the historical criticism wins all too great justification: Yes, a point certainly lies here where only new facts help.

Notes

1. Especially the mathematicians: L. Walras, V. Pareto, Irving Fisher, W. Launhardt; from non-mathematicians, actually only v. Boehm-Bawerk. But the ones that are mentioned do also make some uses of the theory that we must reject (Schumpeter, 1908, pg. 300).
2. And one can finally hope to gain even more statements through further data and more specific, more audacious assumptions. I share this hope and only a consideration for space keeps me from lingering at this point that is interesting in more than one regard (Schumpeter, 1908, pg. 304).

Part III

The Theory of Distribution

1

The Income: General Things

I

If one were to be asked what practically useful results the pure theory provides, then one could most notably allege two things: That it particularly explains "what the prices are" and that it gives certain laws of motion of the same. We have taken care of the first point in essence; we will get to the second one in the fourth part of this work. We are now dealing with the most important use of the price theory here, with the theory of income. The importance of the problem does not need to be emphasized—to comprehend the essence of the scientific distribution processes has always been a primary goal of the economy. Yes, one can say that this was and is the only purpose of many systems of the economy.

Here we encounter similar difficulties as by the price problems in general, only to a greater extent. The title "theory of distribution" already evokes an abundance of perceptions and emotions: bitter battles, sorrows and enjoyments, a part of the history of humanity seems to lie in it. Every discussion of this theme evokes hopes and concerns, and science has to date also not yet advanced to an entirely delineative approach of the same. Its eminently practical interest that also takes the scholars captive makes this so difficult. There are even enough people who resent a pure scientific approach to these questions, a distant objectivity, and consider it to be a lack of social thinking. So then a tendency to advocacy or combating the existing conditions can be proven in almost every work; one could and can almost never refrain from making practical conclusions that must have naturally been uncomfortable for one or the other party, and their superior tone, their representation as inviolable scientific results, and as absolute truths were especially agitating. If one tells the proletariat that all of its destitution is "natural," even corresponds to a maximum utility, then one can count on agreement from the side of its representatives even less so than it stands in the flagrant conflict with the fact of the success of social political efforts of a most different nature. Finally, one nervously explained that general truths do not exist here, and denounced this attempt to state the same as an unfair political maneuver that only serves the purpose of checkmating various efforts and hopes. It is indeed known that this conception is shared by a large part of the scientific world, and that reproaches of this sort against another large part of the same are justified. We will come back to this shortly.

We have furthermore repeatedly said that the social aspect, the circumstances of power, the development, and suchlike are virtually the most interesting things, and that our theoretical picture is not able to contribute anything to it, also, that it is so unrealistic, that only the trained eye can even discover a similarity to reality in it, that an abundance of facts eludes the ascertainment through our method and from our standpoint. But this is not supposed to be executed here. In fact, this has already been discussed, and we have abandoned wanting to gain something significant for the practical discussion and for the concrete development. Here we are primarily dealing with those difficulties that are specific to the problem of distribution.

One could approach this from different angles, discuss the same for the most different purposes, and every purpose and every point of view has its own method, which only has regard for that, which justifies it. Far be it from us to want to give a verdict about any of these methods and purposes. We do not declare any of them as unjustified or wrong, but one must *separate* them; one must above all *separate* theory and practice, scientific description and political discussion. It is now especially important for us to explain that we absolutely do not want to have anything in common with those attempts of the theorists, to want to give a verdict about the value or worthlessness of the existing conditions time and again, whereby that specific opposition between the socialistic and social-political direction on the one hand, and the so-called "middle-class" economy on the other hand emerges. We have already pointed this out, but especially for the distribution of income, this moment comes forward so abruptly that must return to it again. The necessity of the separation in principle is indeed recognized, but then we do read statements like the following time and again: "Competition, perfect competition, affords the ideal for the distribution of wealth."

"Competition affords the only absolute security possible for the equitable and beneficial distribution of the products of industry." "The question whether the labourer gets his product." One speaks of the "justification" of interest, of the "demands" of labor, to count as producer of the entire product, the question of the "fair" wage is time and again blended with the one of the "natural" one, etc. This is entirely unsustainable. It could arise that for example, due to overpopulation, the wage is so scarce that it does not even protect from hunger; despite this, we will consider it as the "natural" one, yes, we must even speak of a maximum of utility that is caused by this distribution, as we have explained this. This is not supposed to be stated again; the solution to all these paradoxes simply lies in the separation of description and value judgment. One also sees that one *can* very easily separate the two, and *can* therefore go quite well without a political attachment that strikes the essence of a science in the face. We must place so much emphasis on it, because the discussion of the problem of distribution that is so lively conducted at present leads to such points time and again.

The interest in theory is newly awakened. We must guard against making the former mistake again and thereby incurring the same attacks, misjudgments, and defeats for the new theory that the former has brought down. Every economist who loves his science for its own sake should not ignore this warning: Two things must especially be pointed out that play a special role at present and seem to be especially suitable in becoming downright catastrophic to science. Firstly, the questioning of the problem of attribution that occupies almost all theorists under different names has led to the speaking of the "product of the individual production factors," to ask for their "products." Especially the American theory has adopted this manner of expression that is already unfortunate in itself, after the earlier phase of this conception, as it showed itself in older literature, seemed to have been overcome. One now constructs the phrase that there is no objection against the distribution from the moral standpoint if every production factor gets that, which it produces. Even if the topic of evidence really were to be explained, which is already entirely impossible because the products of the individual factors cannot be separated, because the expression "product of an individual factor" can indeed only be meant figuratively, it would still not be realized why such a distribution should be *fair*. Because the means of production are not "remunerated" as it were for its good conduct, but rather the *owner* of the same gets the product. If a distribution for the labor according to this principle now seems to be quite plausible, then it is obvious that, for example, the landowner, remunerated for the performances of his land, can thereby receive a "fair," as well as an "unfair," portion. Secondly, some theorists have attempted to construct a general and necessary connection between income and personal efficiency for who it concerns. This aberrance is especially dangerous because it very easily leads over to the claim, which is otherwise entirely foreign to the economy, that the proprietary classes represent elements of higher-value, a statement that already suffices in itself to make our entire discipline unenjoyable for many people. Those theories, although independently developed, can reach a considerable meaning in this connection, which explain interest and ground rent from austerity, respectively labor. We do not need to go into rebuttal vis-à-vis this theory which therefore explains a higher income from higher personal performance at all, since the German audience is sufficiently convinced of its falsity anyway; we only need to emphasize that not the slightest bit of anything that would point to something of the sort lies in the pure economic thought processes.

We honestly do not have a reason to offer the flank for the second time to the all too entitled attacks from the side of the historian and the social politician, and nothing forces us to. Whoever wants to exploit the theory for these purposes, misuses it. It stands in the truest sense of the word above the parties and can be accepted by every man, whatever his political position may be.

We believe to have said enough in order to be protected against every reproach of this sort. That, which one can now reproach us with is, after we have stated the reproach of the overlooking of facts, as well as that of social political partisanship, as far as we can see, only the following: One may repudiate the distinct determination of income with pointer to the fact of the success of strikes, etc. We believe to have given a satisfactory explanation about it earlier, and we also want to still say quite a bit about it in another context. We have also already spoken about the role of the ethical moment, and said that we are not overlooking the effectiveness of others as economic moments, such as altruism, the will of lords, and suchlike. In this context we would still like to point to the aversion that the theory incurs through it, that it conceives human labor as a usual commodity in some relations. We only do this insofar as human labor is bought and sold, and attach nothing else to it. One can finally strive against the conception of the formation of income in our way for the reason because the formation of income is a social process, because a social product thereby arrives at distribution through social powers. We do not deny the justification of this view; it is even superior to ours in same regard, as we will shortly see. But for some purposes the proceeding from the individual, as explained earlier, is necessary and no opposition to that social conception lies in it.

In short: understanding for theory altogether and a clear view of what a theory actually says, what the core of its formulation that is often so incomplete is, those are the unavoidable, necessary requirements for an evaluation of the theory of distribution also. Only he, who brings these, can overcome its difficulties and the so often paradoxical-sounding claims. The following result arises for him: Many of the theorists' claims are actually unsustainable. But they can be separated from the core of the theory. However, the terminology of the same still frequently suffers under the influence of false ideas and deceptive hopes, and here lies the point where that clear view is so necessary. And these are not the only deficiencies; some conclusions and even individual theorems must also be renounced. But the essential content of the theory is nevertheless for the most part unobjectionable in principle. Demurs against *it* are often and perhaps mostly based on the lacking of those requirements. But not always, and it is difficult to clearly differentiate right from wrong. It is almost never attempted quietly and objectively. But let us go on.

II

So if we now ask ourselves what we are able to contribute to the understanding of the distribution processes from our standpoint, then we already know ahead of time that it is not *everything*, and expect that it is probably not even *much*. We especially do not know whether we can explain *all* incomes. But even if this were the case, we could not understand them entirely and in all their relations. What we can do is look at our system and ask ourselves what is useful for the explanation of the formation of income from it. One can then say *that we can more or less explain those incomes that can be represented as sums of price*. Goods of the most different type are exchanged in our system, first consumption goods for consumption goods, and then productive goods for other productive goods or for consumption goods. If barter takes place, whose purpose it is to exchange a consumption good *that was determined* for another in order to use it, then this barter is of no further interest to us here. However, if the consumption good was produced or acquired in order to be exchanged, then we simply interpret it as a form of productive services, which we can readily do. According to this designation, we say that *we can explain the distribution processes insofar as they exist in the formation of price of the productive performances*. This is the pure economic "essence" of the formation of income, and now the question is what this moment is able to offer us.

Also here, the reserve is to be made again that we can also simply not explain *everything* for barter. But besides this we can really understand the formation of that income or parts of the income that have this character. The branches of income that we are differentiating would therefore be just as many as there are types of productive goods within our system. But one can condense these into three groups, namely labor, land, and finally, produced goods. Other types of income than those that may arise from these three groups cannot be in our system. Before we transition to closer statements of the same, we have to make the following remarks. One could especially ask oneself whether the "entrepreneurial income" does in fact represent a further branch of income. Here we speak of the "entrepreneur" without defining him further, but other sciences have more to say about this aspect. Furthermore, we eliminate capital interest in the common sense of the word and also that which one calls "entrepreneurial wage" from its income. Now something undeniably still remains, a sometimes very significant magnitude as is taught through experience, and the examination of this "something" is certainly a problem of utmost importance. One has attempted to look at the same as the compensation of any special service that is however essentially different from the wage. However, the majority of theorists explain this income in another way. We want to wait on elaborating this question until later. But at any rate, our system does not give an explanation for the same: We cannot quote a price that could thereto help, and we stand at a *border* of our system.

We first see from this example that there is an income, which does not explain our static system. There may be others. The task that arises for us there is to prove that the pure economic theories, which have attempted such an explanation, are useless, or that we get just as far as they do. If we would not be successful in this verification, then our system would at the very least be in need of a completion, and if this would *often* occur, then we would turn away from the same. But furthermore, it must constantly be shown whether the questionable emergence is perhaps of dynamic character, meaning certainly economic, but not explainable with the means of the static system, or whether we are entitled to assign it to another science. The latter is certainly not the case for the entrepreneurial income, and we have to find an *economic* explanation. It is, however, quite generally accepted that the same only emerges in a dynamic state.

The case of the entrepreneurial profit leads us to clearly realize some deficiencies of our view. There are therefore branches of income (and we will see that besides the entrepreneurial profit another one of such exists) that evade our explanation here. But then there are still incomes, for which the pure economic view fails, for example, the ruling heads of the civilians, furthermore others, for which it achieves so little that one would be better to drop them entirely. This is more or less the case for, for example, incomes from political occupations, for some liberal jobs, for the salary of the civil servant. One can certainly not understand these things without every economic view; that they even exist is certainly only economically explainable in some of these cases; but this contribution is so scarce that one can only agree with the theorists who disregard these types of income as a rule. The laws of motion, such as the rule of supply and demand only emerge a little, and other views, for example, those of the social power relationships fit unequally better, and tell us unequally more. *Our contribution to the understanding of the distribution processes stands in a similar relationship to the entire problem, as the theory of the international values to the entire problem of the global economy.*

What remains with us among all limitations that we have already made earlier and of the two that we were just now compelled to make through the acknowledgement of branches of income, which cannot be economically explained at all, and such which cannot be explained in the framework of static, is still important enough. It was furthermore much overestimated, and all theorists that have ever lived have therefore predominantly directed their attention to it, and the revival of the theoretical interest has, after the new foundation was in place and was adopted in a large scale, had a formal run of the theorists to the problem of distribution as a result. Let us overlook the battle line in order to see how the matter stands, then one could probably say that many positions are taken, and the capitulation of the stronghold lies ahead. But the flag has in fact not struck yet. The static incomes still stand the firmest, but one still fiercely battles in the field of static.

It is difficult to characterize the current position of these questions. In the circle of theorists the matter is approximately the following: In regards to the ground rent, Ricardo's theory still dominates to a great extent, and all oppositions to the same have not been able to deter the majority of theorists from it, not even when their remaining theories do not agree with the same. For the wage of labor, one has concerned oneself more and more with the concrete conditions, than with a general theory, but v. Wieser's attribution theory within the latter has indeed nevertheless remained unopposed. One can only consider the development of the wages theory by the Americans as a version of the same. The third branch of income is called interest. It was always a stomping ground for the most diverse special theories. At any rate, v. Boehm-Bawerk's criticism has forced the same ones back, and his own theory seems to gain more and more influence as I believe, much more than was generally believed or is admitted. Only the productivity theory and the abstinence theory have maintained themselves beside it.

One is allowed to lose track of it during the evaluation of the individual thought, that it, as we emphasize time and again, only has purpose and meaning in its context. As a rule, it is based on superficiality and carries mistakes with it if one simply transplants one individual thought from the system of an earlier time into the newer one, as was the case for the pension theory. One is also not allowed to judge an individual thought from the standpoint of another system, if one wants to be fair: the value of the same is different within the different systems; it can tell us a varied amount from various levels of the scientific development. On the other hand, it does not seem right to us to be of the opinion, along with some current theorists, that the individual thought are always complementary. This is only the case to a limited extent. In general, the case stands in a way that various theoretical views with regard to their formal character have rather little to say to one another, and the basic theoretical problems allow an approach with relatively simple means: The one thought does not complete the other, but rather makes it expendable. It is a praiseworthy effort, to be fair to our predecessors, but one may think very differently about the attempts of some modern theorists, not wanting to find the slightest difference between the most diverse things.

III

The first result that our view gives us in this field is the realization that the branches of income that occur in static as we defined them are *coessential*, meaning that they are based on the same moment and can be explained in the same manner. This result is very important and gives our system a uniformity that must be considered as great progress towards the former ones. These incomes are price sums and are distinctly determined as such. We do not need to look for special reasons that are supposed to clear up the same ones for us, as the classical authors did. This is the greatest success of the attribution theory. The classical authors have also admittedly not completely misunderstood the fact that the incomes are "prices." It is one thing to occasionally see a fact, and another to grasp its scientific significance. A price theory almost constantly stands before the distribution theory in also the older systems, but one does approach the incomes as if they were independent emergences that demand an individual explanation. The only branch of income for which they clearly recognized the nature of the price is the labor wage, but the representation also immediately diverges for it, in order to attract other moments. By contrast, pension and interest were always specially justified. This is connected with the price theory of the classical authors, as it was already indicated.

By emphasizing the consubstantiality of the branches of income, we are by no means misunderstanding those differences between the same ones that do show themselves by the flightiest observation. We only claim that the pure economic "nature" of the branches of income is the same and that those differences lie in moments that are not purely economic, for example, in the social position of those which refer to the incomes. The latter is certainly an important moment which greatly contributed to the clouding of that fundamental realization. The laborers and the landowners contrast so strongly with one another, the manner in which they reach their income is such a different one, furthermore, all living conditions and the entire social and political habitus, all that is different. It is added that the interests of these classes so often collide, that in fact, everything seems to speak for the assumption that the economic foundations of their being are also different, and we can especially encounter the reproach here that our manner of representation whitewashes the social contrasts. But this reproach is unfounded if one understands this correctly. We are only concerned with the fact that these incomes are formed from prices. A formal equality arises from it, which also leads to a similarity in the laws of motion, but which does not reveal anything about whether these incomes are large or small and which social function they fulfill. The contrasts of the classes are in no way denied through this; on the contrary, our view is very practical for illuminating the economic side of the same ones. One has also said that it makes little sense to first treat the production factors as equal, and then to still emphasize that difference again. An equality in principle is useless when the gradual difference exceeds a certain size. This reproach also does not seem to be entirely justified: The equality in principle and the gradual difference are indeed interesting for different classes of problems. Wherever it deals with saying what these incomes *are*,there, the same thought process can be used for all static ones, and this is important enough in order to speak of a consubstantiality; if one were to then ask for further circumstances, which these so interesting "prices" determine, then one will come across varieties, which does not change anything about the fact that the foundation is the same everywhere. Just as the individual drops of a waterfall find various ways through the rocks, unite and separate and have the most variant destinies without therefore ceasing to originate from the same source, the incomes take different paths in this manner, are narrower determined by various circumstances, but it does therefore still remain interesting that they are of the same essence.

This realization only forges slowly; it really only stands on solid ground when it is based on the theory of attribution. Currently, it is also not generally accepted yet, although it is gaining ground. Only when it has been entirely permeated, *is the first phase of our science completed*, the classical system finally overcome, *not due to dialectic discussion, but rather through the power of success*. The newer value theory has not shown what it is able to do until here, and this new clarity and simplicity is already a reason in itself for giving preference to it.

While the classical theory does not consider the ground rent as a price, but rather explains it from a special circumstance, we can set it next to wage all the more for this reason, since it first deals with only the simplest, most basic things. The matter therefore forms itself quite simply: Land as well as labor achievements attain a price in the manner that was discussed, and their "owners" are in the position to use the same one as they choose, since they can count on the same labor and land performances in the next economic period. If one has completed the production process, then one *firstly* has the product and *secondly* the land and the labor power. The comparison to a constantly flowing source lies near and is useful, and there is nothing conspicuous to the fact that laborers and landowners have the income at their command. All further things may then be very complicated, the foundations are clear enough. There is nothing simpler and nothing that needs to fear less resistance than the claim that one rates and pays for land and labor achievements, *because one needs them*. Even the circumstance, that the owner of land and labor power is not completely in the right when he accepts the recurrence of those achievements that secure his income as being certain, cannot change anything on this matter of fact. The laborer will become older, the land will become worn out. It is probably to be assumed for the latter that it will always be acquired through meliorations, etc., at the same level of earning capacity; it does not go on so readily. Even if this were possible, then it would need a special explanation for why a portion of the earnings is thereupon used, and one does not give this explanation if one simply explains that before this operation is made, net yield is not even available. Only the *gross* yield is *given*, and if the same finds another use than that of consumption, then this requires an explanation. We will encounter this problem by the third branch of income that is being led, and we do not want to unravel it here, but rather want to *assume*, to simulate that labor power and land really form two inexhaustible sources that always and equally flow. This is surely fiction, but it is close to reality for short time frames. One could not say the same for tools and entirely for raw materials, and this causes us to not approach "interest" with the same certainty as wage and pension. Only these two are certainly "static" branches of income whose explanation easily and clearly arises from our system. We therefore do not want to speak of "interest" yet: We want to look at it *last*.

2

The Wages Theory

I

The wages theory is really a classic example of certain points that belong to the methodology and epistemology of our discipline, and that, which we are aiming for can perhaps not be made any clearer anywhere else. Let it be therefore permitted to direct the attention of the reader especially to the way of approach. For clarity about that, which has been accomplished, on the one hand, and about the ways in which further progress is to be hoped for, on the other hand, the same should not be without advantage, even if this chapter only offers things that are well-known.

A price of labor arises entirely by itself from our system. Once given, such a result comes out of the same one, as out of a machine, also entirely by itself without a citation of any new observation or hypothesis or any other measure being necessary. The only thing that was necessary was the realization, or more correct, the assumption that quantities of labor are elements of our system, or that "labor" has a value function, or finally, very clear and popular, that labor is an economic good. And this is, according to our conception of the essence of the value hypothesis not only *occupied by*, but rather *equivalent to* the observation that labor is bought and sold, as it is written in the first line of Ricardo's chapter "On Wages"; because we only conclude from this that it is being "classified."

Our result in its essence exists in that the price of labor forms itself the same in principle as all other prices, and that it is distinctly determined. We have the value function of the—direct or indirect—buyers of labor and money, the same value functions for the laborer, and we can then prove it in the same way mathematically as for all other goods.

Furthermore, not only the price, but also the achieved quantity of labor is distinctly determined—just as the quantities and prices for *all* goods. Finally, a similar type of maximum of utility exists for this barter, and price and quantity of labor are in a complete interdependency with all other prices and quantities of goods in our system. And this makes the use of the variations method that is to be discussed later possible for us, which gives us certain laws of motion of price and quantity of labor.

Our result is certainly not worthless. But very many, especially interesting questions do remain open. It is also clear that the older theory knew to raise all kinds of further questions and claims. Now what is our position to it, and what kind of verdict can we form about it? First however, we still want to discuss our result, and this is what we attach great importance to.

Furthermore, there is hardly anything left to desire on simplicity and persuasiveness. However, both unfortunately disappear through further elaboration. One immediately runs into difficulties there, which are generally perceived but not recognized poignantly enough. This branch of our discipline therefore also has that specific trait of dissatisfaction. And almost every author emphasizes this in order to then still present essentially the same again, if he does not prefer to ignore the theory altogether and to turn socio-political discussions. This field belongs to those deadlocks of the social sciences where the entire progress seems to stagnate. We want to briefly depict these circumstances later. Perhaps we will be successful in smoothing the way through calm, impartial observation of the matter.

Our pure theory of the price of labor is initially deductive. Wherever a result arises from our system that is supposed to explain any emergence that was not specially thought of by the construction of the foundation, a deduction, in the proper meaning of the word, is present. This is the case for us. The closest forms of the emergence of price, which the price theory directly proceeds from, are the prices of the consumption goods. If we also use the same raisonnement beyond it, even if we have examined and carefully pondered every step of our though process, then our obligation is much more pronounced than it would otherwise be, for whether our result can be compared to reality.

We therefore have two questions with which to present ourselves. Firstly: Does our result explain the prices of labor? Secondly: How far does the phenomenon of the price of labor reach; let us say more precisely what we mean by the same. The first comes down to the demand for the verification of our result. Let us call the price the labor wages, so then it gives us a theory of wages. This step seems to be endlessly natural and simple, so that one often overlooks the fact that a step forward even lies in it, and considers his foundation in reality as being so evident that one does not need to utter another word about it. That is not so, but it is rather a not so simple problem whether our value and price of labor, as we have derivated them from our system, explain the emergence of wages. We wanted to state this first. We will then turn to the second question which we can now also express this way: Can all incomes that can be ascribed to work performance, or better, for which work performances somehow come into play, be construed as wages, namely as wages in our sense, which was just defined, and not as "compensations" in the moral sense, which we do not consider? Our explanation surely reaches further than that emergence, which one in everyday life considers to be wages in the strictest sense, but how far? Beforehand: *Firstly*, would it result that our price theory which is based on value, readily, at least in principle, absolutely solves the problem of wages in a satisfactory manner, and *secondly*, that all incomes, which present a personal performance can be grasped under the schema "wages": Then this would give us a downright sublime realization. Yes, one could then say that the economy is in a position to give a type of theory of society. It would be the foundation of sociology in another sense than conformable to the economic conception of history. If all "wages" in this broad sense would just depend on the value of the affected labor performances, it would then also not make sense, or just some artificial sense, to say that the laborer gets his "product"; but just as the different prices of different qualities of a consumption good, the *value* would give *the scale of the labor income*, and if the higher-valued labor would furthermore also be performed by the higher-valued labor power, similar to how the better tools naturally give the better use, then all those incomes and the social position of those that they enjoy could be explained by their abilities and the value of their performances: *The social construction would be comprehensible through the principle of value and would lean on a transparent economical foundation.* This profound insight of magnificent simplicity and a row of scientific—especially relating to the developmental tendencies—and practical—relating to the social policy and the value judgment about the social aspects—consequences of a significance that can hardly be overestimated would arise. And this would still be completed if one takes two steps forward. If one were to assume that one could speak in the same sense for the labor power as for a machine that would also be controlled by the value principle, then the circle of emergences would be closed and the value would really be the foundation of the social science. One would then have an exact instrument for the ascertainment of all uses of incomes: Large incomes and luxury expenditures would then have to be grasped as means of the reproduction of high-valued labor power. If this were possible, then we would have made an endless profit, scientifically speaking. The other step consists of ascribing incomes from "ownership of capital[1]" to performances of the owners, be it in the sense of the abstinence theory, be it that one assumes a type of entrepreneurial activity of the capitalist. Then there would only be *one* more category of income, namely that of property, which would form an exception. And even for this, there are two reference devices: Above all, Carey's theory of ground rent. And then still another, namely the assumption that one can simply grasp the performances of every means of production as being performance of its owner; that one could completely analogously speak of "performances of my land," as of performances of my labor power. This does in fact happen very often, and one quietly slides over the difference, which we already spoke of in another section. But then, a magnificent construction would be done.

Someone will not easily want to keep this thought process completely bare and in the poignancy as we have presented it, but elements of the same, which have a tendency to exactly the same consequences are virtually the rule in theory. We must be mindful of its different levels. The lowest one is widespread. Let us now outline the position of important theoretical directions to it in a few points.

The socialists and the German social politicians are adverse, individually or under their influence. The most approving ones are the French academics, who actually consider such a distribution as being natural, and even if they only partially postulate it, they do also realize it to a great extent, and still more, closely believe the realization. But they help themselves by grasping the worst discrepancies as abnormalities, rudiments that will disappear, and letting the painful gap to reality appear as being as small as possible. Natural and artificial monopolies cause deviations, but all incomes do strive to adjust themselves to the scale of measurement. The interest on capital is explained as being the fruit of labor and the delay of consumption; the entrepreneurial profit is ascribed to a special entrepreneurial activity and to a service of the absorption. Such conceptions, perhaps not made to be so useful in taking a political position, also exist outside of this circle. The abstinence theory of interest is still alive. Especially the moment of supply *of* and the demand *for* "waiting" was recently poignantly worked out by Cassel. Carver associated it with a productivity theory. We will get to this later.

This standpoint is almost the rule in regards to the entrepreneurial profit, for example, according to Walker's theory, and similarly according to that of v. Mangoldt, which we will get to know in its place, the entrepreneur virtually appears as the most talented laborer. Only his talent would lead him to his position and to his income. In this sense, Cassel says that high "business-capacity" is a rare, therefore an economic good, and therefore "highly paid for." And even representations where other moments also have a say, for example—it is actually unfair to name individual ones—in Fetters, a row of characteristics is indeed listed, which an entrepreneur must have with the apparent purpose to characterize his ability as labor and the nature of the same, and therefore making a price of the same plausible.

Such thoughts, the intention to make an economic principle not only to the foundation of the theory, but to the understanding of the social construction, can also be verified by Clark and v. Wieser. We see an interesting variety by Walras, whereby we must, however, strictly separate the politician and the social philosopher from the theorist. He seems to be of the opinion that all incomes can simply be explained by the value theory from personal performances, with the exception of the ground rent, and therefore his claim for the country's nationalization. If this has happened, then everything is all right—an interesting example of how practical claims can grow out of theoretical thoughts, which has cost the economical science so much of its reputation. Pareto's theory of the income-curve also belongs here, which lead to an audacious use by Laurent. Let us therefore say an entire theory of the mechanism of the organism, in order to not shock either side, the existence and growth of society lies herein. This leads to the consequence that the ruling classes are the most competent, the best; a result that the so-called "theory of race" also comes to otherwise, a quite interesting coincidence.

But we must refrain from going into this; because all of this already lies outside of the field of economy. We only want to go so far to say that we consider that theory to be radically failed, that we believe that it blatantly contradicts reality, that this proud construction is only a phantasmagoria. Then of course that, which seemed to have been explained has again sunk back into the night of a chaos, and we must conceal our opinion about the possibilities of bringing light into it, if we do not compromise the same through a flighty representation and want to eliminate the justified reproach of the dilettantism.[2] So let us stop at the boundary of our field, and let us content ourselves with proving that we stand on one of such. May it never be injured.

Let us modestly return to the problems of our science for which alone we have the prerequisites, and let us first ask ourselves where the point lies, at which the raisonnement loses the solid ground under its feet. The answer is not difficult to give: one acquiesced in the result of the theory without verifying it, and one made the broadest use of everything that appeared to let itself be molded according to its schema, without examining its limits. This is how one reaches theorems of seemingly absolute universal validity, with which one has approached reality without taking into consideration that, even if "right," an exact construction never suffices in constructing practical consequences. And yet, nothing at all is absolutely true, and the number and the content of entirely universal sentences are scarce. One should not have lost sight of this and would have immediately become suspicious.

We would still like to emphasize something else. A too far-reaching universal validity of the same representative theory, which is based on the exact theory of wages, is by no means a "speculation," as the national economy is often reproached for it. It is not based on any metaphysical sentences, or any that were cleverly thought out through some dialectic. Rather, it is based on an exact foundation and *through its conveyance* of observations of facts, and we believe nevertheless to be able to prove that it is essentially incorrect. Here we therefore have a case of a really scientific theory that, as one should believe, should have to be accurate if its prerequisites apply, and whose prerequisites are based on facts, and it is still not satisfactory despite everything. Shouldn't we go crackers there concerning the economic theory? What distinguishes the theory in question from the theory of any other price, for which we also have to admit that reality will never completely confirm it? Indeed, we just seemed to have admitted that *no* essential difference exists. Now, this is an excellent example in order to present, in turn, our standpoint true to our principle; that we want to study methodical and epistemological questions for the things in themselves and not with general reasons.

Yes, there is really no essential difference between theories that we represent and this one which, in agreement with other theorists, appears to us as a monstrosity. The opposition is seemingly not unsolvable, and lets itself be solved quite easily. The difference is of course only gradual, and the *degree* of the derivation of the theoretical picture of reality, *considering every case and every purpose of research* is the decisive moment. The boundaries are not poignant, but rather change under the mentioned circumstances and the development of the realization. And because of this, we cannot stress often enough that it is entirely worthless and leads to nothing at all when deciding a priori, by means of great principles, about "value of the theory" and "admissibility" of the abstraction. As we said, we completely reject this and examine on a case by case basis, whereby the same result by no means comes about. It thereby shows us the relative justification of all claims that are seemingly so opposing, pro and con the theory, and this is the path on which clarity and agreement seems to be attainable to us. If an opponent of the theory says that the same is unrealistic, then he is—in general, such a claim constantly also contains a heap of *false* and, furthermore, *foreign* elements, for example, social-political considerations, practical political tendencies, etc., that one must eliminate, and which we are not going into again here—quite right. One disproves him through the objection that this only lies in the essence of all theories when he really has no understanding for this essence and has no awareness of it. But otherwise, one proves nothing for the theory. And this is how it is for all reasons, pro and con, everywhere. The same are almost always true, but they are powerless in their universal validity, so that they, as one can actually see it, never convince anyone at all. They are not decisive for the admissibility of the abstraction and the isolation method, and for the fate of the theory, but rather only that detailed examination that has never been properly carried out, respectively its overall result, gives the verdict.

We came to the conclusion that the price theory is generally not worthless, but it nevertheless only conveys a "stylized" one and one of an excerpt of reality; we are getting to the opposing one, relating to the theory that is discussed here. One could also call it theoretically "accurate," since it does not contain a logical mistake, but it is not *useful*, because its result deviates too *much* from reality. And we are only concerned with *usefulness*, as we demonstrated earlier. One could probably make the assumptions that lead to it, but one either does not get far, or goes astray with it. We therefore see that a theory that in itself is "accurate" can lead to "wrong" consequences, and an element of truth therefore lies in the position of those, which reject considering the isolation method as the only formal aid that can only convey *incomplete, but not incorrect* results. It is a valuable, yes indispensable, but not harmless ally, which only gives its good service under strict control. *Exactly the same raisonnement* achieves much better things for the ground rent theory, amongst others; we will immediately see why. Blame and benefit of the exact method lie closely parallel to one another, not separated by a principally easily recognizable wall.

We devote ourselves to the hope that considerations of this kind, can contribute, in the individual case, where they can really be carried out exactly and do not have that acuteness in principle, which make the general argument so bitter, to lead to clarity and agreement, and especially to approach the distribution problem with a satisfactory solution, which at least lets actual insight into the distribution process be hoped for. Let it also be remarked that the difficulties, which we now want to take a closer look at, are perhaps one of the causes why many authors do not want the work to be "true"—one then embellished it with ethical motives, amongst others.

After we have said that we decidedly rejected the theory of the incomes of labor, we can allow ourselves to admit that we do not deny it each and every meaning. Certainly, if our general prerequisites were to be met, reality would have to appear this way. And there are just as certain some emergences far outside of the tight boundaries of the theory of wages, which this view is suitable for. We do not love any extreme claims and want to retain every grain of truth. One will judge differently how much truth now lies in the same. One will approach this question with different dispositions, depending on the land that one regards, and even depending on the experiences and observations that one personally makes in life. We do not want to attempt to decide on them here, but rather only want to exactly examine how far and under which premises our theoretical result verifiably proves itself.

II

We therefore turn to the two questions whose answer we considered to be necessary; first off, as we said, to the first one.

Let us primarily recall what we understand by "explanation"; none other than the declaration of a distinctly determining variable for our unknowns and of laws of motion of the same. Every theoretical construction that achieves this is "right" for us, and that, which does this the best and the simplest we call the "most useful one."

The "variations method" that we will get to know later on will give us the pure economical laws of motion of the prices of goods and quantities always under the same premises, which grants us the distinct determination of the variable of an economic quantity, so that our first question can be reduced to the following one: Is the distinctly determining wage rate that our system gives actually that of reality? Is that, which we have derivated really that moment, which underlies the different forms of wages? Of course, we do not mean a numerical variable; our system does not give us one of such; also not a general proportion, as for example, von Thünen attempted to give. We are aware that both change according to the circumstances. But we still mean more than the mere fact of the distinct determination: We would like to know whether our entire schema is suitable for the emergence of wages.

Now, it seems as if this verification could not have any greater difficulties for the work than for all the other goods. The processes in a labor exchange, as on a farm where a servant is admitted, are obviously no different in essence than those in a commodity exchange, or for another trade by the farmer. A little more outer-economic moments may come into play there, especially in the case of the farmer's convention and habit, as well as personal considerations perhaps play a larger role than here; the main economic features are always distinctly recognizable, and such moments do not suffice for a differentiation in principle, especially for us, since we at least partially include the same in the value function. The picture of the theory may by and large fit a bit less, but it fits. The wages become high wherever a deficiency of labor prevails; they are lower ceteris paribus wherever abundance prevails—this is almost too obvious to be mentioned and pieces of evidence from reality, say from new colonies on the one hand, and "overpopulated" countries such as India or China on the other hand, are overabundant.

One certainly also runs into difficulties here: The factory regulations almost always contain a specific number of hours. The stronger laborer may also have no opportunity to take advantage of his superiority over his comrades. Social power relations, encroachments that cannot be explained economically in his self-determination (bans on emigration, etc.) may obstruct the formation of our theoretical wage rate. An especially important case is that of combination, which not only leads to monopoly-like emergences and therefore disturbs the wage niveau, but can also make achievements through its social and political power, for whose ascertainment the means of static are insufficient.

But this is true for all goods, and the same reasons that motivated us to abide by our theory for these ones, also prove themselves here. The number of hours for the factory regulation will be generally adjusted to that time, which would arise from a theoretically free commerce—at the most, a rounding off of whole hours will be made, whereby the remaining working conditions (breaks, sanitary conditions, etc.) would give rise to balancing out the rest in another way. One also often sees those interfering influences for other commodities, export and import bans or complications of every kind, etc.: and our laws still maintain their place, despite such deviations, as mentioned. The same applies to the combinations and the analogies for strikes, although less frequently and pronounced as this one, they are so obvious that is surprising that so little emphasis has been placed on this in the theory up to now. Therefore, the question that we ask ourselves, that we are so often asked by opponents of the theory and that is negated by the same ones, is certainly answered in the affirmative *to this extent*. The discrepancy with reality is of course great, greater than most theorists are inclined to admit and that, which remains for our result on value of its realization, surely, different opinions about it are possible; but whoever considers this value to be significant nonetheless, in the sense as we do, he cannot help but accept our theory of wages, certainly *to this extent*.

This is a first step. The theory of wages could, according to this, be conceived as a special case of the exact price theory, it could be satisfactorily represented through its schema, and it could also find itself in sufficient agreement with reality, whereby very important results, in whose ownership the classical authors already believed themselves to be, would of course be moved into an unreachable distance. But once, this is not all. We have proven this only for the one side of the matter, the simplest one that is handled first and which is, however, handled alone in the common representations of the price theory, namely for the formation of the price for available, given quantities. For the remaining goods, with the exception of land and other "gifts of nature" we can indeed go further and also stretch the value and price consideration to their cost goods, and thereby capture the economical cycle entirely. Can we also do this for labor? Only then would our theory explain to us the emergence of wages of reality *entirely*, at least in principle, otherwise the manpower must be accepted as being given, meaning that we admitted that we cannot explain its formation and magnitude. The reader knows that the latter is our point of view. We have indeed therefore acknowledged the population and its physical and moral characteristics—but also for the purpose of having constant functions of demand—as data of our problems, as "system-determinant." This does not have to be justified any further here.

On the other hand, however, not everything is clear for even the attained results, and we encounter a difficulty that can force us to modify the same and to even still refine something from the modest realization of value that we attributed to the theory. There I would like to again point out how essential an entirely detailed examination proves itself to be. How easily one could be satisfied with our "first step"; everything seems to work and surely everything is logically irreproachable, and it will nevertheless show that doubts do still exist. And such thoroughness is for the most part not found in economical works. There is still a hard job to do there, which is in a position to give our system more than some intrepid innovation.

The difficulty that we mean here has already been indicated; it lies in the "flat wage rate" as is given by the theory.

One of such obviously does not exist in reality. Despite the fact that well-known circumstances hinder a local equalization in the same manner as for other goods—circumstances that for now do not play a larger role here than for these and should therefore be by-passed, although by no means be overlooked—there are different wage rates for different jobs. This has nothing noticeable about it per se and also does not contradict the theoretical unity of the wage rate. One also pays more for better quality of other goods without one, if one accurately understands the theory in another way, doubting the unity of the price. Goods of the same kind but of different quality are just economically different goods. But between their values and prices, as between all goods altogether, a given relation exists that was just given by the value and price theory. The individual qualities are available in exactly the quantities as the demand demands it and achieve a proportional price. The best piece is also the one that is paid for the best. If a piece of meat under otherwise the exact same circumstances has double the nutritional value than another, then it will be valued as two equally big ones of the latter kind. The "circumstances" will of course never be equal; in our example perhaps a difference in taste, etc. will be present. Such ulterior elements are especially valued, as Clark has emphasized,[3] and it would not be permitted in general to extrapolate proportional price differences from the physical ones. Not only the value of better qualities will always come into question, but also the buying power and number of those buyers, which compete for directly the same ones. A portion of the buyers that wants to or must be satisfied with the inferior ones from the very beginning will not compete for the better ones, and the price formation of the same will therefore have a substantial independence. Housing prices are an instructive example. This stands out even more in those cases where better qualities *serve other needs, but a relation will constantly exist that can be ascertained with the means of the value and price calculation.*

Just as a machine that "produces" twice as much as another, admittedly cannot be valued entirely twice—at least in strict theory the diminishing of the marginal utility of the product must be taken into consideration—

but its value and price will be in a fixed, clear connection with value and price of the inferiorly usable ones. Only when this connection exists is the price formation of a good completely described by our laws.

Now is this the same case for labor? For the purpose of brevity let us differentiate, without going into the subtler differences that tend to be made today, only "common" and "qualified" labor and ultimately again in that for which the qualification essentially exists in the learning of a skill and that, for whom it essentially exists in a higher, natural talent. Certainly not everyone is capable of learning every skill, and the application of a higher talent requires some type of education as a rule. One will nevertheless easily admit that we have two differentiable moments in front of us. The following questions therefore arise from the one that was just asked: Are the wages of every kind of labor in every connection, which is describable by means of our theory? Thereupon: Do the different values explain themselves from a difference in qualifications? Finally: Is the qualification through learning in that connection to the qualification through assessment in which the characteristics, for example of a raw material for its further manufacturing—the best raw material is manufactured the finest—is this also the same case for labor? *These are quaestiones facti*. It depends on their answers whether the value principle explains the wage rates.

Here we stand before a problem whose existence is often indicated or nevertheless felt. This is *one* reason that many economists only want the wages theory to be used for "common" labor, (common labour).[4] A realization of the difficulties that lie in the price formation of qualified labor opinion already lies in this opinion and shows, again, that the realization of the older theorists went much deeper than is often accepted.[5] But only Marx and his orientation have undertaken a solution to the same. They have affirmed these questions, however from the standpoint of the labor principle, and they have suggested the means of reference to ascribe qualified labor to unqualified (labor) for the reason that one interprets the first as a multiple of the latter. And the representatives of the value principle lean towards an affirmation. For them, all labor is explicitly or implicitly ascribed to one unit of value, to one and the same value scale, just as for Marx it is to one unit of work, as mentioned. *And for the "unit of performance" a flat wage rate exists accordingly.*

Now, if one regards the labor force of a company, or even of a branch, or finally of a country, then such an affirmation could at first glance really be suggested. The better performance at least *inclines* towards better wages; its superiority explains itself from a specially learned skill, or larger force, or skillfulness, and even if this is not certain, the "better man" will most likely acquire the former. The higher wage will be the incentive for it, and supply and demand will both be controlled by the value principle. *One* value scale will encompass these types of labor. The same approach is just as suitable for the production of a specific product of expended quantities of labor. All laborers who, for example, play a part in the production of a skirt, from the shepherd to the laborer, who undertakes the "tailor pressing," are remunerated according to the value of their labor. This seems obvious.

But yet, there are also emergences here that can make us apprehensive. May the Chinese man in San Francisco even achieve exactly the same as the American man, he will nevertheless not receive the same wage. And we do not need to search for such cases—which, by the way, are not rare, compare for example, the wages of the Italian laborers in Austria or Southern France. The example of the enumeration of female labor suggests itself entirely. The same is considerable lower even there, where a woman can do just as good of a job as a man, and does so. One could counter that analog things also find themselves by other goods. A renowned company can achieve higher prices for also entirely the same products as its younger competitors. And if we do not attribute a relevance to this case in principle, then we may also not do this here. Maybe. We could admittedly respond that the difference is, however, only gradual, but that, on the one hand, the deviation from reality is not too great, on the other hand, it is not to be neglected. But we do not want to insist on it, since we cannot meet our decisive reservations yet at this point.

But every company, at least every large one, has a category of laborers who are accustomed to be considered "civil servants." In what connection is their "income" to the "wage" of the laborers? The doubtful point is that such a civil servant who belongs to a different social class would never become a "laborer," even if this would pay better. This fact is undisputable and it is just as certain that he also often did not have a choice at the beginning of his education between both jobs, but rather would have had to aim for the one of the "civil servant," even then when the "prospects" of this career had been disadvantageous all along. His education is not only a "sunk capital," which can no longer be retrieved now—*all* productions offer examples of this—but he was already socially forced from the very beginning, *at least* as a rule or *very* often, to tread on this path.

And this immediately leads us further to the wages in all "higher" professional branches. Who could overlook the fact that as a rule everyone strives to stay in his social class, that the same puts him in iron chains? All of the young people, who year-in, year-out pursue civil service in our homeland, hardly account for the opportunities outside of the same. On the contrary, they are most often aware that their prospects in the economic respect are generally not favorable. They nevertheless offer their labor force here, for the position where not the largest, but perhaps the smallest enumeration waves, and where the demand is obviously exceeded. They do not in fact have a choice as children of their country and their class. A military officer *can* in general not change his profession without a very noticeable social "capitis deminutio." In these professions, national and political boundaries also come into play much more distinctly than they could do by means of bans on emigration. One can avoid the latter, but outside of their social relations young people are helpless and are not able to maintain their ground in their present social niveau. Let that, which has been said suffice; satisfactorily explaining this could be a topic of an interesting social study. Let us only still complete it through one moment: The artist, the scholar not always produces his works, but often without regard for demand, even though he also strives for economical results—again, at least frequently—with his labor. Not to mention the works that are done without this intention, for example the magazine articles of a politician.

The entrepreneur, the civil servant, the artist, the laborer, all of them become this through forced circumstances, not through free choice. This is the rule, which is only proven the more by the stir that an exception causes. Now this means none other economically than that the supply of labor *is not controlled by the value principle* as it applies to land and every other product. Our system is broken here, its inner strength of life, the "interdependency," paralyzed. Only within a national and social circle, free movement of labor prevails, *and only if one attaches this clause* and apart from that explains the distribution of labor as a system determining fact, *only then does the value calculation apply*. And that, which is said, maintains itself to the greatest extent in every type of qualified labor.

Moments other than economic ones therefore determine the distribution of the labor quantity of the national economy and the entire world. This is perhaps a great concession that we are granting the ethical orientation. It is right on this point. "Labor" in general is not as easily economically flexible as even the country is. And if one were to counter us *here* that a free movement also does not exist for other goods, then we could satisfactorily counter this. To the extent, under consideration that the freight and toll of the prices of goods during free competition are not the same everywhere, this is based on "friction oppositions" that or not of further interest as insufficient knowledge, missing enterprise, etc. This is different for labor. Great, important moments that one cannot possibly overlook stand in the way of the movement of labor. National sentiment, or better, the moment of antagonism of the races, social relations of every kind, in short, the entire social structure, everything that it holds together, makes every such assumption difficult. While furthermore, the production otherwise constantly follows the value principle, other moments are first and foremost decisive for the distribution of labor. These moments also function *within* the national economy. But also the geographical chains, which *we* spoke of, have an entirely different meaning here than for other goods. Those that also prevail for these also exist here, but in addition, also others, more powerful ones. Therefore, qualified labor is not always enumerated in a way as one should expect it to be according to our theory, and if one speaks of "labor" in general, then the latter is useless. As the value scale, Marx's labor scale incidentally also fails, as one can easily see.

A concern arises regarding the second question. For all other goods, the best piece stands there where the highest performance is necessary, and it receives its value and price, its place on the value scale from this, from its ability to perform it. Now, it seems to me as if this would absolutely not be the case for "labor in general." As a rule, the entrepreneurial position or the opportunity to attain it is hereditary, and its function is fulfilled to a great extent without regard for special aptitude. Despite this, the performance is a valuable one, and the entrepreneur is right in charging a high wage for himself for it. But he cannot at all claim that he is the suitable laborer for it. However, those who would be just as suitable or better for it can most often not compete with him for it. They have no way of reaching it, even entirely aside from the lack of capital; certainly not the common laborer as a rule, but also not the civil servant; only the very superior force, and even it only asserts itself though favorable coincidences. Only someone in an equal social position can *compete* with him; only there, is the sun equally distributed. This is generally applicable. In also the community life and in all liberal professions, the best force that has to bring forth the most significant performances it is not necessary. Besides efficiency, a row of requirements are to be fulfilled, which tend towards eliminating, at least *often*, very efficient competitors. It is not that the more significant performances always demand higher qualifications. The average measurement can be performed by the average man on all, even the highest levels, and one can generally say that the apex of the social pyramid is not formed by the most efficient elements, and its base is not formed by the most inefficient elements. We could show that no complex of these higher characteristics belongs to the common entrepreneur, which attribute some representations to him that he also does not possess them, as a rule. Not he, entirely different things are the driving forces of his enterprise. And I believe, through impartial observation, that it also otherwise shows that the best-qualified labor can by no means bring forth the most significance performance. But let us stop. It is an embarrassing feeling for me to have to indicate problems that reach deep into "sociology" so briefly. But it was nevertheless necessary in order to justify our opinion.

We are not going into the discussion of the question of *which* moments they are that determine the distribution of the labor force, but rather satisfy ourselves in establishing that our economical means towards these circumstances fail, and we want to formulate the consequences of the circumstance that was just discussed for the economical theory. In order for the value calculation to be thorough and satisfactory, it is absolutely necessary that the labor forces are only distributed from the standpoint of the value of the performances, and the demand for performances corresponds to the schema of the value function. Only then will the values of the individual performances be normal in the sense of our system. Now this is not the case for labor. We have already seen that the supply itself of the available labor is not controlled by the value principle; we now still see that the demand also is not. Or more correctly, it only is this under the same limitation as the supply, with the clause: "In the same social and national circle." This goes as far as one being able to ask oneself whether the use of the categories supply and demand even make sense and are of value here.

It is easy to see how we want to answer the third question. We negate it most decisively of all. Not he acquires qualifications—whichever type—or turns to "higher" professions, who is especially inclined to do so, but rather he, who possesses the opportunity to do so, which is in turn primarily characterized by the moment of class. And again: within the same economical and social class a connection between qualification and natural talent, as it is necessary for the value calculation, may indeed exist. One can think differently about its meaning in relation to other moments that also function within the mentioned circle. It certainly exists in a *significant* degree. So "beneficiation" of the raw material of the good "labor" is therefore also not made according to the economic laws, at least this cannot be claimed generally and in this sense, as it can for all other goods.

Let us sum up: I would not have anything against treating labor exactly the same as all other goods in principle, as a "commodity" like one expresses it, if this schema would lead to useful results. To strive against it out of consideration for "human dignity" or out of reasons like the one that man is the subject of the economy and can therefore not be its object seems to us to rest on a misunderstanding of our theory. But our examination of the verification of our result leads us to recognize the same as being jejune. We stand before emergences to which no bridge leads from our system. *Similar to islands, the individual groups of laborers that exist in the national economy are separated from one another in the broadest sense, and there is hardly any "commerce" between the same*. Those social bonds are indeed not eternal and the centuries are approaching the "islands." For our purposes, for our system that is only constructed for short periods this correlation hardly exists. However, the value principle does prevail on every island. And our means of reference lie in it, which we would like to put in place of the one from Marx and the value theory. We assume that every type of labor and laborers once and for all exists and is given: In our area of study there is a set number of civil servants, artists, scholars, and unskilled manual laborers, etc.; every relation, every transition from one to the other is missing between these groups. To us, this seems to fit better to reality, and it being corrected in this manner results in our theory of wages being applicable. For every one of these groups there is a distinctly determined wage rate that does not stand in a simple relation to the other wage rates as one would like to believe. However, a relation does exist, it is only another one. We then want to immediately ventilate it. Of course, we may then make no secret of the fact that our theory from the standpoint of practical results is almost pressed down to implicitness; at any rate, it loses significant meaning that would otherwise pertain to it.

We still want to specify the meaning that pertains to the common construction. Could one not in fact carry out the same in an entirely abstract area of study? Certainly, and then that organization of society would emerge, which we have outlined. But one may not forget that several new premises are necessary to do so, much more advanced than we would otherwise need for our system. You see, it would not be sufficient to simply assume an isolated nation. Because even a nation that seems very homogenous to us contains very many ethnical elements, between which free competition can never exist. We would have to construct one as it, at least currently, exists nowhere. This would be the first premise. Secondly, but even within one of such we would possibly—it would however not be the case according to some theories—encounter the phenomenon of the class formation and at any rate, the numerous individual correlations, which constitute the social milieu, the social basis of every individual. It would also have to be apart from that. The individual groups that form around certain interests and positions will surely oppose every outsider with resistance, and personal relations would quite certainly play a role in even a communistic community, which would, according to selection of efficiency and other qualifications as it exists for every other good, substitute another type of selection. Our schema would have to connive it. Thirdly, ownership of goods and acquisition of qualifications would also be in connection here, which should be more important than the one between natural talent and miscellaneous qualification. If the value calculation is to be thoroughly useful, then one would also have to abstain from it. Here a uniform price would then exist for the unit of *performance*; even then, not for the unit of *labor*, since the natural skill would form an interrupting moment.

But what purpose could such a construction serve, which value would correspond to it? Above all, it represents a *further step of abstraction* than our system does otherwise. This must especially be held on to. We constantly place special emphasis on such differentiations of *different steps of abstraction*, since they are very essential to the correct understanding of the individual theories in themselves and in their relation to one another. One could say that our discussions that we just carried out actually served no other purpose than to give the proof that *this great theory of society and even the common theory of wages represents such a further step* that it carries another character and is distanced further from reality than other parts of the theoretical economy, than the *greatest* part of the same. And it is informatory to remark that in the course of our thoughts, hypotheses can often creep in entirely by themselves, without us becoming aware of it, without us being conscious in leaving the firm ground and working with new moments.

The economic subjects that the construction, about whose value we now want to pass judgment, has to do with are not people, but rather utility machines, which have need of all the characteristics, which are a mark of people who live in the social organization, which *constitute* the social organization. Those assumptions regarding the "hedonistic" motives and the lack of everything non-economical are really necessary *here*, which the economists *generally* and unjustly constructed for the entire system and superfluously limited the application of our sentences. This is also an important result, which seems suitable in showing the individual parts of our theory in a more poignant light, and also in proving that our system in itself is not at all as far from reality as is often believed, that this appearance is only evoked by *some* of the economic theories. Here we have one of the same in front of us. But our system already deviates enough from the facts; this theory should exceed the measurement of the useful one, and since it can and did give rise to radically wrong deductions of social nature, we want to therefore turn away from it. But we want to add alleviation to this judgment. We have already said that it does not lack *every* value. And we now want to complete this in yet another direction. The theory is *not* essential to the explanation of the wage's *essence*. We can also attain this result in a more correct way, by examining the wage on every one of our theoretical islands. It does *not* give us "the" wage rate of reality, because such a flat rate does not exist at all. Insofar as it debauches us to this opinion, its role is corruptive. But if we remain conscious of its essence and its premises, then this theory is not "wrong" as we said. It teaches us in particular through the sensational discrepancy of its results with reality that the value principle regards, not controls, the field of labor as a whole. One can just prove this the best with it. Now in it lies, in my opinion, its most important, practical value of realization. It only gives us a negative result, but this is also not to be scoffed at, and its derivation and discussion gives us an important pointer in the direction where the decisive moments are to be looked for.

One can briefly justify the lack of a flat wage rate with the lack of completely free competition. But this manner of expression is, on the one hand, incomplete; it leaves the individual, important points in the dark, and on the other hand, ambiguous. We have therefore not adopted them. But at this point where we point them out, we do want to still remark that the mechanism of free competition functions less smoothly even *elsewhere* for labor as for the other goods. One is to be reminded of a special reason for the scarce "movement," especially for labor that we, by the way, already touched upon, of the one emphasized by Professor Edgeworth: Only when *every* "buyer" can barter with *every* "seller," complete equilibrium is attained. However, the laborer must generally sell his entire labor to a single entrepreneur. And this alone would prove, as can be shown, a considerable difference between the price formation of labor and of the other goods.

III

We still have to complete that, which has been said through the examination of whether a connection and which connection that exists between the values and prices from every type of "laborer" from his birth on, from the consumed goods and his wage. We intentionally do not say "and the goods that are produced by him" in order to avoid the difficulties that surround the term "product of labor," and that also only seem fixed in part—even though in the largest part—to us through the modern attribution theory.

Such a connection exists for all goods that are not "freely" presented by nature, that are therefore *produced*, and only when it exists, is the value calculation thoroughly useful, at least according to this direction. Again: We have do not have a collected opinion about how this behaves for labor. It would be pointless to philosophize about whether labor should be conceived as a produced good or as a "bounty of nature." A priori reasons for the one or the other cannot help us at all. Even less naturally determining are social, political, or moral moments for our position. Labor to us does not already belong a priori to one or the other of those categories of goods. It is up to us which one we want to class it among. The one or the other is solely a methodological aid, a technical rule of measurement, so to speak, and not the slightest expression of a fact, or a social claim, or a postulation lies in it. We therefore have entirely free choice. We will decide on that eventuality that is better suited for our system and offers better derivations on the one hand, and which lead to more consequences that are fitting to reality on the other hand. But we must constantly not lose sight of the arbitrariness of our choice in principle.

One reason that could affect us for doing the same would surely be the one that we, if we would regard labor as being a produced good, perpetuate our analysis a few steps further, according to an analogy with other produced and reproduced goods, and could gain more results than for goods that are not able to be produced. And if these results are useful, then this would not be scoffed at. But we must remind one of the fact that for us those *imperative* reasons that we established for the classical authors a. a. O.[6] are not there. We do not *have to* do this like they do in order to maintain our system. The fact that we do not have to do this is a preference *of our* approach, a great preference of the modern system. Insofar as that classical theory would only be traceable to this theoretical imperative, we would simply drop it like many other things. But the "theory of reproduction cost" of the wage also has a second meaning, which is to be differentiated from the one that was just mentioned in the interest of its valuation—it is an interesting theory in itself; with the exception of its role in literature: Working within our area, overlooking the value of our system and the field of its usefulness, we find that a shaft opens itself here, which possibly leads to a mine. We see a possibility to enhance our possession of theories. It is not allowed to be neglected, and we want to regard it without insisting on it at all costs. If we discover something that speaks to us, then we will treat labor according to an analogy of the reproducible goods, in the other case equable an analogy of the non-reproducible goods, and then construct the foundations of our system according to this. Our examination has entirely the same character as the former one. Just as we had seen there, whether there is something in reality that would correspond to the flat wage rate of the theory, we have to prove here, whether the results that would emerge from the treatment of labor as a reproducible good fit to reality. Here too, it deals with an attempt of verification.

Now the first result that would have to maintain itself would be the equation between "production costs" and wages. All others that would be aimed at, are dependent on this sentence, are only attainable across this bridge. In the event that we could verify it, we would then have to repeat the same operation for every step. If we cannot do it, we do not need to ask for anything additionally. The reader is already able to see what our judgment will be. We have already mentioned moments that point to this. Since the theory of reproduction cost of labor never quite gained a foothold in Germany anyway and has only a few followers, we therefore want to be brief. It is the most obvious for all "higher" professions that this equation does not exist. Let us again give the example of a civil servant. As his costs he would have calculated expenses related to his studies, etc., and in addition his labor for them, finally, his financial support up to his employment. This sum would be set equal to the discounted value of his further earnings to the time of its calculation. We are not going into detailed questions regarding this calculation, because the same does not seem to be useful to us, and does not seem to adequately come close to the processes of reality due to the following reasons.

Firstly: A portion of the educational costs cannot be conceived as costs for a specific profession, but would at any rate rather be expended, even if an entirely private life would be intended. This is so clear that examples are superfluous. Primarily the views and habits of the social class, which the person concerned belongs to are decisive of the education, and not economical moments. This alone would already have to bewilder us regarding our equation. Let us keep in mind that this not only applies to "higher" professions, but also more or less applies to every type of labor. The common laborer also learns for example, many things in elementary school that cannot count, or not unforcedly count as preparation for his profession, and obviously other reasons are decisive in learning them. One could now want to limit the equation to those special preparations, therefore to the "educational costs" for the entirely unqualified laborer. But this would not change anything on the fact that other costs that were justified as being only economical are being expended on man; on the contrary, it would only emphasize them. Thereupon, this differentiation would not always be carried out easily: Some things, for example, higher education is, on the one hand, a prerequisite for the profession of the civil servant, on the other hand, it would most often by all means be expended for the members of that class, also with no consideration for the profession. However, these difficulties would not be insurmountable. But we do not want to follow this any further, since there are still other reasons, which divert us from this approach.

Secondly, that calculation, which is not abstained from for every other good is *actually*, as a rule, not constructed here. Who would then ask himself whether the equation will exist for him? One will often be *aware* that the success will be scarcer economically than the costs, and one will even more often *hope* for the contrary. Social constraint, ambition, etc., repress the economical moments. And the child of the laborer is also raised without such considerations only existing distantly. However, during the acquisition of a special qualification our equation will often apply, but here too, certainly not without exception and not even as a rule. There are certainly cases that can fit into the schema of the "productive merger." The entire theory which we are speaking of here is certainly not in limbo. But these cases for which it applies are seldom and meaningless in relation to the quantities of the ones where other moments prevail.

Thirdly: Especially the element of cost that lies in its own labor of education jibs that schema. It is almost only effective for "higher" professions. And inclination, the "will to power," etc., is much more important here on the one hand, and on the other hand—perhaps even more so—the circumstance that the member of certain classes *can* do nothing other with his labor force, is consequently socially forced to utilize them in one of the few ways that stand open to him, even if this does not correspond to the economical rules at all.

Fourthly, costs and success most often or yet, very often do not fall to the same people. The former often carry, for example, the parents and in some respect the community, without hoping for an economic success and therefore also without a uniformity of costs to be able to aspire with the same.

Fifthly, finally, a long time often goes by between expenditure and success. All circumstances *can* change during the same and in fact, almost always change. An exact correctness of our equations can therefore not be expected and furthermore, if a calculation were to be made, it would certainly be computed to dynamic changes. In doing so, one must always keep in mind that directly dynamic moments also come into play for education, every type of effort that does not fit into our static equilibrium. For our system, which only leads a so to speak momentary existence, such processes are intangible. Once expended costs will therefore behave similarly to land, since they can no longer be made reversible; it must therefore be taken what can be achieved, without one being able to have an effect on the price through a modification of the supply. And all skills that were acquired through "propensity" have this character.

This moment thus directly points us to not constructing an equation for labor of the type that was mentioned. This is in fact the result that we reach: *due to these reasons, we will not go into the production for labor*. And we just now have the full justification for this representation that we had developed at an earlier point.[7]

We are at the end of this thought process. To some, it will seem that we have dwelled too long upon this. But this did still seem necessary to us, since we are herein laying our eyes on the difficulties that stand in the way of a clear conception of the problem of wages, and form the sources of many misunderstandings and controversies. Our result is not gratifying to the theorist, because it arises as a result that only a modest role corresponds to the economic theory in these important questions.

In regards to the last of the discussed points, we would like to emphasize that we by no means deny the possibility that a static examination could still prove a connection between costs and price of labor. We only claim that from the standpoint of the theory and with its means one of such is not to be constructed, and that it is *more advisable and more careful* not to follow this path. We only solved our question in the sole interest of our system. We ourselves have indeed pointed out denunciations in the sense of one of such connections. But above all, it is the great fact that the majority of laborers only acquires about that, which is necessary for the maintenance of life and labor force, which the representatives of this theory can rest upon. The modern social statistician does admittedly know to cite enough data that show that that neither something general, nor something necessary lies in it, but we do not want to deny that it does by and large behave in this manner. No logical necessity, no great law expresses itself in it, but rather only the fact that the supply of goods for humanity is just a very sparse one altogether.

The theory of reproduction cost of the wage is, in the use of unqualified labor, a theory of a minimum of existence, and therefore amounts to the "iron law of wages." The latter would therefore arise from the theory if labor could be conceived as a "commodity" from all sides like all other ones. Its relation to a corresponding theory of population is clear, yes, one will perhaps be able to say that observations from the area of the facts of wages and the needs of the theory of wages have contributed to that classical theory of population. I do in fact believe that. The latter has not arisen from a, for example, biological study of the increase in population; because this would have lead to other results; also not from unbiased, impartial observations of its facts in themselves; because in my opinion, *other* moments would have had to force themselves through than those from which the theorems of the theory flow, at least also others. No, it was solely constructed with regard for the explanation of certain economical emergences, and *these* represented its point of departure. I am sorry not to be able to linger on these very important contemplations any longer. The essential point is that our approach grants us a clear judgment over the theory of reproductive cost of the wage and over the iron law of wages, which therefore simply represents a special case of the same—already an important result. Let us summarize it again. Both theories represent themselves under two aspects that must be carefully differentiated: 1. as essential elements of the classical educational system, which *requires* it; 2. as interesting theories, also in themselves. Their *first* role is played out in the modern system: We do not need it. The *second* aspect of the same gives us an interesting example for theories that are assuredly based on facts, which lead onto its construction, and nevertheless do not maintain themselves. They are not "wrong," but are rather to be kept under certain requirements. But the latter ones are such that one would be better off in abandoning that which is based on them. One can call the first role the deductive one; the second, the inductive one. Both were relevant in the past, but the present does not need either one. We therefore come to an end that the theory of reproduction cost of the wage, as well as the iron law of wages, no longer forms constituent parts of the theoretical economy. We are abandoning them—their interest is now more of a historical one.

One more thing about the "standard of life" theory: As the attacks and doubts regarding the iron law of wages accumulated, one believed in being able to save the position of the theory through it and simultaneously being able to approach reality with the latter. It therefore originated from the theory of the minimum of existence and is meant as its correction. Now, little that is positive can be credited to it. Above all, it is based on a misjudgment of the circumstance that if that connection between "costs of labor" in the sense of the educational costs or costs of upbringing and the wage does not exist, this *entire* train of thought must be abandoned. Thereupon, this "correction" destroys the foundations of the theory, breaks its core out of it by directly forgoing that, which is *essential*. Finally, it only says a banality, namely that every laborer in the price battle will *attempt* to attain a wage that enables him to at least continue his current standard of life. He is thereby supported by conventions and other moments of persistence so that the current standard of life is actually mostly maintained, and the entrepreneur will not generally go wrong by regulating the wage, which he will have to pay to the extent that corresponds to the standard, in his calculations. But the standard of life gains nothing from the depth and the meaning of the iron law of wages and also from the practical interest of the same. Yes, its foundation—in fact, its entire character—is a complete different one. It is only a superficial emergency construction that spoils the style of the entire structure; a correction of certain evidently inapplicable consequences without reform of the fundaments, and without regard and understanding for the fact that the substructure can not tolerate such an alteration.

We must unfortunately deny ourselves in carrying out, as others too—in my opinion, *all* others—special questions starting from our standpoint can be added to a clear and thorough solution, which radically and satisfactorily brings the endless controversies to an end. The most important question in this connection would be how the laws of movement of the wage are in regards to the other branches of income, those laws that the classical authors derivated with such great certainty, and that played and do still play such a large role in the discussion of economic problems, without one being able to really maintain them or thoroughly disprove them. Citations of facts pro and con—both are simple—lead just as little to actual insight as do general arguments. By the by, this discussion shows that also the historian and the practitioner must in fact turn to the theory or must at least theorize if they want to reach an overall judgment. Here belongs, for example, the question of the effects of a strike, then the effects of an increase in wage for other branches of income, and namely those branches of income, which increase and decrease *simultaneously* and *in contrast to one another*. Plenty will be said about this at a later point, but only so much to show that our theory really is able to achieve something useful there. A complete representation of the results is impossible in the framework of this work.

We only want to touch upon two special questions here; firstly, the question whether or not the wages, as one maintains to say, "are paid from the capital." The answer is simple: If one calls all of those goods of an individual "capital," which he does not use for his consumption, then the question is self-evidently affirmed. But if one asks whether the consumption goods of the laborer are to be simply regarded as "production means," as for example, oil of a machine, then this is just as self-evidently negated.

May this suffice; we cannot elaborate it any further. We want to answer the second question just as briefly: What can be thought of the "wage fund?" Now surely the total sum of the wages is distinctly determined at every given moment exactly the same through our theorem of equilibrium as the individual wage rate, and the same as the total sum of the ground rents. There is therefore a wage fund, as well as an "annuity fund," and the expression is fitting and useful so far. When it was satirically—by the way, very brilliantly—said that one could then also speak of a "potato fund," then this is to be countered that it could in fact be occasionally useful to regard the total sum of the products: Sold quantities multiplied by the price—the "turnover"—for a good, and that the "potato fund" and so much more the same quantity for such an important good as labor therefore fulfills a task very well, and suffices for an economic need. Yes, even the conception that a larger number of laborers will have to divide themselves into the same like a smaller one is not so far removed from reality than one could believe: This sum certainly does not grow proportionally to the quantity of available labor in the *static state*. But this is also everything. The remaining significance of the wage fund in the classical system disappears in the modern one, and the theory of the wage fund of the elders, even though it is certainly not absolutely wrong in itself and even though, namely on the premises of static—a moment that was given much too little attention during its judgment, but whose fruitfulness shows itself again at this point—maintainable to a great extent, and according to its essence, belongs to the requisite know-how, which we have discarded. It can no longer be regarded as an integrating constituent part of our system, can therefore also not be used as a weapon against the same. If we would like to still help ourselves to it on occasion, namely occasionally use the expression "wage fund," then it is in fact important to clearly comprehend that it does not belong to our *foundations* and must potentially prove itself for each individual case.

IV

It can only still be spared to answer our second question, the question: How far does the area of the emergence of wages reach? This can happen very briefly. Not every skill is "labor," not every labor reaps economical enumeration, not every economical enumeration is "wage"; therefore the price which the theory derivates. Some theoretical sentences are certainly applicable to almost every skill. Every walk can be described in the language of economy: One goes so far until the equation marginal utility-marginal cost is fulfilled, therefore until fatigue or the value of another use of power and time balance the enjoyment of going further. And this can also be said for operations of public spirit or of benefaction. This approach is not always suitable: The athlete often works his horse longer than the actual enjoyment justifies, the politician tries harder than one should expect from the standpoint of actual satisfaction. But *insofar as a static approach is even suitable for these things*, this description is also applicable. In a certain respect, one can now include suchlike in the theory of wages, but there, where it deals with one great emergence of the labor wage, one will be better to eliminate skill, which is self-purpose or follows purposes outside the economy. One will only regard one of such that commonly reaps income. The emergences of wages of the theory here now also outreaches that, which is called wage in common life, thus in the case of the self-employed entrepreneur, so especially of the farmer, of the craftsman, etc. But to what extent? One could be tempted to answer: Insofar as job performance comes into consideration. But some labor always comes into consideration for *every* acquisition. The "capitalist" does not only have to cut out coupons, but also has to select his investments, the landlord has to monitor his tenants in the economical sense, etc., without this "labor" being specially remunerated. But much more important is the skill of the entrepreneur, namely that, which is not suitable for the "entrepreneurial *wage*," but rather more specifically for the entrepreneurial *profit*. This is certainly "remunerated," even often times very high, but not through a "wage," which would be analog to the laborer's. A skill is therefore probably economically reciprocated here, however, the wage schema does not suit this remuneration; its use would rather falsify the picture of reality: As for other labor, no supply and no demand of such performances take place on the market, as we will still explain later—they are not *separately* bought and sold. There finally are incomes, as for example, civilians who certainly correspond to a skill, without the economical term of wage being adequate. Other approaches, for example, by means of the moment of *tax* are better suited.

The answer to our question subsequently arises entirely by itself: The emergence of wage reaches as far as one can connect a good, unaffected sense to the schema supply and demand, buying and selling. The area of the theory of wages is therewith defined; attempts to go beyond this are not advisable.

Notes

1. In the popular sense of the word (Schumpeter, 1908, pg. 334).
2. We must rather reproach even some economists. The treatment of the modern problem whether or not the most efficient elements of the nations, due to the scarce fruitfulness of the upper classes are fated to become extinct already justified it on its own, and must let every serious critic of our discipline appear in the most unpleasant light (Schumpeter, 1908, pgs. 336-37).
3. Distribution of Wealth 1899 (Schumpeter, 1908, pg. 345).
4. The other is the consideration for the subsistence theory.
5. But it is to be countered that this would be very doleful for the theory, because only a part of also the manual labor is entirely "common" and the problem immediately arises for every other one (Schumpeter, 1908, pg. 346).
6. In the first part of this book (Schumpeter, 1908, pg. 358).
7. The reader will understand us when we say that no complete abandonment of the equation cost = utility lies in it. The same will still be fundamental to us. But under "costs" one may understand nothing else than "value in OTHER uses," and furthermore, one must constantly be mindful of the limitations under which it applies—of our picture of the "islands."

3

The Theory of Ground Rent

I

The foundations of the theory of ground rent arise just as easily from our system as for wages. It is hardly necessary to be declaratory of the same of the closer one. Every property has its distinctly determined value and price in our system, which explains itself in entirely the same way and is subject to exactly the same formal laws as value and price of every other good.

It is in the same relation of effect and interaction to all other prices in the national economy and to all requirements of the same altogether, such as number, labor force, and the population's direction of needs, organizing of the social organization, level of technology, quantity and type of the available supply of goods, etc. All of this expresses itself in the value and price of every property. Land does not differentiate itself in the slightest from other elements of our system in all these points, and for the foundations of the exact economy, we need to worry just as little about its special characteristics in principle than about the technical features of, for example, a machine. Just as we did not differentiate the price formation of sugar in the theory from that of wheat, we will also not differentiate the price formation of land from that of labor. In fact, in the theory we only speak of goods in general anyway, and when we name special types of goods, this only happens for the purpose of enlivening the representation and has nothing to do with the essence of our approach. Our schema is abstract and absolute in also this sense, and we only occasionally introduce circumstances, which are only specific to one or the other good, for the purpose of handling special questions. This rule also applies here.

I believe that this conception must seem to be of impartial judgment, yes—self-evident. What is more natural than to say that a price is paid for land, because it is useful, because one needs it? But one has almost always described the emergence of ground rent differently, and even still today, one must consider Ricardo's theory of ground rent to be dominant. In fact, it sounds downright paradoxical to say that ground rent is essentially the same as labor wage. One could obviously much rather speak of a contrast. The landlord and the laborer are, as I said, of such different social characters that one automatically searches for differences in the economical foundation of their existence. Their interests are more often opposing than coinciding, even though this contrast may have often and perhaps mostly been exaggerated. One could accuse of clouding the picture of reality if we were to take no account of all this. But by taking a closer look, that, which is paradox of the matter, disappears. Let one realize that, which we have already said about the nature of our exact system. Of course, far be it from us in wanting to deny those contrasts. The circumstance that we are calling on one and the same explanation for the landlord's income as for that of the laborer does not mean that both are to be judged the same from the socio-political or from any other standpoint than that of the theoretical economy, but only that a small group of formal laws applies both to one as to the other.

The laborer surely does not become a capitalist when someone considers labor as being a capital good, and one can only lay eyes on something objectionable in one of such methodological rules of measurement by lack of understanding or ill-will. But I believe to have already said enough about these concerns that lie in this direction. It is sufficient to repeat that socio-political and sociological discussions cannot play a role there, where it deals with the purposes of the pure price theory. They would only be hindering, and consideration for them is contrary to a healthy labor distribution.

But even regarded as being purely theoretical, our conception encounters quite some difficulties. As is generally known, it is certainly common to quote a great deal of characteristics that single out land from other goods. This discussion occupies a rather broad area in especially English literature. We have already had the opportunity to explain that we do not want to pay special interest to this topic. We said that a priori statements about such things lead to nothing, that the actual purpose which one has his eye on alone decides. An example is the non-duplicity of land: On the one hand, it was explained by us that no good is absolutely duplicable, but is rather actually non-duplicable in every given moment of every one. And on the other hand, the quantity of land is given not quite fixed. Despite the fact that the economically used land can still be aggrandized through new cultures and can still be diminished through the task of cultivation, so does the quantity of land, which is dedicated to a specific use, change through the fact that one can feed it land that has so far served other purposes, or conversely, that can allot the quantity of such other purposes that is available to it. And this is also the case for the other differences, which maintain to be commonly emphasized. This not only contradicts the claim that such circumstances can be taken into consideration with utility for certain purposes. One can therefore take the circumstance under consideration during the discussion of the question of how a change in the price of a product affects the prices of the participating production factors, that the supply of land is generally less elastic than that of capital and labor. But this does not matter to the main questions, and it is advisable to represent the same as simply and coherently as possible for now.

The conception of the similarity in monopoly of the income from land is in relation with the just mentioned moment. But the alleged non-duplicity in no way eliminates competition among the landed properties, and it was justifiably emphasized that one can only speak of a monopoly there, where an economic subject has complete control over the supply of a good. But this is evidently not the case here. One could just as justifiably speak of a capital monopoly and a labor monopoly of the laborers. Such an approach may have its advantages for some purposes, and certain theorems can be demonstrated by means of the same. But a universal truth does not lie in it, one can rather consider it to be a fiction that *occasionally* proves itself. It is generally better to derivate the price of land with help of the hypothesis of free competition.

It could seem that we can also not speak of a uniform price of land in this case; because every property has its special characteristics and certainly differs from every other; it is so to speak always unique in its own way. Location and composition of the ground are by and large given fixedly, and one could therefore at least frequently say in another sense than the one, which was just mentioned, that every landowner has a type of monopolistic disposition in regards to his property. While therefore most of the theorists have no decency in speaking of a flat wage rate and a flat interest rate, it is not at all possible and it sounds very strange to accept a flat rate of ground rent, a uniform ground rent rate. One is rather accustomed to seeing a so-called "differential income" in ground rent, therefore a direct contrast to the flat rates of wage and interest, which are determined by free competition. And yet, our derivation of ground rent as a price points to something of the sort. If we can therefore use the latter approach, then much for the uniformity of our system is won by it, and interesting results for the laws of movement should arise from this standpoint.

This is fortunately readily possible with the help of a simple stratagem. Instead of speaking of land in itself, we must simply speak of land performance. Nothing forced or objectionable lies in it at all. We also do not regard the labor *force* for labor, but rather the labor *performance*, not the value of the first one as such, but rather the value of any unit of the latter one. The expression "capital utilizations" is absolutely common. And the uniformity of the wage rate and the capital interest is not asserted by the entire labor force and by the capital goods as such, but only rather by units of labor performance and capital utilizations of similar type. The matter therefore does not behave differently in the slightest for land than for other production factors: Neither for land, nor for labor and capital is there a uniform price if one has the goods as such in mind, but there is probably one of such, namely not any less for the first one as for the latter one if one adheres to the uniformity of performance.

Every property therefore contains a specific type and number of possible performances, just as a laborer is able to bring a certain type and number of labor performances onto the market corresponding to his aptitude and education. A flat price then exists for those land performances, just as for every other good and the price theory, namely also the hypothesis of free competition is just as applicable to it and has the same limitations as for every other price. The fact that one landowner has a greater income than another no longer poses a problem from this standpoint. It is no more surprising than the fact that the owner of a more efficient machine or higher labor force attains a greater income than he, who has a lesser efficient machine or smaller labor force: He simply owns more or more valuable land performances, a more valuable good than the other man, and is in exactly the same position as a landowner who owns a larger but less fruitful property. The fact that someone who has a fruitful field receives a higher ground rent than the owner of a lesser fruitful one is no more disconcerting than the fact that the owner of a larger one receives more ground rent for the same fruitfulness than the one with the smaller one. We do not need a special principle to explain these things; rather, the matter is clear so that nothing remains to be asked. Our system therefore gives as a completely satisfactory theory of ground rent entirely by itself.

It would thereby be in our option whether we want to limit ourselves to only assuming *one* specific type of land performances so that a flat ground rent rate would arise, or to construct a special ground rent rate for different types of the same and for every one of them. The latter may be more suitable to reality, but nothing hinders us in principle than regarding the different numbers of the units of performances that are contained in it as the only difference between properties. This would also work quite well for the comparison of land, which cannot serve for the same productions; because even if it seems that one cannot compare the units of different types of performances with one another—even if it seems that one, in our schema, cannot compare, for example, differently yielding types of wheat-land, but not wheat-land and pastures—one therefore easily sees that we can construct the unit of performance in a way that it is suitable for every type of land. A unit of value would also be suitable for it among other things. While value calculation with regards to the mentioned circumstances does not offer entirely satisfactory services for the different types of labor, the opposite would arise for land: Its use is determined, although not exclusively but still in principle, by economical considerations. One can therefore say for the unit of value of land for every economic subject that it attains a flat price. This calculation according to the units of value is also applicable to land in various locations and furthermore, can be used agriculturally as well as for structures. However, if one would want to, for example, construct a unit of performance of land due to the chemical component parts, then another would have to be assumed for city land and the LOCATION would also have to be considered as an independent moment. To expand on this would lead too far, but I believe that every connoisseur of the theory sees that there is no difficulty in principle here.

II

We have especially derivated the value of land performances, and this is in fact that, which especially—and actually *only*—comes into consideration for the static theory. Significant changes in ownership can indeed occur in the static state of the national economy, and everything that is actually interesting about them gravitates towards the great problem of the development. Besides, since the price of the land performances and not the one of land itself is important for the problem of distribution, we could disregard the value and price of the latter quite well. We would then proceed in no other way than reality often does: For example, the price of land did not come into consideration for the largest epoch of the history of the German economy, and there was hardly a reason to be conscious of its value. The economical development and moments outside of the economy influence the value of land much more in themselves than that of the individual land *performance*, and cause the first one to show a far-reaching independency towards the latter one.

I am therefore giving the answer of the theory to the question of land value not with great certainty, namely not with much self-confidence. It in itself is of course simple enough: The value of a property for someone is equal to the sum of the values of those land performances for him, which he takes into consideration according to his aptitude and his circumstances. It must thereby also be considered that the values of the latter ones are that much more scarce, the further in the future its possibility of realization lies under otherwise the same circumstances. This answer surely is not without significance; in fact, we believe to have to see an essential progress of the new economy in it. But the matter is not as simple as some theorists represented it to be; our formula namely involves a keener abstraction—it is further form reality—as one should believe. The length of the time frame that it refers to carries with it that it is by far not as suitable to the facts as the theory of the price of land performances. Even the contempt of prospective utilizations, which deals with the problem of interest, is a problem whose difficulty, as well as dynamic character, we will see when we get to interest. By the way, it cannot simply be measured by the interest rate, even if an interesting correlation exists between it and the latter one. As a whole, one can say that one will have to call on even much more—and other—factual material before the matter is satisfactorily grasped, and the reader sees at this point how *occasionally* and even *often*, although of course not *always*, a correct handling of the theory quite astoundingly brings us close to the historians' circles of thought. And this would show itself even more distinctly if we could be somewhat more explicit.

Our theory of ground rent then exists from both of these results regarding the values and prices of: firstly, land performances; and secondly, of land itself. We now have to verify the same. This task regarding the second one is by no means simple; one even readily sees that the result would be complicated and only partially satisfactory. But we do not want to occupy ourselves with it any further, since the topic actually does not belong in static. The verification of our theory of the value and price of the land performances is that much simpler.

Does it explain this value and price? Yes, sufficiently, by and large. There are indeed enough difficulties. It is clear that the use of land does not exclusively take place according to pure economical rules, and even less according to static rules; that the *value* scale in no way exhaustively mirrors the *price* scale of the same. Not everyone gives away his multi-family house to a restaurant or for other business purposes, even if this would be beneficial; not everyone uses his property for economical purposes in the narrow sense of the word. Many people also inhabit their family house in a center of business activities, even though the land that it sits on would be used more beneficially for a multistory, multi-family house. Others lay out a wildlife park there where the value of land considering an intensive garden economy is fixed. And there are many of such cases. They really tarnish the picture that our theory conceptualizes; they paralyze our law of the flat "ground rent rate." But only in part; the large mass of the land performances fits into our schema. One also may not overestimate those assumptions: one will constantly observe the disappearance of family houses in central parts of the city to a large extent—even though other moments besides the economic ones are also effective for it—and we do in fact *mostly* only find wildlife parks there where another type of use of land is not or only insignificantly profitable. Other types of cases *are* just exceptions. Even so, it must be admitted that they play a larger role than for other goods; but hardly anyone will claim that they render our theory useless.

There are also *economical* moments that do not grasp the schema of our theory. It often happens that one holds on to certain cultures out of different types of national-economical reasons, even though *others* would *initially* and *purely economically* commend themselves more, and absolutely lie within the scope of the pertaining landlord. One may promote the cultivation of any fruit, which does not yield that return in money, which would *otherwise* be attainable, etc., out of favor to a national industry or out of other national reasons. All of these things disturb our value and price calculation and are not ascertainable from it. They are also *frequent* and of special interest. But one will still admit that our theory covers most of the facts, furthermore, also explains a good deal of strong tendencies and gives so to speak a standard, which every actual state is compared to, whose application one sees as the norm and whose failure forms an emergence that causes our surprise and immediately requires a special explanation.

But is this price of land performances the ground rent; does it represent the income of the landowner in its capacity as such? This question can also be answered similarly. There are also difficulties here that disavow our picture, take a portion of its value from it, but also do not do *more* as a whole, do not render it completely irrelevant. It is especially difficult to isolate this income. Not only because it very rarely appears by itself, but also because it is influenced by those elements that it is associated with. One can, for example, not simply conceive rent as being ground rent; other elements still go into it, house rent for fundus instructus, etc. But then the income that a property provides will essentially be dependent on what one *actually* does with it, and a special interaction, for example, between ground rent and interest on capital, will exist, which is to be differentiated from the general interaction that our system reflects. In such cases it can occur that the ground rent can only be detached from the total income that someone derives from an economic venture by means of a more or less artificial approach. It can thereby occur that *nothing* at all remains which could be considered to be ground rent—this often occurs in the business of the farmer—while a sale of the performances of the pertaining property would nevertheless lead to an income. Our ground rent leads an ideational existence in such cases. Finally, one must be carefully thoughtful of not overlooking a portion of the same: It can often fall to several different people, not only to the landowner. The building lease is such a case, namely only if a "Rekognitionszins" (an interest on recognition) is being paid; a portion of the ground rent, perhaps the largest portion does not fall to the landlord, but rather to the tenant, to the "laborer" or "capitalist," and it would obviously be remiss to want to look for the ground rent here in the rent.[1]

As serious as all these considerations are, which arise from these and other similar moments against our approach, it will be as clear to anyone, who has a taste and understanding for theory altogether, especially during the recital of the same, that our abstract picture gives the undertone for all of these emergences, that the same appear as problems because of this, because they deviate from the *rule* that is outlined through this picture, and that the principle and the majority of emergences of income from land are appropriately grasped through the same.

III

A theory of ground rent that is simple, clear, and - above all - essentially applicable therefore arises from our system, suitable in replacing the one of the older national economy and forming a great advantage for the first one. This theory represents a great progress vis-à-vis the one of the classical authors for two reasons; firstly, because it does not require a new principle, hence the explanation *the reducing of that which is "unknown" to that which is "known"*, which it offers is more complete than that of the latter one and secondly, because the picture that it constructs is also more satisfying in itself than the classical one: It is therefore a *progress* in itself and allows for a *revision* of the classical approach.

In fact, we require the law of diminishing returns—this is that "new principle" as is generally known—nothing more. It no longer forms a constituent part of our scientific arsenal. It is to us, as we said, only a *technical fact* everywhere it occurs—even outside of the theory of ground rent—which is of course very important in practice, but is of no further interest to the pure theory of the economy. The classical authors on the other hand need this law. As we have already explained, they needed a special moment in order to explain the ground rent: The characteristics of their price theory required it. Our price theory, more complete than that one, does not need this bridge. And the crux of the matter for the judgment of Ricardo's theory of ground rent and our position to the same lies in it. It can only be understood from the needs of the classical system; but from this also follows that we cannot hold on to it as we choose, like many national economists do, even though they otherwise stand aground the theory of marginal utility. It is in my opinion that the most important objection to the "American School" in that it places the law of diminishing returns next to that of diminishing marginal utility without realizing that both do not have the slightest thing to do with one another, except for the formal moment of continuous diminishing, and the first one is made redundant through the latter one. But we must also judge other attempts, which lie in this direction, in the same manner. Especially in England one has continued to build on the foundations of the classical authors and has made full use of the principle of diminishing returns. One has generalized the same in different ways, namely has even applied it to labor and supply of tools, and has come to analog residual and differential theories of wages and capital interest, as well as of entrepreneurial profit—more about the latter point later. We are gliding past an entire system of the economy that is based on this principle; it is perhaps more fitting to say that this system is at least partially based on a "KONFONDIERUNG" of this principle and that of the marginal utility. New terms were formed, thus that of the "producer's rent," which embodies the generalization of the theory of ground rent for every production, and that of "consumer's rent," which represents a *psychological* construction "per analogiam" of the *physical* surplus of the production returns over the total costs. We cannot go into this here,[2] but we will only be able to predict a short future for all of these attempts; they are too formal, adhere too greatly to superficial moments, and lead to nothing. Especially the circumstance that such a boundless generalization of the term rent, in this sense, is readily possible should be alarming: This especially shows indeed how little substance it has.

The most important *material* objection to the classical theory of ground rent—and all of its "branches"—is that it assumes a given price for the ground product. This may sound somewhat surprising, but it is actually no different. It explains the landowner's income as a plus over the total costs of production of simply that product, which actually produces the pertaining property. But why is exactly that much produced of it and not less or more? Why does it stop at *this* "boundary" and not at another one? Now, the price of the product decides this—it must therefore be given. But let us go on. This price can only be regarded as the sole factor for the establishment of this boundary, if the prices of the means of production are firmly given; in the sense of the classical authors, these are the prices of capital—of the tools—and labor. But this is not yet sufficient. Why is this agricultural product and not another produced on our property anyway? The classical authors do not say anything about this. They must therefore also assume the type of culture as being given. But if one does not want to do this, then one can only refer to the moment of demand, of value. This moment decides the choosing between the different production possibilities, thereby indirectly decides the monetary returns—and therewith the value of land performances. If the type of culture is firmly given, then the value and price of the land performances must also be. But then we get to the somewhat paradoxical result that the classical theory of ground rent already presupposes the value and price of the land performances, therefore that, which it should explain; and it does actually behave this way. The theory of ground rent of the classical authors has therefore not only been overcome, it is not a theory of ground rent at all. It is only *seemingly* able to explain the price of the land performances whose existence the price theory disavows, as we have explained, it must *actually* assume it as being given. This theory is certainly "correct" on all its conditions; but these latter ones take every value of realization from it.

We are therefore turning away from it due to both of these groups of reasons. A certain significance for the explanation of some moments of interruption remains for it in another direction that we have already pointed out. The "market of land performances" certainly functions not as smoothly as for the other goods; and the approach that the landowner must take what he gets in a certain sense, because it is difficult for him to alter his supply, is not unwarranted. But this meaning is scarce. Furthermore, this is also the case for other goods in principle, which the appropriate expression "quasi-rent" was coined for. But the essence of the matter does not lie in these moments, and we can say with ease—and thereby be conscious of only serving a healthy scientific development, and being free of every destructive addiction or lack of reverence—that the role of the classical theory of ground rent is finished and the future does not belong to it.

One clearly sees this in literature. One can claim that the development of the theory of ground rent really is a "healthy" one. The thought that we represent gains ground entirely by itself in systematic representations, even if its authors do not have the conscious intent to combat the classical authors on this point at all. One theorist after the next explains that the existence of land "without rent," yes, even the law of diminishing returns is not essential to the existence of a ground rent, that the price of land "enters the price of its products" just the same or just as little as that of labor and tools, etc. Piece by piece of the classical theory is being abandoned; the foundation and the entire appearance of the theory change slowly and without clamor through the inescapable power of the progressive realization. This of course only applies to better representations; there are still enough of those which do not experience this progress. Professor Marshall's work shows us the nicest example of a breakthrough to a new theory of ground rent of the most loyal endeavor to spare the classical authors. He initially formulates the classical theory and emphasizes its correctness. But this formulation depresses it to an implicitness, it namely clearly shows that only the plus over the marginal utility *of the pertaining type of culture*—always on the conditions of the classical authors—does not enter the price of the product, but indeed the plus vis-à-vis *other* types of culture. But how is that different than that *this* value and price of the regarding property, which would befit him in *other* uses, forms an element of cost and a constituent part of the marginal price, even of the actual chosen use very well? That *this* value and price must be given if the raisonnement of the classical authors is supposed to be applicable? And does this not lead to our conception, *is* this not simply our theory? Marshall's conception therefore changes under his hands so to speak, without the classical authors being deemed as wrong in principle—only reluctantly, but that's much more significant. And we cannot help admiring this: Therefore—with this clarity and depth on the one hand, and with this sparing of that, which exists on the other hand—every innovation should go on. But the result is the same in this case: All of the adherence to classical skills, all of the expanding and defending of classical thoughts can mask the innovation of Marshall's leading thoughts for only the superficial observer.

According to this, one can consider the construction of a new theory of ground rent as being one of the most certain results of the theory of attribution. It would really be failed to want to hold on to the classical one still today—and soon, no one will do this anymore.

Notes

1. It is important to differentiate between economical control and legal possession during the assessment of such cases: This differentiation clears some difficulties away (page 378).
2. The reader will find greater detail in my essays: "Das Rentenprinzip in der Verteilungslehre" (The Principle of Rent in the Teachings of Distribution). Schmollers Jahrbuch 1907 (page 380).

4

About the Third Static Branch of Income

I

One can consider it as being consensus that there are three static branches of income. A difference in opinion exists at most regarding a fourth one of entrepreneurial profit, which, as a result from some theories, would have to stand next to this third one. Now, the third branch of income is called "interest." But it cannot be defined as simply as the other two: If one would want to regard it as a price, then one would possibly be embarrassed to say as price *for what* it should count; because different answers are possible for it, different ones to a much greater extent than for both of the other branches of income. The least accordance is surely for interest, and one is generally convinced to have the most difficult problem of the theory of distribution before oneself. Those, who did not have this conviction suffered abject failures. We do not have the intention to deliver a story and criticism of dogmas, but want to certainly seek to occasionally learn as much as possible from that, which has been accomplished, and to say quite a bit about other theories of interest with this intention, which is also supposed to contribute to a better understanding of them. But the facts and the problem itself now lie at our heart.

The interest on capital would of course be, as everything else that shows itself in our system (*if* it does this differently, which we can by no means say for certain yet, since we are reserving the verdict whether it is a static branch of income) determines all other elements of the same as it reacts to all. That, which one generally comprehends as being interest and which we speak of in this moment, without still determining what *we* understand by it and whether we even want to use this expression, would of course be another variable than it is and would play another role, not only in the economic life, but also in the entire social life if the *remaining* elements would be other ones. It is obvious that if the population were to have more or less energy than it actually has, if the technology were to be at another level, if the conditions of the external nature were to be other ones, interest would be different. It bears a relation to all these things and still many others, which are supposed to be visualized through our system. To examine the type of these relations is certainly interesting and necessary, and the phenomenon of interest, regarded from different aspects, can undeniably offer a different view. An approach and manner of expression can then be convenient and useful for special purposes, which prove themselves as being incomplete or even as being wrong in some regard.

But this cannot discourage us if we ask about the *essence* of the phenomenon, solely abide by its *foundation* in its simplest form, and to search for a precise and short formula, whereby certainly no termination of the realization of the complexity and fullness of life of the phenomenon occurs. On the contrary, it can thereby only be promoted. If we did not want to go into this *here*, then we would have to impose the same renunciation also for wages and rent on ourselves, where one could repeat the same quite literally. We are also not misjudging the numerous relations there, which one must shed light upon if one really wants to "understand" the matter, and yet, we do consider it being permissible and useful to initially represent the "essence" of the things as briefly and simply as possible. Whoever pays too much attention to everything of interest that exists on one's way will never reach the goal. And this applies only too much to some modern interest theorists, who eventually get to foregoing a clear theory of interest all together.[1]

Our task is the following: We have to see which elements of our system we have not yet "assigned" from those, which we can assign to the explanation of income formations; thereupon, whether something arises from the same in similar manner as for wages and rent, which can be considered as the foundation of the phenomenon of interest. If we are able to construct a picture that suits reality, then everything is alright and we have won a solid foundation in order to go into those complicated relations. If not, then we at least have the negative result that interest is not a static income. So in turn, the matter shapes itself relatively easy, and it will be distinctly easier *to present* our view of the problem than *to defend* the same against all the reservations and objections that it may encounter. The first thing is done with a few words: Those elements of our system that could come into consideration here are especially—and we only want to speak *of it* for now—*tools* and *raw materials*. We already have generally stated their values and prices, and there is therefore no difficulty at all in understanding how the owners of the same get to the possession of a monetary sum or of consumption goods, and how we spoke of a price of land and labor performance for labor and land, and how we considered wages as well as ground rent as being such prices, we will also speak credibly of a price of performances of tools and raw materials here.

But the difficulty that is lacking in this representation immediately comes on when one takes a step further. It is that universally known one, which has already caused many theories of interest to fail: After the harvest, one has corn as well as land; after the day's work, his labor force as well as wages, but it is different for tools and raw materials. There, after a production process or in any case after a number of such, which is scarce in relation to those that outlast land and labor force, probably the products, but no longer the raw materials and tools themselves, and it is clear that this has the result for the value and price formation that the proceeds of every part of the products, for which one attains *more* with the help of tools than without the same, that therefore a plus, which would represent a continuous income whose recurrence one could count on, does not come about. One is easily convinced of these facts of the case if one overlooks the thought process of any representative of the productivity theory, and this was emphasized so pointedly and convincingly by v. Boehm-Bawerk that more on this point could seem to be redundant. We nevertheless want to convey the thought process of those theorists very briefly, whereby we want to make use of the psychological approach for the sake of convenience.

In a number of production processes, a tool is used until it is worthless. One would have also achieved a certain quantity of products *without* the same, but *more* was won *with* the same. Now, one cannot say that the tool of this plus, which is "ascribed" to him quite understandably, produced in the same manner as the cherry tree produced cherries. The difference in this case simply is the fact that the cherry tree still exists and will again carry fruits. But one can compare the products of the tool just as little. They are indeed things of a different nature which are entirely incommensurable. Such a comparison would only be possible if the things were the same, if, for example, a machine would be used for the production of machines of the same type again. The only thing that is comparable, simultaneously the only thing that is interesting to the economy is the value. But it is clear now that the value of the tool (under certain reserves that do not interest us here) is equal to the sum of values of its individual performances and that, since the value of every such performance is equal to the value of whose ascribing products a "surplus" could never arise at all in this way, which could be consumed without altering the asset base of the tool's owner.

We are not standing in line to make a consequence: Either one calls that, which we have derivated, namely the price of the tool's performances, not "interest," this means that one does not acknowledge that the pure economical foundation of that, which is generally considered as being interest, lies in it. It then follows that the static system does not explain interest, that the same is not a static branch of income, *that an entirely stationary national economy would not know any other incomes than wages and ground rent*, a result that would have far-reaching consequences; OR one calls every price "interest"; the owner of the tool can then either consume nothing of the same, or he will spend his fortune. One can also express the latter in a way that in this case, interest does not represent a net income. The terminological question what one wants to call interest would naturally be indifferent; but one remarks that it does not deal with this, but rather in fact with the very essential question whether or not one deals with the pure economical foundation of this important branch of income here. We believe we should decide on the second alternative, not only because the first one encounters the difficulty of the problem of net income, which one cannot possibly avoid, but rather because we are also thereto inclined through the direct study of the phenomenon of interest, as we will indicate later. *Firstly*, we therefore do not have a permanent income here, and the picture of the always-floating source does not fit here. If one would want to use it regardless, then it would have to be clear in one's mind that it deals with a fiction, which must first prove its right to exist, can very easily lead one astray, and above all, seems to skip over, to bypass, and simultaneously to mask the most interesting and most difficult problem. We will still speak about this fiction, its justification, and its lacking, but here, we are dealing with *facts* and can only hold on to that, which has been said. *Secondly*, this price is not "interest."

These two points do not coincide. We do not have a *permanent* income, but an inflow of goods to the owners of tools nevertheless takes place in our system, and we could call this, in accordance with some definitions of income, an income after all; but this income is not "interest," not only because interest seems to flow constantly, but also due to other reasons.

This conception certainly seems peculiar due to different reasons, and very much requires the closer representation. Even if we were to succeed in inducing the reader to accept it, then the problem of interest would not be thereby solved, our system would rather only bring us to the foot of the mountain so to speak. But it is so difficult to forgo something in whose ownership one already believes to be, that we are responsible for the task of indisputably showing that the matter really is this way.

Above all: Do we not limit our system to an area that is too narrow when we forgo the explanation of interest, is this not proof that our limitation is just inexpedient? This is to be immediately answered: We do not limit it arbitrarily, not on a whim, or due to pedantry, and in order to stay true to any a priori reasons of distribution; *we* are not excluding interest, rather, *it* does not assimilate. We are only doing the following: We are regarding the methods and the results of our discipline and are seeking to formulate them correctly, to work out its essence. When we do this, then we see that those circles of thought, which form the content of the pure economy today, are in essence of static character, and that the same, represented in their pure form, *do not explain* the phenomenon of interest. We will have to show that only through the citation of certain aids is such an explanation or the semblance of one of such possible, and we will have to examine these aids. It is very important to plastically withdraw the same from our system. If our conception continues to be correct, then the theory of interest cannot live out in the framework of static. And in fact, in our opinion, *the cause of all doubts regarding the problem of interest and the fact that all theories of interest and so undeniably unsatisfactory* lies here. If this is admitted, then we have rendered the greatest service to the theory of interest that is even possible, to have contributed to the realization of its true area and its true nature, and we then have hope in finally really being able to understand this phenomenon. The fact that our system then appears in an even less favorable light than before may not keep us from it: It is indeed our purpose to shed light on the same from all sides; it thereby arises by itself how and where we are to continue on working.

Let us return to our argument: We will see how right we are from all productivity theories. One can again characterize them there that they are initially correct and frequently derivate the fact, with an effort of arguments, which would not even be necessary, that tools have value and price. If they thereby react against the socialistic attacks on interest, then they charge an open door: A discussion of the claim that capital is a useful aid of production is certainly redundant. But one herewith has, as we have explained, not proven anything for interest, at least not in itself; one could rather say that one has proven its *absence*. What is to be explained is this "plus," is the permanent net income. One approaches *this* task which therefore goes beyond the mere verification of the so-called productivity with different aids. The simplest thing of the same is to smudge and to explain the facts of the case altogether, that everything has already been done by now. We do not want to speak of this, but the other aids must be examined, at least very briefly, namely for the dual purpose of seeing whether they are *static*, meaning assimilated into our system, to get along with its other form, and thereupon, in order to see whether they are applicable, meaning really explaining the phenomenon of interest.

However, at least a few of the many difficulties of our system must first be continued to be presented to the reader. We initially want to say something about the fundamental problem of the "compensation of capital," in our opinion, and thereupon also a few things about the phenomenon of interest itself. Then those remarks about several of the most important theories of interest and finally, such about the direction are to follow, in which we believe to have to search for the solution to the problem of interest. That, which is offered cannot be complete in any direction; no one can be more aware of its lacking than me. I have only difficultly decided to offer the few aspects that one will find in the following. They are recommended for the leniency of the reader. I can only say that my conception has offered quite a surprising enlightenment for myself, and I am very convinced to have paved the way for a new satisfactory theory.

II

One maintains to encounter the following train of thought in the representations of the theory of interest: The owner of the produced means of production rents out the same to the manufacturer, may the same be a laborer or entrepreneur. He puts a portion of the proceeds aside, which is supposed to serve him in procuring other means of production of this type, when the old ones have become outworn and worthless; a risk premium is also consigned as a rule. The remainder is then represented as his "income." Only a small portion of the theorists accept the presence of such a remainder as being self-evident, most of them seek to explain this fact, but however this may be, one is always of the opinion that one is describing a very natural process about whose factuality no doubt could exist at all. If one says that the owners of produced means of production are permanently, without any time limit, living on their income and do not admittedly increase their wealth on our conditions, but can receive it unscathed, one therefore believes to have expressed a banal, but indisputable fact. The greatest differences of opinion regarding the explanation of this income exist between the theorists, but they all agree *on the fact* that one can place interest very close beside wages and rent. Those, who have a special explanation for every branch of income, of course also have one of such for interest, so that no noteworthiness lies in it, and those, who explain all incomes in principally the same way also extend their explanation to interest, treat it entirely like wages and rent. One is to be referred to the representations of Walras and v. Wieser as examples for the latter group, by which this can be followed entirely. J. B. Clark also belongs in this group, but with a special attribute that compels us to specially come to speak of him. v. Boehm-Bawerk, however, bases the explanation of interest on special moments, but does consider it as an income like all others. In fact, this seems to entirely fit the facts. Interest is such a continuous, permanent income, much more secured in same regard than, for example, wage, and a sharply bound economic class seems to constantly live on it. Our conception therefore seems to be in blatant conflict with reality, and it simply is the peremptory duty of the economist to search for a *static* explanation of interest. We cannot give our complete answer, but we will seek to indicate the main content of the same. However, the following seems a priori important to us: We are remarking in advance that we, in consideration for v. Boehm-Bawerk's examinations, do not want to unroll the problem of net income in its entirety, since this has seemed to have become redundant to us through the same; we want to rather primarily handle only those points that we have to join to the same, and assume its fundamental work as being well-known. Our representation cannot tell the reader, for whom this assumption is not fulfilled, what it should; it must also appear as being incomplete.

Now, v. Boehm-Bawerk has completely worked out the problem of net income and has proven that the phenomenon of interest does not arise self-evidently from productivity. But even he assumes the compensation of capital, in which we want to integrate the risk premium for the sake of brevity, since the same applies to it so far. The first thing that we have to say now is that this is *not* self-evident; we want to especially make this very popularly clear: If one were to ask the economist, who proceeds in this manner, why he does this, then he would surely and not without surprise respond to the question that the capitalist would indeed expend his capital otherwise. This can now be countered in that it may be quite sensible not to do this, and that the economist advises well when he refrains from it, but that this is no reason that can play a role here, since it does not deal with pieces of advice, but rather with descriptions of facts. And it is certainly not so clear there that it is always dealt with this way, or only even that it is imperative to all cases. It will be quite sensible in a temporary emergency to occasionally expend *more*, an individual is also absolutely right from his standpoint (popularly speaking) if he expends more considering, for example, an inevitable, early death. In other situations, for example, considering a declining interest rate, or an old man with, in some relations, greater needs and lesser earning capacity, one will have to again give the advice not to expend the entire income. It can, however, be thereupon countered that one is thinking of *normal* conditions and does not consider those changes of the individuals or social situation. We want to admit that. It is therefore possible to precisely *foresee* the manner and rapidness of the wear of tools, and to *disregard* everything unforeseen; but even then, people do not think of an infinitely distanced future, and if they can also see themselves inclined, considering the indefiniteness of the length of periods for which they want to provide, to always repair and replace their tools, then this is nothing that is necessary, unalterable, and especially nothing that is self-evident.

If one claims this, one always thinks of the freeholder who accrues by himself, so to speak, a very specific sum as income, but we are not concerning ourselves with him alone. We will touch upon his case later. The matter is not so clear for the productive means. A new tool must replace the old one, and this new tool does not originate by itself. Seated, the owner of the old one had for some reason decided to produce or to obtain a somewhat better one in place of the old one. Is this occurrence now such an essentially different one than the one that was mentioned earlier? One will say that here, the man *sets* part *of his own income down*; but what happens in both cases? He has a monetary sum or products. He wants to spend those in a way that a maximum of benefit arises, just as it is most advantageous according to him, whereby we also include unegotistical moments in this expression, which is not essential here. He therefore overlooks his current and future wishes, and will use his money according to the rate of intensity to its satisfaction. The monetary sum that he has is indeed a homogenous amount; an insurmountable barrier is not set for his decisions on the limit of his income. It is up to him how much he wants to use for reparation, or for replacement, or for a recreation. To divest a monetary unit from his current needs involves an equal sacrifice for him, may he now use the same for a repair or an improvement. Entirely the same moments determine him in both cases: He will probably do that, which he always does, because this suits his aptitude and his conditions. If he want to equally maintain his conditions, then he will only sacrifice those monetary units that are necessary for reparation, but the effort of will that this requires is the same, whether he uses the same money for reparation or for improvement. After the execution of improvement, he will be able to satisfy *more* needs, less, if he lets a worsening eventuate, and the same if he just makes the reparation. These cases are only gradually different, *the same* occurs in each one. But one is now in accord that such improvements and recreations cannot be handled, or only in such a disappearing way, in the framework of static, that one is better to leave them aside, and since the *reparation* of tools is therewith the same in essence, it too is not a static process, and this was our point.

In order to now get to the same result from the standpoint of exact science: If one wants to place a third branch of income of this type, may one call it what one will, next to wages and rent, then one must derivate it from such an equal, permanent source. One must therefore either forgo it, or one must create a third production factor that behaves in the exact same manner as labor and land. Insofar as this is none other than a methodological aid, there are no objections to it, but one may not forget that no statement about facts may then lie in it, but must rather remain aware of having made a construction whose results must first prove themselves for the facts. There can certainly be reasons that justify such a fiction, and we will not speak of this yet, but one must beware of regarding the production factor as a reality like labor and land and furthermore, one may not forget that one has done that, because one *wanted* to juxtapose our third branch of income with the other two. This could now also be a permissible, economic ancillary construction in itself, which could prove itself to be fruitful. But through the *semblance*, through a flighty observation of facts, such juxtaposition is not justified yet, and insofar as all theorists believed to have unfailingly observed the *fact of expert knowledge* of a permanent source of income—interest—a prejudice, a mistake therefore lies in it. The only *fact* of the matter is that the tools are used up, and the products are now available; if they are replaced, then it can be explained why this happens. The availability of a permanent supply of tools would only be self-evident in two cases: firstly, if the tools would be just as permanent as land and labor force, and secondly, if they actually did reproduce by themselves, not in the figurative sense, in which some economists allege this, but rather actually physical, as, for example, organic beings. *The capital compensation is therefore not a last fact, but rather a problem*, and to not have recognized this is a mistake of, as we will see, great concern, just as great as the misjudgment of the problem of net income altogether.

The questioning of the latter does of course not lose its significance. The value of the products is always equal to that of the means of production, and the fact that MORE falls to the possession of the latter is still the crux of the problem of interest; but it now appears in a somewhat different light. At any rate, we have to proceed from the *gross yield*, it is the only thing that is given, and in our system it is equal to the value of the tool that it is ascribing to. But the supply of tools is a given one, and we cannot handle the replacement by means of our system. One therefore remarks that our static economy is not a "stationary" one. The latter would have to make such a replacement; the *static* economy does not do this. It therefore only counts for a moment. We see here how very unrealistic it is, and it can certainly not be done otherwise: you see, reality is full of life and movement.

We have said that it involves a fiction when speaking of the self-replacement of tools: This is a fiction of the exact same essence as that, which lies in it, that the tools carry interest like the cherry tree carries cherries. This fiction is unrealistic in the same manner, but is perhaps just as little of use for some purposes as the first one. It would have gone too far, wanting to just rule out both: They are only "wrong" as *a declaration of facts*. The tools are being consumed, one produces new ones, which are, however, in short time frames, by and large similar to the consumed ones and come into possession of the same people. But this is not *necessary*, and it is only approximately correct for a moment, which is so short that one can go ahead and hold onto the identity of the tools for the same.

The core of v. Boehm-Bawerk's *critical* work was therefore the working out of the problem of net income. We have to still add another moment to this work, through which the topic has won endlessly much and which also forms the foundation of our conception, *the problem of capital compensation*, which has also not yet been worked out sufficiently by v. Boehm-Bawerk. However, it is just as essential to the assessment of the matter as that of the net income. Only through the understanding of both of these points does the way lead to the realization of the phenomenon of interest.

III

Our system therefore only tells us that the produced means of production have value and price, and that their owners can obtain other goods for it. Which goods they obtain depends on their aptitude, etc. We now have to ventilate the question, which we have already negated, somewhat closer, namely whether we are supposed to see interest in this price? It would nevertheless be possible that we stand before *that*, which underlies the phenomenon of interest, that those prices of the tools represent that element in the phenomenon of interest, which we contribute to the explanation of the same from our standpoint. Just as we had to ask ourselves for wages and rent, whether that, which we derivate from our exact system really is that, which taken purely economically, underlies those branches of income; we therefore also have to ask ourselves a similar question here.

Such an examination is necessary here more than anywhere; to have failed to do it is the greatest mistake of most theories of interest. Every theoretical derivation must indeed be constantly verified of the facts, since it is in its nature that it possibly, even though "correct" in itself, does not achieve what is desired. Even if in a certain sense a process that suits the rules of logic is "infallible," then a mistake can still very easily slip in at precisely the point where it is claimed that a specific, exact result is suitable for a specific phenomenon of reality. The theory of interest gives us many examples for the importance of this principle: The *fact* of productivity, the *fact* of "waiting," of the different valuation of current and future goods, etc.—all of this is not only undeniably correct, but also very plausible, but where interest flows from it is another question, and this one is not yet solved through the proof of such facts in themselves.

We now have to ask about the essence of the phenomenon of interest. We have, however, already said that we cannot give a complete theory of interest; but we must do quite a bit in this regard, in order to dissipate every doubt about it whether the essence of the phenomenon of interest should even be sought in this direction anyway, which is characterized by the words "price formation of tools."

At the brink of these discussions, we want to remind ourselves of yet another principle, namely that it is our task to analyze the *facts* without letting us get led astray by the linguistic use and external similarities between different things, but not "to work on terms." The disastrous method of wanting to grasp economic phenomena by means of analyzing the linguistic use has led to a great deal of mistakes; not to moreover mention a single word about the plaintiveness of this method. A good example of the wrong ways, which it leads to, is the theory of interest. That is to say, nothing is clearer than that entirely different phenomena are termed the name "interest." Especially house rent and the interest rate of a loan have nothing to do with one another. Rent is a more partial purchase, the exchange of certain performances of a permanent good for another good. At the first moment, it is not perceived at all why such different things even have the same name. It would not even occur to whoever approaches these phenomena unaffectedly to consider them as being equal. If one would want to do this, then one would have to call *every* purchase price interest. The legal conception of the matter offers perhaps an explanation. The lawyers have constructed the interest rate of a loan per analogiam of the house rent, partially because this was quite practical for their purposes, partially also because the legal analysis always achieves the most possible by distortion of the facts. One must, generally speaking, guard against accepting legal conceptions, since the same are most often completely useless outside of the purposes of law. If examples were necessary, then one could very well point to the term ownership.

When we speak of the phenomenon of interest, we therefore only have our eye on the "interest rate of a loan" from now on, whereby, however, we must say that much more than logical reasons induce us the observation of facts to the presumption that the essence of the phenomenon of interest is to be searched for here. But even the interest rate of a loan is not a uniform phenomenon at all economically. Even this is almost implicitness, and to feel obligated, in favor of the legal form and the linguistic use, to find only one formula that suits all these phenomena, is completely foolish. So what similarity exists between the process that we are observing when a new industry should be called to life, and for the case of the shylock, who extorts high "interest" from some indebted individual—therefore, as a result of the common terminology, even though it does not seem to be quite fitting, between productive and consumptive loan? Only that in both cases the same or a similar *legal form* and similar expressions are used. Ones says in both cases that "interest" is being "given," but apart from a very useful one, from *the* essential difference, which we will still come to speak of, the fact of the completely different uses of the loan already justifies a completely different nature of business. The capitalist class could really not live on lending to indebted men or poor people, who find themselves in need; also not on government loans, and if we regard the magnitude and importance of the phenomenon of interest, its central position in business operations, in the essence of the industry, then we will certainly do best not to concern ourselves with suchlike trifles. We have therefore proven what forms the core of the phenomenon of interest in our opinion: It is that, which we could call the "industrial interest." As we said, we cannot exhaustively explain this highly interesting phenomenon here, but before we go on to make a few remarks about it, we want to say quite a few other things that also lie in the same direction. What we especially want to hold on to is that at any rate, the price of the performances of the tools is not interest.

And something else is remarked here in passing, namely that from our standpoint, the canonistic ban on demanding interest appears in a completely different light. Not the phenomenon of interest, which belongs to the life of the industrial development, had the church banned. This only had limited importance back then. It only banned something that does not have anything to do with it, the proliferation of the poor and needy, who are in need of a consumptive loan.

IV

It is therefore our opinion that it is failed from the beginning to want to construct a theory of interest in the framework of static. One can never come to a full and healthy realization of the phenomenon at all in this manner, and what the individual theories of interest, which carry out every attempt, contain that is good can always only be a part of reality, a view of a pinnacle that is unreachable to them. We want to also examine those strategies here, with which one can nevertheless explain interest there, where none can be found. But we can certainly not do justice to the individual authors, since a history of dogmas would go too far here.

A productivity and a utilization theory of course lie the closest. One wishes for an explanation for the obviously permanent form of income "interest." After an analogy of labor and land, a permanent source must also exist for this one. But apart from the consumption goods, next to labor and land—but both of these are already assigned—there are only the "produced means of production" in our study area, which have already been accepted as having been given, due to other reasons. One now lets these generate utilizations or products—this is actually entirely the same in essence, since the utilizations do only exist in the generating of products—and believes to have solved his problem with it. But we now have v. Boehm-Bawerk's reasons that are cited against it, which we also consider to be correct, to submit new ones, namely firstly, the one that those theories start from the assumption that interest is a static branch of income, an assumption, which we believe to be able to prove as being a preconception; furthermore, the one that they assume, that in the house rent and in the tools altogether, the essence of the phenomenon of interest is to be searched for; and we believe that also the latter assumption is not corresponding to the facts. We place special emphasis on the first one: To us, the explanation for it, that one was satisfied with such incomplete attempts at an explanation, seems to lie in it. The same have something despairing about them: If one were take their authors to task, one should get the response: "But it has to be this way, where else is interest supposed to come from?" Once, in the catch-22 of the static preconception, there was no longer a satisfactory alternative, and it is because of this that hard-working theorists committed the most obviously logical violations, as v. Boehm-Bawerk has proven them to be; if the matter was not so, then it would be very understandable why the theory of interest shows such numerous failures; the root of evil lies at the brink of the train of thought, over which everyone unsuspectingly enters, in order to then no longer find his way out of the aberrations.

The most recent productivity theory is the one of Professor Clark. I initially assumed that as a result of v. Boehm-Bawerk's objections and of my own concerns, the same is able to be rejected in the same manner as all others. But the repetitive study of the problem induced me to somewhat modify my opinion of it: We have already spoken about the Clarkian term of capital and acknowledged that this fiction has a certain justification, a certain utility could also not be deprived of it. If one would now want to assume that this "fund of productive force" represents a permanent source of incomes, as well as labor and land, *without eating themselves up in the process*, now, one could certainly then speak of interest in the static economy. Only two things would thereby have to be kept in mind, firstly, that all of this is a fiction and one may not search for an *explanation* of interest in it, and secondly, that this has nothing, absolutely nothing, to do with "tools"—the matter would otherwise be *wrong*. This sounds quite adventurous, and we ask much of the theoretical propensity of sacrifice of the reader when we demand that he follow us here. But, let us not be easily scared away, but let us rather ask whether or not a suchlike fiction could have a purpose. And it *has* purpose. You see, in it lies the only means of being able to speak of interest in static. If this is hoped for—and it certainly is—but if our standpoint is also correct, then one can only continue in the following manner: One eliminates the problem of interest from static and somehow solves it outside of the same. But then, one assumes such a permanent source of the same in static, based on the fact of the far-reaching regularity and consistency of the income of interest, and simply juxtaposes interest with rent and wages, which can be practical for some purposes, and whereby one must only be aware of saying nothing that could collide with that solution, and above all, not to forget the fictitious character of the matter. From the standpoint of static, this means that one does equip economic subjects, who do not have an income according to the laws of the same, with one of such, and also regularly gives them a specific monetary sum. And even if we do not want to tread on this path, we are still not able to deny that it is by no means useless. Of course Professor Clark did not mean this. From his theory, just as it is, we can however only say that it constructs a branch of income that does not exist, but certainly also that this construction is conceived somewhat differently, cannot simply be rejected. But we cannot elaborate on this.

But Professor Clark's discussions also have other merits, which we will soon come to. We are now proceeding to another theory, namely Jevons'. For him, interest was based on the possession of consumption goods, as we know. For this purpose, he defines capital as a supply of consumption goods, and precisely this step leads us to a deeper understanding of his theory. How does he get around to defining capital this way? He only does this for the purpose of his theory of interest. He also obviously proceeds from a static system, and one can imagine that his train of thought was perhaps a very similar one as that of those theorists, who we have already regarded. He also steps through those disastrous gateways towards the problem, and believes *to have to* imperatively find a place for interest in the system. Labor and land cannot carry him and only the tools and then the consumption goods in the system therefore remain. It is now Jevons' merit to have recognized that the house rent is not interest. He saw that the produced means of production as such certainly do not carry interest, that, as we said, the assignment of its utilizations is a partial purchase that does not differentiate itself through anything essential from the purchase of consumption goods. But he now searched for another source of interest. His glance fell onto the only, still available type of elements, onto the consumption goods, and there, nothing was closer than the thought that the solving of the puzzle must lie in them, that furthermore, the explanation is to be found in the moment of time of the closer one, because they only differentiate themselves through this from the productive means.

With what right do we allow ourselves to accuse Jevons of this thought process here, which was possibly not his? We *have to* do it. We believe that one cannot understand a theory any sooner until one has the feeling of formally seeing the thoughts of its creator. This feeling gives a lively satisfaction, but in addition, this effort also has a very practical significance: It gives us a means for the judgment of the concerning theory at hand. If we have accurately felt Jevons, then one thing is certain, namely that his theory did not arise *directly* from the observation of facts. It was probably *indirectly* based on it, since our entire system is based on it, but he did not come to his theory of interest *in the way* that he, regarding the economical life, would have thought to himself that, as a result of his possession of finished consumption goods, the capitalist acquires his interest. I also do not believe that he first regarded the psychological fact of the underestimation of the future, and then through its observation, came to a connection with the phenomenon of interest; but rather that he first, by means of a type of "elimination method" so to speak, came to that group of elements that was simply remaining after he, in regards to all the others, had negated the question whether interest flows from them. And then he simply searched for reasons that were supposed to justify those logical necessities. But all speculations will speak against such a theory. We, for example, will be inclined from the very beginning to deny its precept, namely the necessity of a static explanation, and in this case, to cast doubt on this *theory* from already the very beginning. But not the *reasons*, on which Jevons based them: These are rather quite evidently correct. We are only missing the proof that the phenomenon of interest is based on these facts.

This does also not seem to be the case at all to us. But even *if* this were the case, then this theory would not be a static one. And here we come to one of Clark's earlier mentioned merits, namely having proven that in the static state, neither "waiting", nor the underestimation of a future satisfaction of needs can play a role, namely for the following reason: If a specific quantity of "capital" is given, and if a new one is not built—which however, according to our conception, also involves that the old one is not replace—nothing else can happen than carrying the production process out in the best of the well-known ways; and this will happen; even so, if one estimates the current satisfactions of needs higher than the future one—and one surely does this, we are not denying this. This cannot be of significance, since one by *all means already has the goods or has to wait for the termination of the production process*.

Quite similar remarks arise regarding the abstinence theory. It also is one of those aids that is supposed to make it possible for us to win a theory of interest from our system, despite everything. It is obviously rooted in the theory of the "productive services," therefore has a somewhat other point of departure than the ones previously discussed. The most distinguished one among its representatives, Senior, enables us to recognize this quite distinctly. In order to find three sources that are just as permanent for the three branches of income, he places abstinence next to labor and land as third *production factor*. This means none other now than "tools" without a specific form—this is also only "agglomerated productive force" with the only difference from the productivity theory being that this productive force does not already exist in labor and land performances, but rather in a sui generis factor. It is now by no means decisive for the assessment of this aid whether or not something like abstinence actually exists. This is certainly the case, and the efforts of the representative of this theory in proving the existence of this moment are entirely superfluous: No one will deny it. The only question is whether it has something to do with interest. This is, as we are making an effort to work out, always the decisive point for all these theories. They are actually *not* directly based on the observation of facts, but rather owe their phenomenon to our economic needs. Even Senior certainly did not discover a connection between abstinence and interest while observing the gearing mechanism of the economic life. This would already not be possible, because a connection that is so hidden does not directly arise by itself from the observation. We also in no way demand this, but rather acknowledge that once we have built our abstract system based on reality, the same can very well give us some interesting results, further also individually, meaning without having to call on a new observation. Only, one may thereby not forget two things: Above all, that the thought process, which is discussed here pulls in an entirely new fact from the outside, and very obviously brings it into our system *for the purpose of the explanation of interest*. This is not readily done, but rather makes a series of reserves and cautions necessary, if the historians are not supposed to be right in their reproach of unsustainable speculation. Such a fact must be posed very certainly in itself and also be examined very precisely in its connection with the remaining elements of our system. The abstinence theory does not do this. Nevertheless, we are not denouncing such an approach in limine. It can in fact lead to healthy results, at least in the right hand, and every method that does this has its justification; but from the very beginning there is not the slightest reason for us to assume that the raised fact gives the hoped-for result. But then in *all* cases there is always still—and even then when we draw conclusions from our most secured foundations that are based directly on the facts—a *verification* necessary, that proof, which we spoke of above. And we are missing this verification. This is now our main objection against the theory of abstinence. Only a theory that is content with those demands, which we will make an effort to briefly outline here, really is correct, really economic, and is not affected by those objections of the theory's opponents.

Senior and his followers therefore proceeded from the assumption that a permanent source must correspond to regularly floating interest. And this initially entirely amorphous cause that resembles a clothing hanger was then encased by the moment of abstinence. That, which otherwise may still be said about it is "speculation." So this, along with v. Boehm-Bawerk's objections and Clark's proof that there is no "waiting" in static, or rather that the same cannot have influence—these are the "reasons for the decision" for the death sentence of the abstinence theory.

V

It also rests on us to take a stand on the by far most important creation in the area of the theory of interest, on v. Boehm-Bawerk's theory. Because even though we have rejected all other theories of interest, the question still arises how we adhere to this one. To us, a complete valuation of it is also impossible, as well as an analysis that gets to the bottom of things. We only ask wherein its essence lies, what its premises are, and what we can gain from it on our way. We can also not gain a final verdict about it here, it will soon show for what reason. Only some views of different sides of the theoretical structure arise on a few points of our way, which we want to briefly outline, but we do not quite reach it and do not penetrate its interior.

v. Boehm-Bawerk completely acknowledges the fact that the system that is based on the problem of attribution does not explain the phenomenon of interest, only in the form however, that he says, the *productivity theory* does not result in interest. His problem is to explain the phenomenon of interest in spite of that; however, we cannot exactly say whether or not he would consider his explanation as being "static" in itself. This is connected with the fact that he does not place great emphasis on the difference between static and dynamic. To the extent that, also for him, not all elements can suddenly change for some reason, he considers a type of stationary state that does always repeat itself, but does not completely reflect the characteristics of our static state.

He therefore proceeds from the phenomenon of interest and defines interest as the agio of the current vis-à-vis the future goods, and his problem now is to examine the causes of this agio. There are three of them:

difference of the coverage of demands of the economic subject currently and in the future, the psychological fact of the higher estimate of the current goods, of the current enjoyments vis-à-vis future ones, and a fact of production-technological nature, namely the overly proportional, higher productivity of longer periods of production vis-à-vis the shorter ones. This is all that our remarks refer to, as wishful as it is that this theoretical structure actually gets a criticism for once of the thoroughness and depth that it deserves.

At any rate, the point of departure of the theory is the *fact* of the income of interest, and Boehm's theory of capital can also be understood from it. We observe this for all theories of interest. While one asks oneself for rent and wage, how land and labor come to their remuneration, therefore advance here from the side of the production factor to the income that it yields, thus the opposite always happens for interest. One sees interest and asks oneself where it comes from. This is only natural in itself and shows very distinctly that the problem of interest is a methodologically completely different one than that of wages and rent, and this one can only be formed analogously through strategies and aids. This also shows us how much we have to be wary towards all theories of capital, how much we stand here on the ground of the theoretical construction and not on that of the facts.

But v. Boehm-Bawerk seems to take a step further into the area of the facts than the remaining theorists, and enters the theoretical structure one moment later than they do. You see, his statement that interest is this agio seems to represent observations of facts, as his remark seems to indicate, that his theory, expressed very simply, borders on implicitness. And yet, this sentence is only self-evident in a specific sense, it also contains a theory in another. It is only correct for certain then, when we speak of *money*. Only the consumptive loan can be given in any type of goods—and this does not interest us due to the earlier mentioned reason—for every other loan, meaning for the loan for an industrial operation, it exists neither in the consumption goods for the consumption of the borrower, nor in productive means that would already be available. Rather, it exists, according to all rules, in money and at any rate, only in things for which one wants to by others. One now maintains to readily accept that one can simply omit the moment of money, which one tellingly calls a "shell," a "coat" of the phenomena. It is very clear that this is possible very often, but this must be proven every time if one does not want to risk suddenly noticing that money is potentially able to play yet another role in the theory than that of a measurement of value and convenient expression, and that one has overlooked this role. Popularly speaking, interest is therefore certainly an agio of current money over future money. It presents itself in this manner in the money market. But if one says that it is an agio of current *consumption goods*, then a topic of proof still first lies in it, a specific *theory*. It is thereby questioned, not that current goods have a psychological agio, so to speak, but certainly that the same explains that of money.

After these introductory remarks we are asking for v. Boehm-Bawerk's further proceeding. The first thing that is noticeable during the observation of his three reasons is their complete dissimilarity, and if we remind ourselves of what we have said about the dissimilarity of the phenomena that are summarized under the name "interest," then this will not surprise us any further. The first reason has no significance in principle for v. Boehm-Bawerk, since he only regards the consumptive loan of the needy. This reason can still become very important in a somewhat different sense, but it does not interest us any further here. The other two reasons signify the introduction of two new facts into our system, of two new hypotheses. The thing that is especially important to us for the same now is that they are *not* static. The first one, the underestimating of future enjoyments, cannot become useful in the desired manner in the static state, as we had seen during the discussion of Jevons' theory. Does it even have a significance, which we do not want to decide at all, since this lies entirely outside of the task's framework that is now demanding of our attention; this significance can therefore only lie in the area of dynamic.

But it behaves in the same manner for the third reason. The same was attacked from different sides; also frequently mistaken for the "tool" of the productivity theory. To us, the emphasized objections do not generally seem substantive, even though we are not quite clear about the following point: Even if the *overly proportional* productivity is something completely different then the common one, places emphasis on entirely different moments, will the *entirety* of the value of its products not be attributed to a tool in spite of that, so that a surplus cannot arise, in other words, does the same objection that is so striking vis-à-vis the common productivity theory not also encounter this third reason? And furthermore, is it really entirely certain that the essence of the phenomenon of capital is only to be searched for herein? But we did not want to examine this; however, something different must be emphasized. If "time-consuming production detours" are pursued, then one can be doubtful whether this is possible within the static system. At any rate, only the moment of economizing features the same for it: but we have already said that the same does not seem to be adequate to us, to fulfill the role that is attributed to it. But furthermore, when the new production method is carried out, then everything has changed in the system, even nature and people have not stayed the same in their relationships to one another, the entire construction, the entire life of the people is changed through the now different conditions, the role of land and labor shifts, the organization of the national economy becomes another, new tendencies will come to light, and above all, a further progress will now take place due to these circumstances, etc., in an always increasing scale. The discussed theory is perhaps now a quite first-rate means to grasp certain processes of dynamic, it is by no means *static*, already the circumstance that it emphasizes the time lapse, the *long* periods, shows this.

But if we say that we cannot see the key for the phenomenon of interest in the moment of the produced means of production, then we must, however, emphasize that that, as we have meant it, does not yet speak against v. Boehm-Bawerk's theory in itself, since this one, as the reader sees, deals with the matter essentially different than those other theories. We will still briefly come back to it.

Now, what are the consequences that this theory is "not static"? One could say that this is irrelevant if it only achieves what is desired. And this moment is nevertheless very important: We cannot explain interest in its simplest form within our system. But if we go beyond this, then we stand in the middle of development and movement, as mentioned. If we want to hold on to more or less stationary relations anyway, then a new level of abstraction lies in it, a step further away from reality. But we must do this. Because otherwise, an entire series of new problems that lies against the great topic of development would force itself into our way, as we have seen. And this would make it impossible to derivate any clear laws of movement. The matter is completely different for wages and rent. We can carry out our view very well there. It is therefore impossible to place interest next to wages and rent, and to directly coordinate its laws of movement of those of the latter ones. The most unsatisfactory thing of all attempts perhaps explains itself from it, to do this, and the many objections, which were raised against Ricardo's formulas concerning this matter. These facts of the case cannot surprise us from our standpoint, and we believe to be able to consider them as being a validation of the veracity of the same. Not due to our arbitrariness, rather, entirely on its own, the phenomenon of interest falls out of our system, which is nevertheless the expression of that method, which we *have to* pursue.

We have no choice there. One of such stands open to us at the utmost in the regard that we can still squeeze interest into our system with help of fictions and further assumptions. But we are of the opinion that this method barricades the access to its essence and the view of very important problems, and that it at most represents a provisionary palliative remedy that is meant for giving way to a complete observation, which is not possible in the framework of static. To eliminate interest from the same is then the other possibility, and at the moment where we see that we can get to a really satisfactory theory in this way, those strategies have lost their justification of existence.

We now want to indicate the outlines of this new, encompassing theory, whereby we will again revert to v. Boehm-Bawerk's teachings.

Prologue to a Dynamic Theory of Interest

A. Our result is too unsatisfying. We cannot abdicate ourselves of the duty to at least indicate the way that, in our opinion, leads to the essence of the phenomenon of interest, because a theory of interest that amounts to the denial of interest anyway, would be new in the fatal sense. But we have already emphasized that we cannot give a complete theory of interest, and believe to have said enough in order to justify why not. Only the proof that the phenomenon of interest does not show itself in the pure static system, we wish to see as being considered a final result, for which we are responsible, and which may be discussed. However, what we *now* want to say only serves for showing that we know more and are not agnostic about the actual essence of the phenomenon of interest. On the one hand, we cannot give a theory of interest in the framework of this examination that could not be able to live out there anyway, and would demand much more space than the proportions of this work allot it, and on the other hand, we also do not want it, since we are dealing with the essence of the static system here and our task stops at the moment where the proof is furnished that it does not involve a static phenomenon here. But if we still do not feel justified, but rather believe to also be obligated to make a few brief remarks about new foundations for the handling of such a large problem, we therefore ask the reader to want to think about the fact that the same must be naturally content-related and formally lacking, that a great deal of objections, questions, and doubts arise, which I must necessarily leave unspoken here. A critique of my remarks would have to take that into consideration. Namely, I cannot conceal to myself that some of the same can seem to be superficial, and others can even seem to be obviously wrong; hence my wish to exclude the same, if possible, from a possible controversy that can indeed be initiated sometime later about a more complete exposition of my theory.

I have already stated the negative side of the matter. It is here in the fore. If one admits that interest in its simplest and, however, correct form does not readily arise from our system, and furthermore, that I have concurrently worked out the cause of the so undeniably unsatisfactory character of all static theories of interest, if one admits that and why the problem of interest shows such peculiar, crippled forms in static, and that its solution must be searched for in "dynamic," because the static apparatus barricades the view of the essence of the matter—then everything is achieved that I want to achieve here. The following is only supposed to strengthen this impression and likewise show how I think about the further things. It suffices me, if it is sufficient for giving the reader a preliminary mental image of the elements of a satisfactory solution to the problem, and to convince him that at least something *true* is in them.

Our negative results were the following two: *Firstly*, we recognized that despite the opposing appearance of capital, however it may be defined, neither maintains permanently, nor replaces automatically. This appearance is based on the seeming facts that the "capitalist" keeps his "capital" when he expends its interest, and that the owner of means of production frequently, or even mostly, readily places himself in the possession of similar ones after the use of the same, and before this has not happened, does not speak of "income." But we did not recognize a self-evident process in it, but rather a *problem* in our opinion, due to two reasons: Firstly, because capital, whatever it may consist of, just does *not* replace by itself—which is a very banal truth—and *seems* to maintain by itself only in the case of the "freeholder," a case that we will still come to, but which, even though it gave the push for that alleged observation, still only embodies a small portion of the phenomenon of interest, and secondly, for the reason, because *replacement* of capital is a process that is equal in essence to the *recreation* of such. The latter moment also taught us that the capital income cannot be a static process, since the recreation certainly is not. From this followed that one can only speak of *capital as a permanent source of income*, despite all opposing appearances, at least always then, when one understands concrete goods by it, in a *fictitious sense*, and in turn because of this, that it is a *mistake* to simply substitute a supply of tools for the monetary capital of the everyday experience, and to declare of the latter what seems to apply to the first. Only Clark recognized that both are to be differentiated, but he too did not in an appropriate manner.

Our *second* negative result was that neither in the moment of the supply of the means of production, nor in other moments, which act in its place and, in our opinion, were only called on for this role as a result of the realization of its deficiency, the explanation of interest is to be searched for, that herein lies neither the essence of the phenomenon of capital, nor the source for this branch of income. But for us, from this follows that interest is not a static branch of income, and the attempt to derivate it with static means can only lead to radically wrong results.

Let us now still add how in our opinion, produced goods—whether productive or consumption goods does not make a difference—can yield pure income, whose existence may have made many a contribution to leading the economists astray. Whoever lends tools or consumption goods, especially he, who makes a profit from it, can attain "income" from it very well, but only in the following manner: Above all, such an individual will be able to attain an intermediary trade profit, the profit of the retail dealer. The same one would represent a type of "friction income," which is theoretically without significance. Thus, labor, which he thereby performs, will yield him an income, and the appearance can easily thereby arise that it originates from the rented goods. The landlord can finally also be a monopolist and make a corresponding profit from this circumstance. It is now completely clear that all these incomes do not have anything to do with interest, already not, because they are also possible for every *sale*. But nevertheless, they may have supported the advantage that interest originated from such sources, and it seemed important to us to clarify this point.

Now to our prologue for a dynamic theory of interest.

B. We especially asked ourselves, as we approached the phenomenon of interest, whether our system offers an explanation of the same. We came to our negated answer and now have two ways. We can take a closer look at the phenomenon of interest and construct a theory of the same from the facts, since *our* system is based on *other* facts, the same does not exist, *or* we can, through the introduction of new hypotheses, artificially effectuate that the phenomenon of interest nonetheless arises from the facts of our system. Despite the possibility in principle of the latter way, we will prefer the first one, since only it is able to give us actual perception. But then, we must become clear where we have to search for the phenomenon. We have already said that the economists have handled things that are entirely different in essence under this title, and have already isolated the house rent and interest for the consumptive loan. We now have to take another step in this direction. Furthermore, a characteristic difference exists between those loans that are admitted for the purpose of production; and we are approaching a very decisive point here. Of course we have something to say first, what is not subjected to concerns, namely that productive loans can also be admitted in order to maintain the existing enterprise that, for example, is threatened by a sudden accident. Between these loans and those, which serve *new* transactions and *new* improvements, a not insignificant difference exists. Those first ones could actually and in a certain sense be counted among those consumptive loans, and we must therefore hurry to eliminate great social and economical significance that they may also have in life *here*, where we are dealing with the foundation and the essence of the great phenomena, since all accessories, all that is not quite essential, only serves in tarnishing the great forms. It is quite self-evident that the demand of loans starting from this side is not without influence on the interest rate, just as the demand for consumptive loans also is. We do not want to hold ourselves up with such things, as much as we are aware how dangerous such secondary demurs can often become for a theory. The *interest is the essential thing for loans, which are used for the creation of new industries, new forms of organizations, new technologies*, and the one half of the decisive point is thereby stated.

We now come to the other one. An essential difference also exists—and can now be less easily seen and is open to many misunderstandings and objections—between the loans according to the circumstance *where they come from*, where the loan *giver* takes them from. If a farmer lends his neighbor a bag of seeds, then this is hardly any different, I mean, the economic nature of the process and its economic effects are hardly different ones than if he lends him a quantity of consumption goods. The process does not have special interest, and even if the farmer, but which is by no means certain and probably also not the rule in cases equal to our example, gets back *more* than he gave, then we will admittedly call it interest according to the common linguistic use, but easily notice what a great difference exists between this case and the phenomenon that we are dealing with here. Even then, when the borrower uses the obtained seed on the newly plowed land, so that something *new* is absolutely created, interest would hardly have to necessarily emerge. *If someone generally borrows something from his supply of goods, then this does not yet have interesting consequences as a rule*. An element of our system is enlarged, *another* is decreased, certainly, but a *new* one does not emerge. It is something different when, as we have said, something new is produced. Herewith, the matter already steps outside of the static system, and entirely new formations emerge. But the lender does not always need to lend from his supply of goods, another way can also be pursued. He probably initially lends with *money*. This would now not change anything essential, *but the matter becomes essentially different when he gets this money on his own, for example, issues banknotes or opens an open credit*. Both forms of business of course do not always have this characteristic. The banknote can be covered in metal or in a different way, the book credit can simply be based on the active assets of the lender, but this does not *have to* be the case, *and precisely these cases, where it does not apply, are of first-rate interest to us*.

Now of all the objections that one could bring forth against the thought process, which we are at the point of turning into, we must imperatively emphasize two, although very briefly. At first, one could very much be in doubt about the significance of that type of credit of which we speak here. In "normal," meaning quiet times, it may hardly exist now and again, and to what extent it prevails in times of "upturn," speculation, etc., one can be of very different opinion about it. We want to build an encompassing theory on this phenomenon that, according to our predecessors, only covers a perhaps disappearing, small portion of the phenomenon of interest, also, in addition, on a phenomenon that seems abnormal to many. It can only be retorted here: After we had gained insight that we could not penetrate the phenomenon of interest from our system, we decided to gain the foundations of the theory of interest through direct observation of facts. And step by step, the analysis of the facts led us nolens volens to the *money market*. If one examines the facts, eliminating everything unessential, then one finally comes to realize that the heart of the matter pulsates in the money market. I do know that one, when one hears this sentence, is immediately reminded of an abundance of platitudes and blunders of the practical life, and that some excellent theorists can be inclined by this sentence alone not to read any further. And it is not possible for me here to completely satisfyingly show that, which I mean is something new, that very well deserves verification. But let's go on! Let us now assume that it is correct that we have found, for example, in Lombard Street, the heart or "one of the hearts" of the phenomenon of interest, so we will then seek to generalize and to pursue other neighboring phenomena, and thus, becoming increasingly serious. But it is failed to already limit a priori and, in addition, for no other reason at all than because of the legal and linguistic form, a specific area of facts than that of the phenomenon of interest, for which one and the same formula must fit well or badly. This is one of those processes of the theorists, which so strikingly suits all historical objections that some people just find it unbelievable how one can occupy himself with theory any further. Not in primitive relations, of which one indeed actually does not know anything and which can, if we start from the assumption to have to find our phenomena there, radically lead astray, but rather in our experiences, in really reliable observations we must find the building blocks for our realization, and we have to here again single out the most common, most full of form, most lively phenomena in order to observe, and *then only from this observation, if we believe to have recognized the essence of it*, we can isolate, and *then* Robinson is right. But if we encounter a phenomenon that our exact system does not offer by itself, then we may not want to look for it by Robinson; and may the phenomenon that we emphasized as being especially interesting therefore also just have a small scope, then we believe ourselves to be justified in adhering to it. We furthermore believe that precisely this phenomenon turns out to be the driving wheel that all similar phenomena are to be traced to.

The other objection that we have to make is the one that we are working with something entirely fictitious, with a credit to which nothing correlates in the world of goods, and are in danger of vindicating it material existence. It appears to be this way. We are actually not doing it. We are speaking of something that actually exists, but of a *process*, not a *material thing*. We are not making use of Mac Leod's term, even though we would like to point it out, that trains of thought like our theory let us understand, as we believe, what induced Mac Leod to the construction of his term, and that we believe that a healthy core lies in his theory, that it perhaps has a similar position to our theory of interest as to the theory of marginal utility, which it had indeed anticipated.

Only the type of credit of which we speak here, we consider as being the essence of the phenomenon of interest and we are eliminating all other types of the same. Some of the latter could also occur in the static system; it could perhaps be counted among the organization that a specific continuance of debt of a portion of the economic subjects and a certain continuance of debt of another portion exists once and for all. But only truisms could be said about that. There can also be banks in the static system, which let a once and for all specific quantity of banknotes circulate, and credit institutes, which could form the connection between debtor and creditor. But this also offers little of interest. This proves among other things the terrible banality of that, which figures under the title of credit theory, into the system of our science. We lose nothing at all if we forgo all of this, and from this standpoint, it really does not matter whether our system represents a highly developed, even only static, or a primitive economy. It can do both just as well, but the interesting thing, the only interesting thing about credit, lies in dynamic, lies in every part of the phenomenon of which we speak here, and which is in fact something different than those other forms of credit, and has so other consequences economically that the formal moment of lending completely disappears next to it. The *creation* of credit is the essential thing. If, for example, the bank that issues the notes, rather than "benefiting" an industry, would get them itself straight away, then the essential moment would be exactly the same, although there could be no talk of lending.

The source of the phenomenon of interest therefore lies *in the development and in credit*; there, its explanation is to be searched for.

C. A close connection exists between both moments. The production and its entire organization, adjusted to a specific state of demand and of buying power, is in the static equilibrium. If some circumstance leads to a new enterprise or a new organization, for example, a trust, supposing to be created, then "money"—popularly speaking—is necessary for it. Now, credit offers it, *how* to examine it would lead us too far. Conversely: If a new buying power is created—let one forgive the seemingly superficial expression—then the same can, if the economy was in equilibrium and no otherwise extraordinary reason is present, for example, war requirements, etc., and apart from the case that they are distributed among all economic subjects in such proportions that all prices rise equally—only relate to new creations, and form the greatest incentive to step out of the state of equilibrium and to make *unusual efforts*. Here lies a further, decisive point, the moment of "effort."

The means of production emerge and vanish. We have placed so much emphasis on this sentence. *We* now give it a further and partially different meaning. New ones are superseding the old ones; *but not of the same kind*; rather, better ones, better serving the former purposes, thereupon, more numerous ones, finally, such that serve new purposes.

And thus, the productive supply becomes another. However, we have so far seen only *one* reason of this process, namely the productive use of the present supply. But there is yet another one, that means of production are created, which better serve the present purposes, and because of the fact that other purposes emerge, the *existing* supply is devaluated *even before it physically goes under*. This especially applies to, for example, old machines, which may still be quite useable in themselves. But it also applies to old factories, to old forms of organizations and business methods, to patents and monopoly positions of every kind. New foundations, created by means that were virtually not available in former times, equally surface from the standpoint of the static system that does not regard the available possibilities and from nothingness, and force the former back into nothingness.

One says—and the practitioner does this, as the theorist—that "capital" maintains itself. One claims this in a different sense, one partially thinks of an outstanding debt, which always seems to remain the same through all changes of the economic relations, one partially thinks of tools, etc., that are supposed to constantly repaired, respectively, replaced.

But is this true? Our answer will be negating. That claim is based on a deception. "Capital" is certainly always available, but it is not always *the same*. We have nothing against one liking to regard the matter in this way for some purposes. But the change is interesting to us here: *new* "capital" is always available. Especially to this deception contributes the circumstance that one believes to see that the new tools step into the *place* of the old ones and especially into the possession of the same economic subject, who still speaks of "his capital" as such, even that he has pulled the same out of an investment and "invested" it somewhere else.

But is that really so entirely right? Is the class of "capitalists" really a circle of individually determined people and their heirs? Let us watch closer and let us separate the different cases for this purpose. Someone owns tools that he productively uses and that thereby perish. However, we see as a rule that the same are replaced so smoothly that one often virtually says that they replace *themselves*. But we have already seen that this is not right. He must make *efforts* in order to replace them, and he will often not do this. He will also often replace them with others.

Someone owns an enterprise, for example, an autobus enterprise. Let us assume that due to the construction of an electrical tramway, no one uses the autobuses any longer. What happens then? Can he "pull out his capital" like a general his troops from the battle line? Obviously not; he does still have the transport fleet and the horses, but both are, if there is no new opportunity for use which would have to, by the way, open itself precisely at this moment, since there is no room in the static system, *devaluated*. He can certainly sell them, but he will not get the amount with which he previously put up his enterprise. What has happened? His capital or a portion of the same goes under, the horses will be, for example, sold to the butcher, and the busses used somehow, without being repaired or replaced, and what he has gained only represents this latter value. Here, capital has *disappeared, disappeared without a trace*. And such a case is no exception, an isolated misfortune, *it is a type of the regular process*. Forethought, this can certainly weaken. Our man will just, if he hears of tramway plans, adjust to that. But what can he do? Only let his "means of production" wear off without replacing them—only make that process from an acute one to a slow one. The national economy has not become poorer. But what sense would it have made to say that "capital" has "stayed the same"? Only the circumstance that capital was available *before* and capital is available *now* can awaken such an appearance. Let us modify our example a bit. Our man founded the tramway *himself*. Nothing essential has changed. We must describe the process word for word *the same way*. And he will nevertheless say that he has now "invested" "his capital" "differently." Apart from this, nothing is clearer than that his *former one* has perished, and he has created a *new one*. If he has built the Tramway from the money that he gained through the selling of the autobuses and horses, then "his capital" is now less than it previously was, before the *necessary devaluation* of those things occurred. But insofar he has saved something one could speak of a "transition of capital" of the man, but only in the sense as one, if someone exchanges apples for nuts, can speak of a "transition of his possession" to nuts. If the tramway then prospers, our entrepreneur can again obtain the same monetary sum that he previously had. And if he had foreseen this prosperity, then he will *immediately* set up the tram just as high. Then both processes move so closely to one another that they are difficult to separate. We must nevertheless sharply separate them, recognize that they represent opposing processes. The actual process will, by the way, by different as a rule: The man will raise a credit and will create the tramway from it, but will let his previous "capital" perish. Then *both* of his *assets*, the old one and the newly created one, have so little to do with one another, as if they belonged to different people. And both processes—the perishing and the new creation—are impossible in the static system, are dynamic. Professor Clark handles the following case: The "capital" that was previously invested in whaling has turned itself to the cotton industry. Now, we must say that it has perished. I am not acquainted with the case any closer. But when the capitalists, who had invested their capital in whaling actually did not lose anything, and we find *the same people* in the possession of "cotton mills" of the same value as the ships had, then this could have only happened in the manner that they, as they saw that a continuation of their "investment" would have to have the downfall as a result, stimulated by the concern for it, made a new productive effort, namely created new business companies with the help of credit. Two processes are present, a perishing and an economic re-rising. If their asset in money amounted before—as after, really to the same amount—which is highly unlikely—then this is pure coincidence. Only if the industry of whaling had continued, had they been able to exchange their shares in it for shares in other industries. But this would be a process of no interest at all.

But in general, the owner of an enterprise is *not* able to transgress economically intact to another branch of industry when it goes downhill with the same, due to the reason that is discussed here. We observe daily that the position, meaning of business companies, and occasionally "capital," the asset, which is calculated in money of its owners, is altered through the creation of new ones. Old companies that once dominated the market sink into insignificance, and their owners eventually cease to belong to the highest economic class. It is an old word that great assets only go up to the "third hand." This certainly has many causes and perhaps *predominantly* others. This is indeed said often, but has never been exactly examined; but possible, that one of them is nevertheless to be searched for here—problems, which lead deep into the economic life, and which we must prohibit ourselves from examining closer.

Another case—and perhaps he, who has especially given occasion to believing in the longevity of capital—is the one of the ownership of debts. An annuity bond—is it not always the same? Very undeniably not. The paper is indeed the same, and the legal form, one and the same investment becomes something different *economically* in a short period of time. The significance of one and the same amount quickly changes for debtors, as well as lenders. Not only can one not maintain the same, not exactly the same at two different moments of time for them. This is secondary here. Even if this were the case, the fact would remain that now the entire supply of goods is a different one—better or worse—than before, that the people have become others, that the same standard of life is now valued differently than before; in short, the matter has economically become another one, and since we are not dealing with the legal form, but rather with the economic essence of the same, we get closer to reality when we place more emphasis on the change than on the constancy.

The type of "capital" is also not necessarily movable. This is so obvious that one would actually have to be amazed that it is so often overlooked if there would be no explanation for it; the same is methodologically extraordinarily interesting. In equilibrium, all possible investments must ceteris paribus yield the same return, because otherwise a tendency would exist to cause this state. So if two individuals exchange their investments for some reason, then this can simultaneously happen al pari, meaning that both can, if one wants to express it this way, safely transfer their capital from one investment to the other. This is not so readily possible in the dynamic state. One only transfers that, which is right for the one group of problems to another, without being much concerned. And yet, it is obvious that one, if differences enter into the returns, must pay for the better investment through capital loss. A portion of the monetary capital—the nominal amount is completely indifferent—simply disappears there. Even in the most developed money market in the world, nothing is more common than that "good" securities are also non-saleable—and this means none other than that there can be no talk of absolute movement.

Only two things are completely movable. The static fiction of capital for which the movement is the methodical means, the distribution of this productive force to the production of precisely these and no other tools is to be explained, and thereupon, that credit in the proper sense, that buying power that can be arbitrarily created—it can serve every type of production as long as it is only potentially available. And the sentence of the movement of "capital" is to be limited to it.

D. Now, in these things, as we have said, in the creation of new credit for new industries, interest comes to light. We do not want to discuss how this happens for the closer one. The preconditions are not given here for it. With that, which has been said, a complete theory of interest has not been given yet. It was only supposed to serve for positioning the roots of the problem clearly, to contrast the approach, which should finally show completely satisfactory results, with the current one, to bring the lacking of the latter and the causes of its failure to light. A series of problems, of whose nature the reader should now have an idea, has so to speak broken down the theory so far. And not completely without right, since its methods were not applicable to the phenomenon of interest. If one had not been aware that one, with the help of artificial assumptions of a different, more far-reaching nature than the ones that are otherwise necessary for our theory, dodges those problems that one cannot solve, then there would be nothing to remind of. The mistake lies in that fact that one took its explanation for appearance, its helping hypotheses at face value, and drew conclusions from it that were radically mistaken. If that fact, which we have said is right, *then the theoretical approach has distorted the phenomenon of interest beyond all recognition, and ultimately based it on the moments that have nothing to do with it*. During the demolishing of this structure, other phenomena show themselves, new problems. A completely new structure is necessary. But one cannot approach this here. Only a few remarks may be dedicated to the matter, which I hope to be able to represent satisfyingly in not too distant time.

Those new creations are therefore decisive to the explanation of interest; namely in dual-regard. Firstly, namely due to the fact that they bring forth *new phenomena of value*, they yield a "profit" that could not exist in the static state. This "profit" is not quite interest. But the same somehow develops itself from it. Secondly, those new creations and the stretching of credit effectuate that devaluation of available tools and available outstanding debts. And this fact is also very important.

But we shall call it quits at that, in order to only still touch upon a few suggesting points here.

We have placed emphasis on *one* moment among others, which seemed to approach the productivity theory. But we are realizing the moment completely differently: We are concerning ourselves with *new* production goods, created by *new* means; *and interest does not directly come from them, but rather from credit*. We are also not subjected to the discussed objection against the productivity theory, because this analogousness of the values of the products and the means of production can be readily admitted by us. The source of interest lies in the *creation* of the latter itself.

But do the other phenomena, which are termed as being interest have no relation at all to that in which we see the "actual" interest? Some of the same in fact do not, as we have explained. But we are nevertheless not going this far regarding all of them. The demand for *other* productive loans as such for new creations, then for consumptive loans, naturally exerts influence. This has also already been touched upon. Conversely, *such* loans are touched by the one discussed here, and the interest rates of both will certainly be associated with one another. But this changes nothing on our statement in general, and is a so to speak secondary phenomenon. One could call these other two forms of interest as being derivated, if this could not be easily misunderstood. The profit-earning capacity of the new creations is surely the decisive moment for "the interest rate." But the same is not such a uniform phenomenon as one assumes. One proceeds much too carelessly there. If the rates of the shylock, who lends to young people, are higher than, for example, a bank rate, then one simply blames this on moments of friction, need, non-economical moments like necessity to secrecy, etc. But one never asks them whether a tendency to analogousness even exists. We will negate this and at the most, find a distanced connection between these different phenomena. Here we have an example of really unsustainable theorization before us. Namely, one conceives far too much for the moment of "friction." One should never a priori consider something as being such, but rather always *prove* that one can do that. We will still come to this while discussing the theory of entrepreneurial profit. At this point, we only wanted to calm the reader about the fact that we by no means overlook or deny those connections.

Interest has a distinct relation to the progress—let one pardon the use of this vague term. This is in fact a highly important and interesting side of the matter; in addition, a point that has been disregarded by the theory, one of those points that can only be considered in dynamic. But do we not have to fear the objection that precisely in the failing economy, interest is the highest? This is partially correct, but without proving something against us. Capital is also newly created in failing economies, be it only for the replacement of the former. And these creations continue especially difficultly under the adverse conditions. It is therefore quite understandable that interest is significant there. On the other hand, however, we could, if we had enough space and leisure, prove that this phenomenon is not "interest" at all in our sense, but rather on the one hand, risk premium and on the other hand, "excessive interest" for the surrender of *available* goods. We also had to mention this point in order to show that our conception is not carelessly built on sand, and is exposed to the simplest objections. But we do not want to go further into it.

The relation of the phenomenon of interest to the monetary conditions is just as distinct. And the same is even of fundamental significance to us. If one observes the processes of the economic life, then it is also obvious enough. But despite this, our predecessors almost always refrained from, even considered it, as we have already said, as one of the first demands for a useful examination of the matter, to undress the phenomenon of its "money veil." In our opinion, it would however arise that a portion of its essence remains in that discarded shell. To us, it seems that an essential reason for this process lies in the lacking of a sufficient monetary theory, which evoked the wish to freely maintain the way of the theory from the difficulties and ambiguities that lie there. This should not be possible, and strips a part of the phenomenon from the explanation. It is rather by all means fitting to start from a "monetary capital," namely by no means from a supply of means of production that is expressed in units of value, but rather from a *possession of buying power*, which can be increased through the creation of new monetary imprints or through other forms of credit. This capital has no material existence, except for in the case that it exists in value of money in metal; but it does have a very real role in the economic life. *It is that, which is the most likely for us to term with the name "capital."*[2] Now, this conception can appear to be very concerning. Is it not a superficiality to want to attach interest to it? But, we are certainly not doing this without further ado. We are not foregoing a deeper analysis, and believe to be able to assure—but no more than assurances here—that we account better for the facts than those theories, which contemn this capital as point of departure. We cannot present the observations that induce *us* to do it here, so that the argument does not only suffer through its outlined brevity, but is also lacking its staves. The understanding of the phenomenon of interest demands extensive studies of the processes of the market of a most different nature, and cannot readily be handled abstractly. The abstraction then first arises from the examination of facts. We are not evading the same, our theory is the result of one of such, but we cannot lead it here.

Another objection may be that we strive to make credit a good, as, for example, Mac Leod constructs an air structure whose beams are popular misunderstanding and unclear thoughts. We only mention all of this here in order to show that we visualized these thoughts, and to induce the reader not to easily assume that we are encountering basic mistakes that immediately catch one's eye.

E. We have said that we are avoiding a verdict of v. Boehm-Bawerk's theory, since the same cannot be gained from static, and that this theory perhaps maintains itself in dynamic. We also do not want to give a valuation of the same here, but rather only point to an essential point of contact of our theory with that one. We place so much importance on the moment of development. Now, perhaps the same exists entirely or partially in the pursuing of profitable production detours. We are dwelling more than v. Boehm-Bawerk on the circumstances that bring about progress, on the way it is being conducted. Furthermore, we not only spoke of, yes, also not formally of the production of consumption goods for the purposes of those of the *former* state of the economy, but rather of production with *new* means for *new* purposes in a *new* state, whereby the creation, redevelopment of industries and business combinations ("foundations") were especially emphasized. And in this new state, which the *enterpreneur* anticipates, interest seems to be well-founded to us. A moment entirely foreign to Boehm's theory then is that of credit in our sense. But all of these may just be supplements that are not incompatible with the same. Only a complete representation can show that; here we only wanted to point to this specific point.

The law of the increasing returns factors into our view in a very obvious way, similar to v. Boehm-Bawerk's "third reason." Hopefully one will not believe that we are confounding the two things. But a moment of development certainly also lies in it, that this law becomes operative. Its place is solely in dynamic.

A final relation that we must touch upon is the one between interest and entrepreneurial profit. We have already said that both come from the same source, and even if they are not equal, they do have a similar origin. How this behaves cannot be grappled with. But let the reader be mindful of the interesting result that we are approaching the conception of both, which was previously so frequently uniform in English literature, that we are again at a point where it is possible to we can better learn to understand the doyen Ricardo. Because surely a healthy core lies in it and a result of correct observation. One does generally consider it as progress to have carried out the separation that is common today, and will perhaps accuse us of pleading for a regression. Now, we partially do that. Does such a valuable realization really lie in this separation? Certainly, in some respect. Both things do not collapse and their laws of movement are not the same. But one went much too far when one completely tore them apart and placed interest next to wage and rent. One therewith made the mistake that is so frequent in our area: Every glimmer of a new realization is enforced by an energy that borders on vandalism, without the slightest regard for the fact that in life, as in science, something wrong is said almost just as rarely as something right, that some observation is applicable to almost *every* conception, corresponds to some justification. Now, the true thing about that uniform conception of profit is not difficult to see now. According to our discussion, it is clear that interest is distinctly closer to entrepreneurial profit than to wages and rent, that relations exists between them, which are lacking towards the others and which shed a bright light on both of the phenomena. And even if it is not possible to go into these problems that are partially new ones, then it was still important to indicate this relation, since this also contributes to highlighting our conception of the phenomenon of interest, and to indicate the direction into which our attempt to solve the problem is supposed to move.

To regress to a former conception does not always signify a regression; the same very often has an originality and life truth which, during further analysis, gets lost on the way, so to speak. But apart from that, the former conception, when it is adopted again after a long period of time, is no longer *the same*. The work of this further analysis is not *lost*.

We do also say in our case that it has merits; and if one, enriched by that, which it had to offer, reverts to the former again, then this one tells us much *more* now, even though it signifies something else than before. It is rather difficult to find the right balance between the recognition of merits of previous thought work and the continuity of science on one hand, and the complete appreciation of the better new one on the other hand. If one is primarily missing for us, then, as we have already had the opportunity to remark, a reaction against it has again done too much in the other direction, partially not due to a deeper realization, but rather as a result of a scarce understanding for the modern achievements of our discipline. We are looking to keep ourselves distanced from both, whereby we are not concerned with the justice against people in the sense of the dogmas historian—we do not love to gather words and to put "positions" under the microscope, and we could therefore not exactly say *how far* our conception approaches that of Ricardo. This also does not interest us any further, and we suffice ourselves with this consideration: Ricardo has certainly placed his profit next to loans and rent; the analogy therefore does not go *very* far.

But we do not want to come to speak of a *modern* theory of interest, which should contrast ours in a remarkable way: It is v. Philippovich's. The same fall apart into two parts. The first one, which mind you, almost takes up the entire space that is dedicated to the problem of interest, is a productivity theory and is no longer regarded in this connection. But then the remark follows, "productivity alone is not decisive." It seems essential to the author not to separate the creation of interest from that of the entrepreneurial income. It is difficult to understand the scope of this brief remark, and one surely easily reads over it. It furthermore offers different conceptions, for example, one of such in the sense of the exploitation theory. But I believe that something similar is thought of there as in our explanation. In fact, this remark being thought to the end means nothing more and nothing less than that interest is no "static" income, and the mentioning of the entrepreneur almost points in our direction. And then the preceding productivity theory also gains another significance, which could perhaps be construed in our sense and at any rate, differentiates v. Philippovich's theory from the remaining productivity theories. We could instance several of such appeals in which that, which we consider to be the right realization shimmers through, but this would lead too far.

We have already talked too much about a problem that we cannot solve here after all. But we did not want to let it go at that simple negative result that our static system results in, so much the more as this result also gets its complete purpose from further details first, and have rather offered loose building blocks than nothing at all.

The simple consequence of our conception of the phenomenon of interest is that *our* method, to gain laws of movement which we will get to know in the following, are not applicable to this branch of income. Entirely different laws of motion prevail here than for wages and rent, and perhaps it is this realization that effectuates that one cannot so absolutely content oneself in the present attempts to a solution. The new theory will have to give new information here and will have to show its value. We can already indicate one of the results that is to be expected, namely the confutation of the sentence that interest seeks to diminish without a specific limit and to approach zero. We come to speak of the same point for entrepreneurial profit, and since the same applies to the latter in this regard, then the following should be referred to for this point.

Notes

1. An accumulation of explanation attempts that is absolutely hindering to clarity must simply be considered as a characteristic of the current stage of the theory of interest (page 386).
2. We are very much approaching one of Menger's two terms of capital. But a great difference exists between the ways in which we reached it: he, through the working out of the linguistic use, without attaching anything else to it, we, through the analysis of the phenomena and with regard to specific theoretical goals.

5

About the Theory of Entrepreneurial Profit

I

As we have already remarked, we do not find ourselves on controversial ground in general when we withdraw entrepreneurial profit[1] from our static system. We can therefore be much briefer. We also do not want to solve the problem there, but rather only point to a few deficiencies of the present theories and make a few remarks, which are partially significant to our system, partially are associated with that, which was said about interest.

What initially concerns the first point, the unanimity about the possibility that the entrepreneurial income does not show itself in the static state of the economy, is not a complete one. In fact, the entrepreneurial profit shows itself so regularly that the striving to categorize it into the branches of income of static is comprehensible in a similar manner as the same wish for interest. Here now belongs the theory, which has been represented the most complete by Mataja, and which can be considered as theory of rent of the entrepreneurial profit. The same is in particular conceived as a differential rent of the individual companies vis-à-vis the one that works the most unfavorably. Walker and von Mangoldt, for example, have grasped the matter in another way, by ascribing the entrepreneurial profit to the higher personal efficiency of the entrepreneur, be it vis-à-vis other entrepreneurs—who are then assumed here, as working without a profit—be it vis-à-vis the laborers. This latter theory which implies that the only reason that the laborer is not an entrepreneur is because he is missing the efficiency for it, belongs to those, which one must immediately abandon if one even just wants to *attempt* to maintain the position of the theory vis-à-vis the numerous attacks of a most different nature. Because they are *all* justified here: historical ones, political ones, and above all, also a great deal of theoretical ones.

The conception of the entrepreneurial profit as rent of the person vis-à-vis *other* entrepreneurs is of course something entirely different, and we can combine it, at least as a special case, with Matja's. The theory of this form is very frequent. Two circumstances induce us to reject it. Firstly, the one that it does not explain anything. Naturally, the income of the entrepreneur is that, which is left in his hands, and this "something" can be represented just as naturally as a surplus above the output of an enterprise, which does not make a profit. But what does one gain from it? At the most, the realization that the entrepreneurial profit is not a price like wages or ground rent. This is indeed something, but little. Our second objection is that this entrepreneurial profit *collides* with either wages, or with ground rent, or with the price of the produced means of production. Because wherein is that differential advantage supposed to exist, which results in "rent?" There are many such circumstances; but their economical result is always absorbed by one of those other categories: If the entrepreneur *himself* is especially efficient, for example, as a technician, then his income from it is just considered as an entrepreneurial *wage*. This is not a surplus that requires a special explanation, but is rather just as simple to comprehend as the circumstance that a chauffeur receives a higher wage than a dock worker, and *this* on the other hand, requires just as little a new principle in order to be explained, as the different price of two different consumption goods. And entrepreneurial activity in the actual sense of the word cannot express itself in the static state, in the one where the enterprise exists and all economical activities are determined. Rather, this moment points far beyond the boundaries of static. If the enterprise is furthermore *situated* more conveniently, then the "surplus" is ground rent, if it commands special raw materials or machines, then this expresses itself in their value and price, if a monopoly is present, then this finds its other explanation. What is left for the entrepreneurial profit there?

The theory, which utilizes the same moment in a somewhat different way, which namely proceeds from a law of diminishing production returns—*within the individual enterprise*, has somewhat more substance. The manufacturer produces as long as, or rather, as much until a further growth would no long yield a "profit," and what is produced before this limit is reached, yields a surplus. This is correct under certain requirements that we are skipping over for ourselves with regards to the scarce significance of the argument. But this surplus is not in limbo. We have two possibilities: One either accepts that point as a limit, at which the price that can be realized for the uniformity of the product is equal to the price that was given for the necessary raw materials for it, *excluding* land and labor performances. Then a surplus certainly exists, but the same is gross yield, which says nothing about a final income. Or one includes wages and ground rent in the marginal utility, and probably also interest (compensation of capital is indeed generally something very self-evident for the theorists), then the existence of the surplus is more than doubtful. With the same right, one could also include entrepreneurial profit in marginal utility, and by means of the same, formal raisonnement make out a surplus even then.

II

Another theory considers the entrepreneurial profit as the success of the actual entrepreneurial activity, as which is mostly considered to be the bringing together of the production factors with one another. A correct element lies in it, but the same cannot bring itself to apply, as we have said, in static. One now maintains to include the latter into the same, due to the fact that one speaks of a "wage," which is not to be confounded with that, which we call "entrepreneurial wage." Now, *this* conception is completely askew. These "entrepreneurial performances" are not enumerated under the influence of supply and demand, in the sense as other types of labor. What the entrepreneur receives is by no means distinctly determined and may be greater or lesser than the "value" of his performances for someone. In addition, this cannot be a price because no value functions are available for this "commodity"—at most, for the entrepreneur *himself*, but who stands across from him as the new opponent? Every answer other than "no one" is based on fiction. *Morally*, one could—as unacceptably this seems personal to us—speak of a "reward," which this profit represents, but not of a "wage" economically speaking. We have already spoken about this for the wages theory. But in this sense, this theory would be a "social justification," therefore no scientific theory altogether.

The moment of risk was also brought up, partially by itself, partially in connection with other moments; but only if one conceives the assumption of risk as a "service" that would have to be remunerated, which does not apply for the same reason as to speak of a "wage" of entrepreneurial activity, could a permanent income be there. Otherwise, "good risks" would stand vis-à-vis "bad ones," and profit and loss would almost balance one another.

These theories are methodologically very informative, namely for the following reason: the moments, which they are based on, are not downright wrong, but they do not explain the phenomenon that they are supposed to explain. They are vague claims that can be right or wrong, and whose rightness or wrongness is irrelevant to the phenomenon, about which we wish to find something out. The circumstance that so appropriately makes us realize this in this case is that these small causes can not be suitable after all in explaining such a great phenomenon. But let us assume that the discrepancy between "girders" and "load" would be less big. Perhaps we could then be seduced to accept this theory just as the other authors have done. What abundance of false conclusions could this lead to, which could always be garnished with some facts at the same time! Surely, as long as the national economists believe to have solved an economical problem, if they would even know to answer *something* to a question, may the same not even pertain to that, which is to be explained, and never feel obligated to verify points of departure and results, one cannot completely accuse their opponents of being wrong.

Let us return to our theories and let us choose as foil for that, which we wish to say, a further one, the perhaps most frequent, the "theory of friction." The same well-knowingly states that there would be no entrepreneurial profit if all economical processes would run smoothly. But since this is not the case and the competition can never thoroughly effectuate, here and there surpluses arise, which remain in the hands of the entrepreneur. This theory does not say anything wrong, and it can nevertheless not be used, namely essentially because one dismisses a phenomenon with it in a few words for the most part, about whose magnitude and significance one can nevertheless sensibly not doubt. Not without astonishment, the layman will find that in the textbooks of the economy, so extraordinarily little about this branch of income is to be found. Most of the authors can probably not do enough at all in the broad representation of all good characteristics that an entrepreneur must have, or in a representation of the socio-political side of the matter. But to the question: How does this formation of income go on of the closer one, how do companies arise on the one hand, and the palaces of the upper ten-thousand on the other hand? One actually does not find an answer to this question than perhaps this "friction." And one still only needs to analyze this answer in order to recognize its deficiency. From the fact that someone is mistaken, or that he does not act corresponding to the economy due to negligence or for another reason, precisely the greatest incomes are supposed to emerge from that? Of course, one is indeed not limited to such very small moments. Inventions and suchlike are indeed a bit more important. Furthermore, we have the speculation profit there. But the same appears in the system of the economy either as a gift of luck, which occurs completely sporadically, or as a rather limited profit from arbitrages and suchlike. How pathetic are these elements! They do not get better through the attachment of a few socio-political and moral observations of the game of the stock exchange, and the matter becomes positively *wrong* as soon as one gets around extrapolating the tendency for the elimination of the entrepreneurial profit from free competition.

But before we discuss this point, we still want to ventilate something else; namely the instructive question: How would the facts of the case have to be, if we are supposed to be justified in just going beyond this branch of income with the explanation that it deals with friction income? This lies in the same direction as the general methodological question: When is one allowed to neglect something? Because the essence of the theory of friction is no different at all than the claim that one is allowed to do this with entrepreneurial profit. *Not* necessary for it is a tendency for the elimination, and the same would also not be sufficient at all. The essential thing rather is that *it deals with magnitudes from which one can prove that they, each taken separately, are so small in relation to the others with which one is concerned, that one can be sensible enougb to disregard them*, and that they furthermore, from the standpoint of the examination on the other hand, have the characteristic of randomness, so that it *is probable* that they balance one another. The emphasis is especially placed on the fact that that, which was disregarded, may not noticeably influence the result; that the obligation is incumbent upon us to prove that this is not the case, requires no justification at all. The matters certainly now stand differently in our case, the margin of the entrepreneur is much greater, it is *constantly* greater, without showing a general tendency to sink, and from this follows that the theory of friction cannot be sufficient. We have here in turn a contribution to the understanding of "static." Because we see what the result is if one makes the effort of dealing with dynamic problems in static. Because *this* has happened here. These theories gain such a Hippocratic appearance, one feels pressured to limit the significance of the things for which one has no sufficient explanation, and an improvement is not possible any other way than one placing the matter on completely new foundations—freed from the apparatus of static, which becomes a "straitjacket" here.

Now to the alleged fact that entrepreneurial profit has a tendency to disappear. I believe not to have to fear opposition when I repeat that that is generally not the case at all, that there are periods where it appears that way, but others, where the exact opposite is true. And it is also theoretically clear that such a disappearance would only be assumed under both of the requirements that we will now present. The same also apply to interest, and we have pointed to the present things there. That this is not sufficient to accuse us of confounding both branches of income hardly requires emphasis. So when could entrepreneurial profit and interest disappear in reality? Firstly, if the development suddenly stood still; because further development would bring new interest and profit to the entrepreneurs and capitalists. But this is not yet sufficient. Companies of the same type and same line of business would have to be founded at the same time, as they presently exist, so that this plus disappears through their competition. The artificial and controversial things of these requirements are clear. This is by no means the assumption of a static state, it is a partial stand still combined with a partial advancement of a specific type, as it will certainly never exist.

But why the theorist never wants to acknowledge an entrepreneurial profit is obviously only for the reason that he cannot explain it in the static system. The static requirements eliminate it. If one now wishes, in order to liven the picture up more, to preserve the individual of the entrepreneur for the same, then an "entrepreneur faisant ni benefice ni perte" comes out, as it does for Walras. Most of the theorists now do not clearly express that this entrepreneur is only fiction due to methodological reasons, or rather, they do not clearly recognize it. But this seems very unquestionable to me. Once again, one has a construction here that is practical for specific purposes, of course also supported by deficient observations, simply displaced into reality where it then maintains itself badly. Only this should be the source of the theory of friction and the deeper reason for the claim that entrepreneurial profit has a tendency to disappear.

One of the theories of entrepreneurial profit now also gives the result that the same is a permanent phenomenon and its rate naturally is an unequal one, neither strives for zero, nor for equalization. This is the mentioned "theory of rent" of the same, and Mataja has applicably emphasized this. So far the same has a great advantage over the others. But already the next conclusion that one could draw from it would be wrong; namely that one that a tax on entrepreneurial profit would have to fall to the entrepreneur, without a possibility of transference existing. One often claims this for differential rents. And the same is approximately true for the same. But not for entrepreneurial profit, as one convinces himself if one considers that the complication of the entrepreneurial function, which lies in it, leads to a limiting of production and thus to an increasing of the prices, consequently, indeed to a partial transference to a greater or lesser extent. This sentence is never *entirely* true; but for entrepreneurial profit itself, not in this approximation.

Thereupon, this theory does not quite suitably express the longevity of entrepreneurial profit. It probably remains, it probably always shows itself, but not continually for the individual companies, rather, from which it slips in the course of development. The development is the decisive moment for it; it can only be comprehended from it. And it is completely lacking in this train of thought.

Only the development and the movement fully and completely show this so important phenomenon, from which the capital formation for the most part explains itself, in my opinion. And even here, problems now arise for which that, which has been accomplished offers nothing, and which we wanted to indicate here.

Interest and entrepreneurial profit certainly have more to do with one another than with wages and rent. At least we can also state this result with ease, due to our so incomplete explanation. The branches of income therefore fall into two tentatively different groups, which are to be explained in completely different ways. Of course it would be nice, if this were not the case. How much would static and the national economy even gain if one could also assume a permanent source for interest and profit as labor and land, so for example, abstinence and a special "entrepreneurial service!" How clear and simple would the economical theory of distribution then be! One cannot reproach the economists who attempt it; but it just does not work. Such constructions would indeed be possible in principle, but they would not offer actual insight. They would not solve problems, but rather only mask them. And therefore another way must be pursued. Perhaps it will once lead to this clarity and uniformity. But beforehand, a hard piece of work must be done.

Note

1. I am presuming that the difference between "entrepreneurial income" and "entrepreneurial profit" is known as the income of the entrepreneur as such (Schumpeter, 1908, pg. 431).

Part IV

The Variation Method

1

General Part[1]

I

We have resolved the problem of describing our system as far as it is necessary and possible inside the framework of this work, and have furthermore also touched upon several necessary supplements. But before we come to forming a final verdict about its value of realization to us, we still want to take an important step farther; we want to see it work, so to speak.

The observation of the system in equilibrium teaches us—popularly speaking—what its individual elements, namely what the static incomes "are," and thereupon, their distinct determination. Of course we do not find out anything about their concrete magnitude, but we obtain enlightenment about their nature. The very next thing that we now wish to further find out is the laws of movement of those magnitudes. This is the second, large problem, the second group of results of the exact economy. Not only is this the practically most interesting question, at least immediately after that one, whether the prices and incomes are something "arbitrary" or "necessary," but our current results also have to prove themselves, verify themselves, as a result of the laws of movement, which they yield, having to coincide with reality. We have recognized that the same are nothing else in part, than the result of assumptions, which we have constructed ourselves, that they are therefore insofar the creations of our arbitrariness, schemes, which we are constructing because we expect that they will *practically* reproduce the processes of reality. Their *entire* significance lies in this case, all the purpose that they have, solely in the rules, which they give for the relative changes of our elements; they were constructed for this reason alone. Finally, a complete understanding of our system is not possible when one observes how the state of equilibrium produces itself, how the tendencies, which cause it, function. Through it, the idiosyncrasy and the value of our system then comes quite clearly before our eyes, and all its requirements and limitations come much livelier into our consciousness, as if we solely *allege* them while observing the state of equilibrium. They can frequently seem redundant *there*; we encounter them at the same time *here* when we seek to move more freely than they allow it, and their necessity and significance is much livelier understood.

All of this now induces us to turn to the problem of the variations of our elements. We will again place special emphasis on the methodological side of the matter, make an effort to sharply work out the essence of that, which we are doing and what we accomplish with it, to present the pure economical contribution to these questions separate from all impurities with which it maintains to appear intermingled in literature. It is much more important to us to show what the pure theory does there and can do there, than going into the individual sentences in all detail, to limit this branch of our discipline and to characterize, than to exhaust and to further study it, to remove the "undergrowth," which envelopes its forms, to expand as these. The entire subject matter will be new to most of the readers, and especially the German audience must first become acquainted with it. But the older, as well as the modern, economy has already concerned itself with these questions quite thoroughly, as much that there is still left to do. Now, we are serving our purpose better if we dwell longer on the foundations and questions of principle than if we derivate the individual results. The most important thing is to show the distinct determination of the variations, and to make a contribution to the understanding of our system, which, among other things, will also lead to the methodic aid of "static" again. Our principal task lies in it. The concrete results that we present only have the character of examples vis-à-vis it, without seeking quite adequate treatment, whereby the circumstance also hinder us that for it, as we will see, the help of higher mathematics is essential, and we want to exclude the same from this book at all costs. I hope to soon have the opportunity to add that, which is missing here in this regard. We will only attempt to show the necessity of this type of treatment itself, and hope that for the non-mathematically educated reader, the understanding of that, with which the mathematical economy concerns itself, will be facilitated by it, and thus, an understanding of different directions of research is promoted.

We are encountering two entirely different questions when we take a step beyond the explanation of the existence, or rather, a question, which has two entirely different meanings. It reads: How do prices and incomes *change* absolutely and relatively to one another? Now, an entire literature answers it, and we are standing in front of very current problems. But we have to keep two different things separate. Firstly, it can be asked about the actual development; if the commodities become more expensive or less expensive, if wages, interest, or rent increases or decreases, and how does their actual relation to one another shape itself compared to the past? And secondly: Given any state of the national economy in equilibrium and a specific cause for disturbance; how will the prices and incomes change?

The deep gap between both problems is obvious. And in the first approach, one can immediately say that only the latter of our methods can be approachable. This can be shown just as well as the analog claim that we can never explain a *concrete* state of the economy, and is something similar to the differentiation between the economical explanation of unapproachable, "system-determining" facts and the pure economical quantities—we do not want to correct the latter sentence as it actually would be necessary, for the sake of brevity. The *concrete* movements are dependent on *concrete* data; our *formal* raisonnement cannot put it across for only itself. It can only, *if* concrete data are given, predict specific consequences of the same. If one says that the wage increases ceteris paribus when the demand increases, then the theory can tell us nothing about whether the demand, for example, will increase in the future and what the concrete cause of this phenomenon will be. That is obvious. And we also immediately see that while observing the individual phenomena, the moment of development gains special interest, and that always other things than pure economical ones are determining for the same. One again sees how incapable of development our system is. We must therefore limit ourselves to the second one of the distinguished problems.

But it would still not be quite right to express the contrast between both of them there, that one asks about the individual facts for the first one, and about the laws, which control the same, for the second one. One also wishes to gain generalizations, to discover great tendencies for the first one. The sentence that the population seeks to reproduce beyond the scope of food products, a sentence that is very important in this connection, gives an example. We have seen that the same does not belong to the sentences of our theory, is essentially different from them—but it is nevertheless a "law." It thus follows that we do not completely master the abstract problem of variation, and this is ultimately nothing more than self-evident.

By no means is every relation between both problems lacking. One could certainly attempt to purely economically explain a specific state of the national economy from another given one, or to conclude a future one from a given one. As a matter of fact, this must be our ultimate goal. We must come so far that we, if sufficient data are available to us, can carry out those operations. Yes, one can say that every time a claim about tendencies of movement of the distribution, etc., is vocalized, precisely this happens. If one thereby takes away the economical portion of the train of though, then one only does it because one considers it as being self-evident. We are here at an important point. The entire literature of which we spoke, deals with the *first* problem: One either examines the facts historically or statically, or also concerns oneself with the laws, which may arise from the observation of the system-determining facts. One believes to be able to gain results regarding concrete facts in only this manner, and what the pure theory is able to say, one only considers being truisms. This circumstance and then that relation between both problems, which we have indicated, explain that one did not sharply separate them. This would also be neither practical, nor possible for most purposes. But this is what we want to do here.

This confounding also characterizes the older and the by far largest part of the modern theory. Some representations suffice themselves with the explanation of the essence of the pure economical quantities and processes altogether, and do not go into an exact examination of the variations, which evokes a cause for disturbance. But where this occurs, one easily sees that the author has the feeling that the pure economical theory is not able to say enough interesting things about it, and therefore hurries to raise new moments. This is absolutely understandable. The fact that a price changes when supply and demand change really seems too clear to be specially emphasized. But this is not allowed to deceive us about the fact that suchlike is the only thing that our system can give us out of itself. And this has the important consequence that we, as theorists, are not competent in regards to those other moments. The same belong to the domains of the sociologists, biologists, etc., as we showed at a previous point. We can at most derivate the pure economical consequences of these moments, therefore that, which seems so uninteresting. All such new facts are indifferent to us—they are only considered in their trait as "cause for disturbance," and those things that we, as economists have the right to comment on will soon shape themselves, *whatever this cause for disturbance may be*. Beyond this, we are dilettantes or representatives of disciplines other than ours, and this is, in my opinion, very noticeable in the results.

All common systems of our science—the classical one, the socialistic one, etc.—have taken a stand on problem of the "variations," namely on its practically most meaningful version, on the question of the tendencies of the distribution of income. Now, what they say about it is not purely economical, rather, it is absolutely based on non-economical moments. Since this also applies to those results, which have given rise to the most controversies, it therefore seems essential to me to emphasize this. Above all, the discussion of these things would be encouraged if one were to finally realize what questions are actually being dealt with. This would very much contribute to the "localization" of the war and would initiate exact solutions. Thus, the economical theory would gain much if one freed it from controversies, which basically do not touch them at all, and showed that it actually represents a neutral factor that speaks neither for, nor against one of the arguing parties—at least not in itself. Of course, if the theory can thereby gain universal approval, it again loses very much current interest. Not only the politician will turn away from a weapon whose uselessness he has recognized, the researcher too will ask himself whether that, which remains even still has value of realization. It behaves in the same manner here as for some other points, which we have already mentioned. Certainty and correctness cost us much, and we must nevertheless seek them, even if we were supposed to write a death sentence for our discipline: This is *absolutely essential* for the sake of the healthy development of the social sciences.

But if we must, on the one hand, consider our theory in its entire form and consider it regardless of its value, then it is also our job, on the other hand, to carefully represent what it can achieve. It could show that those truisms, considered closer and developed further, may actually be somewhat more significant than the majority of the national economists believe. So to what extent at the very least can we solve our second problem, and is this solution of interest, worth one concerning oneself with it? Just recently has one begun to purely economically approach and strictly isolate the same. For the classical authors and their predecessors, as well as in the so-called "descriptive" literature and in the discussion of practical issues of the day, basic approaches find themselves well, but they are not only, as we have said, immediately overgrown by foreign elements, but are also of little value in themselves. This is partially due to the deficiencies of the former theory, and partially because one, as one on the one hand threw together both of those problems, which are to be separated, thus on the other hand, neglected an important connection: One has—it especially comes to light by discussions of the laws of movement of the incomes—not approached the matter from the foundations of the theory, but rather much more superficially, as if these were completely independent problems. Our results must arise from the price theory and not only from flighty claims, which have lost every connection with it.

We therefore differentiate ourselves from the majority of economists in three points: In the separation of the pure economical problem from others, in a better theoretical foundation, and finally in the belief that our approach is really directly based on the same. If one adequately appreciates this, then one sees, in my opinion that all so well-known objections against the economy, which were certainly partially justified earlier, vanish. Our position regarding socio-political and other judgments is the same as it was previously, and we do not want to repeat that, which has been said in regards to these and also other things that come into consideration here. Finally, if it seems—and this is only natural—that the previous approach has continued and has given especially more results, then it can be differentiated whether or not the latter ones were of a purely economical nature. And only if the first thing is the case, we must prove its incorrectness or acknowledge the superiority of the former approach.

If one therefore forgoes an explanation that offers more materially through raising new facts, and if one limits oneself to a so to speak more formal one, then there is only *one* way that one can pursue. What one thereby has to do, which rules of measurement are necessary, can be generally and clearly given and must be observed by every man, if he does not want to easily encounter verifiable mistakes. There we have a gratifyingly accurate ground under our feet. *This way is that, which we have called variation method*, and we want to make ourselves closer acquainted with this one. Its scientific significance is, completely apart from the possible value of its results, a great one. With consideration for its representation as one of the first accurate achievements in the area of the humanly trade—and at any rate, the first longer accurate train of thought—a similar significance pertains to it in the area of the "humanities," as for the "Semmeringbahn" (mountain railway) in the area of technology.

II

The variations method exists in the following process: Our system finds itself in equilibrium, whereby, as we have seen, all its elements are distinctly determined. One now enlarges or minimizes one of the same to a small extent. Then one observes what happens. All other elements will also change, not to the same extent, some, actually most, only unnoticeably, but all nevertheless. The fact that one or the other stays the same is indeed not completely impossible, but would only represent, if no external force causes that, which we are disregarding just like new encroachments or non-economical counter-influences against our considered disruption, a just as unlikely as principally meaningless coincidence. Because if, as we have seen, all elements are determined in a muddle, then, after one has changed, the same state can no longer yield our maximum utility, and consequently can no longer be the state of equilibrium. It is indeed very obvious that all requirements are then no longer equally satisfied, that the marginal utility relations, due to the change of one of the quantities that determine it, are no longer equal, and that therefore a tendency for change exists in the sense of our assumptions. And the observation of these changes now gives us the laws of movement that we are looking for; it gives us everything that the pure economy is able to achieve for these problems. The variations follow as reaction against the disruption of equilibrium, and cause a new state of equilibrium that is just as distinctly determined as the previous one, and one can also express our proceeding in that we have to find the new state of equilibrium and compare it to the previous one, from which our results then arise.

That is the foundation, the method in its simplest form. Before we continue, we will dwell on it a bit, in order to add a few necessary remarks. The method is none other than a working out of the well-known laws of price formation or, as one can popularly but with little correctness say, of the laws of supply and demand. It takes everything that is to take there from this simple, yes, sparse point of departure. *How the prices form themselves if something changes in the system*, it exhaustively presents this, as far as this is generally possible. The former contemplation did not result in anything special there, as we have seen, and the question is whether the improved instrument is able to squeeze more out of the system. Whatever happens will be grasped under the point of view of the change of an element of our system. A pure economical effect can never arise differently than through the medium of the prices, and the foundation of its laws of movement is experimentally given through the supply and demand function. However, we do not know their exact form, but we know certain characteristics of the same, *and our method systematically draws all those conclusions that are possible from them.* Since we have now limited the area of the pure economy by definition to what is contained in the barter relation, it thus arises not only as a necessary, but also as a self-evident, consequence that our method is the only thing that the theory offers here.

We have indicated three points, which differentiate our way of dealing with the matter from the previous one, or rather, from the generally common one, and which, in our opinion, represent progress. We now have to mention yet another one. If one considers the pure economical consequences of a change of any quantity of a good in the system, then an entire series of effects are always to be considered, which partially counteract one another. If one has, for example, realized that the wage must increase if the quantity of labor is decreased, then this is a rather sparse result. But this is certainly not everything. Certain other prices will also increase, namely the ones of those goods, which the laborers now earn. This also affects the other incomes. And from these, in turn, also yet other prices. The fact of the wage increase in itself furthermore affects the other incomes very directly, as is certainly very obvious. Now, these things are not so simple, although purely economical, and a judgment about it is no truism. There it does not only concern the *facts* of these variations in themselves, but rather their *comparison* between themselves. Only in this way can one come to a judgment that has some value, and for *this* purpose, everything depends on "how much." What use is it to the laborer if his wage increases, but at the same time, the prices of his food products also skyrocket? Or: Does he gain just as much, or more or less than the other economic subjects lose? This is the punctum saliens, if we cannot say anything *about it*, then we have said nothing at all.

One now commonly works at the discussion of such questions, if one even poses them to oneself, with "arguments." Nowhere does this stand out more than in the fight over protective tariffs. The protectionist believes to have done everything when he says that the price of a commodity must increase in order to preserve the life of any industry. The free-trader believes to have disproved him on his part, when he points to the disadvantages that arise from it for the consumer. We will see later-on that one may never juxtapose these arguments altogether, since they have entirely different things in mind. Here we are only dealing with the pure economical aspect and static aspect of the matter. But the relative magnitudes of both moments are thereby of decisive importance. The "arguments" are almost always correct in themselves, they only represent too small of an excerpt of the facts and overlook everything else. It does not matter how beyond doubt one proves them to be, one has not gained anything for the *entire* problem. The examples of suchlike, completely fruitless disputes are numerous. Every economical textbook presents suchlike. To me, an essential cause of the scarce trust in economical arguments seems to lie in it, which we are presently observing so generally. Guidances of proof that completely contradict themselves can be made plausible—does this not clearly show how worthless the moments are, which they are based on? One can come to diametrically opposed "practical standpoints" from completely the same foundations and with exactly the same right—does that not imply that one is dealing with worthless speculations? One actually draws this conclusion frequently. But one could still do something different, namely that, which we want to indicate here, to examine the arguments more closely and above all, to quantitatively formulate.

However, this can not yet readily be sufficient for practical results, since for the practice, as we do not get tired of emphasizing, also completely other things—and perhaps *formally* others—than the pure economical laws still come into consideration. But the latter ones can nevertheless give more than those vague claims that most often serve the platform more than the realization. We are making a case for the quantitative approach here, for the most exact one, the only really exact form of the train of thought, for mathematics. Especially the things that are to be considered here are so complicated that one can express them very difficultly and never entirely correctly with words. But in addition, the foundations are so extraordinarily clear, and the difficulty now exists in a complete and direct derivation from relatively very simple data. This is now precisely a task of the type for which mathematical analysis is created, where it has achieved its success. It becomes indispensable here as soon as one goes somewhat deeper, and it also leads to some results here, which can only be offered by it. Our system in itself can be explained without its help, but only the mathematician can gain *everything* that further arises with completely certainty and correctness. We want to get to know quite a bit about it as a result of our principle, not for a priori reasons, but to rather solve the questions of method from our work. We must also indicate another advantage of mathematical treatment. Only it highlights all requirements and contingencies of the train of thought quite clearly, so that it is almost impossible to overlook them. The latter is extraordinarily frequent in the common discussions. If someone says that the price, as a result of a protective tariff, must increase in a specific case, and someone else, that it must decrease as a result of the suggestions that were given to the industry, one most often overlooks that both claims do not contradict one another at all, since they have completely different things, completely different requirements in mind. But also in the cases where this does not come to mind in this manner, it is important to indicate this moment. Almost every claim is correct under certain requirements, as we have also seen otherwise. To make this plain is completely essential to its understanding and its appreciation. Only for the mathematical treatment does this now happen systematically: what our system of equations requires is clear before our eyes. If we make further assumptions, for example, the remaining constant of certain elements, then this cannot slip from our attention. And this is of the upmost importance for the subject matter of which we speak here. Where everything depends on drawing the greatest effectiveness of realization from little data, the method of the approach has a superior significance, a far greater one than for other problems where it matters more to collect facts. This now leads us to carefully ventilate certain requirements of our method, which shine on its essence and its limitations, and will in turn give us a contribution to the understanding of our static system.

III

We are regarding price variations. How the same form themselves depends on the form of the supply and demand curve or, more correct, of both of the demand curves from which we have explained the price. We must therefore adhere to this form. Because if we would not do this, then we could not say anything at all about the variations. If the value functions become other ones, then we are robbed of an essential datum. Namely, we could then, as we have said, claim *nothing at all*, not even just nothing *exact*. By this I mean the following: One could believe that, if the demand function changes—let us say, for example, if people suddenly cease the use of a specific good because fashion changes—we then do not apply our method, but we could in fact generally say what happens. This is *not* always possible. Because in such a case the entire value system of the national economy changes, new phenomena arise of which we had known nothing, and the new state is in the true sense of the word "incalculable."

If someone wants to nevertheless claim something, then a further—and very alarming—step on the path of abstraction and away from reality lies in it.

The remaining the same of the value functions, therefore meaning human nature, tastes, etc., is thus essential. Here we first completely understand why we have placed such emphasis on it: The demonstration of the ultimate principles of the system would probably also be possible in itself without these requirements. But this leads a step farther. In order for the value functions to be able to remain the same, the quantities are *not* allowed to change *by much*. We have certainly already seen which difficulties lie in the assumption *of one* continuous value function for every good and every individual. The same does not readily apply from 0-∞, even if we make this assumption for certain purposes. It only applies completely correctly to small intervals. If one were to have *much* more or *much* less of a good than one actually has, the entire economy would run differently. New uses would arise or some would fall, so that the value function would not stay the same. And this would also affect all other value functions, initially the complementary ones, furthermore, the rivaling ones, and finally, also the ones *of all* goods. Strictly speaking, the value system and altogether *everything* that is in our area of study, does only apply to a very specific quantity of goods of every type. Furthermore, to only economize for a specific type, whereto very specific bartering acts also belong, whose results already appear in the manner that we have presented, in the value function of the price goods. Nothing is actually allowed to change from all of this, and if it were effectuated by, for example, a "cause for disturbance" that a quantity of goods, which up to now maintained to exchange A for another one of B, is now used for something else, then the consequences are not to be overlooked. Let us only think of the fact that the cause for disturbance is a prohibitive tariff, which hinders A and B that live on this and on that side of a boundary in the barter. Both of them can only attempt to find another opportunity to barter—perhaps in the inland—but the same will *certainly* not be as advantageous if we assume a smooth effectiveness, which we must do here. They can consume the goods that have been exchanged up to now. But it could also be that the same would become worthless to them. The bartered ones could furthermore be "pulled up" at the same time through the disturbance, and start something completely new with the goods, which no one has thought of so far. In *all* these cases, which are all equally possible, our entire system—although this is *especially* clear in that, which was lastly presented—is changed, and we are not in a position to state something really noteworthy.

We had to bring these facts of the case out so poignantly, in order to gain the background for the following, in order to let the essence of our method stand out well. Although this namely is that way—and it is good to always adhere to it at present—there are two comforting reasons after all. Two circumstances make it possible for us to nevertheless push forward. Firstly, the moment that the infinitesimal method is based on: We can nevertheless consider *small* changes, and herein lies the essence, the value, but also the boundary of our method. It is essentially a form of the infinitesimal method. Let us regard this somewhat closer. It always seems alarming to the layman that certain judgments for "infinitely small" sizes are supposed to be true, which are indisputably wrong or impossible for significant sizes. He even uses an opposing method very frequently; which does not seem very apparent for the small one, gets enlarged, in order to move the matter more in the light. And the first impression of the infinitesimal method for him cannot be better characterized than by the expression "swindle." Some professors of mathematics take this well-known feeling as the point of departure of their representations and say, at the point where the transition from the "finite" to the "infinite" takes place: "We now want to allow ourselves a little swindle." This is didactically most practical and serves to emphasize the arbitrariness, the not quite strictly logical thing of the process, its *nature as an aid*. Now, it cannot be our task to discuss the infinitesimal method more closely, and we have also allowed ourselves for the purpose of brevity, not to use a quite correct manner of expression with regards to it. The important thing for us is that our variations method belongs here. We cannot deal with any somehow significant changes in the size of the economical quantities, but well with those that are small in relation to the data of the problem.

How great can the changes be if our method is supposed to be applicable? We clarify this for ourselves the best if we realize *why* the changes must be so small. We respond to this latter question: So that the value system does not change. So when is that the case? Obviously then, when the change in quantity is so small that the concerned individual is not thereby inclined to significantly change his production and consumption combination. He will then use all goods *as* always, and for the same purposes as always. He only makes those changes that are possible within the base lines of his economizing. If someone leaves, for example, his common daily exercise activities completely undone for some reason, then he will have more time and energy for different things. He will also feel different—worse, but perhaps even better. This can now become the stimulus to change his entire life arrangement, to do things or to refrain from those, which he had always done otherwise or which he had never thought of. But if he limits his exercise, then effects will occur, but entirely different ones: his health will stay about the same; the surplus of energy and the—let us say—five minutes that he gains are being used differently, but probably only devoted to one of those jobs, which he had already behooved. He will write a few more lines of his book, but he will not begin a new one. And the job that experiences this increase will probably be somewhat furthered, but in the way that it could lead to significantly different results. If a certain tariff is placed on a bartering act, then the parties will continue to barter if it is not prohibitive, but perhaps somewhat lesser quantities. Then they spare, for example, from the goods that they have bartered up to now, something, which does not however suffice to call forth great, new phenomena, but is rather just being added to neighboring uses. We therefore answer the question, how great our change is allowed to be, not absolutely, but rather only through a rule: It may not be so great that the value functions would fail. The concrete size varies case by case. For some goods, *one* unit will already be too much. So, for example, for machines: We must make use of the means of the differentiation of "elements of goods" here, which we owe to Professor Clark. Also depending on the question, which we have just discussed, this shapes itself differently: If one considers the individual, then another size is of course "very small," as if one examines the entire national economy. "Very small" is indeed an entirely relative term.

Now this again sheds light on the essence of "static." We now livelier understand why this construction is so necessary. Our result that we can only handle small changes means none other than that we must remain within the boundaries of static, because our method fails outside of the same, and those assumptions, which give us our sentences, must then be dropped. Only within the same do we stand on solid ground, do we gain certain results. And theories that are inconsistent with our construction as, for example, v. Boehm-Bawerk's theory of interest, must be regarded completely differently, also have entirely different requirements, so that one cannot readily place them next to the static ones.

Our method is therefore essentially static, which has not always been recognized. We now see why we also cannot completely solve, at least not with static means, the second of those two problems, which we differentiated regarding the movements that occur in the elements of our system. This is a very serious limitation of the area of the pure economy. Our interest is directed towards the great changes, namely towards a few great tendencies of development, and here, where it becomes so very clear to us that we have nothing to say about it, that we can have nothing to do with it, the question again presses of what our pure theory is actually worth. Its results will come bearably close to reality if one considers short time periods. Comfort lies in it in part. In fact, the "system-determining facts" do not generally change quickly. They can therefore be conceived as constant for short periods without one having to fear to deviate too far from reality. The life and the habits of people also persevere relatively tough, and only if one stretches the observation of the same to a longer time frame does one recognize that they are in the river of a continual change. So one can then predict from a specific state of the economy during the entering of a not too great or vehement cause for disturbance in general, with reassurance of its economical consequences, and expect that the same can actually really be recognized *in the nearest future*.

But only in the *nearest* future. Because the stream of development will soon flood it. But for the other part, this makes us aware of an important characteristic of the static state, of which we just now come to expressively speak. We have already used the simile of the moment photography. We now have to go on. Not only is our theoretical picture abstracted from the *state of the same in a moment*, it is also only useful for a moment. Probably nothing, in order to stay with our present topic, would hinder us strictly speaking, to consider a time frame as long as we want it to be. But our picture would then become too unrealistic. What use is it to us to say that as a result of a cause for disturbance, the prices will continually, for example, increase if other disturbances not only mask but also completely cancel this effect?

Not because we *could* not methodically do it, do we have to forgo the consideration of great time frames, but rather because in such, if one looks at an economical epoch, so to speak sub specie aeternitatis—and for the problems, which *then* step into the foreground—entirely different things become interesting than our purely economical results. Examples are supposed to be instanced later-on. Our system is not *only* without development *for the reason* because no tendency for the development is absorbed into the same, and because beyond this, a development of data, which we cannot do without, would fall to pieces, but also because the effects, which can be explained purely economically and admittedly statically, lose every interest next to much greater things. We could probably also say here that we are disregarding these other things—this would logically not be any more alarming than the same process if meant for an "instant"—but we would be less justified in doing this here, and could not strip a justification of the well-known objections.

This has the consequence that we are completely powerless vis-à-vis an argument that appeals to the development. We can at most say that as to it the future, so to us the present belongs, and that, if we cannot prove anything against the same, then the same cannot prove anything against us, that a dispute is redundant. To already clearly perceive that is not worthless. The arguments for the protective tariff, for example, are almost all of "dynamic" character, point to developmental opportunities. The ones for free trade are partially static, emphasize the direct "damage" of an intrusion into the state of equilibrium. Now, to the extent that this difference exists between both of the arguments, one can impossibly accurately balance them against one another, and the discussion will be without result, with the exception of *special* cases: I am only thinking of the discussion of the *question of principles*.

Let it also be remarked here that it does not seem necessary to us, with regards to the fact that our system strictly speaking only applies to short periods anyhow, to make the so artificial assumption of a population, which regenerates completely stationary and to do similar things, which we have previously spoken of. And furthermore, we can actually grasp the individually identical tools and simulate them as being indestructible. This comes much closer to reality than the other fictions, which are necessary in the opposite case, and hardly has a disadvantage.

IV

The indicated boundaries are very narrow ones. Can we really not go beyond them? This leads us to the *second* point. The changes actually may not be so great if our theory is supposed to have any value. If the quantities of goods change, which we see in the possession of the individual, in the way that the same, for example, is relinquished to death by starvation, then we cannot say what happens. If we nevertheless wanted to formally use our method there, then this would only be bauble. We would receive not information, but realization. The boundary of the "minimum of existence" indicates, rather crudely, however, such a point beyond which we can, under no circumstances go; changes, that bring an individual into another class, change his standard of life, also belong here. The chains of our anchor tear here. But apart from that, we are not completely strictly bound to our demands. So we have first shown how our system strictly speaking eliminates every change. We have thereupon nevertheless developed our method into a form, which every man must recognize as being theoretically sound, if he does not want to reject the infinitesimal method. We now want to still take a third step, namely ventilate the question whether we can or cannot still go farther.

We certainly can if we do this, do not prove it in the same way, do not defend it in the same way as previously; and thus, we want to strictly separate it from it, more than this has already happened, so that an objection that may now come upon us is not also raised against that, which was mentioned previously. But it is only natural in itself to attempt to get a bit farther. We have already indicated at an earlier opportunity that the validity of our results often reaches farther than that of its requirements. It is more correct to say that the latter ones are in fact truer in themselves, are closer to reality than its critics often accept and than it seems for its completely correct formulation. The things change, but yet, not too much, and above all, not too quickly, are more constant than one believes in some regard. And if we have carefully worked out all boundaries and contingencies up to now, which apply to our method, then it is again good here to continue audaciously, not fearfully in order to peek, but rather to dare something. If a result does not quite sustain itself, then it perhaps partially sustains itself, but if it does not sustain itself at all, then we must admittedly drop it, but we will not damn our attempt itself and will by all means repeat it in another way. How far one may go there, there is no rule for it; scientific competence, a type of discretion alone is able to recognize the right thing. We do in no way want to steer into these pathways here. It is more important to us to sift that, which is available, to separate the individual levels of abstraction from one another, than to gain many correct, detailed results. We want to calm the opponents, not to, however, immediately make them nervous again. Of course it is an audacious approach and not a discussion of the requirements and a correct formulation of the foundations, which delivers formally new results. Nevertheless, it suffices us to indicate the possibility here.

What affects the first point, the size of the variations to begin with, we are—and this applies to our method in its simplest form, as well as to further aids to which we will soon get—disregarding the boundaries that were just mentioned, certainly not limited to infinitely small sizes in the sense of mathematics. Our approach is, however, only completely correct when one can assume the value system as being unchanged through the variations of a quantity. But one can also adhere to the same value system when *it* changes *a little, but imperceptibly*.

And finally, also then when it does not change *too much*, although *noticeably*. If it is a matter of, for example, a product of little significance, then one can also with our method, especially if one has the national economy as a whole in mind and disregards the effect on individuals who are especially participating, examine the effect of its complete cessation, so for example, that of a change in fashion or a prohibitive tariff—for a product that is not produced in the inland. The results will not necessarily be useless. But one may of course not forget that one allows oneself more than is strictly speaking permitted, and that it is quaestio facti everyone's individual case what value the result has. One has to be clear that the same is of another root than one that was gained with our method in its correct form. And a verification is even much more, and also in yet another sense, necessary here than elsewhere.

The case is similar for the moment of the period of time. The authors, who have concerned themselves with our method, have actually differentiated between long and short periods, and have carried no concern to also draw conclusions regarding the first one. Far be it from us to condemn this. We only want to emphasize the difference of the nature of the results in both cases. The short period is static. The nature of the results is well-known to us. Through the observation of a longer period, yet another requirement is added, namely the one that "all other conditions" do not change in a way that the results lose all significance. This requirement is often fulfilled, occasionally more than one believes. It will often be possible to explain a specific phenomenon in purely economical ways, which is far off, a rather long time, several years perhaps, or even decades from the basis from which the explanation proceeds. But one must always ask oneself whether it is not caused by "dynamic" causes, whether at least the same foundations of the economy still continue to exist. If the latter is the case, then it is irrelevant if our results do not purely come to light into reality, which has been tarnished by other moments. The "practitioner" often errs here: If not that, which the theory predicted, eventuates, then he simply rejects it as being wrong. This is unjustified. However, our laws still have an effect then, and the concrete result would be *another* if they would not. If we can satisfyingly explain the discrepancy, then we have justified our theory. Let us take an example: One has detected that the increase of the Austrian tariff on coffee has not increased the price of the coffee, and deduced its insignificance from it; of course unjustly. Then nothing is more clear than that the same would have decreased much—or better, would have sunk much *more*—if this tariff would not have existed with regards to the great increase of the production of coffee. One can completely justify the result of the theory here, and the difference of the price in the inland vis-à-vis the one of the world market yields a bearable measure for the effect of the tariff.

The matter is different for some American tariffs: The result of the theory is also not "wrong" there. But the same have given a stimulus for developments, which changed the circumstances so much that one can often downright say—an example would be sheep wool—that through the tariff, the manufacturers won, and also the consumers. But this is something else, the effect of the tariff vanishes in the development, but precisely this one makes it possible that it does not make itself noticeable. If all conditions of production would have stayed with the old one—and this would have been more or less the case everywhere outside of America—then one would have been able to prove its effect very well. But even if the theory is not "wrong," one can quite justifiably say that it becomes insignificant in such cases. So truth and falsehood lie closely next to one another here, and the validity of the individual arguments of the party cannot be examined generally, but only case by case. It is always very important to separate "static" from "dynamic," and this would contribute much to a clarification of the discussion. As we have said, this separation approximately coincides with the one between the consideration of shorter and longer periods, and this one in turn with the constancy and the change of the value functions. We speak of a "long period" here, in a sense that is not to be confounded with A. Smith's and his followers' expression "in the long run." The latter expression only serves as a term to exclude "frictional resistances."

So we have therefore discussed the foundations of our method. But in *this* form, we could only still approach the distinctness of the eventuating changes with it, beside very simple cases—for example, the one of the bartering between two economic subjects. If one replaces any element of the system with another one, which is somewhat but not all too different from it, then the equilibrium, as we have seen, is disturbed. But on the other hand, we now have as many equations as unknowns, and thus, the new size (quantity) of all elements is also distinctly determined, but is also readily perceived without such an apparatus. In the same sense as earlier, we will find "normal," "natural," and "essential" values of our elements here, from which the distinct determination of the variations will arise by itself.

But this is also pretty much everything. We do not get to further statements. This is also not disconcerting. All the actions and reactions that they show are numerous, and due to the lack of closer data about the form of our functions, its relative significance cannot be determined. Its price increases to its full amount. The demand will now decrease, consequently also the one for the means of production of the pertaining good. Therefore, also the incomes of the owners of the latter ones and the demand that generally starts from them. The manufacturers do not lose anything on the pieces that are sold at a new price. Yes, even a profit came into consideration, which comes from the increase of the monetary value that is to be expected as a result of the decreasing of the income of many people. But they sell less. One must now furthermore consider that possibly the state or those, on whom the tax amount is placed, develop a demand; furthermore, that on the one hand, those, who continue to buy the product regardless of the increase in price, must strip the means that are necessary for it from other needs. And every one of these effects continues to be effective in a very obvious manner.

If one considers this, then one really becomes aware that the considered changes may only be small. Because every greater one will unfailingly call forth new dynamic phenomena. All of these are actually indeed dynamic changes of the manner of production and life of the entire national economy, and its structure only essentially survives then, when it is relatively small.

V

But furthermore, a path directly presents itself to cope with the problem. An entire series of simplifications is readily possible, and others are possible with a few reserves. We are in fact thereby going further on the pathway of abstraction, but one will see that the entire thing can credibly happen.

Above all, one will not unnecessarily complicate the problem through the consideration of too many goods. The approach forms itself essentially simpler if one only includes two or three, without being in danger of overlooking something essential. It is especially advantageous not to consider too many production goods for one and the same consumption good. In fact, there are indeed a number of them for the most part. But if one only approaches the common, and not a special problem, then nothing hinders us in reducing the same to three, labor, land, and capital—in the sense of v. Boehm-Bawerk—and if one does not directly examine the interactions and the displacements, which occur among these three, then one can probably also allow oneself to assume only ONE and even more, that this one thing is used for nothing else than for the production of precisely the considered good. This is very convenient and, where it is permitted, very desirable in the interest of the simplicity of the results.

Such a simplification does not need to have anything to worry about, and one would be unjustified if one would want to dismiss it a limine as a caricature of reality. Certain general sentences can be demonstrated so very well, and whoever is even sympathetic to abstract science will understand that precisely such so to speak *technical* simplifications do not stand in the way of the use of the theory on reality at all.

Thereupon, it attracts attention by itself that not all actions and reactions have the same significance, that so to speak only those, where the disturbance occurs, are important in the proximity of the point. So once after one has pointed to the generality of the same, one can limit oneself to a portion of the same, whereby one can indeed reserve to draw its boundaries farther or narrower, depending on the nature of the purpose that one follows. One does not see how this suggests itself so much for the general, but rather better for a special problem. If one examines, for example, the effects of a price movement of pins, then one can conveniently disregard those that it has for the price of the wine, for example. For some reason, precisely this relation can be especially interesting, but if one of such is not present, then one can by all means accept the price of wine as being constant. And not only the price of wine, but also that of the vast majority of all other commodities. This disregarding of further remote effects, this accepting of a constant of variables that change strictly speaking, represents a further methodical aid. The title from which this happens is the opinion that one only thereby neglects variables, which in themselves are "infinitely small" vis-à-vis the small ones with which we are dealing here. It must therefore be promoted that one continually *proves* that this is the case. Now this does not always happen; rather, it is a very useful method to simply accept all prices as being constant, expressively or, even much more frequently, silently, with the exception of the one of the considered goods during the examination of the effects of a cause for disturbance. This is none other than the simplification, which is being discussed here, in the greatest dose.

This is certainly not necessarily impermissible. Less significant products as champagne, for example, can be approached very well. But if the considered product is, for example, grain or labor, then the effect on the other prices must be considered, because otherwise, the result not only becomes incomplete, but also wrong. It would become *incomplete* because the distanced effects are in no way "variables of a higher order" for such commodities, but are rather just as important as the immediate ones. This incompleteness at the very least hinders the direct use of the results on reality. But the same would become *wrong* because a change in the price of such important goods alters the entire national economy, and its effect is partially rescinded through strong reactions. For the purpose of instancing: A change in the price of bread significantly affects all small incomes. As a result of an increase of the same, the demand for other goods would have to decrease, namely so severely that one cannot overlook it. But if one nevertheless does it, then one only sees a part of the problem. But this can indeed be defended, would be an abstract consideration of certain phenomena. But reactions do arise, which tend to *directly* reverse the price increase. One of such, which has often been observed, is a wage increase. Through the same, the price increase of bread becomes illusory *in part*, and *insofar* our result is then wrong.

A good from the quantity of the one whose value maintains to be accepted as constant requires a special approach, because it pushes in everywhere—money. The marginal utility of money can generally not be considered as constant. Every occurring disturbance or our system alters it. This is indeed very obvious: If the price of a good increases during constant monetary income, then the marginal utility of money must obviously increase if the consumption continues, decrease when it ceases, and conversely, if the price of a good decreases. It is a product of the prevailing economic milieu and must be affected by every change of the same. We hardly need to explain this more closely. At the same time, one sees that the movement of the monetary value is a very important phenomenon. It reflects the change, which has called the cause for disturbance in the position of every economic subject forth, and also the behavior of the latter in the certain sense. What the economic subject regarding this good, whose price has changed, does, so whether he curtails his demand, and by how much, and how this in turn affects the production of the good—this is only a part of the problem. And one gets to the other part through the medium of the changes' monetary value. But consideration for the monetary value is also essential to the understanding of the behavior of the economic subject towards the good, in which the change occurs. Because the demand function refers to money, and to every one of its points belongs a different marginal utility of the concerning good, as well as a different one of money. Strictly speaking, the variation of the latter is already contained in it, and it would be a different one than it is[2] if it were constant. So one may also not overlook this moment while considering the effects of conditions of the type that is discussed here. This especially becomes apparent for those goods, whose prices directly form the incomes. If, for example, the wage increases, then the marginal utility of money unavoidably decreases for the laborer, and precisely this signifies the broadening of his demand to consumption goods of lesser importance. The discussion of the wage increase can impossibly go beyond this. It is a matter of an essential part of the matter.

But on the other hand, it is clear that constancy of the monetary value is of upmost necessity for many of our discussions. Let us stick with the just mentioned example for now: If the laborer receives a higher wage, then one can, if one disregards our moment, very clearly say what will happen. He will work more. One can no longer claim this so easily if one acknowledges that he now values money less. The affect of the wage increase is much undetermined, and it may be that the laborer will now exert himself less, will dedicate a shorter amount of time to work and more time to rest. We reduce all variables, which we are dealing with, by means of the monetary value to the common denominator, and thereby make a comparison of the same possible. If the denominator is constant, then everything is infinitely simpler than if it changes. Namely, the comparison of both of the states of equilibrium, which our method involves, is significantly complicated if we are so correct in accepting that in the transition of one to the other, as everything else, thus the monetary value also changes. So then in the scientific, as well as in the non-scientific discussions the constancy of monetary value will almost always be accepted expressively or silently. Must we forgo the results that were attained in this manner? Not entirely, although it is certain that through this approach, interesting phenomena—and precisely hidden ones, which would be one of the greatest services to work out that the science of the practice is able to achieve - are often concealed. We will also admit here that for small changes and short time periods the committed mistake is so small that one is allowed to make it. If one has to pay *a bit* more for a consumption good, then the value estimate of a monetary unit is not going to be noticeably altered by it. I do not value a monetary unit significantly more than previously, because now a cigar costs a bit more than before, and the clarity and simplicity of the result is more important than the advantage that would grow out of the consideration for this "more." However, the matter is different for most of the mass products and for the budget of the laborer. But nevertheless, there are a large number of cases where the simplified approach suffices.

Also the brevity of the considered period can make it appear permissible, namely even occasionally then, when the change that is to be examined is not "small." The marginal utility of money for every economic subject is the result of long experience and gradually becomes "second nature" to him. It uses him completely unaware and habitually. It is the barometer and the regulator of his economy. And it therefore does not easily and not quickly change. Even if his conditions become others, then he will nevertheless attempt to continue economizing with the same, wherefore social and other non-economic considerations also contribute. Of course, this cannot go on for long. But if the change is not too great, then a significant amount of time will pass before our economic subject changes his entire thinking and feeling—which does signify the same as the variation of the monetary value. He would have to abandon things that have become his second nature, cut himself off from deeply-rooted habits. He will often prefer to perish than "learn to calculate." This expression "learning to calculate," which one so often encounters in the discussion of the economic situation of classes, which have a standard of life that is very difficult to change—and only with pain, as for example, the landowning nobility in countries of inferior culture expresses splendidly how insecurely fumbling and reluctantly one constructs a new marginal utility of one's money for oneself. Now, as long as neither demise, nor assimilation of the new milieu took place—and the scope of this unsustainable state is rather large in practice—our assumption can be defended until then.

Other simplifications are also still made, *must* be made. This way, if, for example, the price of a good increases and as a result of this, the demand for the same decreases, the production of the same becomes limited and some means of production become redundant. What happens with them? They could probably be used for the production of those things, which the demand of those people turns to, who now no longer want to buy the mentioned good. But first, such people do not need to exist: Even if the demand for the same is limited, then its price is in fact higher, and therefore "purchasing power" does not necessarily need "to become free," as one could express that. And secondly, nothing gives us the right to assume that the demand, which possibly became free, requires precisely *as much* means of production, not more and not less than become redundant. In a similar manner, the equation between income and spending is disturbed for every economic subject. One of the amounts exceeds the other. It could only continue to exist as a result of a coincidence. In general, the same can now *save* more, or have to withdraw an amount from their savings fund. Finally, the equation between the demand and offer price must be newly established. One has the choice vis-à-vis all these difficulties to either acknowledge them, or to break the Gordian knot through the assumption that those equations exist. And this only applies to small changes.

Not only the popular, but also the scientific discussion overlooks these things most often. And they are of too a specialized nature, so that for the reader, the interest in an elaboration could not be assumed. Let it therefore suffice, having pointed this out.

This would be, in essence, what is to be said of general sentences about our method. Now, through more specialized assumptions about the nature of the cause for disturbance, whose effects are supposed to be considered, it can be very productively developed, whereby special aids also still arise, according to the type of individual case. The general discussion of the same would be too dry and incomprehensible, and we want to therefore rather show the most important thing about it in the concrete examples to which we now come.

I may have dwelled on the foundations of our method for too long. I did it because I am of the conviction that here it deals with the theoretical—perhaps some would rather say *epistemological*—foundations of the most important, mostly discussed results of the national economy. Whoever has followed that, which was just presented, with understanding will notice that the outlines of the common approach stand out from it for him. *In fact, what I have called the variations method is none other than the exact expression of that, which occurs everywhere there*, where for example, two politicians argue about protective tariff and free trade, insofar as they employ economical arguments. I wanted to do the same here what I also seek to do otherwise, namely to show *what the essence and what the requirements of the economical raisonnement actually are*. All those simplifications about whose significance we sought to become clear are made in the most popular discussion, though unknowingly and often without consideration for the boundaries that are then drawn for the results. The scientific argumentations also appear now, I believe, in a sharp light. If that, which has been said contributes to better separating different things, and to consider the relativity and limited application of almost all of the common claims that are so generally grasped, more than it, to me, seems to occur, then my purpose is reached and the time of the reader is not dwindled away.

And as I believe to have contributed to the criticism of the common theories, a better understanding of them has probably also been initiated, with which the abstract examinations of mathematical nature are concerned, have shown that their clear forms also have practical advantages and place many a thing before our eyes, which otherwise easily escapes attention. We do not believe to have said too much. The opposite accusation would be more justified. But it is a matter of finding the middle path between exhaustive detail and the common carelessness.

If we overlook that, which has been said, we could summarize it in approximately this manner: If one even just wants to say *something* with the means of the economy about the variations that can arise in our area, then one may not distance oneself from the static assumptions for the current economical situation. Otherwise, one does not obtain exact results. But then a series of requirements are to be made, which only coincide with reality in certain cases. It is no "jeu d'esprit" to carefully discuss them, but rather stringent necessity. No one, not even the historian forgoes saying something economical for or against free trade. But every time he does this, he conducts economical theory and cannot ignore its principles with impunity. And it shows that one moves on dangerous ground there, and cannot take a step without careful restraint.

It is not very much that our method offers. And nevertheless it is *everything* that can be gained on general truths. The attempts to gain more are numerous, from the classical authors up to the present. But its value is a questionable one, or nevertheless very conditional. However—if our method does not offer too much, it nevertheless offers more than nothing.

We now want to discuss the matter again using examples. The methodical approach is always the same and it is only a matter of adjusting "the concrete cause for disturbance" in a way that it can be brought into our schema—changing of the size of one or more elements of our system. For some, this is readily possible. As for the practically most important ones and the most discussed ones there are: impost of a tax, introduction of a tariff, alteration of the normal price of a good through the fixation of a rate, destruction of a quantity of goods through an accident or intentionally, and suchlike. Individual elements of cost, for example, transportation costs, brokerages, commissions, etc., can be treated this way. Not as if the essence of all these things would be thereby exhaustively conceived. Rather, in our approach lies a formalization in which important moments are lost, namely all social, historical, political, and other aspects. But indeed, the pure economical thing on the matter is thereby explicitly expressed and brought into a manageable form. However, this cannot be done as easily for other causes of disturbance. An example is the theory of the influence of the introduction of machines. This is a dynamic phenomenon in itself, but certain effects of the same can nevertheless be discussed in the framework of static. The question now raises itself *which* elements one should consider as thereby being directly altered. This is actually not the case for any of them, and it is a question of purpose how one has to decide that. A methodic device then is present here, a fiction that has to prove itself by its fruits. An actually different phenomenon is artificially conceived as a variation of an element. This has not yet happened so far, however, to us, a valuable expansion of the scope of application of our method seems to lie in it.

Notes

1. Namely the 3rd, 4th, and 5th parts of this chapter, which deal with a very dry topic of the technology of the theory, and are supposed to set the epistemological foundations of a large portion, also the economical raisonnement of the "practitioner" clearly, are very important on the one hand, but also exhausting. They can probably be skipped (Schumpeter, 1908, pg. 443).
2. As we have already indicated previously (Schumpeter, 1908, pg. 471).

2

Examples

I

How a tax that is placed on a specific commodity—which according to that, which has been said must be assumed as being small—distributes itself on the individually participating economic subjects and what all of its effects are, is a much discussed problem. What the theory can offer certainly does not suffice for the complete valuation of the tax. In practice, the budgetary necessity, social and political moments play such a great role that our results may appear to be insignificant next to them. The type and direction of the influence of a tax is also rather clear in the concrete cases for the most part, and small mistakes, which can result in a theoretically incomplete examination, are often, if one gets to the practical use, corrected entirely by themselves. The corrections of the theorist therefore often make a virtually nit-picking impression. But if one wants to theorize at all, then one also has to do it as correctly as possible. And our method with its strictness is essential for this purpose.

The simplest case is the one of an isolated economic subject, who *only* produces a specific good for his consumption, with means of production that cannot be used for anything else. No further simplifications are necessary here. "The demand curve" is formed solely through the function of labor effort.[1] Our man produces so much that the marginal utility of the good is equal to the "minimum standard" of labor. From some external force, he will feel like delivering a specific quantity of his product in every period of production in the future. What will happen? He will now produce so much that the marginal utility of the quantity of the good *that remains* for him is equal to the minimum standard of this quantity plus the one that are to be delivered. This is the exact answer.

If the supply and demand functions are given, then the old, as well as the new product quantity is distinctly determined, and we also have an exact expression for the "damage" that our subject suffers. We can, if we possess those data, see that he will generally—excluding marginal cases—produce a bit more than before, but not necessarily more for the entire amount of the tax, so that he partially withdraws the same from his consumption, but partially produces it. The latter moment gives us the exact expression of the theory of tax production, in which thus lies an important core that same theorists misjudged. If the means of production of this good would also be used for the production of another one, then the result would not be so simple. One would have to consider the effect of the production of a greater quantity of the taxed good on the one of the untaxed. It would represent a further complication if both of the goods would not only be associated with one another according to production, but also regarding the consumption, would complement or replace one another. This would have no difficulties in our simple case, but we can, especially since nothing essential comes out of it, skip over it or leave it up to the reader. We see that certain results can be demonstrated quite absolutely by a very simplified schema, thereby gaining clarity, which would otherwise be unattainable. And this well justifies the same.

We can also give the general answer to the question, what the effects of a tax depend on: They depend on the form, or as one can say, the elasticity of the demand and supply functions. These results are more exact and correct than the common "dialectical" approach brings them forth. But they do not contain special discoveries. Their significance lies in something else. Their obvious correctness namely guarantees us the correctness, or better, the usefulness of our foundations, *verify* the same. The results are indeed, in my opinion, the *only* really reliable criterion for the value of the latter altogether. Now, precisely the implicitness of the results is suitable in calming us about the foundations. Certainly no one doubts the *facts*, which are supposed to describe the laws of gravity. But their accordance with experience is of greatest epistemological significance.

It is also like this in our case. And furthermore, the discussion of the variations first teaches us the complete understanding of our system, pushes its essence and its boundaries into the light. Some claims about the same would have been impossible if one had always paid attention to these boundaries. We now want to show this in a more complicated case, and thereby also simultaneously go a step further into our demonstration.

Let us assume that two types of consumption goods are being produced in a national economy. Only two, for the purpose of simplicity. Both have an equilibrium price and are available in distinctly determined quantities. We consider these prices—which are supposed to be any monetary prices—as functions of the produced quantities. These functions are not common demand functions, which are related to particular individuals, but rather total functions, which are, however, gained in an analog manner: We ask ourselves which ones the equilibrium prices would be if we let the quantity vary. However, we cannot do this between randomly broad boundaries as we have done earlier, but rather only within relatively narrow ones. And we construct similarly for different quantities of a cost-price function. "Cost" is not supposed to mean anything different here than the disbursement in cash (money), which can be done for the production of the individual subsets. The market price is then given by the equation of the demand and of the cost price for both goods. As money serves a third good whose marginal utility is constant and that, once available, does not cause any production costs. This means nothing else than that this "money" should solely be a *measurement of value*. Its role as *means of exchange*, which leads to changes in value, is not affected by our changes—only small ones.

A tax is now placed on one of the two goods. As an example, we are assuming one of such for the unit of the good.

If one now conceives both goods as being completely independent of one another—according to the consumption, as well as the production side—then the same that we discussed earlier can be proven in regards to the taxed one. Generally, buyers will be affected as buyers, to what extend depends on the elasticity of both functions. Nevertheless, there are marginal cases—complete inelasticity of the supply or the demand—in which the tax *only* affects the buyers or *only* the sellers.

This theory only comes sufficiently close to reality then, if that independence is a complete one. This can never be entirely the case, but at least it applies more closely only when the taxed good vis-à-vis the quantity of the other one is insignificant. *Otherwise*, its changes in price and quantity would *always* also affect the other one, even if the consumption of the two had no connection and the means of production were different.

A suggesting train of thought leads to a more complete approach. The demand that someone develops for a good is never reclusively for the same, but is rather dependent on its total supply of consumption goods. In the language of psychology one can demonstrate this very convincingly through the reference to the fact that the satisfaction, which someone attains through the consumption of a good, is never reclusively dependent on this: How one values a food product shapes itself differently, depending on whether or not one also possesses others. This is naturally the clearest in the case of complimentary consumption goods: No one values salt if he owns nothing that he could salt, and it is probable that he conversely, if he owns no salt, will value other food products less as if he did possess some, since they now warrant him less enjoyment. But this applies very generally, even beyond this narrower circle: Whoever has a poor apartment, is less protected against the cold, will need more food than someone—ceteris paribus—who can better satisfy his housing need. Individual luxury items will have little value for the poor man, and a need for them only grows in the milieu that is correct for them. It therefore arises entirely automatically that the price of a good is not a function of the quantity of the same alone, but rather *of all* goods, and this conception, which currently becomes more and more common, allows one to conceive all interactions of the demands of individual goods. This would of course be complicated for a large number of goods—in our case however, it works very well. This approach encompasses even more, namely also the relation of rivalry between goods and finally, that, which exists between all goods independent of all of that, insofar all purchases must be paid out of one specific income.

Similar applies on the side of costs. Complementarity and rivalry between the individual cost goods are also here in an analog way. Every more general relation that lies in it, that the demand for every good is connected with the one for all others, only works for the cost goods through the medium of the consumption goods; there are still quite a few special relations for it here. At one point, the production coefficients are not constant, are rather variable within certain boundaries and *one* moment for their size will surely be the need of means of production for *other* productions. But then it must be considered that if we reduce all means of production to labor, land, tools, and raw materials, those three are necessary for *all* products, and their movement towards the individual uses is controlled by a law of uniform niveau so to speak, therefore, considered in this manner, *all* goods are production-related with one another and *none* are independent. It is indeed clear that not for every good its quantity of labor, land, and "capital" accrues on its own and without consideration for other products, but rather the totality of means of production of the totality of products. As in a reservoir, out of which several pipes run, the distribution of the amount of water to the pipes is not only dependent on the diameter of every single one, but also on that of the others, and a uniform niveau governs the same, as also in our case. This niveau law is that of the uniform marginal utility of the products for every individual—not so readily for "society"—or of the normal price, which is uniform for every product on the market. This analysis that, elaborated, leads rather deeply is only a development of things that have been previously said, under a somewhat different point of view.

It is not free from difficulties, especially in consideration for the moment of free movement. Even though we have directed one's attention to the same previously, we can nevertheless build on it here. No objection lies in it. On the contrary, we want to in fact direct the reader's attention to the fact that our position is a different one for different problems, and that we in no way disdain useful trains of thought because we have stated critical concerns against it. Of course one has to remind oneself of the valuation and application of the results of the same. Here we present an important method in a way that it does not contrast too much with the one that is common to the exact theorists and do not want to repeat that, which was said about the foundations.

An important consequence still arises from that, which has been said about the "cost side." If a good only has means of production, which cannot be used for anything else, then their value is readily given, as we have seen, and we can speak of the "supply" of this good just as well as of the "supply" of those means of production. Both are identical here; but not so in the other case. The supply of every good is probably also distinctly determined here, but not out of its relations alone, but rather through the collaboration of all goods and through that general law, whose effect can only be conceived through the observation of all. The "supply" of a good is therefore something that does not carry its determinateness within itself. And therefore one is actually never to speak of a "supply" of a product, but rather always only of a general one of means of production or productive services, as we have already emphasized at an earlier point.

We will therefore conceive the demand prices, as well as the cost prices of both goods as a function of the quantity *of both*. And here we will seek to present a small and elementary piece of an exact thought process to the reader, solely to show how the variations method that has been generally described by us appears of the closer one.

Let the quantities of both of our goods that are available on the market be x and y. So then the "demand price" of one of the same is a function of x and y, $f(x, y)$. Here, x and y *themselves* are, for the purposes of this thought process, thought of as independent variables and especially also as being independent of one another, and therefore the values, which are assumed by the demand price of this good if one adds more and more different values to x and y, are graphically illustrated in the following manner. In the common coordinate plane, one familiarly uses the chosen x and y for the fixing of a point C, constructs a perpendicular to the coordinate plane within the same, and writes the value of the measure of the demand price on the same, which corresponds to the pertaining quantities x and y. Thus, one obtains a point in the space D. For polyvalent functions, one would find more than a point D, for us only *one*, as a result of the assumed definiteness of our function. The paragon of positions, which the point D can assume as a result of all possible changes of x and y—its locus—is a surface.

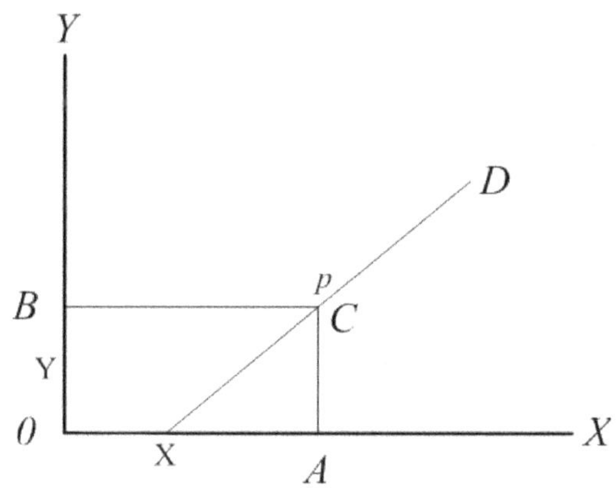

A change of the value function $f(x, y)$ can be caused in three ways:

1. As a result that for fixed y only x goes into; x_1
2. As a result that for fixed x only y goes into; y_1
3. As a result that x and y simultaneously go into x_1 und y_1

x_1 und y_1 as per that, which has been said earlier, are to be assumed as only slightly different from x and y, and can be expressed through the equations $x_1 = x + \Delta x$ und $y_1 = y + \Delta y$, whereby Δx *und* Δy signify respectively small increases.

Corresponding to this, three different types of differentials must also be differentiated:

$$f(x_1, y) - f(x, y), f(x, y_1) - f(x, y) \textit{ und } f(x_1, y_1) - f(x, y)$$

In both of the first cases, it is a matter of partial differentiations, in the latter, a complete one.

Our approach of the price as function of *both* quantities allows us to conceive the effect of every cause for disturbance, even if it only directly affects one of the goods, to the quantities and prices of both. Since furthermore, the quantities of *both* will change in our case, we are therefore dealing with a complete differentiation. The same of course applies to our other functions, namely the *other* demand price function *(F [x,y])* and the two corresponding cost price functions, which we want to identify with. $\varphi(x, y)\varphi(x, y)$ und $\psi(x, y)\psi(x, y)$

In equilibrium, the equations now apply:

$$f(x, y) = \varphi(x, y) \textit{ und}$$

$$F(x, y) - \Psi\ (x, y)$$

The same is now disturbed through the placing of a tax on the unit of a good. This effectuates nothing else than that the costs of this unit are increased by this amount. *So this is the form in which the exact economy allows to conceive such a tax.* This is only *one* of the uses of always just one and the same thought process on different problems or better, always just one interpretation, according to the situation of the case, of the variables with which it is concerned.

The pure economy can only constantly contribute *such* results for the solving of a concrete question, which is connected with the theory of supply and demand, and it constantly says *the same* in principle, be it that it deals with taxes, transportation costs, changes in the size of other cost elements, tariffs, or anything else. There are basically no separate purely economical theories for these things, but rather only *one* theory of variations, which can encompass all of that and is only formed differently according to the concrete data of the problem.

Since we have developed this one method, it is only still spared to show how one has to conceive and "stylize" the different problems that reality poses us, so that they fit into our schema. Some do this better, others worse, we can state quite a bit for some, for others, only make a small contribution. But this effectuates that the tax theory and the transportation theory or international trade often form entirely different disciplines; these are, as we will still briefly show, moments that lie outside of the pure theory.

The effects of, for example, a tax and a tariff are certainly very different ones, and both are used for different purposes. The pure economical *essence* of these effects is the same. Now this naturally does not mean that we want to smudge the differences between these areas, condemn their separate approach, and advocate their increase. The latter would be very impractical. Here it only deals with the economical core of the matter, only with the fact that the methodological differences are not essential ones to that extent. If we have pushed that, which the economy can actually accomplish into the proper light, then we are free to entirely withdraw this consubstantiality for other purposes. Here, as everywhere, a differentiation of different classes of problems and different purposes of research is imperatively offered and is essential to the understanding.

Moving on. The equilibrium is disturbed through the tax. However, a new state of equilibrium must fabricate itself, as we have previously seen; equations will again apply in the same, which are analog to the ones that we previously had, again, marginal proceeds and marginal cost must be equal, as we have also seen in our simplest case.

We place emphasis on clarifying and memorizing the thought process for ourselves step by step, but it must again be emphasized that we are not doing anything different than what everyone else is doing—more or less complete, but everyone in principle—who seeks to form a judgment about economical relations of this nature, be it as a researcher or as a father who discusses the content of his paper. If someone says that a grain tariff increases the price of bread, then our entire, exact raisonnement lies in this judgment in nuce. The corrections that we can add are not insignificant, but *they* are nevertheless not what we are primarily looking for, but rather the scientific nature of the thought process itself. The new state of equilibrium, which is characterized by such equations, will present other quantities and prices. And we want to find these first. The new equations simply are:

$$f(x_1, y_1) = \varphi(x_1, y_1) + a \text{ } und$$
$$F(x_1, y_1) = \Psi(x_1, y_1)$$

or in another form corresponding to our definitions of x_1 and y_1:

$$f(x+\Delta x, y+\Delta y)=\varphi(x+\Delta x, y+\Delta y)+a \text{ und}$$
$$F(x+\Delta x, y+\Delta y)=\Psi\ (x+\Delta x, y+\Delta y)$$

which is readily understandable. We are now especially interested in the ($\Delta\ x$ *und* $\Delta\ y$, in which the change is expressed for the quantities, namely not so much their size—since both are small anyway—as their algebraic sign, and then their price. But here, higher mathematics gives us a means for an important conversion, in the development through the Taylorian series. This development represents an *approximate* value, and it has to continually be proven that the difference vis-à-vis the *exact*—the "remainder"—can be neglected without too great of a mistake. But we do not need to conduct such an examination here. Because already, $\Delta\ x$ *und* $\Delta\ y$) are *small* in relation to x and y, its higher potential is therefore even smaller, and thus, we want to neglect the same, whereby the examination of the remainder is dropped on its own. One of the developments is simplified like this:

$$f(x,y)+\left[\frac{\partial f(x,y)}{\partial x}\Delta x+\frac{\partial f(x,y)}{\partial y}\right]=$$

$$\varphi(x,y)+\left[\frac{\partial \varphi(x,y)}{\partial x}\Delta x+\frac{\partial \varphi(x,y)}{\partial y}\right]+a$$

and the other, completely analog. We can now make further simplifications. Above all, we know from the equation, which characterized the FORMER state of equilibrium,

$$f(x,y)=\varphi(x,y)$$

that we can cancel out these two terms. If one does this and if one also properly positions the terms, then one has:

$$\Delta x\left[\frac{\partial f(x,y)}{\partial x}-\frac{\partial \varphi(x,y)}{\partial x}\right]=\frac{\partial \varphi(x,y)}{\partial y}-\frac{\partial f(x,y)}{\partial y}+a$$

An arithmetic expression that is exactly the same—only, of course, without the term "+ *a*"—arises for the second equation.

We therefore have two equations between Δx *und* Δy, and it is only a matter of seeing what the remaining terms of the same—apart from "+ *a*"—mean. That, which we say there is very elementary. But it is only a matter of making a simple case as clear as possible for the non-mathematician. This has not yet happened. And yet, only such a broader circle can be won for this method, as it appears desirable to us in the interest of scientific progress. Of course, that, which has been said can still not be completely clear yet to the one, for whom higher mathematics are *very* far away. But he nevertheless receives an approximate picture of that, which the mathematical economist does, and referring to an encyclopedia would make complete comprehension of this simple case possible. We even believe that such a demonstration will be welcomed by some serious friend of the theory for the current state of affairs, and thereby consider ourselves pardoned for its elementary character.

So let us continue: Both of the arithmetic expressions in parenthesis, what do they mean?

$\frac{\partial f(x,y)}{\partial x}$ gives a relation, namely the rclation of the changes of the price to the changes of the quantity of one of the goods, whose consequence is the first one. If the quantity of the good increases by $\partial f(x,y)$, then the price changes by $f(x,y)$

But how; does it also increase, or does it decrease? The form of the curve *f(x, y)* teaches us this: If the quantity increases, then the price decreases. "Unequal changing" is present, and the quotient $\frac{\partial f(x,y)}{\partial x}$ is therefore *negative*: It gives us the rate of the decrease of the price vis-à-vis an increase of the supply.

The same applies, as one easily sees, mutatis mutandis for the arithmetic expression $\frac{\partial \varphi(x,y) \partial \varphi(x,y)}{\partial y \quad \partial y}$, which we interpret as the elasticity of the cost-price curve. Here, however, arises an important remark: The elasticity of this curve means nothing else than the rate of increase of the cost-price, and this in turn means nothing else than the law of diminishing returns, whose exact arithmetic expression we have therefore found here.

It is thereby interesting to see in particular that it is completely indifferent to the same and operating with it—at this point and *so far*—whether we are thereby thinking of the *physical* law of the classical authors or of the costs as a *value phenomenon*, and so we understand that the former could also prove itself as useful instrument to a certain factor. As you know, we have decided on the latter eventuality.

And something else: If we integrate our function $\varphi(x,y)$, then we obtain another, be it $\theta(x,y)$, which gives a curve whose ordinates illustrate the total costs of the quantities that are given through the abscissas for us, and this curve is none other at all than the picture of the law of diminishing returns in the form, in which it commonly appears: It shows us that the *total* expenditure—again: For one, so far, by which cause—increases overly proportional, as this has again and again since Ricardo, or even longer, inconveniently been made clear to us with many words and numeric examples, especially in tabular form. Our $\frac{\partial f(x,y)}{\partial x}$ now appears in the form $\frac{\partial^2 \theta(x,y)}{\partial^2 X}$, and here we have the arithmetic expression for the content of those demonstrations. This only appears as a sideline.

We can also similarly integrate *f(x, y)*. This integral curve, be it $F(x,y)$, would analogously give the "total utility" of the quantities that are realized through the abscissas and their second differential quotient $\frac{\partial^2 F(x,y)}{\partial^2 x}$ would then give the measurement of the diminishing of marginal utility, so that the Gaussian Law and the law of increasing costs would be completely coordinated, of course only *formally*. They are *one* in essence if one also conceives the latter as a law of value—then there is no coordination, but rather just *one* law. *Otherwise*, however, both laws are coordinated. (Cf. AUSPITZ' AND LIEBEN'S approach.[2]) But many difficulties surround the terms "total utility" and "total costs", which we cannot go into here.

But what do $\frac{\partial \varphi(x,y)}{\partial y}$ und $\frac{\partial f(x,y)}{\partial y}$ signify? How obviously they express how the cost and demand prices of the first good change when the quantity of the second one changes, meaning the rate of the increase and decrease of the cost and demand prices, its elasticity, in regards to the quantity of the other good. The moment of the relations between supply and demand of both goods is therefore embedded in both of these terms, therefore complementarity, rivalry, and also that general relation, which exists as good as always.

Let us again make use of the approach by means of the integral curves, thus, $\frac{\partial^2 \emptyset(x,y)}{\partial x \partial y}$ Und $\frac{\partial^2 F(x,y)}{\partial x \partial y}$ arise. As one sees, these arithmetic expressions are two-dimensional. They represent the rate of variation of the integral functions in relation to the quantities of both goods. It again can only be remarked in passing that suchlike arithmetic expressions express v. Boehm-Bawerk's "third reason" and the variation law of the Americans brief and to the point, without charts, numeric examples, and lengthy discussions.

Now, if such a rate is not present, meaning, is the demand price or cost price—or both—of one of the goods insensitive to the quantities of the other one, then our arithmetic expressions—as differential quotients of constants—become zero, and we then have our equation in the form:

$$\Delta x\left[\frac{\partial f(x,y)}{\partial x}-\frac{\partial \varphi(x,y)}{\partial x}\right]=a$$

We have therewith now gotten to the discussion of our equations, (*which presents the manner of how we gain concrete results from the same*). And with it, we then have completed the demonstration of our method: If our equations are set up for the former, as well as for the new state of equilibrium, and its terms are indicated, then it only spares to remind ourselves of that, which we know about it and what arises from our basic assumptions, and this indicating of the individual sizes and this examining of the relative meaning, of its *algebraic sign*, etc., *gives us everything purely economical of the matter in exact and irreproachable form.*

Let us consider a few simple cases: If the costs are also non-elastic in our last equation, meaning constant, then $\frac{\partial \varphi(x,y)}{\partial x}$ becomes zero and we have the result:

$$a=\Delta x\cdot\frac{\partial f(x,y)}{\partial x}$$

which means nothing else than that in this case, the tax falls completely upon the "buyer": The price increases for the entire amount of tax. However, the effect of the tax is therewith not exhausted. Less is offset at this higher price, so that the "seller" also comes to grief. But yet he loses nothing from the offset quantities. The exact method helps us here in distinguishing between two different types of effects, namely *transfer* and consumption *cut-back*. The same are only all too often—although not always—confounded in the common discussion, and clear insight into the processes of reality are thereby significantly facilitated through our method. We find an entire series of such confusions in literature.

Direct and further, static and dynamic effects are namely not adequately distinguished from one another.

Of course, the same also applies to the inelasticity of demand. Let demand and supply now be inelastic. Our equation, as is obvious, fails there. This means nothing else than that there is no distinct solution. It is not difficult to make clear why this is so. Inelasticity of demand means that a specific quantity of a good is demanded without consideration for the price, a case that occurs within adequate further boundaries, for example, for certain luxury items. If the supply function of such a good were to now also be constant, then nothing can be said from the standpoint of the theory about the effect of a tax. The same was dependent on the result of a "price battle" that would have not been bound to its boundary. In "practice," where so often—or most often—one does not strictly produce up to the economical boundary and our functions are not realized as smoothly, this case occurs more often than one should believe while considering its theoretical requirements, and one of the reasons for it may lie herein, that the theoretical picture for tax problems often contrasts so much with the facts. Yes, one may be in doubt about whether one ever—namely during retail trade—can sufficiently grasp the processes with theoretical means, and whether the "practitioner" is not completely right in applying himself very little to the same. How a tax affects, for example, luxury horses or dogs, or certain types of some semi-luxury items, for example, cigars, is quite ambiguous. Perhaps it is carried by the "consumer" as a rule, even if one should not expect this according to the theory. It is then thereby important that it is not felt very much at all by the same with regards to his most significant buying power. In these circumstances lies a distinctive feature of the so-called luxury taxes, which assigns a special position to the same, completely apart from the social and political moments. However, other circumstances also come into consideration, thus, the lacking of completely free competition for some luxury items—one thinks that the reputation of a company plays an even greater role here than it usually does: a piece of jewelry that originates from the store of a small gold-smith can also be significantly less suitable for an otherwise identical nature of gift purposes than one of such, whose etui carries the name of one of the great and fashionable companies—but it is important to point out that apart from this, some approaches of the theoretical conception can in fact slip away. But we do not want to follow this thought process further, since we do not intend to give a complete tax theory. Let it suffice to have pointed out that our method, even there where it failed, accomplished valuable services for us, since it sharply highlights the pertaining point and thereby shows us the place where an approach other than the economical one has to be utilized, while one easily skims over such gaps without it.

That, which has been said can also be represented geometrically, whereby it is practical in order to make a representation in the plane possible, to again only consider the price and the cost as functions of the quantity of *one* good. But something, wherein our more complete approach leads to an important, new result is the following. In general, and excluding special cases, one can say that the price of a commodity cannot increase for the entire amount of a tax that was placed on the same. How important the *proof* for this result is, one becomes really aware of it when one surveys the popular-, but also a portion of the scientific-, but namely that discussion, which stands in the middle of both: there, I think of the material and the argumentations of enquêts, commission reports, parliamentary reports, etc.

This result readily arises from our simplified equation when we bring it into the form,

$$\Delta x \cdot \frac{\partial f(x,y)}{\partial x} = a + \Delta x \cdot \frac{\partial \varphi(x,y)}{\partial x}$$

in which the moments on which the distribution of the tax burden depend are expressed so succinctly and concisely that from the opponent of the theory, *who does indeed still have to work with essentially the same thought*, a certain approval can be expected.

But an important exception to this rule is taught us by the more complete form of the equation, in the form:

$$\Delta x \cdot \frac{\partial f(x,y)}{\partial x} = a + \Delta x \cdot \frac{\partial \varphi(x,y)}{\partial x} - \frac{\partial f(x,y)}{\partial y} + \frac{\partial \varphi(x,y)}{\partial x}$$

The left side signifies the price increase and is positive, since Δx, as well as $\frac{\partial f(x,y)}{\partial x}$ are essentially negative variables.

The same is equal to the tax amount *a* modified by three terms. $\Delta x . \frac{\partial \varphi(x,y)}{\partial x}$ is negative, because the second factor of this arithmetic expression is essentially positive and expresses the above-represented truth, that the tax does not increase the price by its entire amount, as well as the moment, which determines how much of the tax will not appear in the price. The next term is essentially negative, but also has a negative algebraic sign, so that this works towards increasing the price through the same expressed moment, and counteracts that, which was expressed secondly. And the same applies to the last term, which is essentially positive and is provided with a positive algebraic sign. The final result is therefore dependent on the relative variable of the second term on the one hand, and the sum of the third and fourth term of the right side of our equation on the other hand. We cannot say anything in general about it, and the possibility is therefore explained—and the reason for its existence proven—that a tax on a commodity, which bears those relations to another, *can* increase the price of the same by more than the tax amount. Namely this—let us recall the meaning of our arithmetic expressions—is dependent on the rate of increase of the costs with increasing quantity of production and the measure of the relations between both commodities.

This result is now very important. Not as if the fact, that a tax on his product would be able to offer the manufacturer a positive *advantage*, were new. This is well-known to every house wife. But one will always be inclined to ascribe that either to a monopoly-like position of the manufacturer, or to any other defect in the mechanism of free competition, or to the "law of increasing returns." Every one of these moments can in fact be effective, we also admit that the same are far more frequent and practically more important than that, which is being discussed, and it is always quaestio facti *what* this phenomenon causes every time. But that, which is important to us in the matter is that such a possibility also arises from the standpoint of the pure theory.

This is a result that can hardly be reproached with implicitness. I do not believe that one is able to find it and prove it without our method. We therefore have a case here, in which mathematics teaches us something that we cannot otherwise come to know. Especially the significance of the complementarity and rivalry in this connection that was first discovered by it and would be difficult to explain without it.

We must deny ourselves elaborating these things, which would lead us far beyond the framework of our task. Perhaps that, which has been said already suffices in showing the reader that a fruitful area lies here, whose handling first lies in the beginnings and that it does not promote the progress of science, to go past it quite carelessly or with brief rejection. I believe to have shown that the variations method is in fact the only way, the only means to get something out of all of that, which they can offer for the pure economical moments, and a first reminder follows from it to get acquainted with higher mathematics. Otherwise, it could happen that the progress of the economical theory completely falters, and this area appears unfruitful solely through the faults of its representatives.

The case of the monopoly, which has already been handled altogether by Cournot in a classical way, especially presents itself to a mathematical treatment, which has acquired a high degree of completion through Professor Edgeworth and Marshall. The taxation of monopoly profits has a special interest primarily today for well-known reasons. And yet, as diligently as this question is being discussed, one can say that one is also generally not clear about the elements of the matter. Thus, a popular theory claims that every tax on a monopoly good can only affect the monopolist. In fact, what seems clearer than that the monopolist, who appointed the price in a way that his profit is a maximum, can also not gain an advantage through the changing of the same after the sanction of the tax, will consequently have to carry the tax. This is nevertheless not generally true; and if I think of the mathematical proof of the opposite possibility, then I cannot imagine how one is supposed to make the latter one clear without the help of higher analysis. But how up to date is this problem, for example, considering the punishments that are administered for some American trusts, which belong here indeed! By the way, also the proof that and why such a tax falls onto the monopolist *as a rule* is not so simple, and its exact form is not without interest. Just as important is the case of limited competition, perhaps even more important. However, we must deny ourselves of going into it. I believed it was better to linger on the presentation *of one* exact thought process and on the general principles of our method longer, and now no longer have room for anything further in the framework of this work.

What kind of tax applies will also prove itself in a quite analog way for a premium; a simple changing of algebraic signs allows us, as one easily sees, to also stretch our thought process onto this case.

But we may not forget to which limitations our result is subjected, especially that it only applies to *small* taxes and *short* periods. Regarding the first limitation, Cournot had suggested to break up a large tax into small parts, and thus successively also prove for them that, which initially only applies to every single one of the latter. This aid does not clear this difficulty away and also does not avoid it; because it does not make it possible for us to grasp the effect of a larger tax, which is indeed always issued at once. It requires that a small tax is issued and so to speak absorbed, and only then when the equilibrium is established again, the sanction of a similar, just as small one follows. Since it is clear that the effect of one of such processes would have to be an entirely different one than the sanction of the tax at *once*, since furthermore, as we have presented earlier, a deeper intrusion into the state of equilibrium would fundamentally change the same and would evoke phenomena, which are not even able to be presented with the means of static and perhaps the economy, thus, we must renounce this stretching of our method. That fact that we are thereby not strictly limited to the "infinitely small" has also already been emphasized, but it will always be a question of each individual case whether and how much our method can accomplish for it.

The same applies to the length of the pertaining time periods. We can only regard short periods in principle. Of course, some requirements, as for example free movement of the production factors in the area of study would be more suitable for longer ones. But regardless, it is generally not possible for us to pass judgment on such without further ado. This would be very fatal now. Some taxes, for example a house tax, can only express a part of their effects immediately. Further effects, for example the ones that are dependent on the transfer of capital into other branches of production and on the limitation or stretching of the supply of houses would evade our approach. And we in fact see that a dynamic moment regularly gets involved in discussions about the house tax, namely increase of the demand as a result of the increase of the population; certainly not without justification. One can impossibly disregard the same during judgment of this question. But this leads to ambiguity regarding the theoretical foundations, which are distinctly verifiable in all debates. In addition, our method would become inapplicable.

But it is not quite so. Periods, which are long enough to fully show us all pure economical effects, are often not long enough to grant the dynamic moments too many developmental opportunities. We will therefore be able to avail ourselves of our approach in many cases, in which their static requirements do not quite apply. Only, we must then always be aware that we do not have entirely solid ground under our feet and cannot be surprised if our raisonnement does occasionally not correspond with the facts.

However, we can also easily stretch our case to other taxes, as such of the kind that was just discussed, by ascribing real taxes of every kind to those, and finally even to personal taxes. This gives us an important way of conceiving the same at hand, whose applicability is however different from case to case: The general costs of a production are increases by a tax on an enterprise and can be reduced to the commodity unit.[3]

It is by no means necessary to grasp taxes on "rents" and "surplus" as a sui generis case, as the classical authors have done. As our method makes continuing education of the realization, an increase of our insight possible and puts us in a position of adding some corrections of the generally accepted way of handling these questions, it also gives us a firm standpoint vis-à-vis the approach and the results of the older economy. One of the methods similar to ours, or better, the same method, only in incomplete form has applied the latter to only the taxation of the product unit, for example, through a tariff. Apart from that, one operated with general principles and handled each case by itself. Our method places the entire tax theory, insofar as it is purely economical, on a uniform foundation. We could not have shown its merits better than through a brief discussion of the classical tax theory.

But we can also not go into this here. Let us only give one example, the house tax. One of such would have to always fall onto the landlord, according to the classical authors, since, corresponding to the law of rate of profit and the wages theory of the same, neither on the "building trade," nor on the wages can some of it stick. At any rate, this is the great principle; for houses that are already finished, one would really have to acknowledge exceptions. If one only acknowledges the formal principles, on which this thought process is based, as being correct, then the latter itself is also rather unobjectionable; not completely certain, because the analogousness of the rate of profit only then suffices for the conclusion, which is drawn here from it, if one can regards the "building trade" as insignificant vis-à-vis the mass of other possibilities of use of the "capital"—otherwise, a tax on the same would influence the total niveau of the rate of profit and so very well, a portion of the tax would fall on it. But how superficial and unsatisfying is this theory, how little it corresponds to reality! *Ours* on the other hand, not only enables a more complete and more correct representation of the fundamental principles, but also a consideration of a myriad of finer moments, thus, the influence of the structuring of means of transportation on the effect of a house tax, a differentiation between the different needs that are adequate for tenements, the "rivalry" between different parts of the city, etc. A good deal of very nice and theoretically, as well as practically, equally interesting results thereby arises. This was best elaborated by Professor Edgeworth (Econ. Journal 1897). However, the common discussion, which, as is well-known, is currently led in a very lively manner, practically overlooks these things completely. It can experience quite a number of corrections and enrichments through the use of our method. This question is an excellent example of what a great difference the moment of the *method* can make for the results. The data are indeed the same for the theorist as for the practitioner; and yet, such a different effectiveness can be attained from them. In every step it shows how important a careful working out and correct handling of the formal instruments of the thought process is—therefore, how little redundant approaches of this type are, as the general portion of this section has brought them. I do not believe that someone, who has seen our method for this problem of the work, will make a contemptible judgment about it.

Let a further use of our method in this area also be indicated, namely the theory of the income tax. Certainly, this one does not offer itself as easily for the grasping from our standpoint, and our contributions are less significant here than for the just mentioned problems. But nevertheless, two things can be done here. First, a theory of the progressive income tax, of the tax progression altogether, can be developed, due to the Bernoullian Hypothesis. Thereupon, one can conceive the monetary income of our individuals quasi as *a* good, which has a specific value—and a just as specific cost function. It is then possible to apply a similar raisonnement to the income tax and to gain similar results regarding its effects, as we have seen for our simplest case—in which only *one* good was produced and consumed; yes, therein should lie the most important practical use of this case that appears to be so unrealistic. To my knowledge, this has not happened yet; but I do believe that it is worth the effort and that certain processes, which are not so completely clear to everyone, can thereby be accurately described. Finally, one can also grasp an income tax as a tax on the individual branches of income. We would encounter the difficulty here that only two of the same are "static" and therefore easy to handle. This is nevertheless a path to different, not uninteresting results.

II

Let us now skip to a second example, to the theory of tariffs. We also want to be very brief here and only say some things for epistemological reasons; but apart from that, we want to proceed differently here than for the first example. Have we primarily placed emphasis *there* on exemplifying the concrete process by means of which our method achieves its results, so *here* we want, with consideration for the fact on which we place so much emphasis, namely the fact that this process is always and everywhere the same in essence, in all ever so different areas, to only mention a few points, which are suitable for setting apart that, which the theory can achieve from that, which it cannot achieve, and to contribute to the better understanding of the essence and value of its results, to also free the theory from some misunderstandings and attacks, which it had been and is subjected to.

Above all: During the discussion of the protective tariff, *everything* depends on carrying out both of the following differentiations. Firstly, one must differentiate the theoretical problem from the practical one. Whatever the result of the theory may be, it can never suffice to recommend or to damn a specific course of the trade policy for oneself alone. It lies at hand that the moments, which encompass the theory, always just form a portion of the matter and can be urged into the background by other considerations. And one therefore likes to possibly attack the *politician*, who only placed emphasis on economical moments, but it is certainly unjustified to condemn the *theory* for this reason. The tirades of the party-conflict can therefore not direct themselves against *it*, and as long as the theorist remains a theorist, he will never be a politician.

One must secondly differentiate between the static and the dynamic problem, between that, which one, although not quite correct, calls "direct" and "further" effects. In part, this differentiation coincides with the one between short and long periods, insofar as dynamic moments most often require a certain time in order to become effective: Developments need time. Now it makes no sense at all to simultaneously pit both groups of effects against one another. They are completely different from one another and most often quite incommensurable. If one were to realize this, then some controversies would become silent. In the consciousness of the politicians, dynamic moments mostly play the lead, which is, however, to be strictly differentiated from the question whether the parties, which they lean on, are also led by such contemplations or by the consideration for direct advantages and disadvantages. Now one can certainly claim that the aspects, which dynamic offers, are unequally greater than those of static; the future of the nation, the war of the races, etc., are certainly things next to which static arguments often appear petty and picayune. But this changes nothing on the fact that static and dynamic considerations are independent of one another and, each one for itself, has a healthy reason; furthermore, also nothing on that fact that only the static ones are currently open for exact evidence and the only thing, which is able to offer strict science today. One can smile about it—this can only be partially resented—but one cannot deny these facts.

Thereupon: The theory approaches the problem of the effects of tariffs with both of the following weapons. Firstly, it considers every tariff as a tax that is placed on commodities. From this follows that the problem is methodologically entirely the same as that of the tax theory, and results of the same nature and form can be captured. From this further follows that every other aspect of the problem of the theory is inaccessible. The second instrument of the theory is the assumption that between different national economies, the means of production are not freely moveable. Therein lies the characteristic that this problem separates from that of tax. Insofar as free movement nevertheless exists, these processes do not distinguish themselves from the ones within the national economy. And insofar as it there is also no completely free movement *here*, the difference between the two is an even smaller one—we will soon see that incidentally the latter moment allows for an important use. As a result from the not all too great significance of that difference, the topic of the "international values" nearly materially coincides with that, which exists within the national economy. It is only separated historically from the general price theory because for its purposes, an approach was first worked out, which was different from the price theory at that time and is closer to the modern one. But today, where this approach is also applied to the general problem, there is actually no longer a reason for separation—at least from the standpoint of science.

Further: In the way, which we have demonstrated the tax theory, a tariff theory—it would perhaps be better to speak of theories of the *effects* of taxes and tariffs—can now also be attained, which can be formed very completely and interestingly and, *insofar as the standpoint of the theory suffices*, just as satisfyingly as correctly through the introduction of different data, of rivalry and complementarity of goods, of different forms and variables of the tariffs and of other circumstances. A series of corrections on popular and also scientific claims and quite a number of results, which cannot be captured differently, thereby arise, which are of undeniable value. Now, one may not forget their static character and everything that this involves in particular while assessing them: This cannot be repeated often enough.

We can now not think of even just presenting a portion of these results here. Nevertheless, we want to say one thing. It arises that in general, a tariff diminishes the utility profit of both parts. But this indeed means nothing else than that this formal maximum of utility, on whose character and requirements we have placed so much emphasis, by no means that the welfare of both parts is also diminished. This basically just means something self-evident, namely that *now*, the same bartering acts are no longer made at the same price as before; this is self-evident because it follows directly from the distinct determination of both conditions. So far, this sentence is indisputable, but also without special interest. Its significance lies in the fact that one goes beyond it, over to the determination of that, "which now happens," to the determination of the new prices and sales. Thereafter, our theory gives us a series of exceptions for this rule. J. St. Mill has already realized some of them, but they can only be completely captured with the help of higher mathematics. It is possible that the tariff is occasionally only carried by *one* part, yes, even that *one* part has an advantage from it. Our general rule is already not without value. That the tariff is generally carried by both parts is not self-evident, even if it seems to be clear enough. Those exceptions are furthermore also well-known to the practitioner. But they are often overestimated, often also impugned. To really satisfyingly prove them, but to simultaneously limit to their actual meaning is only possible with the help of our theory. As an example of its value, let the catchphrase of the "taxation of the foreigner" be quoted, which plays such a great role in England. Our theory delimitates very clearly what can be true about it: First, the foreigner carries a portion of the tariff in general. And furthermore, it is in individual cases, whose characteristic of exception, however, comes forward in the exact raisonnement, that he carries the entire tax and possibly even *more*. Or another example: The claim that measures, which are of the nature of protective tariffs, amount to the destruction of machines, etc., has also stirred up much dust. In regards to the theory, the matter can be straightened out without every necessary echauffement: they are similar *insofar as* both measures lead to a limiting of supply; and insofar as a limitation of the supply can provide the opponent advantages, which are smaller *as a rule*, but not *necessarily* than the damage that thereby arises for the other one, they are both "advantageous" in a certain sense—but this is also all.

If one also considers the profit of the treasury as a result of the customs revenue—our theory naturally also applies to the essence and the effects of the financial tariff—and further, the possible backlashes of the tariff on the domestic price of the commodity that is burdened by a foreign country, as well as its effects on the price *of other* goods, therefore, a very complicated problem arises, which does not allow for a simple solution and is very much in need of a correct method. As a whole, we can say that neither the free-trade argument can be based on our *rule*, nor the protective-tariff argument can be based on our *exceptions*, which generally gain strength through the complications that were just indicated: The answers, which the theory gives, are very different according to the situation of the case. It is certainly possible, for individual groups of interest, as well as for the entire national economy, to make profits through corresponding tariff-political measures. But whether the same are significant enough in order to outweigh the effect of retortion measures cannot be said exactly, since that depends on the importance that one precisely gives credit to the interests, which are in question and those, which thereby suffer. In fact, that, which has been said should reproduce the standpoint of the most advanced theorists, who are turning way from short and easily ready rules about our question more and more.

Finally: We can therefore state the sentence that the static theory does not support the free-trade argument, or nevertheless not in a significant way. Our "general rule" seems to do that, but if one first-off considers its requirements, and secondly its exceptions, and thirdly, complicated cases altogether, then one comes to the realization that its practical meaning is very scarce. Our static theory therefore does give us many important results, but—and this is, in view of the complexity of the problem, virtually a testament of its accuracy and life truth—no simple, general answer. It is only to be added that the most important arguments pro and con protective tariffs are not static, hence, still evade the exact conception today. Ones sees this most pronounced for the theory of the educational tariff, but this also applies to most of the others. Namely therefore also for the free-trade argument; because this one is by no means based on those small building blocks, which the static theory can contribute to it, but rather to a far greater extent on the opinion that free commerce of the economic *development* is of greatest use. But all these things require "longer periods." But let us conclude. We must deny ourselves of going into the discussion of individual arguments, as compelling as the task of collecting the granules of truth is, which are contained within them—one only thinks of the catchphrase of the "protection of national labor"—and to battle methodic and contextual errors. But it must suffice us to have said those things, which we believed to have had to say in the interest of the static theory and above all, to have emphasized that they are completely inadequate for the role of a political weapon in the controversy of great principles. It may indeed solve smaller, clearly transcribed problems.

III

In a similar manner, the possibility arises to work out a pure economical, static theory of the assignment of income, which is subjected to the same essence, the same value, and the same limitations as both of the theories that were just outlined. Above all, one may not confuse them with a theory about the concrete tendencies of the assignment of income, as it has already been elaborated in the general part of this section, namely for two reasons: firstly, our laws can only be formal ones and cannot say anything about the concrete relations, for example, at present, and secondly, one can also not readily want to find the result in reality even then, when the necessary data were to be given, because other, dynamic moments are also effective here, which are missing in our static picture. But despite that, enough is left for being able to extract interest for this branch of our theory.

Already the classical authors have constructed laws of movement of incomes in regards to one another, and one will have to say that that, which has been achieved by them is nearly the only thing that we possess in this area. Despite many rudiments, the modern theory has not yet made an advance to a systematic answering of this question, and there is still much to do there. From our standpoint we encounter the difficulty that there are only two branches of income, but in the few remarks that are supposed to follow here, this will no longer emerge disruptively. We want to therefore nevertheless speak of the prices of the means of production, even if in our opinion, a group of the same does not represent a pure income.

The first thing that we can say, a first, general rule is that every arbitrary increase of the price of one of the means of production "damages" the owners of all of them, once as a consumer and thereupon, by and large, also as a manufacturer. This sentence sounds very controversial, but is just as true and just as innocent as our "general rule" in previous paragraphs. Quite similar to there, the primary interest pertains to the clarification of all effects and to the exceptional cases, and just as there, a very complete theory can thereby be captured. One will sooner admit that a limitation of the quantity of one of the production factors damages *all* constituent parts of the national economy. This rule also has exceptions. It can happen—this depends on the form of the supply and demand curves—that the limitation of the supply, for example, of labor for *all* laborers is advantageous in the same way as the destruction of a part of the supply of another good for its seller. It can therefore by proven that, which is so often impugned, that a general strike can not only nominally increase the wages, but also the amount of laborers—*of all* laborers—of the amount of the available consumption goods.

There is a good deal of such results—these include many very complicated ones—and much can happen for the clarification of some discussions through working them out. But our theory does not give a general answer to the question, which incomes fall and rise simultaneously and which move in contrast to one another, of the determination as the classical authors gave. This is nevertheless only an advantage. Such stark, firm rules do not exist, or better, one can only construct them for the price of the acceptance of requirements, which then do have too little to do with reality. Precisely the circumstance that our theory gives a good deal of special answers and that different results arise from different data begets its life truth, the great progress, which it shows vis-à-vis the classical system. If, for example, a price of a product rises as a result of the increase of demand for the same, then this increase will generally benefit all its means of production. We can thereby express the relation of its participation through a formula, which very jubilantly unites strength and clarity with suitability for every possible situation: It is the relation of the elasticities of its respective demand curves. Next to such movements, which take place for all production factors in the same sense, we can then also consider others for, which the opposite is the case, without contradicting ourselves.

Our results can still be enhanced by means of different methodological measures. One can conceive the three production factors as three separate national economies, and then directly apply the theory of the international values to the commerce between the same, as Professor Edgeworth has suggested. The group of the consumption goods could form a fourth of such a national economy. And this aspect is very frightening. One can furthermore touch the matter from the side of the monetary income and examine how an increase of the same functions, which also leads to self-evident results and much more.

What are the classical laws of movement supposed to do for us vis-à-vis this? Insofar as they affect the wage, they are dependent on population-theoretical requirements. According to this, the laborers cannot win or lose under any circumstances. The price of the produced means of production must sink during the increase of their quantity, and it therefore arises that the landowner primarily has the advantage of "progress," which corresponds with the result of the formal raisonnements of the classical theory of ground rent. One can go ahead and say that this is correct under corresponding requirements—on the other hand, Carey's law of distribution, for example, is completely mistaken—and still be convinced of the lesser value of this theory. It is therefore good that we have other things to put in its place.

IV

One is able to capture yet many a thing with our method. In fact, all pure economical problems can indeed be brought into this schema, insofar as they are not concerned with certain primary questions, such as the essence of the incomes, etc. And the primary difficulty lies there, as we have said, most often more in the "stylization" of the facts, so that they fit into every schema; the discovery of the individual theories then is, if this is successful, mostly very simple—in fact, these theorems are indeed the same for all the different problems, which cannot be emphasized enough vis-à-vis the difference of the forms. It deals with gaining a standpoint from which the things can be grasped in a way as we need it to be. According to the situation of the case, one can overlook such a greater or a smaller part of the matter, the results will have more or less value. But nevertheless, everything that is "purely economical" and "static" about it arises in this way. And there lies a broad, fruitful field of research, whose exploitation is just in the early stages. One can say that currently, even the most elementary principles of the method are foreign to most economists, definitely as a disadvantage for this circle of problems; it is very distant to them so much the more in questions, which have not already been discussed since the beginning stages of the economy. But the modern theory must rise to the occasion for precisely such new tasks. We want to limit ourselves to the following remarks. An important part of economics, which so to speak offers itself to the application of our method entirely on its own, is transportation. As one can easily see, the effects of the transportation costs on the price and aptitude for sales of the commodities can be grasped without much difficulty as the ones of tariffs, so that one can reduce this problem to the first one of the ones presented by us—and therein lies the entire economical theory of transportation. In the same manner as in the case of taxes and tariffs, we are introducing the tariff rates into our system of equations and observing how the state of equilibrium changes under its influence. Data from practice help us to give our sentences concrete content matter, and to bring the same in closer relation to individual problems. We can thereby exactly examine the influence of differential tariffs, of "discrimination," of tariff wars, etc, insofar as these things are purely economical and insofar as they can be statically explained. This certainly does not suffice to *completely* understand, for example, the tariff policy of a country or even just of an enterprise. Insofar as it has its eye on far-lying purposes, especially being supposed to promote or hinder a development, insofar as socio-political and other non-economical moments also affect it, one will always find a discrepancy between theory and facts. But one will mostly explain it satisfactorily and will always be able to understand a significant part of the phenomena with our means—perhaps a greater one than many a national economist is inclined to accept.

The theory of monopoly performs services that are especially important, since a monopolistic or even monopoly-like position pertains to most of the large transportation enterprises. One can say that all questions, which can be brought into the schema—price formation of the transportation performances and reaction of their price on the one of the other goods and their turnover—can be answered very satisfactorily. The freight tariffs in the sense of our "interdependency system" do not only affect the commodities that actually reach the transport, but also all the others. There has to be an influence on the price of a good if it, for example, has to be depleted at the place of manufacturing due to the tariffs being too high. The effect of a tariff is not exhausted with its influence on a concrete commodity, this in fact affects all prices and incomes of the national economy through the increase of some incomes on the one hand, and through the decrease of others on the other hand. All of these things are made clear by our method. Finally, we can put the collection of tariffs in relation to the manufacturing costs, or at least the costs of operations of the transportation enterprises, and examine these relations. But what does the common theory of transportation offer?

Above all, it offers truisms about the importance of transportation, about the influence of its progress in the development of the people. We hear that without the same, a higher level of culture is possible, that it overcomes the moment of the local distance and pushes the markets closer to one another, that it is an essential factor in the formation of a global economy, and so forth. One presents that the commerce by letter, by telegraph, and by telephone is an integrating moment of technology, of the modern economy, and is indispensable to the same. The trains and steamships have made new production combinations possible and have created new economies. And for all that, data are most often given to us, also most often overviews of the historical development. What scientific worth does this have? Everyone knows all this quite well, and I believe that one is not able to read suchlike remarks without disappointment. Descriptive examinations of this area certainly have value; yes, they are indispensable. But the general discussions of the theoretical economists offer extraordinarily little of interest.

But thereupon, one maintains to discuss questions of the transport policy. A railway enterprise is a very important factor to the entire national economy; it is furthermore a great power in itself. The question how it makes use of its influence and whether or not one should entrust it to the hands of private ones, then the discussion of the advantages and disadvantages of the government enterprise concerns the economists much more than theoretical problems. The national-economical and legal questions that are connected with the phenomenon of "discrimination" and the like, this is what one primarily means by the theory of transportation.

The same are certainly very important; but they are by far more practical than scientific questions, and they are the arguments of parties and groups of interest that one also encounters in scientific literature.

In a similar manner, one can single out every element of cost of a good and finally every good altogether, in order to continually gain such general sentences about the effects of small changes of its quantity or its price, in the same manner as we have presented them. Nothing else was that, which we did for the theory of the assignment of income, also nothing else for the theory of transportation. There are many similar applications, although they are of lesser significance: The daily life gives them to us in profusion, and in view of the relative complexity of these questions and their undeniable importance, a careful development of the method is certainly not without value. Of course, for practical purposes, it is mostly only a matter of concrete facts. The conditions, under which the price, for example, of cotton changes and which effects this has on the sales of the makes and on the involved industries, finally, on the entire national economy, all this can only be examined due to static material of any kind, and the practitioner will turn to his experience in business and politics, and not to the theory; but the theory itself is able to gain new suggestions and problems, data for its abstract schemes from business experience and statistics, and will certainly be in a position to sooner or later approach the facts with its system of equilibrium and its theorems. The practice of the economic life, especially that of the stock exchanges, has led to the development of an entire series of popular theories about price movements, etc., which, may they be as incomplete as possible, do represent the sediment of extensive experience in a similar manner to the rules of weather of the farmer. Without giving much thought to the deeper connections, the experienced stock broker knows to anticipate the changes of the bank rates and takes advantage of the interaction between the prices of the stock values. The finance article of every newspaper contains more theory—and more *for* theory—than one should believe.

Of course these theoretical elements only seem rudimentary and disconnected, but our system gives us the means to prove and to adjust it. We can also expect something of the future here, may it also stay far behind the keen hopes that one dedicated oneself to in earlier times.

The tax and tariff theory, or better, the sentences that the national economists initially developed in connection to and in view of these questions, therefore only *represent special cases of a thought process, which is capable of a very broad application*, insofar a general case, as there is thereby no talk of a specific good, and a change for the production relations is demonstrated the simplest through a tax or a tariff. And this entire broad circle of problems is able to experience an essentially perfected approach. This basing of the exact tax theory on a concrete scientific foundation on the one hand, and its generalization on the other hand, these are progresses, which I may recommend for the attention of the reader indeed. It is deep insight into the gearing mechanism of the economic life, which our system opens to us here.

We want to give another example of a somewhat bolder application of our method, however, only very briefly, namely the examination of the effects of technological progress, therefore primarily in order to name the catchphrase under which the pertaining discussion is known well, the effect *of the introduction of the machines*.

In typical life we already find both of the views being supported, between which science also fluctuates: the type of one of them is the feature section of a newspaper, which enthusiastically celebrates the achievements of technology and predicts all beneficial consequences imaginable of the same; the type of the other one is the conception of the laborer, who curses and occasionally destroys the machines. We can be certain from the very beginning that both views are not unjustified. Because the practice of daily life only rarely grasps something completely wrong: What appears as aberrance is often quite consequential from the standpoint of the negotiator, and the one judging forgets too easily that his standpoint is also a subjective one. That fact that a "laborer-saving" invention is *initially and by and large* advantageous to the consumer is just as indisputable as the other one, that the laborer *also by and large and directly* suffers damages in his work opportunity and in his wage.

The scientific discussion of the topic shows the features that are well-known to us. Without bringing the question into organic connection with the foundations of the theory, one attempted to argue with general arguments for one or the other conception and to get to just as general of an answer, until one saw that one did not get any further and constantly ran into the same arguments, which do in fact not convince anyone, even if they are not unjustified. Then one tiredly turned away from the theory and fell into the other extreme—namely to despair of it and to suffice with the awareness to have realized its worthlessness. Always the same drama: pretensions and mistakes, justified attacks—but which go too far and "throw the baby out with the bath water"—and then that state, which one could consider as disorganization of the discussion. But is there no other remedy than radical rejection of the theory? Certainly, namely a better theory. How can we reach it?

Two remarks thereto: For one, we can—and actually must—relegate the question to dynamic. A primary reason of there being no result for the controversy certainly lies in not distinguishing between "direct" and "further" effects, between short and long periods. Marx and his students have above all emphasized the first one; the compensation theory has especially placed emphasis on the latter one. But then we can also attempt to introduce our new machines into the static system. This is principally, as no longer needs to be explained here, inadmissible; but if its influence is not too great, then we can nevertheless try it. It can also not be done readily; but we can help ourselves with different devices. We only want to indicate the latter ones: It would not suffice to simply assume an increase of the available supply of tools. But it is perhaps possible to somehow express that fact that through this increase, labor becomes "dispensable." But perhaps the assumption would be better that the acquirers of new machines are suddenly *in the possession of a specific quantity of labor*. Once one has adjusted the new machines to our system in this manner—or somehow—then the variations method will automatically give us all effects of its introduction, *insofar as they are static*, in an exact and clear manner—and an abundance of interesting and really sustainable results will arrive. And these will probably also maintain themselves under conditions that cannot be called "static" strictly speaking.

So we are finally also able advance against the problems of dynamic with our method. How far? This is always quaestio facti. We can *never* penetrate the core of the same; the great developmental tendencies surely go beyond our system, play on other stages. We only hear their voice like a growling of distant thunder. But, as the case may be, our method is nonetheless able to give us a great deal of practical results and, what is more important than that, a series of valuable realizations. We must learn to forgo the demands of the older national economists; however, enough valuable things remain. For us, it was only a matter of presenting *that* this is the way it is, and we cannot go into the details of the matter. Of course our method is a powerful instrument for the mastering of facts, which protects us from being mastered by them, to lose ourselves in them. Once one has realized its value and has paid heed to its teachings, then the scientific discussion will have been lifted to a higher niveau. Only through the understanding of the variations method does the path lead to certainty in the solution of concrete economical problems, to that certainty, for which we envy the natural sciences today—and also the path to the results, which are worthy of universal approval and will meet with it.

Notes

1. We have a case here where we can use the thought process of the cost theory—at least halfway—very well (Schumpeter, 1908, pg. 479).
2. Examinations of the price theory (page 491).
3. It is interesting to emphasize that that EXACT tax theory is based on the moment of supply and demand, proceeds from a "specific" tax on the commodity unit, which subsequently appears as the main case of the tax theory from this standpoint (Schumpeter, 1908, pg. 500).

Part V

Summary of that, which arises out of the previously stated for the judgment of the essence, the value of realization, and the developmental possibilities of the theoretical economy.

1

Nature or Essence of the Exact Economy

I

I have strived to present the essential content of that area, which is generally understood by the term theoretical economics. This term has indeed gained a somewhat further, altogether different meaning in especially German, and one may say that that, which is offered only covers a portion of the same, for example that, which one could consider as pure traffic theory. But at any rate, our theorems and the foundations of our system apply by and large and at least in essence to every state of the economy, especially also to the "commerce-less," "closed," or "isolated" one, as we have attempted to work out. In addition, we saw that all other constituent parts of economics are either worthless or belong to essentially different areas and demand other methods. We therefore consider ourselves justified in considering that, which has been said as the core of the economy. But we do not want to insist on it; let one call our discipline as one may, it is only decisive *that* it is a self-contained, autonomous province of the kingdom of knowledge. We only adhere to the former name for purposes of practicability. We are not dealing with what the modern German sociologist, social philosopher, or even economist defines as his area—we are also not passing judgment on him and his research—but rather simply that former type of economics, which he often considers having to shelve, that type of economics, which one condemns or defends without actually really knowing what is to be considered of it.

The purpose of this last part of our work is to say the latter or, better, to once again summarize our results regarding this question. It is no longer supposed to bring anything new, but rather only contain that, which arises out of the previous, in my opinion—a final judgment of the value of realization of our discipline. The same lies *in* and arises *from* that, which has been said; and if we will speak somewhat more generally here, then one nevertheless does not want to forget that because of it, we are not basing on the practical scientific work, on the experience that arises from it, and on the concrete scientific goals any less than for our earlier approaches; not on general premises or on meta-physical speculations. The reader will soon see that he has nothing to fear in this regard: Our intent is primarily only to dryly and clearly sum up, and the simplicity and austerity of our executions will dissipate every suspicion in this direction and, as I hope, make the impression of complete composure and reliability. I gladly forgo colorful phrases for this price.

In fact, I should have to leave that, which I want to say here, up to the judgment of the reader. I basically have no right to anticipate the same. Such an appendix of the actual exposition would actually not even be necessary in any other discipline, also not in works that place more emphasis on epistemological questions than it commonly occurs. Goals and methods, value of the results—all this is much too clear there to have to be especially grappled with vis-à-vis a further audience, even today where criticism also does not stop in front of the proudest scientific structures: *few* are there who doubt, *many* trust. But it behaves conversely for us. And if I myself were to not say plenty now about that, which I consider to be the truth, to point out the jumble of opinions of parties, then I would be nothing less then reassured about which final judgment about the essence and value of the theoretical economy would be taken from that, which has been said. The power of the phrases of the parties about the ghosts is too great; the latter are too little accustomed to look at the matter themselves and not their political or philosophical theater cloak. So once again: what is the situation that surrounds the little, exact island of knowledge that we recommend one's attention towards? What is its nature; is it a sand bank or a boulder? Is there organic life on it or not; is it fruitful or fruitless; is it useful as a coal station or in some other way; *what is it worth*? And how does it behave towards the large mainland of the remaining exact knowledge of humanity on the one hand, and towards the sea of facts that surround it on the other hand? We will seek to answer these questions briefly. But we will not be allowed to thereby forget that the decision is in the hands of the reader, of what *he* wants to thinks of it. A number of viewpoints that seem important to me may therefore only be very briefly and almost solely suggestively emphasized, and apart from that, we want to distance ourselves from every absolutism and not only enforcedly grant everyone the freedom of his opinion, but rather emphasize ourselves that one *can* be of different opinions about many points, yes, even has to be, without one of them being able to claim the privilege of sole accuracy.

But in addition we will still have something else to discuss or nevertheless touch upon here. Not only what one should think about that, which the economy offers *today*, is so unclear, but also and perhaps even more what one has to hope for it *from the future*. In which direction and how should one continue to work? Is there even anything new to discover or have the basics already been achieved? And where does this "new" lie; which paths lead to it? Is the current foundation of our discipline capable of development or are fundamental changes preparing themselves as some "reformers" believe? Must other methods be found in order to advance further, or can significant things still be gained with the old ones? These questions have also already been answered in the previous part, and it can only be spared to formulate this answer, which gives us our present executions by itself; it is, however, also *necessary*. Several outlooks will therefore arise for the great question "now what?" and for the nearest future of our science. That, which we can offer here can only be brief and incomplete. And here too the reader will have to decide for himself: What there still is in our area, beyond the achieved; this can only be precisely stated to a limited degree. And we want to suffice ourselves with it. Every man can only *feel*, *anticipate* further details, and his hopes will be different, according to his strength and inclinations. The point of view that everything has already been done is just as comfortable and superficial as the one that everything has yet to be done. Both are not to be taken seriously or nevertheless not literally. The truth lies between both extremities, but by no means at the same point for everyone; to one, the achieved seems to be more complete, to another, in need of reform according to his personality and the standpoint that his concrete work instructs him. Whoever works in ground-breaking areas has less insight into the smaller defects of the theory's detail; whoever is directly working out the latter often has little understanding for the work of the other. Both will think differently about the direction and the means of the further progress. And each of these subjective opinions has its justification, and an exact verification of the right or wrong of one or the other is impossible. Everyone ultimately has to arrange that only with himself.

II

The question of the essence of our exact system can now be answered very briefly and clearly due to that, which we have already said about it. The purely static economy is nothing else than an abstract picture of certain economical facts, *a schema that is supposed to serve for the description of the same*. It is based on certain assumptions and is *insofar a creature of our arbitrariness*, just the same as that every other one is exact science. So if the historian says that our theory is a figment of our imagination, then he is correct in *a* sense. Surely, in the world of phenomena itself there are neither our "assumptions," nor our "laws." But an objection against the same does not follow from it yet; because this does not prevent that they *suit* the facts. Where does this now come from? Simply from there that we have indeed proceeded arbitrarily but rationally during the construction of our schema; *we have simply constructed the same with regards to the facts*. To make use of the phrase of a deep thinker: The tailor does produce the skirt and the same is insofar a product of his arbitrariness as he could have certainly also cut it differently. We will nevertheless expect that it fits and not be surprised about it at all if this is the case; because he will tailor it to measure. We will therefore also not misuse our sovereignty, but rather make such assumptions which are forced upon us by the facts and from which we can reasonably assume that they will not become disavowed from the same. This can nevertheless happen constantly, and all that we can do for it is choose our fundamental assumptions in a way that we can calmly face this eventuality. We work in order to adhere to our picture, not constantly "to measure," but rather wish that our schema also suits the facts that we have not observed. But like the tailor who upholds a stock of ready-made skirts, we expect that our product suits a sufficient number of customers. And our expectation confirms itself by and large. The tailor then says that his skirts would have "fit"; we say that our sentences are "universal."

Now the latter does not mean, and we hardly still need to emphasize it, that they are some "laws" that are stipulated to the universe, or even that they rule the world of phenomena like beings outside the same standing, metaphysical world, but rather nothing else at all than that they maintain themselves to a *significant degree*, to such a significant degree that their construction is worthwhile. However, they do not absolutely do this. We often encounter contradicting instances. Now, great tactic is necessary for such. One will soon neglect them, soon control them with ancillary hypotheses, soon ascribe them to different areas and abstract from them in our theory; but it will occasionally commend itself to drop our other approach for them. As we have said, to properly proceed here is difficult and a criterion of scientific competence. We must truly quote the facts; this is the entire purpose of our approach, but we may nevertheless allow ourselves to be mastered by them. Just as an artist must carefully observe his object, but may nonetheless not lose himself in details, we also must meet both of the contrary demands and simultaneously defend the overgrowth of the individual facts, which smudges the great lines; and not deny the nature of truth, to so to speak discipline the facts and still let them run free. Hardly anyone steers entirely unscathed between this Scylla and this Charybdis, and there are no absolute rules for it at any rate. It is now extraordinarily important for the correct understanding of our, and ultimately every, theory to remain aware of this arbitrary character of the same and to not look for the expression of some "absolute" truths in it. It is none other than a descriptive method, and it must be judged as such and be equipped rough and ready. If one says that one expresses the "essential thing" or even the "necessary thing" within the theoretical laws, then this does not mean that an essential difference exists between the categories of facts termed as such, that one group of them are the consequence of great laws and the others are "only" causes for disturbance; this does not even mean that the first ones are absolutely "more important" than the latter ones, or that these would have a tendency to disappear; *only a rule of measure lies in it*, to simplify the representation and to prevent it from becoming hopelessly complicated. Once one has understood this, one especially knows that only the purpose justifies the theory, only the success justifies it; many objections, of course, also many pretensions are thereby eliminated that otherwise barricade our path.

There is nevertheless an inclination in which one can say that the theory is absolutely valid, yes, unfailing and even independent of factual observations. This is sustainable by its "logical accuracy." As one has said that the theory of light is "independent" of the existence of any phenomenon that suits it, one could also claim this of the pure price theory. But it would be a great fallacy to believe that one has thereby gained something for the theory, has also conferred a higher dignity on it; because what does the sentence mean if it is supposed to be accurate? Obviously none other than that a system of somehow defined terms by means of the rules of logic allows a derivation of certain judgments, against which no objection can be made from the standpoint of these rules, if only they had not been defied. This is of course true, even an implicitness, a truism, and applies from every system of concepts, as also from the one of the economy. But of what use is this to us? None, absolutely none. A system of such could therefore be completely unfounded of every usefulness, yes, of every meaning. Its value of realization can only come from the supply of facts, which has given rise to its construction; it is only characterized by this and can only be understood from it.

This is all that we want to say here about the question of the nature of the theoretical economy, about the question *what the economists actually do* when they theorize. One has most often asked oneself the same in the form of one asking whether the theory is deductive or inductive. The answer was for the first, and a quite intense fight about the advantages and disadvantages of the deduction was the result. We can only express our sympathy about it for the involved parties. In spite of the fact that it cannot be the task of a special discipline to try a logical method, the entire question has failed; one could have just as well fought over the "Modus Barbara." What does "one-sided deductive approach" mean? What use is a glorification of the deduction to us? But above all, it is inconceivable to me how the representatives of the theory could admit that the latter is solely deductive. If they meant to say that the theory represents a deduction of certain eternal, inalterable laws, then the reproach of most unfounded speculation would come upon them; how the latter in a certain connection with the deductive approach even stands, however little importance such a connection may have by itself. But let us drop this and rather briefly answer the question: In what sense is our theory deductive? Now, in the same sense as every exact science, let us say, for example, as astronomy. It can nevertheless not befall on anyone to deny the latter its empirical character or its justification in the facts. So how does the matter behave? Our points of departure are certainly *induced*. Further inductions as well as deductions follow it without an unbiased observer being able to find something objectionable or even noticeable in it. This is as simple as possible. Was have also already stated what is to be considered of our fundamental assumptions. It no longer needs to be emphasized that they are not demands. But even apart from this, hypotheses can still play different roles, namely the following two: A hypothesis can be a statement about facts, express an assumption about an actual occurrence, or it can be a formal assumption, to which nothing in reality needs to correspond in itself, but which must lead to healthy results. For example, the hypotheses of history, as for example the one about the creation of cities are of the first type; the ones of exact sciences, as for example the molecular hypothesis, are of the latter one. Both varieties are different according to the essence, as well as the scientific role. According to the essence; One of them attempts to reconstruct one of the facts inaccessible to the observation and requires verification, the others are arbitrary assessments and do not need to be "true" in themselves if they only achieve that, which is desired. According to the role; The first ones already represent results in themselves and want to convey to us knowledge that is the purpose of their construction; the latter ones are methodological construction aids, which do not tell us anything by themselves, but are rather only supposed to lead to other results. Both are based on facts; the "historical," as well as the "exact" hypotheses, but in an entirely different manner: One of them is based on factual material—it would otherwise be in trouble—only on an incomplete one that it is supposed to complete; facts also *induce* us for the construction of the other ones—otherwise "our skirt would not fit"—but in principle, the assessment of these hypotheses is arbitrary and unnecessary; it is dependent on the lack of counter-instances. The first type of hypotheses can finally be a cause for serious differences in opinion, but the latter one is indifferent in itself, and only its purpose can be discussed, not its "accuracy." Now, our hypotheses are only of *this* nature. They are fundamentally innocent in themselves and involve nothing, at which one could take offense from any standpoint in principle. And if theorists and opponents of the theory had always realized this, then our theory would have been spared many unfruitful discussions.

What the historian actually means when he accuses the theory of its "deductive approach" and demands a factual study is not that the theory takes *no* account of facts—misunderstandings on his part and encroachments of the theorists aside—but rather something else. He believes, and perhaps partially with good reason, that facts other than the ones described by the theory are more interesting. At least this is the most important content of the historical objections, although not their only one. But we do not want to speak about it here; rather, only the relation of the theory to its own factual material is supposed to be indicated at this point. This can be done in brief: That every theorem and every result must be verified by the facts is clear and is acknowledged by everyone in principle, even though it is often, very often neglected in practice. It is just as clear if one were to believe that the points of departure of every theoretical reasoning can also only be facts, and that all results only flow, although often indirectly, out of factual observations. How is it that this is not always realized and even less often emphasized accordingly? This would be difficult to explain. But it is certain that for the opponents of the theory, their task was thereby unseemly alleviated. However, this is not yet everything. Factual observations also influentially, correctively, inspiringly, and warningly play into the theoretical reasoning itself—and *this* is comprehended the least. It was hopefully successful to convincingly instance it in the previous example. This moment uncovers a much closer relation between theory and "description" than even our verification that both are fundamentally essential: They must also go hand in hand *in practice*. Just as one goes beyond the simplest elements, new views into reality will become necessary, new data indispensable. And as the theory is able to sharpen the view for the facts—let it be said under any reserve—these react fructifying to the theory in every step: The smallest observation can lead to a surprising change. We have finally still become acquainted with points at which the pure theory completely fails and where it must clear the field for an entirely new factual study. To sum up this portion of our argument: The structure of the theory appears very independent in itself; but it is nevertheless entirely based on factual observations; yes, the necessity and the influence of the same reaches much farther than is generally realized and admitted. The deciding point that everything depends on is in the separation of two different aspects of the matter: On the one hand, we have the principal arbitrariness of our theory, on which its system, its strength, and exactness is based, and on the other hand, its adequacy for and conditionality through the phenomena, which alone give its content and value. If one distinguishes between these moments and if one puts them into the correct relation to one another, then a clear conception arises, which successfully overcomes the difficulties and doubts, as they encounter us in the common discussion of these questions.

One could say all of this about every exact discipline. In fact, the theoretical economy is an exact science according to its essence, as we have already stated previously and as it probably now arises in an evident nature, as for example, pure mechanics, with which it is so often compared. We now see that an actual moment lies in this comparison. One could even say that all exact disciplines, including ours, are not only essentially equal, but actually only one and the same: Namely one and the same system of equations; the same problem of equilibrium always forms the core of all—the only difference lies in the interpretation of the individual variables of the equations. We are thereby certainly aware that a healthy meaning lies or nevertheless can lie in the objections that were raised in the circles of the economists against such comparisons. These objections are however partially based on prejudices, but they are certainly justified in part, and a mechanistic conception of, for example, the essence of economics must appear as certainly being questionable, yes, failed, and nevertheless as being outdated. But we are keeping ourselves free from the possible mistakes that lie here. We did not proceed from such a premise, but rather unbiasedly approached our tasks, whereby it only arises *afterwards* that the structure of the pure economy is also a system of equations of the kind as we find in other exact disciplines. But then we do not extract any material conclusions from these facts, neither such social or political nature, nor any altogether; rather expressively acknowledge that no such thing not possible. This analogy only applies formally and methodologically, and even there only for certain fundamental theorems. This cannot appear any more questionable than for example, the claim that similar, logical rules prove themselves for the economy, as well as for mechanics. However, to the extent that we believe that our comparison offers good services to the highlighting of the essence of our discipline, we will not go any further.

I believe that this conception leaves little room for a controversy. Let us go ahead and look at this latter one as it has actually been led; we in turn find, as we have said, that right and wrong lies on both sides. One often looks for objections against the pure theory with reference to confute the exact sciences. But we observe that such arguments make little impression on the opponents; partially unjustifiably. To scoff at "economy in vacuo" is certainly superficial, as proper and effective as it may be. However, this aversion is partially justified; because one certainly has a right to demand that the methodical questions of our science are solved by their problems and subsequent to their goals, and not through vague analogies. For this reason, and also for the reason because the mechanical analogy can definitely be misused and was misused, we have absolutely foregone such arguments in general and also express ourselves with every reserve here, where we nevertheless make use of the same for the purpose of the clarification of the nature of our system.

A remark presents itself here. It is one of the most favorite activities of the modern philosophers to unite the subject matter of the individual disciplines, in order to make use of their expression, to an architectonic, whole one. We are not allowing ourselves to pass judgment on the worth or worthlessness of such endeavors, which nevertheless make tremendous demands on every one that behooves them. But we can certainly demand that no harm is thereby done to our discipline. Certain universally-known classifications of the individual sciences into different groups now apply to this purpose, namely the ever so modern one in "natural sciences and humanities" and several other, similar ones. It appears quite innocent in itself, but it is actually nothing less than harmless. A judgment on the essence of the individual disciplines also always hides itself in it, which can lead and actually has led to the construction of a priori demands for their goals and methods. It seems to us that a range of prejudices, misunderstandings, and unscientific tendencies lie here now, which must be regretted all the more, for these circles have a significant influence not only on public opinion, but also for us, on the experts in each area—in contrast to the other, more self-assured sciences. A serious obstacle to progress of true realization in the area of the social sciences is growing there in Germany, under the protection of authorities of philosophical nature and metaphysical catchwords. But apart from this, and assuming that one carries out these attempts entirely unbiased, the economist by discipline can only have a nervous feeling in doing so, similar to that, which one feels when one is in an automobile whose steering is entrusted to a novice. One can only peremptorily caution against trusting those shimmering phrases, and cannot preach a type of economic Monroe Doctrine urgently enough. Let us only briefly and dryly formulate the conception that arises from concrete work: According to its methodological and epistemological nature, the pure economy would be a "natural science" and its theorems "natural laws" in the sense that was defined in the first part of this work. This claim applies entirely independent of a priori contemplations of any nature. One could still admit that the economy is in another sense—concerning the contents—a form of "humanities" and *insofar* of another character than its methodological sisters. Only, this factor does not come into consideration for the treatment of its problems. We, who do not want to philosophize or politicize, never had occasion to therefore assign an exceptional position to the exact economy—although we would have absolutely been ready to give one of such its right to have it. Only its minimal development and the organization of scientific operation brings with it that it appears to be excluded from the realm of the exact disciplines.

III

As many reservations as a comparison of two sciences to one another always has against it, as much as it must always be "limping," it can nevertheless not be denied that it can contribute many a thing to the understanding of its essence. And precisely in the study of our discussions, in which we currently find ourselves, we can avail ourselves this aid with greater freedom than during the examination of concrete problems, and need to fear less than there that it can lead us astray. Even otherwise, apart from the purpose of the analogy, the contemplation of the relationships of our science with others contributes to enlightening us about its essence; namely to show us its independency again. We therefore want to still dwell a bit upon these things, as much as there has already been said about them, and as dry as the subject matter is.

Deterred from the many attacks of exposed, mechanical analogies, one resorted to the biological ones. No one inferior to A. Marshall has recommended it to us, and one finds it in every textbook today. It must immediately be emphasized that this has nothing to do with the ominous, organic constitution and so forth, even though such views may have greatly contributed to the popularity of this analogy. It only deals with a *comparison* here, not with the drawing in of material truths. Now, if we want to figure out the significance of the same, we must ask what its motive was and what it is supposed to achieve. This becomes clearly apparent when regarding Marshall. The only reason that compels him to give preference to the biological analogy over the mechanical one was the striving to bring the moment of development into our discipline. The mechanical system of equilibrium gives a resting state and offers no analogies for the phenomena of progress, etc. This is correct. But unfortunately, Marshall does not say *that*, but rather only indicates the motive that the economy is a "science of life," a motive that is far too general to actually be useful and to belong into the category of those general catchwords, which are only obstructive to a clear conception. Of course if one, like Marshall, attempts to further our system in a way that it is also supposed to grasp the phenomena of development, then this analogy actually presents itself. But this attempt has not brought the desired results in my opinion, rather showed that this way does not lead very far. For this situation, I find it better to acknowledge and admit an essential difference between static and dynamic; that the system of the pure economy is essentially without development, insofar as it has actually been worked out today, which we will still come back to. Precisely the fact that compelled Marshall to give preference to the biological analogy is a reason for us to prefer the mechanical one. According to this, the first one—let it be understood for the static—seems to be of little fortune to us, and rather brings the danger of bewilderment with it. We would rather recommend the old, mechanical one to the reader's attention, in which a healthy realization manifests, in spite of everything; also, because to us, it, among others suggests the use of exact methods and the avoiding of phrases more. We fear the misuse of strict forms of thought less than straying off from its principles—however, also contrary to Professor Marshall. The latter danger should at least be the greatest one currently in Germany. Others have already preached enough against the first one; with too much success, as it appears to me.

The relations of biology to other areas are certainly numerous. For example, the essence of the economic trade and the one to comprehend the humanly motivations, which, as we have said, we cannot do—*it* achieves this. And its results in the scientific worldview will therefore perhaps not be far from ours. But because of this, our discipline can still be very close to biology epistemologically, and neither receive stimuli from it, nor can it give such to it; and this is not only insufficiently clear to the layman, but also to the experts in each area; and the situation actually is this way. Even the realization that all trading must ultimately let itself be biologically explained, and the economy is determined to merge into biology content-wise this way, in a certain sense; that, as long as a treatment of the economical phenomena by themselves and without going into their most inner being, is able to offer us more than such an entering, as long as an independent discipline of economy even therefore exists, is also independent, and suffices for itself. But then biological arguments are able to tell us quite little for our problems, and then both of the areas have little to do with one another—at least for now and the near future. Of course such a support point was welcomed by the opponents of our conception, and one can often observe how much the enemies of exact methods like to seclude themselves to biology. However, this thought process proves itself as empty when examined for its actual contributions, and the result of every serious entering can only be a disappointment today, in my opinion.

A readily apparent connection exists between the economy and sociology. No one can be more convinced of the necessity of this young science than the economist who sighs at the division of labor in the area of the social sciences. It is not a collective term for the latter ones, but rather an individual discipline with its own goals and methods, and it must be. Even today, one can often hear doubts about the justification of its existence and few clear views about its function. But even if its content were to exist in nothing else than in that, which we can allot it from our area, then this would already be sufficient. We have seen that under the title "economics," important topics are discussed, which—as we have said—cannot run free in the same and require other approaches, namely the organization theory. On the other hand, we have to say similar things about the relationships of the economy to sociology, as about to ones to biology. The fact that other methods apply in this neighboring area brings with it that the results, like the arsenal of conception of the same does not allow for a direct application to ours. Sociology can achieve many things that we cannot offer and what nevertheless interests us. It can therefore, for example, figure out the essence of economics, while we only talk about a "study area" that only has a few characteristics of the first one, and it cannot be considered its life-like replica, out of risk for serious misunderstanding. But it cannot offer us anything for our own results, as little as we can for theirs. The points of contact between both disciplines can be easily indicated: they are certain data of our system, especially the given organization of the economic subjects of our area. *But this "given" means nothing else than that we do not want to debate on this moment in question any further, but rather leave it to other disciplines*. The pure economical processes, with which we are dealing, are in the same sense something that is given for sociology, and it is a mistake to believe that it could give us teachings about their treatment, as we had the opportunity to emphasize for the question of the individualism. In my opinion, one can not even say that sociology stands *beside* our science. It would rather suit the facts to place it *behind* the same. Let us express ourselves more clearly: The situation is not in a manner that one could perhaps say that the economy deals with the economic commerce of man and sociology with the remaining commerce of man. In fact, the first one is a sui generis area whose content and methods cannot readily be placed next to the one of the latter, but are rather closer to other sciences whose material content has nothing in common with economizing.

But it is nevertheless in the best interest of the economy to welcome sociology and to advocate its recognition, but namely to advocate that all those "economists" who are actually sociologists—and there are many, in Germany especially—actually consider themselves as such. The development of sociology and its general introduction into the organization of research work and teaching will provide the greatest services for the economy and contribute much to the clarification of the situation; of course, only when one lets it get to the calm possession of a field of work that is circumscribed well and does not expect the economy to become sociology. At any rate, both fields have nothing in common with one another methodologically and epistemologically.

IV

We furthermore have to summarize what we have previously said about psychology, and add plenty more. In the broadest circles and for the most different directions, we encounter the viewpoint that the economy is virtually based on psychology. This can mean two different things. First, it can be meant in the sense in which one can say that all sciences are based on psychology, in so far they are products of the observer's and thinker's psyche. According to this conception, the area of psychology grows into an indeterminate thing; it not only becomes the most important science, but actually the only one. The economy also belongs to it in this sense, of course. However, we do not want to elaborate on it, as many followers as this conception may currently have among the psychologists; because this is not what the economists believe; they are concerned with a much more direct relationship—namely with the psychological explanation of the economic acts.

Gabriel Tarde probably gave this standpoint the most poignant expression,[1] by virtually turning the economy into a branch of psychology. But the demand for "psychological deepening" of our discipline is being raised quite generally—and rather *was* raised, because a reaction is currently exerting influence. One must now clearly determine what this general phrase means.

We encounter the indication of psychology in two different connections; once, subsequent to the newer value theory. We do not need such a foundation. It is based on a fallacy if one believes to be able to thereby justify our results more soundly. The point of departure of our thought processes are certain assumptions about the value functions, which are completely independent of the psychological explanation, as well as of parts of the voluntary theory, as of parts of the teachings of feelings. The same are particularly not identical to Weber's Law, are not dependent on the same and cannot be struck by the objections against the same. The economic facts, not the psychological ones induce us to their construction. A connection can nonetheless exist, but the same is only of philosophical interest. The same is irrelevant to the economical *results* in themselves, and it can never be the economist's job to go into these things. And it is good that this is so; our discipline would otherwise be in a bad situation.

The theory of motives of human trade, the questions about the meaning of egoism and altruism also do not play a role for us. The entire development of our discipline tends to eliminate these discussions.

It is therefore very similar here as it is for sociology. We are coming up with our assumptions entirely on our own. It is redundant to go into the science, to which the same *materially* belong; it would not be worth the effort. We have to adhere to our facts *in themselves* and cannot follow the same into endless distances. The entire science field may certainly once be able to be uniformly constructed on another level of development; but currently, each discipline works with its own methods for its own purposes, and the economy also does this. It is possible that when the boundaries of the special sciences are punctuated with the flow of development, we are then compelled to change our conception in favor of a "psychological deepening." This is not allowed to keep us from initially regarding our facts by themselves; may this type of proceeding only be a provisionary one. All scientific systems are indeed only provisionary structures when regarded as "sub specie aeternitatis," which are determined to yield to other, more complete, more special ones after a few decades. However, this cannot lead us astray on our path, which leads farther step by step, and only rarely opens such broad outlooks. Just as his views about the development of humanity in the concrete case play no role for the trading of the individual, such broad prospects are also irrelevant to the current questions of a science. And even if the hour surely comes, where the same determinedly step forward, it is nevertheless only damaging to let the practical research work be influenced thereby. It is only a loss of time, and only he, whom the rocky way has fatigued or who does not know how to continue on the same dwells upon it.

Of course, the individual disciplines interact in yet another way: their methods and material results allow applications that are very frequently extraordinarily fruitful to other areas of knowledge. The history of science offers many examples; and especially younger sciences can learn much from their older sisters. But we do not believe that psychology plays such a role for us. Which methods or results would we have adopted from the same? Let us only distinguish between experimental and introspective psychology for our purposes; thus, we see that the methods and results of the first ones, which are primarily dedicated to the "perceptional analysis" and lie against psycho-physics and physiology, are as far away from our area as possible; and we have seen well enough that introspection offers us nothing. Even if we wanted to make use of the same, which can indeed occasionally prove to be unharmed by the principal inaccuracy of this approach, this occurs entirely independently, solely on the basis of everyday observations, which so far do not interest the psychologist in the least. This leads us to the other group of statements, in which we encounter the word "psychological" in economic works.

We can summarize our present argument by stating that *no* connection exists between economics and psychology, neither a methodological one, nor a material one of the type that we would have to follow the latter one in order to attain our results.

An example of those psychologically seeming claims is perhaps the expression "psychology of crises." The expression is generally well-known and almost every economist uses it. But what is actually meant?

I believe that one formally thinks of two phenomena, of the feverish activity in periods of lively speculation and of the sudden change of the situation in the moment of panic, in approximately the manner of how this stands out in Engel's description, which has become classic—although in my opinion, it is rather vapid. Under the same title, one furthermore currently mentions the fact that the panicked behavior of the parties concerned is now a somewhat different one than previously, and that the entire phenomenon tends to take on another character.

Another example is given to us by the expression "psychology of entrepreneurship." By this, we mean the entire behavior of this class, namely towards the laborers. One especially thereby thinks of phenomena like "feeling of dominance," "awareness of power," etc; phenomena, which are adequate for others as those motives, which one is accustomed to identifying as the pure economical ones, namely a form of heightened egoism, which cannot be explained by "hedonism" or by eudemonism.

Finally, the phrase "psychology of primitive man," which is accustomed to emphasizing the fact that the economic trading of the "primitive man" significantly differs from the one of the cultivated Indo-European of our days; that the first one shows a peculiar lack of foresight and energy, as well as clear capability of assessment.

These examples could easily be increased; but we want to be content with these, since they sufficiently show us what we mean. Our claim that the same does not interest the scientific psychologist very much refers to these things. They do not belong to his system, but rather to that popular, everyday psychology, which has nothing in common with science. It is a matter of facts of experience that everyone knows and often observes; and they are not supposed to be analyzed any further than the practitioner does.

But then it makes no sense at all to give them a scientific character as a result of one interpreting them as being "psychological ones." This also only happens very frequently in order to cover up their triviality and to confer a higher dignity to many a doubtful claim. We have every reason to attribute distrust to the phrases that fill half-scientific literature under the title of psychological sentences. Many an inexact, illogical claim is sought to be pushed through in this manner.

Our examples show us this very well: the indication of the "psychology of crises" means almost nothing else than that one is not able to give an actual explanation of that peculiar upward and downward movement of the economy. The psychology of the entrepreneur very often serves only for the embellishment of political demands. We will soon say quite a bit about the moment of "effort" and thereby show that we are not mistaking the healthy core that lies in it. However, it is not discounted that they are often absolutely questionable and mostly not very scientific claims, which sail under these colors. Finally, the psychology of primitive man has played a not so meritorious role in literature. Ethnology teaches us that the influence of the environment, etc. does, however, lead to an essentially different mindset and conduct for the primitive peoples than for the civilized peoples, but at the same time, that primitive man is no fool, but rather deals logically within his narrow scope of view. But one has summarized observations under that title, which are supposed to show the inapplicability of the economical sentences to it. This does not apply to the correct understanding of the latter; in fact, it follows that this entire "psychology" is rather irrelevant to us.

But apart from this concern it must be emphasized, and this is the decisive moment, that only the visible *behavior of man*, not his psychological processes are of interest to our purposes. In fact, those psychological statements are only statements about *facts*, about the behavior of crises, about the *behavior* of the entrepreneur or of "primitive man", etc. The psychological manner of expression is only an attachment, does not touch the essence of the matter, and one easily sees that one can replace it with another, without affecting the value of the observations for our area in the least. It solely proceeds from the effort to *explain* the observations. However, this is a vain effort, and if one knows to add nothing else to the simple presentation of a social phenomena than the mere indication of the psyche, and it is nothing more, then one has only produced a tautology, as we have explained at a previous point.

We therefore reach the result that our discipline is currently completely independent of psychology, and whenever it deals with representing this one purely, we can and must disregard the latter and should also avoid every psychological manner of expression. With this reserve, we can then nevertheless make use of this, wherever this is convenient and wherever it does not come down to strict accuracy, but this does not change anything about the principle.

A brief remark may again be made here about ethics. Entirely unharmed by the role of ethical motives for the economic commerce of man, the fact alone, that ethics still currently do not describe must prevent us from dragging the same into an exact discipline. But furthermore, the same considers the commerce of man from another standpoint, even if it is describing, and for other purposes than the economy does. It cannot be foreseen how our results could be influenced by the ones of ethics, and conversely, a claim that cannot bewilder him, who stays current with that, which has been previously said. Specific ethical dispositions belong to the *data* of our problems and cannot be discussed from the latter ones. "Ethical" simply means "non-economical" to some economists. Would it be surprising if this cannot play a significant role in a theory of economizing?

V

What does ethnology now teach us, to which also a portion of the area considered as being "psychology of peoples" is attributed for our purposes? In the economical textbooks, in which one so regularly finds remarks about psychology and biology, this question is most often not treated as "ex professo," even though most of the ethnological facts are utilized. In fact, the attention of the economists has just recently been directed towards this field with the rise of the ethnological literature. One followed the influence of sociology there, which proceeded in this way. The theoretical economists have nevertheless also given rise to it themselves through their preference, the assumption of a simple economic state, which is of great value didactically; although only principally necessary in few cases, it is constructed livelier through the representation of a primitive economy. Instead of admitting that one proceeds on unrealistic assumptions, which scares away so many people, one believed having to make the same more plausible by embellishing them with actual or alleged examples from reality. It is possible that this was practical; it was not very scientific. Aside from the fact that it represents a flaw in a strict system, the imagination was thereby awakened, as if our deductions are dependent on the actual existence of such economies and nothing was more obvious than examining whether the economic process actually ran in the manner for the primitive peoples[2] as the theorists assume. It then followed that those examples, which were mostly just constructed, were actually not completely realized.

Therefore, if there is talk of the economy of primitive people in an economical work, one must strictly distinguish between phrases with which the theorist embellishes his abstract constructions, which furthermore have no significance pertaining to them, and which can by no means be conceived as cultural or economical historical claims and actual, ethnological collections of facts; the latter, as we have said, are becoming more and more common. Ethnologists and sociologists advise us to utilize the ethnological material for our theory, and many current economists, especially German ones, virtually expect the salvation of the same in a restructuring on this foundation. One could speak of an ethnological direction, which appears to steadily gain ground.

Ethnology has recently very much come our way and has turned its attention to the economic relations more than it has done in previous times. For example, the 9th volume of the Ann. Rep. Bur. Ethn. of the Smithsonian Institution contains such material as the economists of that orientation desire. What is to be thought of it now? The reader is able to predict what answer we want to give to this question. The demand of a verification of our fundamental assumptions of the facts of ethnology is based on a misunderstanding of the nature of the same, and we dare to claim that it proceeds from a circle that not only faces the pure economy, but rather the exact approach altogether. The misunderstanding is dual one. For one, we have emphasized again and again—and we believe to have done enough in this direction—that those assumptions do not represent factual statements and can be neither validated, nor confuted by observations from the realm of primitive economizing, but are rather abstract aids, whose only purpose and whose possible service only lies in the fact that a schema for the facts of the price results from it. Even if economical phenomena are introduced into genetic language, so that it appears as if the theorist would want to tell a story about the same, it does not mean that the processes actually ran this way. It is probably of culture-historical and also of sociological interest how these things developed; furthermore, it is important for dynamic problems, but completely irrelevant to our exact system. The theory of money gives us an example of this; the theory of barter gives us another. Some theorists present these things in lively speech, let individuals or hordes, who have been content by themselves until now, meet and readily make transactions. The objection that primitive peoples do not have the conception of barter, but rather that robbery or gifting occurs, is entirely irrelevant if more is intended by it than simply the elimination of that naïve manner of representation. And furthermore, barter, price formation, and the phenomenon of money would not be explained by the prehistorically correct representation. We could not derivate any laws of movement of value from it. This shows better than anything else how different the goals of both sciences are. Let us assume that barter arose from gifting. What does that tell us about the point, which interests us alone, about the relation of exchange? It would at most be interesting to us to know something about the relationship that the gifts of both parts have to one another; and we can at most form a conception about it through economical discussion of theoretical nature. However, we do not need ethnology for it, just as we do not need the history of the earth for pure mechanics.

But the economists of that orientation are still guilty of making a second mistake. Even if our sentences were to require the testing of the ethnological material, one should not act as narrow-minded in doing so, as it occurs. Dominated by the fact, which is obvious to the eye, that the "savage" thinks and acts so very differently from the "cultured man," one explained that the sentences abstracted from the economy of the latter one could not possibly be suitable for the ones of the first. Here, one mentions the phenomenon of the "silent trade," for example. One says that this one and other phenomena do not have an analogy in developing economics, and especially that the "savage" lacks the ability to carry out an exact calculation of value. Similar applies to the European farmer, and the entire argument amounts to limiting the application of the pure economy to modern conditions. This runs parallel to those objections, which were raised by historians, etc., against it, to transfer terms of the modern, economic life to former periods. The same are partially justified. For example, in finance, one must guard against operating with the modern term of tax by the observation of former times. It is very evident that the same is only applicable insofar as no general validity befits the term of the modern state and the sentences, in which it does not play a role. But this does not apply to the foundations of the pure economy. As for so many controversies we must also be aware here of distinguishing the right core of general arguments from the one, which is false about them. Those difficulties that made an agreement so difficult are immediately omitted when we do this. It always depends on the individual case. The fact that the economic process now appears differently on different cultural levels, continues in different forms, changes nothing about its essence. One has no right to smile at the "speculative economist," who realizes the analogousness of essence in the multiplicity of the form of appearance. *Every* act can be brought under the value schema, and if we want to avail ourselves to the psychological manner of expression for the sake of convenience, we can say that *every* act and therefore also every economic one assumes value processes that are as precise in their nature as the ones of the stock broker. If a guest gives a present to the other, then this must either be a completely meaningless gift, which does not play a role for the economy, or a comparison of value must be possible between the gift given and the gift in return. When Cook says that a savage, whom he met somewhere, was so unfamiliar with the process of bartering that he did not want to comprehend at all that he has to forgo the "price commodity," then it is to be commented on it that this savage must have certainly known the "inner barter": he must be clear about whether or not he wants to take on the effort that the bringing down of game requires—and this presupposes valuation processes. By the way, only a misunderstanding of the "causa donationis" was apparently present in this case, which can happen on every cultural level, especially when difficulties in a sense of language are present. But the following two moments are decisive: if one wants to definitely verify our theory by such facts, then one is first off, not allowed to be so narrow-minded as many people are; otherwise, one would also come to the point of denying the law of gravity, because not everybody always and readily falls to the ground. If a "savage" or anyone else would always barter differently as is to be expected according to our rules, for example, always divest oneself of one's commodities without getting something for them, then he would have to quickly perish, and this exception would therefore vanish. The basic principles of our theory presuppose so little that one can go ahead and argue the scarce significance of the exceptions. Of course, one may not count on it too much and every longer development must be verified, which often leads to negative results; we have often emphasized this ourselves, but now we can also say that some of such verification attempts are virtually caricatures of healthy thoughts. But secondly, one must distinguish between the culture-historical *fact of barter*, to stay with our example, which assumes the most diverse forms, which undergoes the greatest changes and can also fail often, and our abstract *barter schema*, which is only a scientific instrument and very generally applicable. How can one mistake the dissimilarity of the two things?

Ethnology is therefore able to offer us very little, but of course, only for the foundations of our static system. It may have a similar position beyond this, just as the economic history and the literature about the current, great problems. What is written in such a "descriptive" book? Well, presentations of facts and theories about actual events. And both are surely of fundamental meaning to the theoretical economist, as soon as he leaves the narrow boundaries of his exact system. Is this position not almost self-evident? But the foundations for *new* theoretical work lie here, by no means for a new construction of *static*. We have already outlined its significance for it; only this should still be added here. But one sees: Brief, general answers to such questions are nowhere; everything depends on the individual case; the same principles can lead to "right" or "wrong" results in different hands, can be fruitful or fruitless. For example, one can expect very much from ethnological material and nevertheless take that position towards some attempts that we have just developed; no contradiction lies in it, and this is ultimately also just self-evident. But we can say this much: all those relationships of the pure economy to other disciplines, which make themselves at home in prefaces and occasional utterances, only have little—or nothing—to give us. In the interest of clarity, it is imperative to emphasize their voidance and to throw this ballast overboard.

Notes

1. Whereby it was useful to him that our formal schema can also be applied quite easily beyond the boundaries of the economy, for example, to ethical actions, etc (Schumpeter, 1908, pg. 541).
2. I sometimes remember a little friend of mine and his desire and wishes to always look underneath the surface.

2

Value of the Pure Economy

I

What we have just presented is everything that we want to say here about the nature of our discipline and about the essence of our pure economical realization. The great question about its *value* arises now. We now know what the theorist actually does, what the core of those abstractions is, at which he slogs away, and now want to ask again whether that, which he achieves is worthy and deserving of the effort and cultivated, known, and worked out to be handed on to our followers; and we believe to have presented what this is in the main point, and we can view it on this level of our discussions and assume it as being known. Is our exact static system an "aere perennius" work, in spite of everything, which can fill us with confidence and will be maintained in the storm of time, or should it be laid to rest and considered a closed matter—with or without regret? Is it similar to a flourishing market place or to a necropolis? Be this as it may, the matter is very deserving of austerity and loyalty, and be it only out of consideration for its circumspection that is devoted to it, and no one who does not give it this right can be spared of a heavy reproach.

Everyone, at least everyone that we can speak to, encounters the question about the value of science altogether in his path through life, and everyone will answer it differently; quite naturally, not only because everyone brings completely different dispositions with him according to aptitude and course of education, but also because everyone has a special purpose in mind as a measurement of value. Some are interested in the great traits of things, some in the details. The first one may claim, for example, that all people are the same, the latter that all are different; an agreement is difficult there, actually impossible, and a substitute for it only lies in the acknowledgement of the difference of the standpoints. A banality is more attractive to one person than the most passionate political speech if it can be expressed in an elegant, exact form; the results of a work survey are more interesting to the other person than the most profound functional-theoretical development. Many demand practical results, rules for concrete action, or at least a practical use altogether; other realizations for their own sake. Just as everyone has his own world, everyone also has his own science: It has a different meaning for everyone, and everyone values what it tells him differently, namely from individual standpoints *and* with individual measurements. This is his good right; *if* there were some "natural right," then it would be certainly be seen in *his* eyes. Only, no one may forget that every retina other than his own gives other pictures. Whoever forgets this is truly the biggest tyrant of all. We are not dealing with this question, but such moments certainly also figure into our problem; and we therefore emphasize again and again that the final judgment is at everyone's own opinion, however, only applies to him, and we can arrogate forcing an absolute result upon the reader just as little as unifying the religious opinions, for example. We are not striving for agreement in regards to the judgment of the value of our discipline, but rather for a better mutual understanding at most, which nevertheless leads to agreement in many, but not all cases. We want to be brief in doing so and limit ourselves to primarily such points, which have a more objective character and are capable of precise treatment; from these again to such, which to us do not appear appreciated, or not appreciated enough.

Some things could certainly also be achieved through general arguments. In this manner, we could surely combat the standpoint of those who, for every theory, primarily or even solely ask about their practical uses. We could present that science is the sole-purpose for us, furthermore, that theories of humanity can achieve greater services through the conveyance of knowledge than through technological successes. Is it not clear that one is not allowed to value, for example, astronomy with *the* value that it has for wave resistance, that the latter would have simply never led to the great structure, which we admire today and of which one can claim that it has impinged upon the entire being and thinking of humanity through the broadening of our mind. Must it always be emphasized that only disinteresting mental work leads to really great achievements, which often also carry practical fruits later on, of which the first pioneers did not think, could not have thought of? It is just as mistaken to demand practical achievements from a young science as allowing a child to work hard; this will damage the child and just lead to insubstantial results after all. We could certainly defend this standpoint with enthusiasm, and we would not fear the answer of the opponents. But we do not want to do that, but rather touch upon general arguments only to the extent that is unavoidable. We also do not want to evade the "begging question"—"what is it good for?"—but also seek to highlight this side of the matter and put the judgment of the reader forward. It is of course even more peremptory to come to a result about whether the theoretical interest of our discipline is a sufficient one: The two questions, to whose answering through the reader we want to offer quite some material, is firstly the one, whether it is worth the effort in our field to even construct an exact system and especially ours—whether the same is sufficiently interesting—and secondly, the one about its practical meaning. A summarizing outline of its boundaries and deficiencies will be added unforcedly and then lead over to that, which then follows, in which we want to talk about the desired reforms and the paths and outlooks of further work.

Firstly, turning to the first question, there is hardly any item in the world about which something general could not be stated. For example, a science about those moments would therefore be possible, which is similar to all ethical judgments, despite the fact that its concrete substance is different according to place, time, cultural state, race, etc. There are certainly moments as such, and it follows from it that there could be exact ethics, which would be strictly descriptive in contrast to the common one that raises demands and falls out of the framework of true science for this reason. But it could come about that the substance of its theorems would be such a "general one," meaning so inferior here, that one is better to abstain from the construction of such a structure; it would be a shaft that leads to nothing. Perhaps this will change in the future, and perhaps this future is imminent; I even believe this with regards to certain, new achievements of sociology; but currently, such exact ethics do not exist yet—*they would not be worth the effort.* I am not sure whether exact psychology of introspective orientation is not also in this position, and is also not able to extract much interest for the friend of exact thought processes the way it is today. Perhaps also, for example, an exact theory of human migrations could be conceivable, and basic approaches are also available for it. Every population movement surely goes about in a way that it can be described in the language of the maximum theorem: It takes place in a direction of least resistance, and it is certainly possible to speak of an ethnological balance, a state, in which any "forces" balance one another, and which strives to maintain itself as long as no cause of disturbance operates "from the outside." But as long as one can say no more than this, someone who wishes to carry on "exact ethnology" will not be found easily, and no one will be able to reproach even the most passionate theorist.

We have instanced these examples for two reasons. Above all, we wanted to emphasize again that "sufficient interest" is just as necessary for the justification of existence of a science as "sufficient power" for the emergence of sovereignty, according to several teachers of constitutional law. The question about its existence is by no means to be confused with the above mentioned "begging question," which opponents, as well as representatives of our discipline, have often overlooked. Is it in such a bad situation as the one of those imaginary, exact theories of ethics or of ethnology? Well, the general answer to this question, as will be easily declared, will be in the negative. We will still engage in it further and highlight it from different angles, but by and large, the core of our argument, which we, as we believe, can offer to the reader with the greatest ease imaginable, can be specified in the following manner: No, the theoretical economy is not as worthless as the indicated types. An actual worthless or nevertheless premature, theoretical structure would look like *these*, and the comparison between both says everything that is essential in this regard, to the extent that another word about it would be superfluous. However, the economy of the "accepted" exact sciences stands just as far as from these, from those that impress the layman. Some of its components apprehensively approach the first ones, some of them the latter ones, and if one is allowed to speak of an average level of our discipline, then one can say that it lies in the middle. So since the judgment about whether or not a discipline is worth something, as we have emphasized, is necessarily subjective, and also the boundary between the worthless and the valuable is not a concrete one here, as everywhere, but is rather a fluid one—even for the individual ones—then that, which has just been said is by no means sufficient for an absolute judgment. But for this reason, one will admit that we have now moved a bit closer to one of such in a natural and inoffensive way. But let us go on.

We are not holding it against anyone if he rejects our theory. If one says that it does not interest him, then not a word is to be uttered. We are reserving to make use of the same right towards other directions. Such judgments do not always flow form mulishness, but rather from subjective impossibilities. But it can occasionally be interesting to hear the justification for the same; firstly, because this difference in opinion gets some color and it's complete meaning through it first, and secondly, because the justification can contain actual claims, about which an exact discussion is possible. As we have said, we would like to contribute to one of such. No one can be understanding of especially the pure theory, which is far off from the exact science and its methods altogether. This is certainly the case now for many colleagues in the field. Many an economic politician or historian, who judges the theory so harshly, would think about exact mechanics in the same way if the firmly-founded character and its connection with the achievements of modern technology would not hinder him from doing so: its pure system and its epistemological premises would interest him little. Many a man, who condemns the modern, nice literature, similarly pays his reverence to the "classical authors"; not because he actually understands them, but rather because the attack on their well-secured position is much more difficult. Some condemned judgment about the value of realization of our discipline, which is justified externally through the reproaches of "speculation," "aprioristic," etc. flows from this source. Such influences will always affect our pathway to clarity impedingly. We can not go into it and relating points again and again, and want to turn to other things, during whose discussion we will have the opportunity to show that we acknowledge that, which is correct in the arguments of the opponents of the theory and their merits, and have actually learned much from it.

It lies in the nature of the matter that in the previous part, we have already said that, which can be led into the field for the theory and which lies in its concrete achievements, and can only add or even summarize very little here. It is the downside that is primarily discussed here, and the reader always has to keep sight on the previous discussions if he wants to render us justice and maintain a passably complete picture in an approximately accurate light. When we view our work, primarily the concern is forced upon us whether we have not abstracted from precisely the most interesting aspect of the things, with which we occupy ourselves, excluded them from our consideration; we cannot deny this—the opponents are right in this regard. Does a rather bare framework not remain in our hands after all the work? It may certainly be correct, logically indisputable, and also, as far as that goes, applicable; one could also object that this is also not certain beyond any doubt—we will still come to this—at any rate, we saw that our rules suffer from many exceptions; but on the whole, I believe to have put aside the most profound concerns in this regard. However, precisely this happened by means of a far-reaching abandonment of content-related, highly significant results, as one will recall. Is that, which we are left with not just as worthless as it is lifeless? It could almost appear this way; it is entirely indisputable this way, in part. That, which is really relevant, which is noticeable through its significance in the chain of causes, which determine the course and the state of the economy, that, for which it is battled and that, which is being discussed lies quite formally in the data of our problems, so outside of our circle of power. The distribution of land and the remaining means of production, the social power relations and forms of organization—these are the factors that control the formation of the economy, and these are, at the same time, those moments that we assume as being given. Everything further follows from them so naturally and almost self-evidently that it is almost forgivable when some overlook that there are still other problems besides those. In this sense, it is not only true, but altogether indisputable that economizing is "historically contingent." In addition, it is of course clear that we are never able to offer anything concrete, but rather always just general realizations, which, on top of everything, are also often still disavowed from reality.

Our response to it is simple. The reader already knows it. Although all of this is true, the theory gives us a group of sustainable and precisely not self-evident sentences. The previous part must speak for itself in this regard. We do not believe that the insignificance of that, which was just said, follow from it, but we do believe that it will be limited to its true content. Accurately conceived, it does not contradict the famous statement that whoever has grasped the theory of value, has thereby also understood all economizing. It suffices to realize that the authors of both of such seemingly contradicting dicta—*this one* and the one about the historical contingency of economizing—thought about different problems, in order to easily be able to combine them. A small area still remains that is contained and can be described by a single, great principle of clarification, an area that carries significantly more fruits than perhaps an exact ethnology. The difference primarily lies in the fact that at first glance, there is a phenomenon of great importance, which can be described exactly and generally, namely the price relation. Its significance is still heightened by the fact that its schema, in which the theory grasps it, can be easily and naturally broadened to the phenomena of the commerce-less economy, and thereby gains a high universality, which is a fact of great, very great significance, despite the necessary limitation, which we have already emphasized often and will soon touch upon again.

Two other moments are still added: First and foremost, it can be shown and we have shown that the price relation contains all factors in itself, which are necessary to distinctly determine themselves and to derivate a single state of equilibrium and also, under the same requirements, the quantities of goods that must find themselves in the possession of the regarded economic subjects; also that, under limitations, which reduce the significance of this moment, but do not destroy it. And this does not already follow by itself from the "historically contingent" facts of the organization, of the milieu, etc.—if it appears this way to some, then a *verifiable fallacy* lies in it—but is rather a result of our theory, which it possesses from its own strength and with good reason: Solely with *its* means can it not only be made plausible, but also be *proven*. This has a dual meaning, a dual value of realization—we will get to the question whether it also has a practical one and which one it has later: For one, it is an interesting truth in itself. We see here with a type of clarity, for whose beauty one may, however, have more or less understanding, that there is a type of logic of facts in our field, whose pressure must be felt by everyone, and we certainly obtain a contribution to the understanding of economical events from this source. But thereupon, precisely the "evidence through action" lies in it, that these things form one, self-contained whole, to which exact forms of thought are applicable, despite their seeming "unpredictability." And this is a scientific fact of an importance that can hardly be overestimated, as it has already been emphasized. We do not want to emphasize this too much; because one can nevertheless think very differently about it, and we would like to avoid compromising our representation through inexact moments at all costs. May the reader therefore see for himself what he wants to do with this suggestion; just let him not *overlook* it, despite its brevity. A gap exists in the scientific worldview there, where man stands. The mere fact of the applicability of exact methods is therefore very important here, even if the results of the same were to only be insignificant. It nevertheless opens up significant outlooks and possibilities. *And to us, the upmost interest of the pure economy seems to lie in it, that is represents an expansion of the area of exact thinking*. Of course, this judgment is subjective in part, and we do not want to force it upon anyone to that extent; others, along with A. Marshall, for example, like to search for the value of the theory elsewhere. But under all circumstances, that, which is being discussed, is also a not too neglected moment. And it seems to me that one can defend the demand of the pure economy for acceptance better from it than from some other one, namely better than from the "practical one."

One point has yet to be added to the far-reaching universality and to the distinct determination of our state of equilibrium. It allows for different applications and provides the same results, of which not every value of realization is to be deprived. The monetary theory, the distribution theory, certain laws of movement of prices, these are the most important examples. One will be able to maintain the claim that the contributions of the theory are only difficultly dispensable for the discussion of these topics, and its lack of knowledge in many points, which do not, however, have to step forth often, involves a significant disadvantage to a clear understanding. One may attribute a greater or lesser significance to it, and the same will surely vary case by case, but one will indeed occasionally claim that one is able to manage completely without it, but everywhere there, where realization and not so much the solution to practical problems is at stake, one will most often or nevertheless quite often not be able to prove it.

This is *one* of the sides of this argument. The other exists in the following: Our system, which is so universally valid theoretically, whose elements are distinctly determined, and whose applications nevertheless contain a healthy core, which significantly stretches beyond the area of implicitness—this system covers an enormously great amount of facts and is in a closer connection with reality than it is perhaps apparent to the opponent of the theory, who is shocked by its apparatus. We had to again emphasize the opposite in contrast to other theorists and in substantial agreement with the opponents of the theory. Above all, we were necessitated to eliminate many allegations of the elder and even some of the modern economists from the theory as not corresponding to reality, like the hypothesis of the individual egoism, or to restrict in a way that they lost their most interesting content, like the maximum theorem and the theses that pertain to free competition. This has been done and we are not speaking of it here. Thereupon, we saw that our static system does not explain all economic phenomena by far, not, for example, interest and entrepreneurial profit, not even all possible types of price formation and everything that is important to the latter in its simplest form; moments that belong here will come up for discussion immediately and then at another point once again. Finally, it continuously occurred that even the accurate results of the theory in themselves did not quite sufficiently sustain themselves in the reality of the facts, for example, in the wages theory—yes, nearly everywhere to a certain extent. But especially the opponent of the theory, whose great merit was to give the same its right, overlooks these kinds of considerations too easily, that the amount of facts, which unforcedly falls in line with the schema of the theory, is an extraordinarily great one in spite of everything. This is the great mass of phenomena of everyday life, that, which one can see daily and everywhere, and from which one knows that it happened daily and everywhere, and will repeat itself just the same with great certainty. Precisely this "everyday occurrence" in the true sense of the word effectuates that these things are less noticeable to us than others that are fewer and less important, to the extent that one overlooks them and is little inclined to give an account about it, just as how one does not give thought to the nonetheless so unusual phenomena of digestion or of sleep in everyday life. This entails that many people are not able to give special interest to the discussion of those economical phenomena, "which every cook is well acquainted with," and so often find the lecture of a book about pure economy boring: Because the things that it deals with are so banal; one therefore believes that every representation of the same could also only be banal. But in this connection it is an argument *for* us, and more strikingly shows than everything else how broad the bases of our system are. They are much broader than it would be necessary, broader and more reliable than we can strictly prove, and maintain themselves better than our suppositions had speculated, to which we attached such a great number of reserves for the sake of strict correctness.

So if one says that our system of equilibrium portrays precisely that, which is banal or even self-evident and abstracts from everything really interesting, then this is only a half-objection. The interesting thing is the unusual thing, and then every sentence *partially* amounts to acknowledging that we are actually grasping the common thing, the regular thing, in short, the great mass of those phenomena that we want to grasp anyway. The scientific significance of our discussions therefore even gains something by it—it is admitted that only a relatively small, although precisely therefore noticeable arrearage of "price facts," in our sense, inexplicably remains behind. But only partially, as we have said, does this save the value of our discipline, and we are far from denying that this argument is double-edged. The fact still remains that precisely those things, for which our system is customized, very much withdraw from interest vis-à-vis other scientific and social phenomena. How insubstantial our picture of reality looks next to the colorful fullness of life, which presents itself when we look around us! The great questions of life, of time, the problems of the past and future, which force themselves upon us there, cannot fail to fascinate us. And then precisely the newest progresses of the pure theory of static teach us that we cannot understand anything, nothing at all, or as good as nothing about the same from it. The attempts of the older economists have deplorably failed, and we cannot do more, as economic theorists, than to prove just that exactly. Those great analyses of economics, which have occasionally been attempted from the pure economic standpoint, are especially instructive, for example, Marx's and many others. We cannot go into an evaluation of the same here, namely also not touch upon their merits, which we do not completely deny. But I believe, the final result was nevertheless always a negative one, and only a few will dispute that the insufficiency of the foundation thereby arose. One has deviated from it today, and even though almost every textbook attempts such an analysis, it does also pull forth other and even formally different means than those, which the economic theory offers in our sense. We cannot even think about grasping the problems of the races and classes, and the great questions of politics, the magnitude and the reduction of the peoples, their hopes and aspirations, and the dangers that threaten them, their past and future, from our standpoint. And all these things nevertheless have their economic aspect, of which one will be easily convinced. We will discuss this with greater benefit if we speak of the "practical" value of our system, but they already had to be mentioned here. We like to admit that the most interesting problems of the social sciences lie in them, that they attract the intent look with a magical force, and that we cannot blame he, who forgets our theory due to their magnitude.

But this is not even everything. The common course of the economy is also full of life and movement and grasped in continuous development. We now helplessly stand vis-à-vis the developmental phenomenon and the "great problem" of the economic progress. Not only this makes the grasping of highly-important, economic phenomena, which appear daily and never fail, impossible for us now, as we have seen and will touch upon again; but also our picture of everyday life, to the extent that we portray it, is in danger of being virtually falsely convicted, since it feigns a resting state to us, which never and nowhere exists. What pitiful countenance our economic subject, who nervously searches for the balance, is, without ambition, with no initiative, in short, without strength and life! And where are all the wants and actions that also raise everyday life out of the dust?

More can be replied to it, even if there is certainly something true about it. We want to sharply contrast one and the other against one another. As a side-remark, the reader is able to see here in how complicated a manner the threads of opposing arguments are engulfed, and how easy it is to go too far to one side, how much patience and love for the matter belongs to it, in order to push towards the truth. The following can be *replied* and instanced *for* the value of realization of our system: As good as everyone is such a boring "balanced-person" for the greatest period of the common life by far. Everyone only braces oneself up for energetic wants, for new paths in certain cases, which carry an exceptional characteristic vis-à-vis the numerous daily events. This may appear obvious, but it is well-founded. Precisely the stir that deviation causes from that, which someone "commonly" does and which one expects from it with great certainty, proves it. After quite some pondering, one will be—perhaps not without surprise, but certainly sure—that we only actually *live* in relatively seldom moments, but otherwise "mechanically" chip away at the common workday. Of course, no one does this completely. We cannot assume this of anyone, especially from our standpoint, since we have already conceived the production of a new tool and similar things as an extraordinary event. We have therefore always attached great importance to emphasizing that our system is only applicable to very short time periods. From these, we can claim that nothing of the sort happens without going very far astray. In any longer one, in which the energy of the individual one, as well as that of the masses has time to, so to speak conglobate to jump, it generally does not work. New pathways will be pursued there, which change the foundations of our system. But within all of our suppositions, the same actually cover the great mass of phenomena. In addition, we still have a reserve in *one* regard: We have suggested a method, according to which it is possible to circumvent the suppositions of a pure hedonistic-egoistic method. The effects of non-economic motives, etc., can be included in our value functions to a certain extent. As the reader knows—our economic subjects are not complete calculating machines; but it is however a bureaucratic, quietist, narrow-minded world that we are sketching, or better, it is precisely the quietist, narrow-minded *aspect* of the commerce of man, which is reflected in our picture. But this aspect simply is important. Even if it is not everything, it is nevertheless much, if not the most shimmering, then nevertheless the broadest problem, that, which must be solved first and must be understood before one can continue, that, which consciously or subconsciously is never lost sight of and can never be lost. It is the great headquarter, from which all "interesting" movements begin, and they are simply interesting and unusual in comparison to it. This is the aspect that would offer itself to the unbiased observer—to a being that would not know anything about the trading by man yet—would especially offer itself at every given moment, and whose laws can be verified the easiest.

In fact, while being eager to emphasize the counter-instances, one overlooks how strikingly our system of equilibrium can be verified. The laborer generally goes to his daily work rather "mechanically," in the same manner and with the same dispositions as yesterday. The civil servant goes into his office in also the same manner, the merchant to his market stall, may the same be located in the "Kaffir-Circus," in the stock-exchange in London, or in the fruit market of a small city; and what all of them experience there daily is by and large the same as yesterday, and every novelty is noticeable and encounters a significant resistance. Of course, everyone speaks about the changes that are consummatory to himself, and if one were to believe him, then one would have to believe that all economic relations change daily from the ground up. Not only the man in the practice of economic life—and every housewife—believes this, but also the agitator and the politician. But that is not the case: The things only change slowly; their essential characteristics even slower. It is based on a fallacy in a large part, if one speaks of ground-breaking developments within a few years. This is recollecting of the popular belief, which one can hear so often, that the climate has recently significantly changed. But it should not have changed at all according to current belief of the circle of experts in historical times. The changes that take place are certainly not complete, but significantly more than one believes, in words, in the popular—for us, unfortunately also the scientific—phrases; and even these remain the same in a surprising way. They are always the same arguments and fears that we hear and that are hardly ever actualized de facto; namely, it is an old trick of the parties to accuse one another of *changed* behavior, *new* demands, where opposing class-interests collide. One always believes to possess an especially effective counter in it. A classical example is the relationship between servants and their employers. The latter ones claim that the first ones now behave differently than a short time ago. But a bit of contemplation teaches that considering the fact that the character of this employment *slowly* changes, that combinations within the same are difficult, and finally, that many servants considering their occupation as only being a transitional stage can insist less energetically on an improvement of their position than other laborers; at most, this position goes along with the progresses of other working classes, but can in no way stand at the top of the upward movement. It can actually also be shown that all essential characteristics, for example, the long labor period per day, can by and large have changed only a little, also vis-à-vis the middle-ages and even antiquity. And furthermore, one also sees how the smallest *actual* change causes the greatest stir, leads to the liveliest discussion, and therefore often attains undeserving distinction—especially when worried interests of property are considered. One could certainly go too far with this thought process; especially we, who cannot explain this enough, are exempt from such a suspicion and perhaps even misunderstanding of different kinds; but if one believes that we have gone too far, then one should consider that we want to help *one* neglected aspect of the matter to justice, while to us, the *other* one seems to be sufficiently appreciated. We have always emphasized which limitations the applicability of our raisonnement is subjected to and will do it again soon; but here, it was about time to emphasize that our system nevertheless maintains itself, although not *as good* as the theorists most often believe; can survive better than its opponents believe. What one may think about our argument, in turn, depends on personal opinions. We are satisfied when one admits that some truth lies in it.

We only want to mention one more point. As we have seen, our theory is based on those connections between the quantities of goods, which the individuals possess, and which we considered to be the law of the marginal utility niveau—the law of the marginal utility level. We said that the entire pure economy lies in a nutshell within the same. Now, this fundamental theorem can be easily verified. A great fact suits it. It is the fact of the budgets' constancy of most people by far, the fact that as good as everyone tends to consume the same goods in always the same quantities within long enough periods—periods, which are long enough to be interesting—as well as how one by and large extraordinarily, tenaciously adheres to ones productive activity. One can speak about laborers' budgets and easily construct types for every place and every time, which, whatever one may say, sufficiently correspond to reality; and the same also holds true for other classes than the ones of the laborers. Of course, differences exist there, and the construction of types will not be easy everywhere; but for every individual one, there is a rather set budget—one only has to ask oneself—or, as one can also say, one and only *one* rather set production and consumption combination, a very constant standard of life. Let us also not exaggerate this fact; there are many significant limitations that would have to be made, namely there is simply, in no way such a fixed standard for *everyone*; but all of this does not destroy the great scientific significance of this fact, and no generous criticism will contest with us that a sufficient verification of the theory's main content lies in it. If one accepts this—and we have the best hope pertaining to this—then one will also agree with us when we say that the great phenomenon alone suffices in carrying a scientific structure, and this latter one is of value, even if it did not describe anything else at all other than this one moment. But one can by no means reproach us with the claim that the ground, in which the theory anchors, is an insignificant and worthless one.

So this is what one can present *for* our system, and *something* is undoubtedly won by it. If one had ever appropriately pondered that, which has been said, then, I believe, one could have never gone so far in the rejection of the theory. But, it is now incumbent upon us to also acknowledge on our part that something of truth, even much of truth lies in the arguments of the opponents. We have already emphasized this so often ourselves in individual cases that we only want to suggest two moments of the reader's attention here. One of them is hardly more than a banality: Namely all that has been said does not completely help us, but rather only partially beyond the indisputable fact that our picture itself, as far as it even reaches, is incomplete and does not contain a series of important phenomena. Its exceptional characteristic is only halfway comforting when faced with the indisputable interest of these exceptions. We cannot regard the same as being a "quantité negligeable"—or nevertheless only from the standpoint *of our* results—but must rather admit that their study is necessary and interesting, because they are in no way inclined towards balancing one another or disappearing, but are rather the foundation of constant developments; and we cannot forebear to grasp the standpoint of those who smile at our theory, even if we do not share it for the instanced reasons. We have thereby already touched upon the second moment that is important here: The economic development and all the more significant causes for disturbance of the state of equilibrium—meaning all with the exception of errors, etc.—lead away from the latter without there being a tendency to come back to it. It is therefore not an abstract, but a nevertheless always available gravitation center of the "economic powers." However, we are certainly not describing a concrete state of the economy, but rather a formal one, which we can always observe, even at every moment of the liveliest development, things, which actually remain constant, just as the concrete data change. But one can still not say that our state of equilibrium resembles the level of a sea that is constantly disturbed, yet constantly strives to produce itself, yes, seen from a sufficient distance, constantly offers a picture of tranquility: The waves of the sea come back to the level of the same, but not the waves of the economic life; and despite that, which we have said above, the economic development continues faster than, for example, geological changes or even systematic changes of the astronomical bodies. It therefore has a much greater significance to man than this one, and it is unavoidable that the intent look falls upon it. The dynamic phenomena therefore play a larger role than in the one of other exact disciplines, in relation to the static ones in our field—this remains in effect, despite our previous argument. From there now surely follows a great limitation of our system's value of realization, and also a, if perhaps only gradual, then still not any less significant difference vis-à-vis its exact relatives. The comparison with pure mechanics is more comforting: This one is also just an insubstantial picture of colorful, vigorous nature—and yet, who will reproach it with it?

From all of this, in cohesion with our discussions of concrete problems, however, the reader may now form a verdict about our discipline's value of realization. I believe that one will not rebuke me for the indeterminateness of the result and the many "ifs", "buts," "howevers," "then agains"; this was intentional and can, in my opinion, bring more use than finished, brief, general claims, which can indeed be countered so easily. The reader finds enough of *such* in our literature. Here, we wanted to try it differently for once. What we believe to have shown is only that a ray of realization proceeds from our theory. One may think differently about it, and we have *therefore* only offered material, not an absolute opinion; but the reader should *feel* its presence.

II

Let us complete that, which has been said through yet a few words about the question what significance approaches our system for the solving of practical questions. We thereby want to deposit a moment—an important, too little appreciated one, and reserve a later discussion. Here we understand the problems of practical politics, etc., by those practical questions. Now, in principle, we do not think highly of that, which can currently arise for it from pure economic contemplations. Bearing in mind the strict lessons, which the history of our discipline has given us in this regard, we therefore want to rather be too careful than too sanguine, all the more as we believed to have observed, not without concerns, that the theorists, in turn, stand at the point of forgetting the same, or more correct, that they have never sufficiently paid heed to the same. One only slowly manages to push oneself through to the yet unavoidable renunciation, and the number of the entirely irreproachable works in this regard is still deplorably scarce.

So let us immediately say that we agree with the opponents of the theory to a great extent. The practical applications of the same are partially based on misunderstandings of their methods and on misjudgment of their task. What we thereby reproach the opponents with is that they concluded the worthlessness and even falsehood of the theory from it. But we do not want to repeat this, but rather only briefly summarize our results concerning this matter. They are supposed to be offered to the reader without further justification, since we, tired of the endless mistakes and the failed attacks that followed, doubt to convert anyone to our point of view anyhow. We can communicate with the historian, but not with the politicizing theorist. Whoever wants to absolutely solve the greatest questions using the pure theory as a starting point—he resembles Ikarus in an alarming way—or whoever does not use theory at all, in order to utilize it for the political discussion, is its worst enemy. It is based upon a *misjudgment* of the essence and the tasks of the theory if one wants to demand something, or justify or attack something due to the same. The reader knows well enough how much the theorists have sinned and are still sinning in this regard; that this contradicts the essence of a strict science and that we do not want to have anything to do with it, but especially that such aberrations can be separated from the theory, and that this does not stand and fall with them, we do not need to develop all of this again, regardless of how lively we wish that the reader imprints these points on his memory. It is also a *misunderstanding* of the essence and also of the methods of the pure economy if one applies its terms and theorems outside of its closest field and especially to reality, without further ado. This is nevertheless more forgivable. The same can be observed in all areas: The first glimpse of a new realization gives rise to fulsome hopes, and one overestimates the significance of that, which has been achieved; and this also has its advantages, but the disillusion is unavoidable and it will be necessary to decide on painful abandoning. This is also the case for us. We must be clear about the fact that we cannot solve the great problems of our time from our standpoint. Some strategist, Napoleon or another one has said that during war, everything depends on having the superior forces at the right moment. A good word, which we also want to be able to say to ourselves: It makes no sense to attack great problems with insufficient means, and the secret of scientific success also lies in encountering such only then, when we can cope with them. It is not the pure economy, because its weapons are not even made for this. Believing that *our* atomistic term of economics tells us something about its actual life and weaving, or that our maximum theorem is adequate for social politics, means misunderstanding both.

But even there, where not such misunderstanding is committed, the attempt to gain much for "practice" from the theory must currently fail. What do we want to say about, for example, the problem of British Imperialism? Only truisms or inexact philosophies would be our offers; but can we not contribute to certain special questions of that great problem, for example, to the fiscal problem? Certainly, and we will come to this shortly; but one may not forget that, which we have already highlighted in the section about the variations method, namely the static character of these contributions. The same entails that we can always just grasp the direct effects of the things, and exposes us to the objection that we are missing the decisive point. We are then in the unenviable position of having to let ourselves be told that we are considering the things from a worm's-eye view and in the most short-sighted manner imaginable. What does it matter if a tariff directly "damages" someone, where the future of the nation is at stake? What use is the exact verification to us that a socio-political invasion lessens the maximum utility of the parties concerned—even in a case where it really works—if we have to sit with a "ceteris paribus"? "Cetera" do not simply remain the same, are not supposed to remain the same. We are examining the effect of a tax. These examinations cause the politicians, who have appropriately learned from the economist, to very much be for conservative budgets; justifiably in part. It is certainly true that boundless expenditures eventually will reach the limit of that, which is possible, and steadily increasing taxes will have to become alarming. But to the extent that something true lies in it, this is indeed self-evident; we need the economy just as little for it as the private citizen needs it, in order not to be a squanderer; and on the other hand, the social politician will smile about it: he surely does not want the things to remain the way they are, he wants to continue on, higher up—and our tactical position will again not be an advantageous one.

But for virtually all questions of the industry and its development, the matter is the following: The interests that come into play, due to the combinations of the individual ones to groups, among others, are so great that the people and the state must take it well or badly. Trusts, etc., must be impinged upon, it must be arbitrated between laborers and entrepreneurs, new outlets must be established, possibly with force, and occupational opportunities must be made available for the industry through the state and its diplomacy. The acquired orders must be distributed more or less arbitrarily, and frequently according to non-economical points of view, etc. There simply is no other way for all of this, and it is completely pointless to argue about whether it is good or bad, vis-à-vis this. The facts are more powerful than the principles, and the most vigorous doctrinaire could not do otherwise but put all those tasks on familiar terms and conduct industrial expansionism, etc., when put in the relevant position. But if we want to have the courage of truth, all of this means not much less than that our theory, insofar as it is well justified, fails vis-à-vis the most important phenomena of the modern economic life. In the great battle of the world market, which is led with such different means, the future has the say, and our system becomes silent. *If* it achieves something, then it is only the fact that it teaches us, especially in its exact form, to separate the individual moments that it comes down to with clarity, and not to confound them, as it usually almost always happens; it can do this up to a certain degree: The differentiation between static and dynamic, and the specification of the necessary data of our system already achieve much there; but that is also it.

We are also unfortunately not in a position to let the reader have much hope for the current development of our science in this direction. Those problems are certainly not hopelessly difficult; but we believe that *our* discipline, the pure economy, will never achieve anything substantially better for it. To step back, not move forward is offered here in our opinion; sincere renunciation "sans phrase." We will get to know another direction, in which a developmental opportunity seems to present itself to us—but *those* problems will probably be forever unworldly to us. I believe we can only answer one thing to the question what the pure economy has to achieve for the questions of practice: There is a series of very special problems of practice, which the theory can solve in many cases. These are those complicated questions of the price formation, for which an exact expansion of the general rules of logic, a type of special "logic of prices," is not worthless. We have gotten to know examples. Of course, data from reality are always necessary, and *if* the same are given, then the result also often arises entirely on its own; but nonetheless not always, and one will not be able to completely deny merits of the theory here; it is nevertheless possible to add a series of corrections to the popular discussion of these things in this manner. The reader knows that we are talking about the complicated applications of the variations method here; but is that really all? What we can say about the essence of the branches of income, does this not have a practical significance? It hardly does, apart from the fact that this realization enables us to apply that method. The result is certainly interesting, just as the distinct determination of wages and rent. But what use is that to the practitioner? The fact that they are economically explainable gives no higher dedication to incomes as some theorists believe. The first one will be very indifferent to whether he can directly influence the distribution of income or only by changing the "data of the system," if an exertion of influence is even possible. We have seen that from the economical derivation of incomes that a "justification" or even its absolute "necessity of nature" does in no way yet follow; and if the owners of the sources of income would not defend themselves, then they would protect our discussion very little from socio-political intrusions; and this is the situation for all of our theorems; they are interesting, scientific results and promising beginnings of further development. But let us suffice with that and let us not expose them to the endurance test of practical applications—they cannot endure it: They are observation towers, not fortresses; they cannot endure a bombardment.

A brilliant man has once expressed his astonishment about the fact that the practitioner most often understands nothing about theory; the theorist understands nothing about practice. This is extraordinarily relevant. The greatest statesmen and business people are often agnostic about the most elementary things in a very astonishing way, not only about the pure theory, but also about phenomena that *directly* concern them. The best men of action have written the worst critiques about economic questions, and have given speeches that would not withstand cool scrutiny. But this cannot surprise us, and we will not rate it *according to this*; that, which we would expect is much more straightforward. One can indeed also digest very well without knowing that one even has a stomach, and we know that correct thinking is by far not necessary for correct action, as one believes: The motives and the principles that are *conscious* to the doer are often other than those, which actually guide him. It would be terrible if we had to first teach the economic subjects their action. We want to learn from them, meaning to characterize their doings to our intellectual satisfaction. Our sentences must be partially self-evident and partially incomprehensible. It will signify the dawn of a new period for the social sciences, when this will someday be accepted on all sides.

3

Once More the Boundaries and Defects of the Economy

I

We want to present the boundaries and defects of the theoretical economy once more, according to its current condition, before we move on to that, which we wish to say about the necessary reforms, the question about the direction of further work, and several developmental possibilities. We will thereby in a sense proceed somewhat differently than during the discussion of the value of realization of our discipline. While we left the final judgment to the discretion of the individual *there* and only made the effort of fully and truthfully presenting its so to speak material substrate, we believe that *here*, not only the layman, but also the expert of another orientation must surrender the reigns to he, who devotes his entire strength to the theory and knows its structure exactly. So there, the pros and cons are supposed to be represented in a corresponding relationship; here, brief and precise answers are supposed to be given to the reader to questions, which he is justified in directing to us. We want to suggest a ready standpoint to him in these questions, something that he can adhere to, in our opinion. But here as there, we are constructing our views in front of the eyes of the reader, and are making an effort in being careful, but also reliable. But we do not want to create as many words here as there, but rather be as brief and dry as possible.

After all that has been said, we can present the boundaries of the pure economical realization, which makes our static system possible, without further justification in approximately the following manner. Our area *positively* reaches as far as the applicability of our *barter schema*, as we want to repeat again; so in one regard further than the phenomenon of prices in the typical sense of the word, especially also into the field of the commerce-less economy and even beyond that of the economic processes. The latter point is, however, of relatively little importance; the results that are thereby attainable hardly deserve an elaboration, or not to the extent of the economic ones after all. But in another regard, our area does not reach as far as the barter; because we can by no means explain *everything* about the barter altogether, and also not all bartering relations and all types of the price formation. Only as far as the economic "everyday life" goes, especially the great factum of the *constancy of the budgets*, does one get by with our picture of reality. One can then express this more precisely, in that this picture is useful insofar as *the assumption of continuously and always decreasing marginal utility functions* do not collide with reality. It cannot be emphasized often enough that all concrete prices can in no way be described on this basis. Our reduction of the entire pure economy to the barter relation will already meet with opposition; but the claim that was just constructed will be even more noticeable; and yet to us, both seem to be essential for the correct understanding of the economy.

A delimitation of our area already lies in it. We still want to *negatively* complete the same by indicating those moments, at which we notice its failure, meaning so to speak its boundary stones. This is also just a repetition. We have established four of such boundaries. They are the following: *firstly* and above all, the *data* of a problem also always represent its boundaries and those of the method, with which the same is solved. But *our* data were the value functions, in which the entire nature of the economic subjects were reflected—their race, history, etc.—as we explained, a given geographical milieu—climate, composition of the ground, etc.—a specific organization of our individuals—state, law, economic organizations of every kind, etc.—and finally, a given distribution of *all* goods—as well as of all productive and consumption goods. The last-mentioned limitation is insofar the most important one to us as it is often overlooked, and in this sharpness that was first worked out by us, it represents a very serious and perhaps peculiar limitation of our area. It is so important to the evaluation of our system and for the understanding of some points of the methods controversy that it is recommended for the reader's attention again. *secondly*, one of the boundaries of our system that it is a practice of many and is to be very much emphasized vis-à-vis most economists in its descriptive, meaning, strictly scientific character, which excludes value judgments and demands; *thirdly*, in its formal and *fourthly*, in its static nature. These boundaries entail that nothing about concrete conditions of the economy can be contained in our theorems *in themselves*, and that they generally fail for the phenomenon vis-à-vis the development. We do not want to elaborate these things any further; that, which has been said, only represents a resume of previously won realizations, and the same also applies to the following.

If we ask about the *defects* of the economical theory, then we must carefully separate two different types of the same, namely those, which cling to the prevalent scheme and those, which cling to the theory itself, quasi inhere to it and cannot be removed or are only difficult to remove. We want to sum them up separately, and very much regret that this did not always happen.

The number of the first ones is significant. They are to be grouped in the following manner. We saw that this scheme above all, contains quite a number of *worthless* constituent parts. As examples, let certain parts of the monetary theory, certain discussions about economizing, about transportation and the insurance industry, furthermore, things that one could consider as perhaps the "study of trading," be mentioned. Thereupon, it contains *non-pertinent* elements. The same can be combined into two groups. The common justification attempts of incomes can be considered as the type of one of them, considerations about climate, question of race, etc., can be the type of the other. We are not theorists at all for the first one; for the latter one, we are probably theorists, but dilettantes. The theory of population partially belongs here. Thirdly, if we now skip to the actual economic theory, we detect an entire series of sentences, which one could consider as perhaps being "*weak points*." If one recollects, for example, the theory of interest, the theory of capital formation, the theory of entrepreneurial profit, apropos also others—the common monetary theory certainly belongs here, but it is on the point of outgrowing this stage. But one can still enqueue the quantity theory today—and one could have just recently enqueued the theory of ground rent into a fourth category, in which the "dead points," by which we mean the topics about which an endless discussion is led, whose arguments constantly repeat themselves without any type of progress being noticeable. One will partially count the theory of population, and nevertheless the "iron law of wages," hereunto. A fifth group of defects is of another type: It repeatedly occurs that one and the same representation contains thoughts, which jar with one another, as for example, a classic theory of ground rent and in addition, another theory of entrepreneurial profit that is based on the moment of differential rent. Even the acceptance of the modern abstinence theory and the adherence to the classic theory of ground rent can also not comport with that. Furthermore, the theory of interest, precisely in most recent times, is overrun with such mistakes, and the striving to highlight the phenomenon of interest from all sides, or better, to cover up the lack of a satisfactory explanation through the accumulation of explanation *attempts*, has led to aberrations in this direction. These are only some symptoms of the deplorable fact that not every economist appropriately reflects about his system and is sufficiently clear about the nature and the mutual relationship of his theories. Instruments of different origin and different age are used side by side. In the works of authors, whose primary interest does not apply to pure theoretical questions, different systems of our discipline are confounded, which do not abreast in their developmental process, but are determined to take turns. For the most part, no conscious and beneficial unification of different standpoints, just as we aspire to them, lies in it, but rather, as we have repeatedly shown, a misjudgment of their differences, a *mistake* that is extremely damaging to the discussion and also stands in the way of clarity and unity of our system. While some inconsiderately and uncomprehendingly drag along new skills, others drag along old skills "in infinitum."

Examples for this already offer themselves to us in the most superficial overview, in the outer appearance of our science. In order to name only *one* important one: one still adheres to the old classification of our theory today, into the sections of production, consumption, of trade and distribution. But production and distribution are based on trade, as far as it comes into consideration for us, they *are* simply just bartering acts, and the consumption does not offer us any interesting sentences, if one does not think of culture-historical and psycho-physical discussions for a "consumption theory." This classification is therefore entirely inapplicable and shows with alarming clarity that some economists, who *classify* and *judge* the theory, do not quite know what it is actually about; regardless, it lives on.[1]

That, which was last said leads to the sixth point of our criticism: Finally, the common methods are *inadequate*. We only want to stress two instances and forgo other points; above all, that method of word discussion, of the revision of conception, that method, which gives itself away though the introduction: "in which meanings does one use this or that word?" We are certainly not denying that many of the best thoughts of our science, actually the most, appear in this form, and that this method for many a good achievement is nothing more than a figure of speech, for which it therefore only has the meaning of an imperfection and does not touch its essence. But in principle, one can only consider them as being deplorable and will also have to see one of the reasons in it, as to why economic discussions impress the layman, as well as the educated public so little. Thereupon, we would like to point out, although with all reserve, that for more complicated problems, there, where the language does not suffice, the economists avail themselves to a highly primitive aid, namely the construction of tables of concrete numbers. Ricardo already does this, and this has become very common today. This is also just an imperfection for the time being; but these tables furthermore complicate an exhausting representation of the problems and easily lead to incorrectness, which would avoid the language of higher analysis. If one is already conducting theory, then one should also do this as correctly and completely as possible and not be left behind that, which can be achieved.

Let us now move on to those defects, which are inherent to our system, which still exist then, when it is represented completely accurately. There are also many of them, and not all of them can be stated again here. Only the following may be summarized here. Above all, some "boundaries" of the system are to be mentioned there, and many a thing that is a "weak point" for the common scheme and is being excluded from static can therefore be considered as a defect of *our* system as well, although from another title, because we can only partially excuse ourselves with "excluding," when "solving" is demanded of us. It is probably of little use in itself to complain about that, which one cannot attain; but this does not prevent that for every theoretical system, it is more or less reproached for its failures and testifies against it especially then, when its acceptance or rejection is at stake. It is just that these defects are inalterable.

In this sense, one will certainly reproach us for the fact that we are constructing a system, which does not explain several very important and undeniably purely-economical phenomena, especially capital interest and entrepreneurial profit; and we respond by stating that we just cannot do differently and feed with hopes of "dynamic." However, a further comfort lies in the fact that we, as we believe, are then able to grant a far more suitable approach to these problems, but these are painful deficits for static, and this one alone has already been worked out halfway satisfyingly today, so that we almost have to identify it as "theoretical economy" altogether.

It furthermore fails vis-à-vis *every* phenomenon, which can only be conceived from the standpoint of the development, as the ones, which were mentioned in our opinion.[2] The problems of capital formation and others, especially the one of economic progress and crises belongs there. Especially the latter must be emphasized, since we have not mentioned it until now: The static systems and its methods do not give us a means of explaining this phenomenon. Just as there would be no interest, there would also be no crises under the requirements of static, even though some *effects* of the same can be demonstrated by it quite well: In a static economy, there is no room for those moments, which cause a crisis, and all crisis theories, whatever their nature or value may be, are essentially "dynamic."

In connection with it, it also states that we cannot even adequately treat the recompensation of capital; that our people, strictly speaking, are not allowed to alter or otherwise change themselves, that great changes in ownership[3] of land and capital, which would result in a change in the direction of production, cannot take place, that the savings activity must keep itself within narrow limits, that we cannot do justice to the law of increasing production return, insofar as it can function as an element of progress and influence the size of the "real incomes," etc. Now, all of this is not as despairing as it appears. If one considers that our system only applies to every given moment, and if one also knows that everything that our system limits in principle and according to its essence, and because were are primarily concerned with the realization of its essence, we have so distinctly emphasized this; but nothing prevents us from going somewhat beyond it in practice, if one only remains aware that one thereby carries out *further*, more audacious abstractions, then one will calm oneself about it. However, the nature of the aid thereby shows itself in a bright light, the artificial, not quite adequate thing of our system, and also the necessity of a dynamic.

We only want to instance one more defect of our system here. We have seen that the exchange theory does not yield a distinct exchange relation in all cases, namely not then, when two or more monopolists face one another. This is very unfortunate, because this case is very important practically and does paralyze our system of distinctly determined actions and reactions. This defect is even more serious than even when the exchange relation between monopolists is certainly distinctly determined: If we could grasp its economic power and energy, etc., just as exactly as other moments, then a distinctly determined result would also have to arise here, which would have just as much justification of existence epistemologically as our competitive price. And yet, this is a point, about which one can justifiably demand an explanation from us. If we admit our inability to give it, then we cannot deny that a great defect of our approach lies in it.

Notes

1. I am foregoing to suggest another classification "ex professo" in place of the one that was criticized; the same does indeed easily emerge, almost by itself. A notable attempt in determining another classification, which better suits the current state of the science, has been undertaken by Prof. F. A. Fetter (Schumpeter, 1908, pgs. 585-586).
2. The reader knows that this "defect" is serious, especially because our delimitation of static is a very strict one and even the slightest "systematic" change signifies "development" (Schumpeter, 1908, pg. 587).
3. Not even the value of land can be completely understood from the static standpoint. The reader saw how hesitantly we spoke about it. One must actually differentiate a third market, besides the market of consumption goods and that of the productive services, a market of land (and capital) itself, which can only be fully presented in its function in "dynamic." The relations of this market to the other two are very interesting: A seed for a new theory lies here (Schumpeter, 1908, pg. 588).

4

About Reforms and Attempts at Reform

I

Our views about the reforms that are necessary in economics will arise by themselves from the previously stated. They are, as I believe, clear and natural, and can be presented in brief. I furthermore believe that they correspond to a healthy "communis opinio," which slowly but surely seems to break ground, and differentiates itself from others by its practicability and also due to the fact that it is equidistant from radicalism and from quietism. Through composure and measure, we would like to achieve that they seem just about acceptable to everyone. In turn, we would like to distinguish between the reforms, the one which is to be carried out for the common scheme and that, which is to be done to our system in correct form. The latter will then lead us to the discussion of the further paths of research and several developmental opportunities and perspectives. Both of the different points fall apart on their part into the presentations of our views and a judgment about the other economists.

Our suggestions for reform in *first* regard are the following—they simply amount to the demand of the elimination of "defects"—let one separate theory and practice; whoever can never forgo the value judgments and politics, even within his scientific activity, he should at least *say* every time he touches upon these areas that he is doing that and momentarily leaving the ground of strict science, in order to thereby facilitate a separate criticism of his theorems and his political position, but he should not hide behind the theory. One should furthermore separate theory and metaphysical speculation; one should never forget that for the sake of truth and clarity, for the sake of the serious obligation towards the science that one is dealing with. Thereupon, we are demanding distribution of labor in the area of the sciences of the trading by man; the very first thing that the unbiased observer in our discipline must notice is the characteristic of its parts that is so different methodically and content-related; in the beginnings of the same, it was possible and even advisable to combine them; this is no longer possible today. No exact science is allowed to consist of a conglomerate of different things, just as, for example, medicine or finance, if it is supposed to fully develop itself. Such unifications are essential to many practical purposes, but none of the contributing sciences can run free within the same, but rather the latter must still find their separate maintenance—and their progress is achieved in this alone. The separation of static and dynamic is still necessary, meaning the general acceptance of the fact that our static system, even though it achieves enough for problems, *which could otherwise not be treated accordingly*, in order to justify its existence, but it is nevertheless not able to solve all pure economic problems, and that this lag is better to be worked out separately, by means of other presuppositions, other materials, and other methods. In it lies the demand for the foregoing of the attempt to jam things into our system, which do not fall in line with its schema by themselves, and furthermore, the ones of the discovery of an adequate approach, which gets rid of the "weak" and "dead" points. These points are especially the ones that should be pointed out to those experts who either consider the economy as being completed or doubt its developmental ability. Here lies a large, fruitful area of work, in which there is too much to be done, that has to be cultivated first: a colony for all economists who complain about shortages of theoretical work. And finally, the most secured area of our discipline has not been fully developed yet by far: A thinking through, working out is still necessary there, a really satisfactory conclusion of all the pending controversies. An improvement of our methods is also a necessity.

In these brief sentences, which arise here as a consequence of our work and which we strived to carefully prepare and secure, lies our view about the reform of today's economy. Again, we sought to be clear and also modest, and have limited ourselves to salient points, about which a difference of opinion should actually not exist. Precisely this will contribute to its acceptance, as we hope; but now, yet another word about other views about this matter. Most of the economists admit the necessity of a reform altogether, and most of them also have a more or less specific view about it. But the same often has a commonality, which very much complicates the practical implementation of suggestions. One of such is often not even attempted; it is often just a matter of a coining of catchwords and of a type of "window dressing." The fact that these suggestions for reform do not grow out of concrete work and occasionally originate from people, who must be denied of having sufficient expertise, contributes to this. We cannot let the philosopher point us in the right direction, but rather he should turn to us when he wants to find something out about it. But unfortunately, the economy is able to gain just as little from the majority of the methodologies and epistemologies, which economists have to draw up; because the same only rarely glance back at their own theoretical work, are often not adequately acquainted with the theory and rest on their task much more subsequent to the philosophers and their manner than it is good, and whether they actually *further* know the work of devoted economists.

But the catchword and the general phrase also prevail here, and all misunderstandings, which only exist about the topic of the essences and the value of the economy, are rendezvousing here. Wherever truth is contained in there, it must first be liberated from a shell of falsehood, correctly formulated, and limited. The call for facts in its commonality belongs here, just as the demand to avoid a priori sentences, and the one to consider non-economic moments. We have already mentioned all of this; we have therefore shown, in regards to the first-mentioned demand, that one must differentiate between those facts, which form the foundation of our system and to which its results refer, and those others, which lead to the problem that lies outside of the same, and thereupon, that and at which points the latter affect the first. However, we do not want to elaborate these things at this point.

Let only one more type of reformers be mentioned, namely those who step forth with the demand of wanting to newly construct economics from the ground up. The self-confidence that is expressed therein is enviable. Newton and Laplace have worked consequent to that, which exists; but they do not consider that as being necessary. The brain work of a century—and even longer—seems meaningless to them vis-à-vis their own productivity. An endeavor like ours could surely only fill them with contempt. But is it not narrow-minded to deny the possibility of such a recreation? We do not do this; we do not know of one of such. If it stands in front of us, then we will not withhold our sincere admiration from it. But the *demand* for a completely new construction by itself seems idle to us, and to us, promises regarding this do not seem to be fulfilled. I do not know who the brilliant scoffer was, who wrote in the "Globe" during the time of Polignac-Labourdonnaye's Régime, under Charles X: "M. de. Polignac is certainly very determined, only he does not know whereto."

I also have the same impression in our case, which does not prevent me from showing complete appreciation for every actual achievement and even for every good apercu, which may find itself in such a work.

Our view now about what there is to be done for the core of the static theory, so therefore for our system when it is accurately presented, correctly delimited, and methodically irreproachable, is simply this: An actual reform does not seem to be necessary to us. That is certainly not supposed to mean that it is absolutely complete and that there is nothing else to change or to better about it. But it seems to us that the way it is, is as good in essence as it can possibly be, even if it is just for the present and the nearest future. We are not mistaking its defects because of it; we just believe that they are unavoidable in part, and that it is more advisable for the other part to accept them, to deal with them as those fundamental changes, which would be necessary for their removal. To us, the reform, which demands time and scientific development, seems to have been realized, whereby we of course have to emphasize that we thereby not only mean the newer value theory, but also several other points, namely the more accurate formulation of the foundations and of other, individual things; the acceptance of our variations method and the separation of static and dynamic, which also has the result for the theory of capital interest that was affected by us. But if all of this is accepted and spread, then *we* would like to withdraw from the row of reformers, because we consider it practical to hold on to the foundations that have been gained for a while unchanged, in order to let them consolidate—"sit down"—and bring themselves into effect. We believe that *essential*, further reforms would currently be possible indeed, but would harm the clarity and simplicity of our system more than the probable result warrants, insofar as we can look past it. Of course, every moment can expose us; and then it would of course be the greatest pedantry to adhere to this standpoint. But if one asks us about our opinion whether further great *reforms* of our system are to be expected in the nearest future, namely, whether we believe such to be desperately needed, then we can only answer in the negative in the sense, which we have just explained and which will hopefully not be misunderstood.

Completions of methods and content in detail, careful working out of many individual points, this is certainly necessary; but the great characteristics of that, which this work is supposed to represent are not expected to change so quickly. Beforehand, a battle for their acceptance is to be partially ended and partially begun; and then they are supposed to still carry further fruits first, before they are thrown on the scrap heap, and new ones, which are, as we must emphasize, not yet available, not even in basic approaches, and of which we cannot conceive a clear idea yet, take their place. Before we say something little about these further fruits and other ways of further work, we want to still make some remarks about several suggestions for reform, which are expressed from a different side for our system.

II

These are the desiderata, which are of a more particular nature than the just-mentioned catchwords, and furthermore for the reason that they absolutely bear witness to insight and expertise, they deserve more attention. And if we believe that they are better to currently remain unrealized, then we are still aware that another view about it is possible and may even seem more correct by deeper insight into our science than I possess. We are alluding to the following points, all of which we have already mentioned: above all, one has also demanded a social approach in the theoretical circles. This demand, which is to be strictly distinguished from the one of the consideration of socio-political moments and which aims for the introduction of social categories in place of the individual ones into the pure theoretical thought processes themselves, especially in Germany and America, and our standpoint vis-à-vis it, apart from all misunderstandings, which it so easily encounters, exposes us to the objection of backwardness. But we have already talked about this topic and can only repeat here that we still find "*methodological individualism*" to be indispensable today, and that a social approach, of course, only in our narrow area, seems to offer us neither essentially new results, nor any other essential advantages, which is confirmed by the fact that no one is serious about it anyway. But it would probably complicate our picture and take clarity away from it. In consideration for demands and attacks from the outside—and herein, not in requirements of our system, is the origin of this tendency to be searched for—and in the attempt to fend off false suspicion in the political and social orientation lies no sufficient reason for an improvement, so much the more since it mostly only exists in the utterance of a principle.

This is not quite the case for the desideratum of the consideration of the moment of "effort," with the attempt to create an "energetic" theory of economy. This moment is certainly necessary for the understanding of important phenomena and must be grasped somehow. But, as I believe, just not through the progress of the static system, but rather separately: namely for a similar reason as the one, which induced us to eliminate the social moment, namely, because the essential characteristics of static would thereby be complicated and tarnished without something special arising from it. And entirely the same applies to the phenomenon of development—of "movement" altogether. Attempts to consider them inside of our system have led to little, valuable results, at least up to now. We believe to be able to continue in another way and would like to keep our static system, whose most beautiful adornment is its clarity and unity, free from all of these things.

Let us only mention one more of these desiderata, perhaps the most important; it refers to the moment of time lapse. Apart from several attempts to consider this moment, which are less significant and at any rate, uninfluential, there are mainly three noteworthy theories, which realize the same. To begin with, it is the abstinence theory. Thereupon, Professor Marshall's theory of "long period curves," which distinguishes itself from our demand functions by the fact that they do not just count for the moment as this one does, but are supposed to cover a longer period of time. But v. Boehm-Bawerk's moment of time was especially studied, and it powerfully penetrated into literature from his work, so that today, almost every systematic representation talks more or less about it. Where do we stand in all of this with our system that only applies to one point in time? Well, what we have to say about it is the following: It is not the mere time lapse that these theories have in mind. Rather, they refer to that, which happens in this time—this is hardly more than self-evident—and *this can be nothing else than "development," in our sense*. One can be easily convinced of this. The abstinence theory considers the significance of productive efforts for the purpose of changes, elevation of the level of the economy, and plays, as we have seen in agreement with Professor Clark, no role in static. Furthermore, one readily sees that Professor Marshall's long period curves just have the purpose of grasping phenomena, which escape our demand functions. But these can only be developmental phenomena, which involve the changes of the data, which we are necessitated to determinedly accept. Of course, one can also interpret them as pictures of "further" effects of causes for disturbance, which we also treat in static. But only then can they have a form that is different from ours of static curves, when these effects drop out of static; *otherwise*, the time lapse, which must take place up to its entrance, has no significance, and nothing prevents us from disregarding it. We have already proven that v. Boehm-Bawerk's theory finally is not static. His "third reason," on which the main emphasis is placed, has a distinct relation to economic process.

Since the most important thought processes, in which we encounter the moment of time lapse, therefore do not fit into the framework of static requirements, the conclusion arises from it for us that we are not forgoing anything essential when we disregard this moment and adhere to the belief that our system only applies to given points in time, which suits its essence and enlightens us about so many of its peculiarities, as we, however, cannot demonstrate again here; in fact, it is one of our most important methodological results, without many a theorem not being able to be correctly understood. By the way, here still lies many a problem, and if we do not go into it—as into many, interesting questions of detail—we are only reluctantly conforming ourselves to external requirements.

We are therefore answering the question whether the basic approaches to a future development lie in these and related attempts for reform in the negative, insofar as the formation of static is thereby considered. But we want to emphasize again that we therein differ from many, precisely the most progressive economists. We constructed our judgment in front of the eyes of the reader and believe to have justified it, as far as this is possible in such things. At any rate, strict verification of its validity is *not* possible; only the future will tell whether or not we are mistaken.

5

The Developmental Opportunities of the Theoretical Economy

I

Finally, after all that has been said, the question "now what?" is raised. It has been discussed what is to be improved on the scheme of our science and the question whether ground-breaking reforms are imminent for our exact system in the near future, for the exact system *as we presented and delimited it*. It is now worth saying quite a bit about what is to be further done on this system and which paths the further work in the area of pure economy will presumably pursue. Everyone who really feels "at home" in his science must be able to answer these questions, and as long as they are left unanswered—even if it is in brief and with due reserve—the representation of our discipline is not complete, the reader has no clear picture of it. It lies in the nature of the matter that a good measure of subjectivity must also lie in such discussions, and there is certainly not only *one* way to continue; but the matter is nevertheless, as we have said, of lesser subjective character than a judgment about the value of the discipline, and the reader can, and also must, trust the "specialist" *in doing so*. So to begin with, we want to indicate the direction of further work on our system and several of its developmental opportunities, at least in an outline, and thereupon, say something about the problems that lie outside of the same, which essentially amounts to a perspective of the area of dynamic.

Now above all, our system must still be elaborated. The variations method has nowhere near given all the results that it can give, and especially the mathematical analysis can still get much, more than one thinks, out of these things. We could only indicate how rich this area is. May the results not even be very "great," they are not worthless, but rather certainly of significant, theoretical and not without practical interest. But this has already been said and should only be mentioned here for the sake of completion. The expansion of our system therefore especially resides with us, and one can say that it makes gratifying progress daily.

But thereupon, those connections, which we can currently clearly define and which give us our secured results today, are in no way everything yet that can be won on our basis. On the contrary, the same can still be substantially enhanced, its fruitfulness increased, namely in a different way. One can characterize these opportunities by three catchwords: specialization of our assumptions, construction of new assumptions, and new combinations of our elements. What we mean by our first catchword is a methodological rule of measure, which exists in the fact that we *give* our assumptions *a more specialized content*. One of such would be, for example, to lend a more specific form to our value functions, which must suffice for the same requirements as the current one, but also contains others. Bernouilli's curve is such an attempt; W. Launhardt probably went the furthest here. One harshly criticized this, but too harsh, in our opinion; because it is indeed true that such further assumptions must not be as one chooses, but rather carefully verified and limited to the purposes, for which they prove themselves; thereupon, that the gained results will have a narrower application area, are distanced a step further away from reality, in short, represent a keen *attempt*, which only success can justify; finally, that both of the mentioned ones and also other authors proceeded too carelessly and either became guilty of many a mistake themselves or in their followers; but this changes nothing about the fact that their proceeding was not a principally failed one, but rather corresponded to very correct insights into the essence of our discipline, and that future, basic approaches for a development lie here. To have realized this it is a much greater benefit than one may believe, it is also much greater than the mistakes that were made in the process. We cannot get closer involved with this point any further, but would like to express our conviction that here, a path leads forward, upward to a worthwhile look into the gearing mechanism of the economy, a path, which only he, who was educated using exact methods can completely appreciate, but which *must* be, will be treaded on sooner or later.

This is the first of the opportunities of new development, which we consider as being really fruitful, unlike almost all of the experts—also unlike most of the commonly suggested improvements. I am well aware that this lies too far from their goals, desires, and their developmental process, than that agreement could be counted on. Let us therefore suffice with that, which has been said and let us go to the second point, the *construction of new assumptions*. Entirely the same applies to it, the same hopes and concerns. New assumptions signify the introduction of new facts—because, as I said in the first part, the same always enter our system under the guise of assumptions. Examples would perhaps be the hypothesis that the total demand of all economic subjects of our area of study for one good behaves similarly to the individual demand of each of the same; that a total function of similar form to the individual functions can therefore be constructed; or the hypothesis that the value functions of the individuals only differ for the same goods through constants. Such assumptions can then also lead to new results, which are of course to be realized, but with great caution.

Finally, a third opportunity is represented by *new combinations of the elements of our system*. We are generally speaking of the ownership of goods of the individual economic subjects; we are using it as our point of departure. But for some purposes, one can combine, for example, all quantities of work that are available in the area of study, and contrast it with the quantities of the other production goods, and finally also the consumption goods that were combined in the same manner, just as this occurred in our picture of the "islands." This leads to some results, which are certainly worthwhile. As a rule, we are furthermore only speaking of consumptions goods in general. If one separates them into different groups, nourishment, housing, clothing, etc., then one can add further characteristics to each of them, which together, are not adequate for it, and perhaps more specialized results will consequently be gained from it, which may have more or less value, but must certainly be *looked at*, before one blows over them.

Therefore, our tasks are the elaboration of the current foundations of our system and their enrichment in the manner that was just mentioned. A further point is now added to it—the appointment of concrete data into our formal theorems. This moment is already partially contained in both of the others, and there is nothing noticeable about it so far. If we want to examine the effect of a tax, then something must be told to us about its type if more than very general sentences are supposed to arise, so for example, whether it is placed on the *profits* of the entrepreneurs or on the unit of the commodity, etc. During the discussion of the influence of every cause for disturbance on some price, the result is dependent upon the elasticity of supply and demand, meaning on new facts, on further data. But, what interests us here is the fact that one gets very far with this *appointment of facts*, that an entirely new perspective can present itself to the economy, a developmental opportunity, which is "unimagined" in the true sense of the word and perhaps appointed, to induce a complete revolution in the conception and evaluation of the economy, to bring it into a new era. One does not readily see this by looking at these modest sentences that we just stated, and we must therefore be somewhat more explicit.

When we introduce the datum into our "raisonnement" that a tax is placed on the unit of a good, then our result still remains very general; it will apply to all of such taxes and tell us nowhere near all that we would like to know about every single one of the same, in regards to the pure economical aspect of the matter; or when we examine any other price variation with the help of a special datum, in regards to the demand function—one of such is the "degree of elasticity"—then this result will also apply to many cases, to the variations of the prices of all goods, whose demand function has a similar form, but since the form characteristics that are given to us are always so little, we will therefore not attain a concrete—let us state the decisive word: *numerical*—result. But can one not continue on this path, which already thereby proves itself, even more, has proven itself as indispensable and generally used? Can one not determine the demand function more exact, so exact that we do not just achieve a "distinct" result, but rather a concrete result? I believe to hear the answer: what a fantastic endeavor—unpredictability of the economic processes, constant change, etc.! But we can also generally counter such universalities: so where does the utopia of such a proceeding lie? One can only press towards it difficultly and slowly; the path leads through tedious collection of facts, possibly through unsuccessful attempts, through mistakes and disappointments; but this is only natural, if the matter were simple and everything was already done, then every word would be redundant. Every progress encounters doubts and failings, and one only needs to throw in the towel a priori, in order to actually cause nothing to be achieved. We are only further opening a way, whose beginning already clearly and surely lies ahead of us. Why should we not be serious about the "inquiring," about the experimental determination of our value functions? I can readily construct *my* value function for cigarettes, especially since a circumstance comes to my aid. And we are therewith entering the realm of *exact* arguments.

This circumstance is the following: It would be difficult for me to say what the quitting of smoking would even "cost" and what I would pay for a cigarette daily. But I do not generally need to say that, it rather suffices for many cases—and these are the ones we are concerned with—if I can indicate a relatively small interval of my value function, for example, that portion of the same that applies to the 10th or 20th cigarette; and everyone can do that, and the effect of price variations is felt in everyone's budget. Each one of its influences is *almost* deliberate—meaning, let it be understood, the form of its value function in the so-called *actual* interval—is one not supposed to be able to press towards a great precision of an indisputably existing moment? The difficulties are great, and we cannot hope for practical significance of the results for the time being, but theoretically, even convergences would be of great significance. Another moment helps us further: It is the total demand. Every merchant knows—or if he does not think about it, then he feels it and acts accordingly—how the price of a commodity influences the demand of his customers for the same and furthermore *his* demand for the same, namely in no way just almost, but rather quite exact, meaning he knows about the total demand curve of the concerning commodity within his area and in his street more than we include in our curves. This applies much more to a fortunately especially important case, namely to the one of the great world trade articles. And especially today—and this will pertain even more to the future—where all kinds of organizations unify the price formation and the news service makes an abundance of data generally and quickly accessible, demand curves of gratifying convergence can be constructed relatively easily. Can one not follow quite well, how a tax on corn influences the food supply of a nation? Do we not have quite a number of methods to determine this quite satisfyingly? Can the pricing policy of a trust not be analyzed here with the greatest success? The examples would be so numerous that an explanation of each individual one is completely redundant.

But of course, a great change in price could lead to such changes, for example, to the abandonment of consumption, or to the introduction of surrogates, that our approach fails. Thereupon, it cannot be denied that the phenomena of development figure into this here, and not only let our results become quickly obsolete, but also complicate the construction of our value functions. It is certainly clear that the pricing policy of a trust is very significantly determined by the consideration for the future, that the wrestling down of competitors, combat and distribution areas, attempts to introduce a commodity or to stretch its use to further classes of consumers and other moments, form great difficulties. But also nothing more than that; we are pointing to earlier explanations for the justification of the claim that we are left with a significant stock of facts when we forgo them. However, we must do this; but if we are paving our way step by step towards a higher goal, then we do have the right to ask that one does not immediately demand *everything* from us; those, who have already denied the possibility of the first step, have the least occasion to do this. We must suffice with this one for now, but we can and *will* do it. This is only half of the matter, but it REALLY is THIS; and if it is possible to come to this problem solving through static, then the gained results can then in turn serve as a measure for the "development": if our method sufficiently proves itself and one has gained confidence in it, it will be confronted with the latter in cases, in which its results do not correspond with reality, and then it will show us how great that difference is, that unexplained falling behind, which is ascribed to moments other than those that static offers.

Our sharp delimitation and our detailed discussion about the essence of static methods prove themselves in precisely this point. Short periods, small changes, all of that, which we have acknowledged as belonging to this essence achieves practical services for us here: It namely instructs us to separate those facts, which especially lend themselves to the scientific conception, from others, and makes us aware of the availability of an essential difference between both groups. So it was not the mood or any other speculative premises, which induced us to all the formulations and discussions, but rather moments, whose real significance show themselves in problems that are just as real. We wanted to so to speak adjust the methods and theorems of the economy, which, in our opinion, press towards directions, which lead to nothing, for exact, theoretical, and practical, well-circumscribed problems—and suppress that, which seemed harmful to this goal. One must not misunderstand me; that, which has just been said is certainly not what the economy "is all about": We are certainly not infringing the theoretical significance of its result in themselves; but it does show us one of our future paths well, one, which is very important to the value and the reputation of our discipline. Our exact system shows itself to us in a new way from this standpoint: It is also a workshop, among other things, in which weapons are forged, which, although not by themselves, but together they can nevertheless *also* serve further purposes of science and practice.

We are making the case for "computing operation." The connection of our discipline with the methods and the factual material of static becomes readily clear to us here—in turn, from our work and not as a result of some general phrases. The popular question, what static can accomplish for the economy now answers itself completely automatically, if one wants to signify our system by economy: we require it for the determination of the value functions that are so fundamental to us. We expect much from it; even the smallest result will signify an enormous step forward on the pathway of the development of our discipline, as much as it may be sneered at or criticized, as it will surely happen, and nothing is easier than such a criticism about first attempts. We must of course limit ourselves to this indication of a great "developmental opportunity" here. But that, which has been said is only one aspect of the matter; we now want to turn to perhaps even more important ones.

Let us immediately say what it is about: About the connection of the theoretical economy with the technical sciences in the broadest sense of the word—"aesthetics" if you will, although we would prefer to avoid this term. This change of our discussion can actually not surprise the economists, namely for two reasons. For one, one had indeed conceived the economy itself as a type of "aesthetics" in earlier times, as aesthetics of the practical, economic life or even of politics. This has of course been overcome, and it should hardly be necessary, especially to emphasize that we do not mean something of the sort. But thereupon, one has always said something about "technology" in the economy, in the usual sense—and this still happens today: About the significance of the same, above all, for scientific progress. We have, however, already mentioned the fact that this has little value. Furthermore, one has also always touched upon technological topics, meaning topics, which the "engineer" typically deals with, as, for example, transportation. Of course, one limited oneself to universalities, and all of this moved into another direction altogether than that, which we want to say here. For example, in the "economy of agriculture," agricultural-political topics are mostly discussed, and possible schemata about the technical methods of agriculture, which we encounter very frequently, have no independent significance, serve as introductions or even as pointless embellishments. But nevertheless, one may possibly claim that within the constant return of such things, the feeling is expressed that the relationships between economy and technology are closer ones and partially of a different nature than one principally believes.

By the way, it is also clear that the facts of technology impact on the process of the economy, and the laws of the latter on the progress and the practical application of technological methods. Particularly the latter point is important to us: for the question, which technological methods should be applied, for example, which operating system should be chosen for a piece of property in a given moment, what type and how many machines recommend themselves for a specific factory, etc., certainly not only the level of technological knowledge is decisive. If it is concerned with explaining a specific, given "modus procedendi" of the agriculturalist or the factory owner, then different moments are regarded, which we can combine into three groups for our purposes: The level of technology, economic considerations, and finally, still other moments, as indolence, destitution, ignorance, etc. It is now essential to distinguish between the second and third group. The third encompasses "causes for disturbance," about which we can say, in the same sense as for error, etc., in the economy, that they are without principle significance. This is of course not the case for the second group. Even the most technologically developed machine will not be used, as long as it is not "worth it," and much has already been said about the difference of the agricultural operation systems, which recommend themselves under different conditions, even if "better ones" are known. So if we find different technological methods parallel to one another in their application, then this does not need to involve any "backwardness" whatsoever, but this can rather be "correct" and be based on much more interesting moments.

So while the pure economy on the one hand, and "technology" as an independent field of knowledge on the other hand, face one another as independent in themselves, there is still an area, in which the moment *of technological efficiency* and the moment *of economic efficiency* meet. It is thereby especially important that these two moments do not stand next to one another without diffusing, in an approximately similar way as it occurs in the finance economy and socio-political chapters, which are completely independent of one another or whose points of intersection do lie outside of strict science and only in the psyche of the politician; but rather that the two can be combined exactly and bring forth a new, third area. This area is that, which one can describe with the words "practical business operations" in the broadest sense. The agricultural business operation, the theory of forestry, the one of transportation—"railway economics"; commercial routing, tariff theory, etc.—are parts of the same, which we want to cite as an example; but the entire area of practically applied technology belongs here. This area lies in the middle, between those two other ones, and it can only be treated with the help of both.

However, up to now, it was as good as exclusively in the hands of the hands of the engineers. Which discovery is to be established now for the economists, that the same are already actuating economic theory and that one recognizes the forms and theorems of the economy in works of this nature; incomplete and insufficient, which actually results in the fact that not quite that is accomplished in those works, which could be accomplished, and that they still play a rather minor part today—very satisfying to us! But the fact in itself is without doubt, a glance into a popular book about such topics, or into a magazine that is dedicated to the same—for example, the "Annales des Ponts et Chaussées"—convinces us of it. The fact gains a special significance in this connection, that an engineer belongs to the first discoverers of the "law," which is carried under Gossen's name, which means none other than that he is interested in the form of the demand function. There are already works of *economists* in this area; to just name the best one that I know, let the one of Luigi Perozzo[1] about the Italian trains be mentioned. Furthermore, one more of the mentioned, somewhat remote topics must be thought of—of the theory of insurance. The fact that one can consider an economic hypothesis as its foundation,[2] teaches us two things: Firstly, how little "airy" and "speculative" at least *this* economic assumption is and secondly, that we at least connect in one point with the theory of insurance. I cannot elaborate on further relations to it here.[3]

We can only indicate what is to be done, perhaps best in the following way: let one consider works about commercial routing and others, in which the questions about technology do not emerge *by themselves*, but rather with economical ones regarding the costs and the returns, and let one attempt to express this about that, which has been said last with the help of our theory, just as exact as the technological aspect of the matter has already been expressed; and our system allows us to do this quite beautifully—the economic aspect about it then appears just as scientific and of surprisingly similar form as the technological aspect about it—and one *will* find that this not only essentially increases the clarity and correctness of the entire thing, but also enables us to gain complete unity and many new results. This is the *principle*; we have already given examples. Even if the difficulties are great, and that, which can be directly achieved is nothing more than a start, no reasonable person will let himself be scared off by it. The matter functions like the first locomotive functioned, and maybe the hope is not unjustified that a distant future will look back at doubts, objections, and derision, which this new pathway will surely encounter, just the same as we did at that, which was said about those of its time.

But we emphasize the conquest of a new application area, *the introduction of new data into our "raisonnement,"* is not a vague hope, but it has rather already begun, its day has already been broken. Even though it is not entirely correct, it will perhaps contribute to the highlighting of our thought when we say that just as statistics substantiate the "demand aspect," technology—also supported by statistics, however—substantiates the supply aspect of our equilibrium problem, and will fill it with life and facts. Our exact methods now prove and justify themselves here, particularly also the application of mathematics; the analogy also proves and justifies itself here with mechanics. All of this now appears in a new and very significant light. One cannot get at these things with the "literary" economy and even less with the common universalities; and with consideration for the same, the opponent of "theoretical gimmickry" will hardly still sneer at our efforts. But we want to be content with these insinuations; let us now conclude.

We believe that here, and not in the attempt to solve great political and social questions, lie the prospects for the further development of the economy. This is the moment that we skipped over during the discussion of the practical value of our discipline. We believe that the introduction of methods and theorems of the economy into the area of technology will lead to practical, as well as theoretically valuable results, and is readily possible in principle. This is now of very great importance for our discipline. The smallest gain is that individual ones of its area, which only offered the saddest implicitness up to now, like the theory of insurance and transportation, can thereby be filled with very interesting content that is based on the foundations of our system. The verification of our system is of great, principal significance, which is achieved the moment at which the practical usefulness of the same shows in an exact way, in which no doubt about it can exist, that our value functions and that, which is based on them proves itself in a similar way—in the considered area, actually entirely in the way—as the foundations and theorems of mechanics that are not less abstract by themselves. We are thinking about the *scientific* importance of this fact here—the practical one is clear, although by no means as great; as we finally want to admit here, only then, can we be sure that we have thought correctly and have constructed our thought structure solidly and appropriately when such practical applications prove themselves. The importance of technology for the exact sciences also lies in it indeed, as a great physicist has said[4]: If the latter were not to lead to correct, meaning beneficial acting, then "we would not know how we should conclude." Now, this last and most convincing manner of verification does not lie in the area of economic policy for the economy. One could almost say that it does *not* prove itself there. It is therefore fortunate that we find the necessary verification elsewhere.

The conception of the economy as a piece of economic logic also carries its fruits here. Furthermore, our claim appears in a new light here, that the economy is closer related to the exact natural sciences than to other science fields; it does not only belong to them methodologically, but also according to its practical results, it comes into direct contact with them. This partially makes an entirely new conception of our discipline necessary, and perhaps even *a transfer of the same into other hands*. At any rate, that, which has been said lights fire under those who would like to separate the economy from the other social sciences; its character and its direction proves itself as being completely different from the ones of those, and as we have said, the demand for exactness and for application of exact methods receives significance, which should also be taken seriously by those who rejected our other reasons—it shows that more lies in all of this than one expected.

This may encounter resistance. The outer difficulties of a development in this direction are actually already great. What mistakes are being made, what objections are being raised! Even the change in the entire conception of our science that lies in it will only penetrate slowly. The upmost sparing objection that we have to expect will be a smile of superiority from the sides of all involved; and in the brevity of our presentation, as well as in the lack of practical examples, lies a partial justification of this standpoint. But in spite of everything, we believe that the developmental opportunity, which we indicated here, has a future that lies ahead of it. Despite everything, the prospect that presents itself is great. Finally, despite everything, a new time announces itself, in which the historian and the social politician will not deny it of its acceptance, and the engineering student will also *visit* the college of economics. It is not meant by this that the first ones will now have to be interested in the theory, on the contrary, they will only realize the difference between their tasks and those of the theory even more distinctly. But the meaningless and fruitless battle of directions will be weakened or disappear, and if the pure theory is set aside, then this will not happen without compliment.

II

We still want to touch upon the "economic problems that lie outside of our system," whereby we want to be even more brief. Every modern economist knows the fact that there is an area—which one, as we have already said, has not very befittingly been called "dynamics"—which belongs to the economy, but lies outside of our system. But if we acknowledge that one of the most important progresses of the newer economy lies in the differentiation of static and dynamic, and also one of the most secured, then it can still not be concealed that the most far-reaching differences dominate over the essence, tasks, and the content of dynamic, that still only very little has been achieved in its area—although nevertheless some things—and that the expression and its content is virtually in danger of solidifying into a phrase and of increasing the amount of the unclear and inexact expressions, which already exist in our area, by one more. Even the misuses, which just seem to belong to the destiny of one of every economic thought, we can already detect here. They threaten dynamic like bacteria a yet unborn child, and will probably only disappear after a long battle, endless discussions. Many a man already inserts this modern-sounding word there, where he knows nothing to say; many an other covers practical demand and hopes with it, because it is absolutely not able to support the static system of science. Since much to our regret, our views about the matter differ from nearly all other ones that we know of—even though very gratifying agreement exists in principle and in many individual points, also for us—it is necessary for the completion of the picture, which we attempted to draw, to also say quite a bit about dynamic, even though this does not actually belong into this work; but we want to indicate the following points only to the extent that it absolutely necessary for the general information, without discussing other views or even just stressing the "points of difference."

Let one especially spare us the good deed of a priori "pointing us in the right directions" or giving us the essence and methods of dynamic. We or our followers will see what our paths are and where they lead to, after they have been treaded on, and not sooner. The fact, from which we proceed and which we no longer need to prove here, is the one of the existence of such problems that lie outside of our system, but are yet economic. The formation of capital, the interest of capital, the entrepreneurial profit, and the crises—these are phenomena, towards which the pure economy[5] currently fails. One will nonetheless have to accept them well or cursedly, as "economic" or even—in another sense, in that, which will perhaps recommend itself in the future—as "pure-economic"; no one would accept the opposite. One must therefore somehow attack them in themselves, and insofar as they drop out of every other discipline, which actually shows itself, in our opinion, one can fittingly combine them—possibly with several other problems—and characterize this group of questions with ONE name, so let us say "dynamic." But this certainly does not mean—and the reader will recollect that, which has been previously said about this matter—that this dynamic represents a system, just like static, and also like this one has a uniform method and things that are conditional of one another at its disposal. Those, who have already included the variations method in dynamic may believe this; but we do not believe this due to the simple reason, because we have recognized the most valuable component part of static in it. In fact, we do not think anything else of our dynamic other than a—in no way logically concluded and non-duplicable—group of problems, which satisfy both of the indicated requirements. *An exact, enclosed system crystallized itself out of former economics*, which forms its nicest and most valuable component part—of course, "nice" and "valuable" is always just *subjective* in this manner. But, if we consider what remains when we have salvaged this crystal, then it shows that the backwardness does not only consist of elements that belong to other sciences, but also of such, to which none of the possibilities apply. We can only attempt to nevertheless integrate the latter ones into our system, or to treat them separately and by themselves. We have decided on the second possibility, due to reasons that we have already presented—and our dynamic thanks its creation to this decision, whereby, as I believe, enough has been said, in order to give a first and clear perception of this area and of our conception of it.

How is one supposed to treat this problem now? Nothing is easier than presenting this in principle: We will consider the fact, as many as we can provide, first off—historical ones, more specifically, descriptive ones, static ones, and also those, which we directly see around us—and when we have done this for some time, we present the question: Is it necessary to continue on with it, or will it arise that a further accumulation of material details no longer teaches us so much that is new, that it is worthwhile? Another question is of similar character: Do we have to be satisfied with our collection of facts, or can we somehow describe the facts more briefly than it is possible through merely cataloging them? If we can answer these questions in the affirmative, then our actual, theoretical action begins and we will begin to proceed with assumptions, isolations, and abstractions; or better: *Attempt* to proceed, because it can arise that our venture was premature and we would have been better off answering those questions in the negative. Of course, this will not scare us off forever, but rather, we will continue our work and make our way towards exact pictures and phenomena through mistakes and failures. Others may proceed differently, and we will be able to demand a privilege for our proceeding all the less than we are aware of, that everyone naturally sees his special path, that there are many good paths, and finally, that even a *logically* questionable one often leads to at least partially valuable results in a quite wonderful way. All of this is certainly easier said than done, but we are allowed to bring forth these remarks all the earlier as they seem to be so natural and clear as possible to us. Let it still be remarked that we are of the opinion that at this moment, although very soon no longer, the economic history and description prevail almost exclusively in dynamic, and not in theoretical works, but rather in the works of that character—and not lastly in the *German* ones—are the most valuable achievements in this area to be searched for. It is irrelevant that the authors of the latter ones possibly know nothing about such considerations and the significance that their works have for the theory, and that they follow completely different goals with the same; and that they have not bred abstract methods yet, of the type that we finally aim at, is to be permitted in the current state of the affair and even imputed to them as a merit, especially towards hasty attempts of some theorists.

A further point is the following: The opportunity offers itself to us to let moments be expressed, which we could not consider in static. Yes, we can non-reluctantly exclude many a thing from static, and thereby preserve its purity and clarity, if we know that we can come back to it here, as if this were not the case. We will make use of this opportunity and come to another aspect of dynamic: Even apart from the fact that the problems, which we ascribed to it demand consideration of such new moments, we will also attempt otherwise to treat interesting things here, which do not fit into static. Such new moments, whose significance lies in the solution of those problems for now, but does not necessarily exhaust themselves in it, are for example, "abstinence" and—even more importantly—"effort." We will keep our system of equilibrium free from these things and turn to those more brilliant, more significant phenomena, which one can commonly characterize with the words "will to power," "will to be master," etc., and will seek to come to more general theories with their help. The great battle for the world market and the economical aspect of the being and becoming of the social classes will become the item of our efforts. Some other types of price formation, as static explains, and perhaps even other social, ethical, and national influences will encounter us in the process. But should always remain as our premise to keep quiet about things—or to limit ourselves to factual presentations in regards to things—about which we have nothing *exact* or sufficiently *interesting* to say.

The circle of our topics is growing under our hands. The phenomenon of credit represents an especially important moment. Nothing actually prevents us from already speaking about it in static. But I believe that only definitions and otherwise only truisms come out of it. Its significance lies in dynamic, in the movement, in the development. Only here, can its effect be observed, its essence understood. In a static state, it only appears in connection with a momentary emergency situation, if any, and its treatment in static leads to a stunted picture. Therefore, only outside of the same can a new, complete, naturalistic theory of credit be given, and it will form an important chapter of dynamic.

Another topic that belongs here is the question of the tendencies of the distribution of income. As we presented the variations method, we said that static cannot say anything about the *concrete* movement of income, at least nothing about the great tendencies of the development. Now, more can be achieved outside of the system of static, with other methods, and due to other facts. But this example teaches us, compared to the other, mentioned topics, how disparate the items of dynamic are, how little they have to do with one another, and how little prospective exists—this may indeed change—to unite them into an enclosed whole, which could be based on one or a few principles: some of the dynamic problems easily offer themselves to a THEORETICAL solution, others do not at all tentatively, some will be able to be treated, due to daily experience, like the ones of static, others only will with the help of statistic examinations, some are of superior magnitude, others are relatively small.

One could reproach us for combining things that are so different. We, on the other hand, must see something very suitable in it; because to us, it would seem to be a mistake to systematize and categorize too early, to possibly squeeze the problems into artificial schemes. The individual ones should be treated freely and independently, from their own needs, without shackles that would have to soon be torn apart again. The opposite appears to contain a serious danger to us. And yet another must be indicated. It is the one to improperly expand the circle of dynamic and to get there in this manner, to make invasions into neighboring areas again, like the older economists. Attempts, to seize on an economic theory of population again, to come to a scientific economic policy by means of dynamic, or to expect it to explain the economic history—in the end, history altogether—all of this would only be obstructive to peaceful work and true progress, and the tendencies that exist for it would only instill worry. This must suffice. Since we are only able to offer so little at this point, we are not allowed to permit ourselves to give others good teachings.

Only one point remains to complete this panoramic view, as far as this can even happen here. It concerns the problem of the economic development in its commonality, if one wants that of *progress*—although the latter expression hardly fits into strict science and the dynamic in it will perhaps recognize something like a mantrap in it, whose removal could possibly be associated with difficulties and battles. Above all, is there an *economic* development? The question is not as absurd as it could seem. It does not mean that we are in doubt about whether or not the economic things change. But one could very well doubt whether the causes of these changes lie in economic moments. In fact, the economic principles in our sense do *not* evolve; the economy that we actually possess today gives us a system, such as mechanics, does not tell about *development*, such as biology does. One has called our theory scientific logic—does this not point towards *lack* of development? Well, not necessarily, the economic development could simply lie outside of our static system. But there is still another fact that points in this direction. You see, we can very often and possibly always attribute that, which we call development to causes, which are not economic—neither static-economic, nor dynamic-economic—for example, the increase in population, changes in human nature in needs and motives, progress of technology, changes in the social organization, and others. Does this not indicate that the development can never be "economic," meaning it can never be explained by scientific moments? Again: not necessarily; it could be that there are also economic moments, which lead towards a development out of themselves; for example, economizing could be one of such. Even further, other things could be utilized, as for example, the moment of "effort" for an "energetic" *theory* of the economy, which could say something about an economic development. Furthermore, the changes of human nature, the social organization, etc., *often* have economic causes themselves. Finally, there are always economic *consequences* of a development that cannot be explained economically, so that we can probably contribute *something* to its understanding. But all of this is surely not certain. In connection with this, the question is also raised how a possible economic development even compares to the social one. Is it possible to construct a theory of the first one on condition of the constancy of the social conditions? If this could happen and yield results, then so much would be gained. Finally, there is still the question whether something like that exists or whether something like that can be assumed, like a *dynamic balance*—or whether only a static one exists.

We cannot answer any of these questions. We only want to emphasize how important it is to approach them impartially, and to not *want* to find certain things. For this reason, it is also very important not to attack these problems with the apparatus of static, in front of our eyes. Despite everything that has been said, we are not denying the connection between static and dynamic; during the discussion of the variations method, it has already been indicated that its power reaches into the area of dynamic to a certain extent; we still want to add here that we also consider other aids of static being capable of a reconstruction, which will possibly grant a utilization for dynamic one day. But today, one has all the reason to beware of such attempts; one would surely almost go mad in doing so. All in all, one can still say today that only the historian and the statistician can say to themselves that they are on the right path and that their works are of value. Beyond this, we must keep very close to our goals and are not allowed to hope to achieve great success with little effort.

And now, we still have a word to say about the future of the pure economy. Even here, on the last step of our path, we want to refrain from that moderation, which we constantly seem to have endeavored. It would contradict the spirit of this work if we wanted to attempt to simultaneously say "inaudita" and gush about keen hopes or dreams. Several sobering words will provide better services than great prophecies. We do live in a time of cool criticism of that, which has been achieved and that which can be achieved, in a period of limitations and the correct formulation, and even the modern physicist no longer shares the hopeful pretensions of his predecessors. But much more than he, do we have reason for modesty, because our discipline is just starting to recover from a difficult crisis, from a crisis that was largely caused by such pretensions. We have to be glad when only its justification for existence is admitted, when it is granted only one spot, although a modest one, in the kingdom of knowledge.

So we modestly ask ourselves, after all that has been said: Will the economic theory disappear as is often claimed? Namely in the near future, which we are able to disregard, not in the development of the centuries, which can cause and actually will cause unpredictable changes in our realization and its technology? No; it will continue to exist—this is the great, final result that we come to and which, as I believe, every impartial judge will sign. There was a time where it appeared as if the theoretical economy was based on unfounded speculations, frivolous generalizations of temporary phenomena and halfway-true demands, would be recognized as a mistake and swept away by the current of the scientific development, where a significant proportion of truth for the benefit of its opponents existed, and where the best and most advanced spirits of time turned away from it. This time has passed. One can clearly indicate today where individual pieces of right and wrong are in this dispute, and it thereby arises that so many points must be recognized as being unsustainable and so many as being in need of reform, a discipline of significant value under the title of theoretical economy remains. It may experience new reforms in the course of time—and it surely will—be based on new principles, gain a new form, which is so far from the current one, as this one is from the classical one; it may be the subject of general interest and carried by the current of the scientific development, or it may only be fostered by some and simultaneously appear to be washed up on a sandbank; it may finally also be overestimated in the future or unfairly criticized; but that it will even have such a future life, can no longer be doubtful today.

I will say more. It is not only incorrect to believe that the pure economy *has been*, but I actually prefer to believe that it still *will be*: In my opinion, it is in its early stages of development today. Is this disconcerting? Let one regard how numerous, detailed questions of the theory have not only not been solved, but have not even been generally felt yet, as many great problems have only found pseudo-solutions. One finds examples on every page of this book—but I have not even attempted a complete representation of all these points, as much as it was my endeavor, precisely to show the developmental capability of the economy.

And this also teaches us how very energetic work on its problems is necessary and also worth the effort, despite all of the limitations that the results are subjected to. Superficial observers often believe that the pure economy is stagnating, that no actual progress shows itself. Will the reader still share this belief now? Even if this was true—and many a backward representation evokes this semblance—this is not the economy's fault, but rather the economists'. The work has not been done yet by far, and only the corner stones have been laid. We have already said in which direction one should continue to go and what is to be expected of it. We only still have to ask ourselves here, whether great, epoch-creating things are to be hoped for, whether we are standing at the eve of a development, which can be put at the side of the one of the exact natural sciences.

Now, it has seemed certain to me from the very beginning that results of our science will never make such an impression on further circles like the ones of physics. What the stars are made of is a problem that impresses the layman; the questions of his own action are much less interesting to him, would also interest him less if the exact same brain work would be related to it and just as brilliant methods would be developed for it. Besides, our science is indeed centuries behind its exact sisters, and the prerequisites can only be obtained little by little for similar developments, in lengthy work. But it would be vain pretentiousness to want to indicate where they will lead to. The history of the sciences gives us enough examples of such prophecies being deplorably disavowed. The decisive factor is only the existence of developmental opportunities. Let one follow them and one will see—or our followers will see. *That* there are paths, on which one can press forward further, that the area, in which we work, has not been exhausted yet, that there is also a tomorrow for us—and not only a yesterday—a future and not only a past, this is all that we can claim with ease, but at the same time, also everything that we need. So "To work and not despair" can also be shouted to the economists. The economy is not a corpse yet—and as long as this is not the case, unlimited opportunities also exist for it in a certain sense, as for every living being. Whoever believes to be able to a priori condemn it, precisely shows that he has no actual insight into it in doing so; and whoever believes it to be exhausted, shows that *his* strength is exhausted.

If the reader has gotten the impression that viable powers bestir themselves in our area, that this discipline, which is certainly worthy of honor, of having first regarded the action and suffering of man in an actual, scientific spirit, will also have new things to say in the future, then everything has been achieved that I desired to achieve, may it also be admitted that the number of interesting theorems is only a modest one today; and even this small group of secured truths is after all a beacon in the middle of a sea of darkness.

Notes

1. Giornali degli Economisti 1906.
2. Namely Bernouilli's.
3. Since it only deals with several primary points here, we are thereby skipping over things that are less important, for example, the theory of speculation, that, which one could call the exact theory of banking, and others.
4. L. Boltzmann
5. The terminology is indifferent; let one say "pure economy" in place of "static economy." This makes no significant difference, as long as the economy has not gone beyond static (Schumpeter, 1908, pg. 615).

Index

www.ingramcontent.com/pod-product-compliance
Lightning Source LLC
LaVergne TN
LVHW011103300926
849160LV00008B/262

9781412865340